*George Frisbie Hoar and the*
*Half-Breed Republicans*

# George Frisbie Hoar and the Half-Breed Republicans

*Richard E. Welch, Jr.*

*Harvard University Press*
*Cambridge, Massachusetts*
*1971*

*To C. M. W.*

# *Acknowledgments*

I am indebted to all of the manuscript libraries cited in the bibliography and most particularly to the staffs of the Library of Congress (Manuscript Division) and the Massachusetts Historical Society. My obligation to Dr. Stephen T. Riley and Dr. John D. Cushing, Director and Librarian of the Massachusetts Historical Society, is immeasurable. They gave me free access to the two hundred and more boxes of the Papers of George Frisbie Hoar, as well as encouragement and assistance at many points. Those papers were initially opened to me by the late Mrs. Reginald Foster, the granddaughter of Senator Hoar and a lady of great charm to whom I shall always be grateful.

I would also express my appreciation to the President and Board of Trustees of Lafayette College and to its Committee on Advanced Study and Research for grants of time and money. I am equally indebted to the secretary of the Lafayette History Department. Mrs. Carl L. Cooper labors endlessly, cheerfully, and efficiently, and I am grateful on all counts.

As the manuscript for this book went through various permutations, it received the aid and criticism of many persons. I would particularly thank Professor Frank Freidel of Harvard University for his courtesy in reading the manuscript. I wish to express my appreciation to Mr. Gregory Wilson, Curator of the Theodore Roosevelt Collection, Harvard College Library, who selected the cartoon illustrations, and to Catherine Helen Welch who read copy hour after hour.

Richard E. Welch Jr.
*Lafayette College, Easton, Pennsylvania*
*June 1970*

# Contents

| | | |
|---|---|---:|
| | Introduction | 1 |
| 1 | Born to the Cause | 5 |
| 2 | The Loyal Reformer in the Age of the Stalwarts | 28 |
| 3 | The Hayes Interlude | 59 |
| 4 | The Eighties: Years of the Half-Breeds | 99 |
| 5 | The Harrison Years: Protection and Sacrifice | 145 |
| 6 | Suspicion and Tolerance: Cleveland's Second Administration | 169 |
| 7 | Party Unity and a War for Humanity | 199 |
| 8 | The Start of the Last Crusade: The Treaty of Paris in the Senate | 221 |
| 9 | The Election of 1900 and the Inevitable Decision | 251 |
| 10 | The Uncertain Patriarch and the Cautious Innovator | 290 |
| 11 | The Man and the Partisan | 313 |
| | Bibliography | 343 |
| | Index | 357 |

# Illustrations

*Frontispiece.* George Frisbie Hoar. Photograph in the Papers of George F. Hoar in the Massachusetts Historical Society, reproduced by permission of the Society.

"The Modern Cassandra" from *Puck*, February 8, 1899. Theodore Roosevelt Collection, Harvard College Library.     223

"The Bugaboo of the Anti-Expansionist" from *Puck*, January 18, 1899. Theodore Roosevelt Collection, Harvard College Library.     252

*George Frisbie Hoar and the*
*Half-Breed Republicans*

# Introduction

Some twenty years before he died, George Frisbie Hoar began to look like a scholarly Mr. Pickwick. His hair turned white; his face and his figure became very round. His life-long interest in his Puritan and Revolutionary ancestors became increasingly pronounced and he seldom spoke on any topic without reference to the heritage and ideals of the past. When he died, in 1904, three quarters of the editorial eulogies referred to him as The Grand Old Man of the Republican party and at least half declared that with his death passed the last of the Men of '48.

The implication that Hoar was the last representative of an earlier and purer day in the history of his party was a judgment cultivated by Hoar himself and was a judgment partially true. But only partially. If the relationship of Hoar and the Republican Party had been only that of the Free Soiler lingering on into the age of Quay and Hanna, of the idealist adrift in a world of power politics and commercial greed, their relationship would be easily described but of minor historical importance.

The history of the man and the party were shaped by similar forces, to which they responded in divergent yet parallel fashion.

The compromises each would make varied considerably in degree, but far less in kind. Hoar's was not a career without change, nor a simple evolution from idealist to conservative. By the same token any history of the Republican party that attempts to portray the party of Lincoln and Sumner as one characterized by undiluted moral fervor and its subsequent development as a continuous descent into the swamplands of spoilsman politics and big business domination is an account where truth is perjured in the interest of simplicity.

George Frisbie Hoar was neither a guileless simpleton nor a political anachronism. He was a Republican Half-Breed, and his career illustrates the manner in which the Half-Breeds provided a significant note of continuity for the Republican party in its varied transitions of leadership and policy between the administrations of Ulysses S. Grant and Theodore Roosevelt.

The Half-Breed Republicans have frequently been dismissed as a band of supporters of James G. Blaine who figured in the Republican convention of 1880 as an expression of the personal and factional divisions within the Republican party. Their longevity and significance was far greater than is usually acknowledged.

The term "Half-Breed" was one awarded them by their enemies, the "Stalwarts." Designed as a term of contempt—implying an insufficient commitment to the requirements of partisan allegiance —it became if not a badge of honor, a mark of identification. The Half-Breed Republicans in Congress were never an organized, disciplined bloc; they had no clearly constituted national following, nor did they wave banners emblazoned with the hyphenated label, "Half-Breed." These men were nonetheless an identifiable and increasingly influential component within the political leadership of the Republican party between 1878 and 1890. Far from being half-hearted Republicans, they possessed in fact a greater allegiance to party than did their Stalwart enemies. The touted loyalty of the Stalwarts was directed to the claims of individual chieftains and the operation of their machines; the loyalty of the Half-Breeds was directed to the Republican party as an instrument of political accomplishment and industrial progress.

Identifiable first in distinction to their enemies—the Stalwarts and the political Independents—the Half-Breeds fashioned in the

1880's a coherent if ambivalent set of ambitions for their party and country. The Half-Breeds wished simultaneously to encourage economic growth and maintain social harmony. Associating the future of the country with its industrial strength, they advocated the expansion of foreign markets, the protection of industry, an improved standard of living for the American workingman, and a national currency system suitable for the needs and safety of American business. They sought in effect to adjust the mixed goals of the early Republicans to the social and economic complexities of late nineteenth-century America.

The two decades following the inauguration of Rutherford B. Hayes saw America move into modernity. An agricultural-commercial nation was gradually transformed into an urban-industrial country characterized by national consolidation in many spheres. The Half-Breeds did not fully comprehend the changes being wrought by urbanization, industrialization, or mass immigration but neither did they ignore them. Aware that the changing economic pattern of America raised new political problems that deserved the attention and perhaps the intervention of the national government, the Half-Breeds erratically sought their solution and in the process bore witness that the post-Civil War years were not the era of "dead-center politics" that has frequently been portrayed.

The convictions and labors of the Half-Breed politicians—however restricted their policy expression—provide an essential note of continuity in the postwar evolution of the Republican party and its congressional leadership. They served as a necessary link between the Whiggish orientation of the earliest Republicans and the national, urban orientation of the administration of Theodore Roosevelt. Seeking to reconcile the idealized social harmonies of the past with the needs of industrial expansion, attempting to balance the old values and the New Industrialism, the Half-Breeds sustained in the Gilded Age and after a needed note of political ideology and thereby foreshadowed the efforts and the limitations of the Roosevelt Progressives of the succeeding generation.

A study of the career of George Frisbie Hoar is a study of the origins, convictions, and compromises of the Republican Half-

Breeds. It is as well an illustration of the divisions and evolving leadership of the Republican party in the half-century after the Kansas-Nebraska Act. The son of a Free Soil Whig, Hoar would enter Congress as a Radical Republican and the self-acknowledged disciple of Charles Sumner. Over the next four decades he would support the Freedman and defend the New Departure. resist the Stalwarts and excoriate the secessionists of 1872, fight for cautious federal regulation and damn the Populists, urge the expansion of trade and battle the Imperialists. Only during the years of Half-Breed dominance would he share the leadership of his party, but for forty years he bore witness to the tensions of change and continuity that determined its evolution.

# 1

## Born to the Cause

> I became of age at just about the time when the Free Soil Party, which was the Republican party in another form, was born. In a very humble capacity I stood by its cradle . . . No political party in history was ever formed for objects so great and noble.[1]

The influence of family tradition and inherited standards is strongest for those who relish their debt to their forefathers and lay no claim to individual genius. George Frisbie Hoar serves as example on both counts. During a long career as a Republican politician, he would revise his position on various reforms and policies but he would die possessed of the same set of ultimate convictions that were his inheritance by birth, time, and region.

Hoar was born in 1826, the son of Samuel Hoar, descendant of the Puritans and the friend of Emerson, and Sarah Hoar, daughter of Roger Sherman, signer of the Declaration of Independence. He was born in Concord, shrine of the Revolution and the acknowl-

[1] G. F. Hoar, *Autobiography of Seventy Years* (N.Y., 1903), I, 132.

5

edged capital of "simple living and high thinking." He was born at a time when New England intellectuals were prepared to combine the sense of duty of the Puritans with the more optimistic strains of Unitarianism and Transcendentalism and produce a blend of moral certitude more powerful, more "American," and perhaps more self-gratifying than any like movement in American intellectual history.

The formative influences of ancestry, Concord, and the Unitarian faith were supplemented but not altered by a careful and traditional education in Greek and Latin, a degree from Harvard College in 1846, and legal training at Harvard's Nathan Dane Law School.[2] When Hoar was admitted to the bar in 1849, he possessed a conception of the order of the Universe and the relationship of God to man and man to society that would sustain him throughout his life.

God was innately benevolent; so natural laws that dictated the evolution of human society tended to the continual improvement of that society. Divine in inspiration these natural laws left man in large measure the master of his fate; their direction and rate of progress was largely his doing. How man should proceed to fulfill his divinely appointed function to advance society and its institutions was most easily discovered by a study of history and most particularly the history of the most favored of peoples. By studying the secular scriptures of William Bradford, John Winthrop, and Thomas Jefferson, by keeping forever fresh the glorious struggle for liberty of the heroes of Lexington, Concord, and Valley Forge, man could best determine his own individual moral code and so his social and political ideals and duties.

The rather rapid transition from God to George Washington inherent in this conception of the universe posed no worry. The universe if created by God was the current responsibility of Man. Hoar was a traditionalist, not a fatalist; if he worshipped the Puritans, he went to church with Channing. He never doubted the existence of God nor God's wish that Americans be true to their history and its heroes. A firm belief in the necessity of individual responsibility and orderly social progress; a conviction of the

---

[2] *See* Faculty Records, XII, XIII, Harvard College Archives.

identity between individual morality and public well-being; a belief in the dignity of all men and a strong suspicion of unrestrained egalitarianism; a faith in reform and a deep respect for historical precedent: such comprised the intellectual heritage of George Frisbie Hoar.[3] During the course of a long political career Hoar's convictions about the propriety of labor unions and the beneficence of industrial growth would waver, but never would he doubt the existence of an orderly universe, wherein God's natural laws were shaped by the actions of men and the actions of men shaped by their individual sense of right and wrong.

Possessed of such a view of God, man, and society, George Frisbie Hoar had he lived in Virginia in the year 1800 might have become a Jeffersonian. As a proud son of Massachusetts in the year 1849, it was virtually inevitable that he would see in the new Free Soil party the political movement most congenial to his idealization of the American past and the American promise. The strength of family authority and personal ambition both pointed in that direction.

The father he worshipped had but recently bolted from his long association with the Whig party and joined the new movement, disgusted by the Whig nomination of General Zachary Taylor in 1848.[4] The elder brother he held now in awe and always in admiring respect, Ebenezer Rockwood Hoar, had coined the phrase, "Conscience Whig" and then followed their father into the Free Soil ranks, convinced that the dictates of conscience demanded association with a party untainted and unafraid. When George Frisbie Hoar first took an active interest in politics, during his last year in law school, it was as much a matter of family duty as personal conviction to take the affirmative in discussions of the con-

[3] Supporting evidence for Hoar's early allegiance to that heritage will be found in some twelve College Themes in the Papers of George F. Hoar, Massachusetts Historical Society (hereafter cited as Hoar Papers). *See*, too, draft of a practice lecture on "The Place of the Lawyer in Society," evidently prepared by Hoar in 1849 during his last year in law school, Hoar Papers.

[4] Samuel Hoar served as president of a "People's Convention" that met in Worcester on 28 June 1848. Composed largely of dissident Whigs who had opposed the Mexican War and were now outraged by the recent nomination of General Taylor, it marked the beginning of the Free Soil Party in Massachusetts. Boston *Daily Whig*, 30 June 1848.

stitutionality of the Wilmot Proviso and to demand that the evil designs of the Slavocracy Power respecting the Mexican Cession be frustrated by all "rightful and constitutional means."[5]

Admitted to the bar, Frisbie, as he was known to his friends, determined to establish himself in practice in the fast-growing town of Worcester. Worcester was one of the leading centers of antislavery sentiment in New England, and identification with the Free Soil party there was professionally advantageous.[6] Most of its "rising young men" were increasingly restive under the patronizing authority and compromising measures of the Massachusetts Whigs. In the years 1849–1852 the magnetism of the God-like Daniel Webster evaporated and the younger members of the Worcester bar gravitated toward the rebellious Free Soilers. After the Compromise of 1850, Webster was in the eyes of Frisbie Hoar but a sorry ruin and the Boston Whigs a shortsighted and anachronistic oligarchy. In his maiden political speech, Hoar declared that by their continued support of Webster the Whigs in Massachusetts gave undeniable proof of their unwillingness to cooperate with men of conscience in behalf of human liberty. As for the national Whig leaders, they had with the Fugitive Slave Law endorsed a measure "which the Saxon language does not contain words strong enough adequately to condemn; a Bill, to decribe which, is not to gild refined gold . . . but to increase the blackness of Egyptian darkness."[7]

Hoar's opposition to the Whig party was based almost exclusively, however, on its willingness to compromise the moral issue of slavery in the territories. The Whig doctrines of protection of native manufacture, federal aid to internal improvements, and support for a more national banking and currency system were still worthy of allegiance. Such doctrines were of subsidiary importance, however; party allegiance should be determined on the score of the issue of slavery and the threat it posed to the free men and institutions of the North. In 1852, at the age of twenty-six,

---

[5] *See* J. A. Faulkner to Hoar, 22 October 1848, Hoar Papers.

[6] *See* B. F. Newton to Hoar, 6 January 1850, Hoar Papers.

[7] This speech was delivered before a county Free Soil meeting in the Worcester City Hall on 5 October 1850, and was reported at admiring length by the antislavery paper, the Worcester *Daily Spy,* 10 October 1850.

Frisbie Hoar would be elected by Worcester to the Massachusetts General Court as an avowed Free Soiler.[8]

With the early 1850's Hoar's dislike of slavery became a consuming hatred of slavery; his distrust of Southern politics became a certitude that there existed a conspiracy to fasten the tentacles of slavery on all parts of the nation and in the process wreck ruin on the economic prosperity, social ideals, and intellectual freedom of New England. The influence of the South in Washington and in the Whig and Democratic parties was a fact; Frisbie Hoar became convinced it represented a clear and present danger to a way of life he identified with Concord and its leading citizen, Samuel Hoar. The prosperity and liberties of New England demanded that the territories between the Missouri and the Pacific be reserved for freedom. This was the basic issue, and the foremost duty of a northern man and party was an uncompromising effort to prohibit the expansion of slavery into the territories by every constitutional means possible.

By every constitutional means possible ... Hoar's inherited conception of an orderly universe supervised by a God who blessed constitutionalism and liberty with even-handed benevolence would not allow him to become a Garrisonian Abolitionist. Reform must come through accepted and constitutional political processes. The Free Soil rebel was also the lawyer and the son of lawyers. If he disdained the "cowardice" of Webster and the northern Whigs, so, too, did he express strong disapproval of those who would question the sacred writ of the federal Constitution or encourage Southern secession.[9] Equally scornful of extreme Abolitionists and cowardly Whigs, Hoar found in the Free Soil movement a natural object for his political idealism and ambition. In the transition of that movement to a new and broader identification as the Republican party of Massachusetts, he played an illustrative if modest role.

At various times in later life, Hoar would make preparations for writing a biography of Charles Allen, the leading Free Soil

[8] Henry Wilson, Chairman, Free Soil State Committee, to Hoar, 23 June 1852, Hoar Papers.

[9] *See* Scrapbook, 1850–1879, Hoar Papers.

politician of Worcester in the early 1850's. That biography was never written, but in the scattered notes that remain the intended theme of the volume becomes clear. It was Hoar's desire to show that the Republican party had been baptized most falsely at Ripon, Wisconsin and Jackson, Michigan; its true birthplace was Massachusetts. He would have had a difficult time in proving this contention; for Massachusetts had missed its opportunity in the year 1854.

Conventions at Concord and at Worcester on 22 June and 20 July 1854, attended by Frisbie Hoar, saw efforts made to fuse the Free Soilers with certain of the more dissatisfied Massachusetts Whigs into a new party. In both conventions there was but a scattered attendance by the Whigs and in both cases recrimination and heightened mistrust were the chief result. The birth of the Republican party in Massachusetts had to await the beginnings of a new crusade and survive the diversionary eruption of old nativist prejudices. The crusade was in behalf of a Free Kansas; the eruption was that of the Know-Nothing movement. The former provided the stimulus to weld the Free Soilers and converts from the Whig and Democratic parties into a new political union; the latter provided a crucial test of the vitality and ideals of that union.[10]

The Kansas-Nebraska Act and its repeal of the Missouri Compromise aroused strong opposition in New England and nowhere more than in Worcester County. There such Free Soil leaders as Charles Allen, P. Amory Aldrich, Frank W. Bird, Dwight Foster, and young Frisbie Hoar attacked it with mounting fervor. On 20 September 1855, a "mass convention" was held in Worcester City Hall. It passed by acclamation various resolutions denouncing the Kansas-Nebraska Act and pledging unyielding opposition to the admission of "any more slave states irrespective of whether they lay north or south of 36°30'."

This convention was attended by many men not previously associated with the Free Soil movement and bore witness to the continuing disintegration of the Whig party in Massachusetts.

---

[10] The best study of the confused and confusing political situation in Massachusetts in the 1850's is still the unpublished dissertation by William G. Bean, "Party Transformation in Massachusetts with Special Reference to the Antecedents of Republicanism, 1848–1860," Harvard Archives, 1922.

As much as any other single gathering it marked the birth of the Republican party in the Commonwealth of Massachusetts.[11] It marked, too, the beginnings of a four-year effort by certain citizens of Worcester County to secure the Kansas territory for the Free States, an effort that gained its most dramatic expression in Eli Thayer's Kansas Emigrant Aid Society. Hoar would be among Thayer's most prominent lieutenants in the task of equipping and dispatching emigrants to Kansas and raising capital for their new settlements.[12] When, in July 1856, he accompanied Eli Thayer to the Free Kansas Convention in Buffalo, he had been for six months a self-designated Republican. As it was the Kansas-Nebraska Act that assured his position as a charter Republican in Massachusetts, so it was the struggle to defeat the "Border Ruffians" in Bloody Kansas that saw Hoar for the only time in his life work for a cause outside the pale of political action.[13]

On the very same September afternoon of 1855 that saw the birth of the Massachusetts Republican party at the Free Soil Convention in City Hall, another meeting was held in Worcester. At Horticultural Hall several dozen men convened in behalf of a political movement that had sprung up a year or so earlier in various parts of the East, the Know-Nothing movement. The Know-Nothings—or, more officially, the American party—would furnish both an opportunity and a test for the Massachusetts Republicans. In that test, Frisbie Hoar wavered on but one occasion.

In Massachusetts the Know-Nothing movement began, as elsewhere, as primarily a conservative movement inspired by a desire to avoid the divisive issue of slavery by means of a concerted attack on the Immigrant and the Catholic, and the threat they allegedly posed to the public school system, the purity of elections, and the old values and institutions. In Massachusetts, however, ambitious

[11] *Ibid.*, 318–321.

[12] The extent of those efforts is indicated by the following letters: A. G. Fay to Hoar, 14 June 1856; A. G. Hill to Hoar, 29 July 1856; George L. Stewart to Hoar, 25 June 1857; George L. Stearns to Hoar, 5 May 1858; Daniel Foster to Hoar, 14 December 1860, Hoar Papers. Stearns, a Boston lead-pipe manufacturer, was an ardent abolitionist and one of the "Secret Six" who subsidized John Brown's Raid.

[13] *See* Hoar to Professor W. H. Carruth, University of Kansas, 26 March 1903, Hoar Papers.

Free Soilers and Anti-Nebraska Democrats saw in the movement an opportunity to advance their own ambitions and the antislavery cause as well, and the Massachusetts Know-Nothing movement appeared, for a time, to preach antislavery sentiments as well as nativist prejudice. It was consequently possible in 1856 for various members of the embryonic Republican party to make a plausible case for alliance with the Know-Nothings in an effort to end the last remnants of Whig power and unhorse the state Democrats as well. Such pragmatic young veterans of the antislavery movement as Henry Wilson, Nathaniel P. Banks, and Anson Burlingame openly advocated fusion between Free Soilers and Know-Nothings.[14] Hoar initially opposed the idea, allowed himself to become briefly and indirectly involved in certain efforts at electoral cooperation, and then, after the presidential election of 1856, denounced again and now more firmly any further trafficking of the newly-christened Republicans with "those faceless partisans of secrecy and proscription."[15] His brother, Ebenezer Rockwood and his neighbor, Frank W. Bird were more influential in their efforts to end the flirtation of the Republican and Know-Nothing forces in Massachusetts, but young Frisbie Hoar was by the winter of 1857 firmly aligned with the antifusionists, those who denounced cooperation with the Know-Nothings as discreditable and self-defeating.[16] By the late summer he was commenting with relief on the eroding status of the American party and acknowledging with praise the agency of his new hero, Charles Sumner.

[14] Bean, "Party Transformation in Massachusetts," 375–383.

[15] In the fall of 1856 Hoar was nominated as the candidate of the Worcester Republicans for the state senate; he was also appointed a member of the Republican county committee. In both posts he gave tacit approval to the erratic efforts of the Republicans and Know-Nothings to agree upon a common ticket for certain county and state offices. *See* memoranda in Hoar's hand, dated 21 October 1856; A. Prase to Hoar, 15 October 1856; James Allen to Hoar, 23 October 1856; P. Emory Aldrich to Dwight Foster, Chairman of the Republican Committee, Worcester County, 24 October 1856; William Mixter to Hoar, 24 October 1856, Hoar Papers.

[16] For evidence that Hoar had determined by the time he took his seat in the state senate to foreswear any future cooperation with the Know-Nothings and to stand forth as a "straight Republican," *see* William S. Robinson to Hoar, 7 December, 22 December 1856; E. F. Stone to Hoar, 25 December 1856; J. S. Brown to Hoar, 8 November 1856; Erasmus Hopkins to Hoar, 1 January 1857, Hoar Papers. Also, Robinson's nostalgic letter to Hoar of 10 March 1869, Hoar Papers.

Sumner's attacks on Stephen Douglas and the Massachusetts Know-Nothings were the objects of equal admiration. Over the next dozen years it would be Sumner who would offer the inspiration that earlier had been provided by his father. Hoar's position in the Secession Crisis of 1860, his conception of the nature and objectives of the Civil War, his support of Radical Republicanism in the postwar period would all be influenced by his near-idolatrous admiration for Charles Sumner. When later he followed Sumner in the Senate of the United States his unstated but constant ambition was to be acknowledged the equal of his predecessor.[17]

As the decade of the 1850's came to a close, however, Hoar had no thought of succeeding Sumner; he was content to play the role of a county lieutenant in the Republican Party of Massachusetts. Never without ambition, despite later protestations to the contrary, his ambition at this time was fulfilled by professional success at the Worcester bar and recognition as a hard-working committeeman in the increasingly effective Republican machine of Worcester County.

He had served a single term in each house of the Massachusetts General Court; as a Free Soiler in 1852 in the lower house, as a Republican in 1857 in the upper house. In both terms he had performed various well-regarded labors in behalf of the reorganization of the Massachusetts judiciary, and in the House of Representatives had given the first speech in behalf of state regulation of the hours of labor.[18] But his tenure in the General Court had been too brief to secure wide prominence. At this time he preferred to view politics as an avocational duty and to perform that duty within the confines of the county where he practiced. In the presidential campaign of 1860, Hoar gave the keynote address to the county convention and directed the Republican effort that secured for the Lincoln ticket a large majority in Worcester County.[19]

[17] *See* handwritten draft of Hoar's address on Sumner before the Worcester High School, 26 April 1889; Hoar to Samuel May, 10 September 1890; Hoar to Edward L. Pierce, 26 October 1895, Hoar Papers.
[18] *See* William S. Robinson to Hoar, 30 July 1852, Hoar Papers.
[19] Handwritten draft, Hoar Papers.

   When Lincoln was elected and the South chose to secede, George Frisbie Hoar was a figure of only local importance, whose views on most political and economic issues were dictated by a narrow conception of the interests of New England. He was allied, however, with a party soon to gain national predominance, and with a cause that having helped precipitate a rebellion would soon change the nature of a war. In his concern to assist Lincoln in defeating the rebellion and to assist Sumner in transforming the social, economic, and political position of the Negro slave, Hoar moved slowly but logically toward the national political scene. He moved with equal pace and logic toward the ideology and policies of a Radical Republican.

   For Hoar as for his generation and his party, the Civil War was the most significant event he would ever experience, but he experienced it only vicariously. In compensation he was untiringly optimistic of victory during the four years of struggle and an unceasing admirer of the Boys in Blue for forty years thereafter.

   The fervor with which Hoar embraced the war is not, however, to be explained primarily in terms of guilt feelings. Together with most of the charter Republicans of Massachusetts, he saw the war as a culmination of the great struggle with the Slavocracy Power. The defeat of the South would be the defeat of slavery, of agrarian obstruction, and of the Democratic party. The victory of the North would represent the victory of human liberty, of political and economic nationalism, and of the Republican party. For Hoar the war was from its very beginning both a war for Union and a war for Freedom, a war to defeat secession and end human slavery in America.

   Professional ambition, the urgent pleas of his former law partner, and the demands of two motherless children persuaded the recently widowed Hoar to fight the war in a civilian capacity. He was but thirty-four when Lincoln issued his first call for troops, and in the months of April–June 1861 appears to have given serious thought to requesting a commission from Governor John A. Andrew. It was then he received an anguished request from Charles Devens, the newly appointed colonel of the Fifteenth Regiment, Massachusetts Volunteers, that he remain at home for the sake of their law office. "I really do not think I should ever have consented to come," pleaded Devens, "if I had supposed so great an interruption to our business would take place as the withdrawal of both of us would occasion."[20] Hoar, aware that his own aptitudes were more scholarly then martial, complied. By October 1862 he was remarried, and again to a wife of delicate constitution, and was certain that he could best serve his cause and country as a civilian soldier. In that capacity he labored zealously and in several directions.

The least essential of these labors were those concerning the promotion of the rights and rank of the commissioned sons of Worcester County. Typical were his efforts in behalf of Devens, a man whose valor was only matched by his eagerness for continous recognition.[21] Devens was simply the most prominent and able of the Worcester men who requested Hoar's help in assisting them to receive commissions and then transfers to positions and companies more conducive to fame and glory. The prima donna quality of the military amateur was less noticeable as the war lengthened into a bloody test of endurance, but especially in its first months—when it yet retained the features of a martial picnic —Hoar's correspondence mirrored the military politics that would plague Lincoln, Governor Andrew, and lesser officials.

During the course of the war, Hoar served as a member of the county committee on enlistments, raised money to furnish "extra comforts" for the Fifteenth Regiment, and took rank as the main speaker at all patriotic meetings in the county. His increasing prominence was signaled by a request that he serve as the mayoralty candidate of the Republican City Committee of Worcester. The honor was refused. Hoar doubted his administrative capacities and was convinced that he could best serve the Union as the champion of Governor John Andrew and Republican "radicalism." In this role the civilian patriot found his greatest satisfaction.

By the fall of 1862 a split had developed within the Republican ranks of Massachusetts. It centered on the figure of Governor Andrew, but more significantly revolved about the issue of the

[20] Devens to Hoar, 6 May 1861, Hoar Papers.
[21] *See* Charles Devens, Jr. to Hoar, 11 May, 18 May, 16 June, 23 June, 28 October 1861, 1 May 1862; Arthur L. Devens to Hoar, 1 May 1862, Hoar Papers.

central purpose of the Union war effort. The dissatisfaction of various eleventh-hour Republicans with the domination of the state party by its Free Soil element was accentuated by the dislike of these same Republicans for Lincoln's Emancipation Proclamation and the increasing "radicalism" of the national administration respecting Negro slavery. These men were for the most part social conservatives, and were reluctant to see the objectives of the war broadened to embrace Emancipation as well as Union. Governor Andrew, and such staunch supporters as Ebenezer and George Hoar, had from the beginning urged Lincoln to proclaim slavery and secession enemies equal and inextricable, and it was against the figure of Andrew that the malcontents concentrated their fire in the fall of 1862. They formed a People's party, persuaded the politically naive Charles Devens to serve as its gubernatorial candidate, and sought to contest the political predominance of the former Free Soilers in the Massachusetts legislature.[22] The forces of Governor Andrew rallied to the challenge. Renewing their suspicion of too-recent Whigs and Democrats, they tightened their organization, swept the fall elections, and held the field.

In the struggle Hoar confirmed his position as Andrew's chief lieutenant in central Massachusetts, and reenforced his own conviction that the war against the Confederacy was but a continuation of the antislavery crusade and Negro emancipation the proper and inevitable consequence of Union victory. As early as November 1861 Hoar had attended semisecret meetings designed to promote abolition as a war objective and encourage antislavery operations in Texas.[23] A year later he publicly declared Lincoln's proclamation an act of simple justice, though sadly incomplete; by 1864 he was an active member of the Emancipation League. George Frisbie Hoar was by that date a Radical Republican.

"Radicalism" was the single most important theme in the history of national politics and the Republican party for the years 1865–1870. As with a majority of the Radical Republicans, Hoar's radicalism is to be defined and understood almost exclusively in

---

[22] *See* Charles Devens, Jr. to Hoar, 17 October 1862, Hoar Papers.
[23] *See* James M. Stone to Hoar, 6 November 1861, Hoar Papers.

terms of the issues of Negro rights and southern reconstruction. Not only does the term obviously bear no connection with socialist theory or economic protest, it can not be associated in any historically useful pattern with the values and political ideology of business. Radical Republicans and businessmen alike varied in the late 1860's on such political issues as the contraction of Greenback currency, the revision of the National Bank Act, the proper level for the tariff, the role of the government in the construction of railroads. Recent studies have shown that though the program of the Radicals indirectly served to pave the way for the increasing political influence of various financial and industrial interests, neither those interests nor the politicians most associated with Radical Reconstruction enjoyed the homogeneity that would make meaningful an identification of Radical Republicanism and big business.[24]

Hoar stands as a case in point. In the immediate postwar years he is to be identified as a Radical Republican because he believed in the power of Congress to dictate the terms upon which the states of the Confederacy would be readmitted into the Union, and he believed that Congress should insure the unhindered operation of the Fourteenth and Fifteenth Amendments in the South by military intervention whenever necessary. Economic issues he considered subsidiary to the overriding concerns of southern repentance and Negro rights. It is true that he was already an advocate of high protection and hard money, and a man convinced that the economic prosperity of Massachusetts was closely associated with the expansion of its manufactures, but it was not these views that made him first appear on the national political scene as a Radical Republican. His radicalism was inspired by what he referred to as "Southern outrages" and the "needs of the Freedman," not by a desire to serve as a political puppet for the manufacturing community of Massachusetts.

If Hoar's position respecting the rights of the Freedman reflected the crusading fervor that had led the Hoars of Concord into the ranks of the Free Soilers, his position respecting the status

[24] *See,* for example, Robert P. Sharkey, *Money, Class, and Party: An Economic Study of the Civil War and Reconstruction* (Baltimore: Johns Hopkins Press, 1959), especially 281–293; 304–308.

of the Confederate states reflected as well a desire for sectional vengeance. Among Hoar's papers there is a handwritten draft of a speech evidently delivered in Worcester in the winter or early spring of 1865; its title, "Do the Rebel States Exist?" The answer was an unqualified No. Those states by rebelling had "lost their political organizations as States under the Constitution" and were "resolved into the condition of unorganized territory." "The iron hand of the nation must not unclasp itself from the throat of these rebel communities until they are powerless for purposes of present or future mischief." The rebel states must not be readmitted until the political authority of the slaveholding gentry of antebellum days was broken and their social and political institutions completely reconstructed.[25]

Throughout his life Hoar was a great admirer of the Constitution and the balance it fashioned between the powers of the central government and those of the states, but in the immediate postwar years he entertained views that if permanently adopted would have destroyed that balance. In conjunction with many Radicals he was ready at this time to upset both the division of powers as it related to the central government and the states and the division of authority between the President and the Congress. In the latter connection, his correspondence illustrates a growing suspicion of the loyalty of Andrew Johnson and approval of the unsuccessful effort to expel him from the presidency. Hoar entertained certain doubts respecting the validity of the charges and methods of the managers of the impeachment trial, but persuaded himself that on balance impeachment was both constitutional and necessary.[26]

With an inconsistency typical of several of the more extreme Radicals in the years of the Johnson administration, Hoar had criticized Johnson for his opposition to the Fourteenth Amendment and then criticized that amendment for its failure to guarantee the Freedman the vote. He felt so strongly on the latter count that he published a letter to the Massachusetts General Court urging the legislature to refuse to ratify the amendment. His views were one with those of a special committee of the Massa-

[25] *See* Box, 1865 and Scrapbook, 1850–1879, Hoar Papers.

[26] Hoar viewed the Tenure-of-Office Act, however, as excusable only on the score of emergency conditions, and would later fight for its limitation and its repeal.

chusetts Senate that declared: "to ratify said amendment is consenting to the re-establishment of that very aristocracy—a white man's government—out of which grew the rebellion."[27] The General Court ratified the Fourteenth Amendment, however. on 2 March 1867, by a large majority, and Hoar was before long convinced that its decision was wise. The role of the Fourteenth Amendment in the Reconstruction Acts of 1867 and 1868 assured its virtue in his eyes, and he would in the next decade acclaim all three Civil War amendments. They redeemed the promise of the Great Declaration.[28]

The fact, however, that he had initially opposed the Fourteenth Amendment throws added doubt on the popular thesis that this amendment—and particularly its "due process clause"—was the product of a conspiracy in behalf of the propertied rights of big business. Surely Hoar's admiration of the business men of Worcester has little relevance for his initial opposition to the Fourteenth Amendment. That opposition was the result alone of a simplistic belief that Negro suffrage would serve as the instrument for a salutary reconstruction of southern politics and society.

Prior to his election to Congress, Hoar expressed his support of Radical Reconstruction policies by means of speeches, public letters, and service on the Executive Committee of the Massachusetts Reconstruction Association. The latter was an outgrowth of the Union Clubs of the Civil War, and was both an expression of opposition to the "moderate" Reconstruction theories of Andrew Johnson and a device to enlist Northern opinion and money in support of the organizational efforts of the Union Republican Congressional Committee in the South. The Massachusetts Reconstruction Association offered a very distinguished list of supporters on its printed circulars and was particularly active in

[27] Worcester *Spy*, 2 March 1867; Edith Ellen Ware, *The Political Opinion in Massachusetts, During Civil War and Reconstruction* (New York: Columbia University Press, 1916), 180.

[28] Hoar was in Congress when the Fifteenth Amendment was in the process of ratification, and he cheered the affirmative action of each state in turn. *See,* for example, the letter of Republican representatives and senators to Governor Rutherford B. Hayes, 21 January 1870 praising Ohio "on her ratification of the crowning measure of reconstruction." Hayes Papers, Rutherford B. Hayes Library, Fremont, Ohio.

1867–1868. Not only did it offer encouragement to the "loyal vote" in the South, but it supported various agents who were paid to organize the Freedman and to make it safe as well as patriotic to vote Republican. The association's admitted purpose was to "establish the party of freedom and the Union upon a firm and permanent basis" throughout the South and thereby: "To secure for all time the glorious results already achieved, to give the deathblow to secession and slavery, to bury the spirit of rebellion beyond all hope of resurrection, to establish the integrity and peace of the Union in such firm majesty, that its most malignant enemies shall never again dare to raise their heads."[29] With his election to Congress, Hoar's efforts broadened and assumed a more positive character, but his views respecting the rights of the Negro and the danger of the Bourbons remained those of the Massachusetts Reconstruction Association.

Hoar's election to Congress in November 1868 was the result of a well-planned campaign for the district Republican nomination engineered by his political friends and a group of influential Worcester County manufacturers. Hoar refused actively to seek the nomination, but was well aware of the efforts of his supporters.[30] His attitude toward political office would always be somewhat ambivalent. He desired it strongly but felt political self-seeking to be discreditable and corrupting of character. Anxious to play a part in the determination of the policies of his party and nation, he was grateful to those who would work in his behalf but scornful of opponents who built personal machines. The honest candidate should leave electioneering to others, though always ready to make his views clear to those who would demand his services.

The voters of the Eighth Massachusetts District were made well aware that they were sending to Congress an advocate of the congressional plan of Radical Reconstruction. In his address to

[29] Printed circular sent to Hoar by the Massachusetts Reconstruction Association, 13 June 1867; Harrison Ritchie, Secretary of the Association, to Hoar, 30 July 1867, Hoar Papers.

[30] *See* L. Fullam to Hoar, 18 September 1868; Alvin Cook to Hoar, 21 September 1868; M. O. Ayres to Hoar, 28 September 1868; T. G. Kent to Hoar, 5 October 1868; F. M. Ballou to Hoar, 5 October 1868, Hoar Papers.

the Republican county convention, accepting his nomination, Hoar played down such subsidiary concerns as the volume and redemption of the Greenbacks and declared that the prime issue was "to place the rights and security of all men of all races and conditions beyond peril." He hoped that with the election of General Grant, the country would begin to enjoy an economic prosperity that would raise all the securities of the country "to the level of specie," but the immediate problem was to insist that the South reform its ways before it was allowed the right of full participation in the national government. The national legislature had every right to dictate conditions for the return of the former states of the South; for "the Constitution was made for the country and not the country for the Constitution."[31]

During the Forty-first Congress (March 1869–February 1871) Hoar achieved swift recognition as a self-acknowledged disciple of Sumner: a radical on the issue of Negro rights and an advocate of a national system of primary education for the permanent reconstruction of southern society.

He opposed and deplored the readmission of Virginia and Georgia, convinced that the professions of loyalty by the provisional legislatures of those states were unproven if not false. Influenced by letters from fearful Republican carpetbaggers in the South and from old Free Soil allies at home, Hoar wished to see both states forced to subscribe to the full course of redemptive treatment provided by the Reconstruction Acts.[32] He was certain that these states, though belatedly ratifying the Fourteenth Amendment, were determined to subvert its true purpose. Hoar now saw that amendment as an essential instrument in behalf of the civil liberties of the Freedman and was anxious to see Congress strengthen it by enforcement legislation. His major oratorical effort in that connection was delayed until March 1871, but by that date Hoar had frequently expressed his opposition to South-

---

[31] Scrapbook, 1850–1879 (7 October 1868); Charles W. Upham to Hoar, 9 October 1868, Hoar Papers.

[32] Sumner Fitts to Hoar, 10 January 1870, Daniel W. Crosby to Hoar, 17 January 1870, Thomas W. Ward to Hoar, 22 January 1870, Petition of "Walpole constituents," 7 February 1870, Hoar Papers; *Congressional Globe*, 41st Cong., 2d sess., 490 (14 January 1870).

ern Black Codes, vagrancy laws, and secret societies. The Enforcement Act of 1870 was supported as vigorously as was the Ku Klux Klan Act a year later.[33]

Although Hoar believed that "Southern outrages" on the Freedman and his supporters made the Force Acts necessary, he had by 1870–71 come to the conclusion that military intervention alone would never reform the South. Only a nationally administered reform of the educational system of the South offered a permanent solution. In his speech supporting the KKK Act, Hoar had concluded by declaring: "I hope and trust this necessary measure of relief will be short-lived. The permanent remedy for the evils of the South is deeper and milder. There is one panacea, only one; that is, general education. The key to these difficulties is the key of the school house. Among the fundamental civil rights of the citizen is, by logical necessity, included the right to receive a full, free, ample education from the Government, in the administration of which it is his right and duty to take an intelligent part. We neglect our plain duty so long as we fail to secure such provision."[34]

Hoar had first expressed interest in an educational solution to the division between races and sections in the fall of 1867, when he had labored with his good friend Edward Everett Hale to raise money among the Unitarian congregations of Massachusetts in support of the "Southern Free Schools," but it was not until 1870 that he was ready to propose to Congress a plan for "Universal Education."[35] That plan reflected not only the pioneer effort and influence of Sumner but Hoar's life-long conviction that as human happiness was to be associated with material progress, so the latter

[33] Hoar's speech appears in *Congressional Globe*, 42nd Cong., 1st sess., 332–335. A carefully prepared effort, this speech saw Hoar offer a long exposition on the full power granted Congress by the Constitution to secure the civil liberties of all citizens. Its chief theme was the inherent superiority of national to state citizenship and the primacy of the national government in the protection of the civil rights of the individual. As respects the Ku Klux Klan Act, possibly the last piece of legislation that can properly be attributed to the radical program of Reconstruction, Hoar took upon himself considerable credit for persuading President Grant of its necessity. *See* letter from Congressman Samuel Shellabarger to Hoar, 11 September 1871, confirming Hoar's "recollection" of an interview between Grant, Shellabarger, and Hoar on 20 April 1871, Hoar Papers.

[34] *Congressional Globe*, 42nd Cong., 1st sess., 335 (29 March 1871).

[35] Hale to Hoar, 8 November 1867, Hoar Papers.

was dependent on widening educational opportunity. The strength of Massachusetts lay ultimately in her system of public education; the prosperity of her manufactures, in her schools of industrial science. What was true for Massachusetts was valid for the nation, and particularly for the troubled and backward South. If it was too late to fashion the South in the image of Concord, it was nonetheless essential to diminish its sectional difference and to protect its black citizens by insuring compulsory primary education for all. This was a national need and duty, and the national government should provide both tax support and the element of compulsion.

In his first term in Congress, Hoar was appointed a member of the Committee on Education and Labor, and in that capacity he addressed both the President and the Congress in behalf of his theories. Hoar requested an interview with Grant on 1 April 1870 and three days before sent a note timed to coincide with the official ratification of the Fifteenth Amendment. He assured the President that "the framers of our Constitution well knew that a republican government could not endure without intelligence and education generally diffused among the people." This consideration assumed new force "when by an amendment of the structure of the Government all citizens without distinction of race or color are hereafter to be entitled to take part in the Government." The President should recommend to Congress to exert all its constitutional powers to promote education and expand it universally among the people.[36] Congress was addressed in more detail but, at least initially, with even less result.

Hoar delivered his first speech to the House on behalf of a national system of compulsory primary education on 6 June 1870. It was a long speech, directed primarily to the task of proving the constitutionality of congressional action, and was filled with quotations from many sources and authorities, but its argument and intent were expressed in the following sentences: "I believe with my whole soul that the preservation of my country is as certainly dependent on the adoption of this policy of universal public instruction as it was on the overthrow of the rebellion . . . I would

[36] Hoar to Grant, 29 March 1870, corrected first draft, Hoar Papers. Grant did make such a recommendation to Congress but without enthusiasm or subsequent mention.

not undervalue the strength of congressional legislation, or the inestimable blessings of the Fifteenth Amendment; but I say that all these are a snare and delusion unless they are followed by ample provision for the education of the people. No legislation, no constitutional provisions . . . can protect your newly enfranchised citizen in his constitutional rights unless you give him the defenses of intelligence and virtue."[37] Six months later the House Committee on Education and Labor introduced a bill "to establish a system of national education," and on 7 February 1871 Hoar rose briefly to explain its provisions and necessity.

In all states where there was not in operation a compulsory common school system by 1 July 1872, the national government should require the immediate establishment of primary education. The national government would offer financial aid and encouragement to these states by means of "the assessment of a direct tax, amounting to fifty cents for each inhabitant of the Union." Such an arrangement would be simple, constitutional, and of great national benefit. He could not understand the timidity of his fellow Republicans: "If this measure or some better or kindred shall not be adopted the members of the Republican party will go down in history as feeble, timid, base, blind statesmen, who undertook the work of emancipation which they were incompetent to carry on to its final results."[38]

The bugbear of direct taxation, the tradition that education was a "local affair," and the pressures of the congressional calendar combined to defeat the National Education bill. Hoar would try on three different occasions in the next four years to persuade Congress of the propriety of federal aid for primary education— shifting the financial burden to indirect taxation and revenues derived from public land sales; attempting to conciliate and join forces with the congressional champions of the land-grant colleges; protesting the nonpartisan nature of his bills and multiplying their

[37] *Congressional Globe*, 41st Cong., 2d sess., Appendix, 478–486 (6 June 1870). This speech was warmly praised by John Eaton, Commissioner of the Bureau of Education in the Department of Interior. He began now a long correspondence with Hoar, offering the latter statistical evidence and steady encouragement. *See*, for example, Eaton to Hoar, 14 October 1870, and two manila folders, "Papers Re Education," Hoar Papers.

[38] *Congressional Globe*, 41st Cong., 3d sess., 1041 (7 February 1871).

statistical support—but to no avail.[39] The defeat of 1871 proved permanent. The burden of Hoar's last conversation with his idol, Charles Sumner, on 4 March 1874, was their mutual regret that Reconstruction had failed to receive its essential security, "a system of universal education."[40]

Hoar's persistent labors in behalf of federal aid to education reflected not only a continuing concern for the Freedman but an appreciation that legislative dictation and military intervention had failed to reform the society and institutions of the South. He never questioned the propriety of the Reconstruction legislation of the years 1866–1871 and never ceased to attribute to Southern obstructionism the chief blame for its failure to accomplish its desired ends.[41] Reluctantly, however, he admitted that failure, and came to see in widening educational opportunity throughout the country the surest means to accomplish those ends—a strong middle-class democracy in the southern states, an expanding role for the Negro in the economy and politics of the South, a Republican party ascendant in virtue and power in all parts of the country.

The term "Radical Republican" offers little assistance in identifying factions within Congress or the Republican Party after the

[39] *See* E. E. Henderson to Hoar, 23 January 1872; General S. C. Armstrong to Hoar, 12 February 1872; John Eaton to Hoar, 31 October 1872, 4 November 1875; Charles Eliot to Hoar, 6 February 1873; Andrew D. White to Hoar, 20 December 1873; "Thirty Public School Teachers of Washington, D.C." to Hoar, 27 February 1874; Hoar to Ruth A. Hoar, 10 December, 15 December 1874; W. Townsend to Hoar, 23 December 1875, Hoar Papers. Hoar's bill of 1872 passed the House, but never came to a vote in the Senate.

[40] G. F. Hoar, "Charles Sumner," *North American Review*, 260 (January 1876), 1–26; Edward L. Pierce, *Memoir and Letters of Charles Sumner* (Boston, 1893), IV, 317.

[41] In the fall of 1900 Hoar would write: "The [Reconstruction] plan of the Republican leaders . . . was a very simple one. It was to confer upon every man, born or naturalized in the United States, equality before the Constitution and laws; to secure to him the elective franchise, equality in such social rights as are the proper subjects of legal protection, provide for him a good education at the public charge, and to secure all these rights, especially the right of a free and fair ballot, by national authority and power . . . It is the theory on which the Constitution of Massachusetts was established in 1780 . . . If the white man in this country had welcomed the black man to citizenship as they have welcomed men of all other races from abroad . . . things would have gone as smoothly throughout the whole country, as they have gone in Massachusetts." G. F. Hoar, "Party Government in the United States," *International Monthly* (September 1900), 424–425.

middle of Grant's first term. By the early seventies it was the figure of Grant and the issue of Grantism that served best to demarcate the politicians and factions of the Republican party. Various issues related to the congressional program of Reconstruction lingered on, however, as a sort of postscript to radicalism, and this fact made it easier for such devoted sons of the party as Hoar to gloss over new divisions as they periodically renewed old battles. Troubled by the need to expose the corruption of former allies, Hoar would find relief as well as duty in such battles.

In the year of Grant's second administration, Hoar would express renewed horror at the disregard of Negro liberties by the "redeemed states" of the South, promote the passage of the Civil Rights Act of 1875, and serve as a member of a special House committee investigating subversive efforts to overthrow the carpetbag government of Louisiana.[42] He continued to insist that the old battles had not yet been won, and he fought against a realization that they had somehow become outmoded. Refusing either to doubt or dishonor the old crusade, Hoar was frustrated and angered by its perceptible evaporation. The fervor of the crusading years of the sixties seemed to have disappeared. A period of scepticism and reaction appeared to have succeeded a decade of enthusiasm and faith.

Hoar judged the quarrels and feuds of the declining band of Republicans in the South stupid and dangerous. They distracted the Republicans of the North from what remained "the living, vital issues of the hour": the continuing attacks in the South "against the loyal men and against the freedom of election." The Northern businessmen must not ignore those attacks under the false assumption that in appeasement lay the path of expanding trade. "Send down Freedom and Education in to the South" and

---

[42] *See* Benjamin F. Butler to Hoar, 8 November 1872; two pamphlet boxes and seven manila folders marked "Re Southern Outrages" (1873–1877); William P. Kellogg to Hoar, 13 January, 18 January, 22 March, 1 December 1875; William A. Wheeler to Hoar, 8 March, 22 March 1875; William P. Frye to Hoar, 1 May 1875; James S. Matthews to Hoar, 10 March 1875; S. B. Packard to Hoar, 21 April 1875; J. M. Edmunds to Hoar, 17 September 1875; Hoar to Ruth A. Hoar, 17 December, 18 December 1874, Hoar Papers. Also, *Congressional Record*, 43rd Cong., 2d sess., 1645–1652 (23 February 1875); 44th Cong., 1st sess., 5373–5380 (9 August 1875).

the Southern labor force would prosper, its market expand, and "all branches of economic activity would flourish."[43]

It was only with reluctance that Hoar turned his attention from the freedom and education of the southern Negro to the mischievous friendships of President Grant and the conduct of Grant's Stalwart supporters.

[43] *See* Hoar's campaign speeches to his Worcester constituents, 14 October, 28 October 1874 in Worcester *Daily Spy,* 15 October, 29 October 1874.

# 2

## The Loyal Reformer in the Age
## of the Stalwarts

On three counts, George Frisbie Hoar cast himself in the role of reformer during his four terms in the House of Representatives: as spokesman for Negro rights in a reconstructed South; as advocate of woman suffrage and the rights of labor; and as the cautious opponent of the demands and tactics of certain leaders of the Stalwart faction of the Republican party.

His continuing concern for the rights and status of the southern Negro has been noted. His advocacy of the rights of women and labor, if less ardent and less illustrative of the history and divisions of his party, was no less sincere. Hoar's inherited faith in individual responsibility and the continued improvement of mankind naturally led him to an interest in reform movements that promoted the intention of a beneficent Providence that republican government become ever more pure and equitable. That faith would waver in the 1890's, as the threats of industrial warfare and William Jennings Bryan cast doubt upon the certitudes of social amelioration, but in the 1870's, Hoar was still the optimistic son of Concord, and his earlier interest in reform movements concerned with the conditions of labor and the rights of women continued. For the most part he would seek the gradual accomplishment of these reforms through the instruments of public opinion and education, but he was at points prepared to call upon the intervention of the state and federal governments. Ideally, however, reforms for the improvement of society should be accomplished by the spontaneous spread of moral sensibility, reason, and good will. Hoar's role in the woman's rights movement offers a good example of his attitude toward the proper objects and methods of a reformer.

Together with other antislavery leaders in New England, Hoar had first become interested in the women's rights movement in the 1850's. The efficient efforts and discreet discipleship of certain New England matrons in the antislavery movement had won his admiration, and by the war's end he had come to believe that for a republic to bar citizens from political participation because of either sex or color was illogical and unjust. But not, perhaps, equally illogical and unjust. The South must be coerced by the Fifteenth Amendment to give the Freedman the vote, but constitutional adjustment in behalf of woman suffrage might await the tactful re-education of the American male. Modest petitions and lucid argument should work a gradual revolution, with women obtaining first the franchise in school and municipal elections, then the ballot in state elections, and ultimately an unrestricted national franchise. Social habits and inherited prejudices being what they were, the effort must be one primarily of moral suasion. Missionaries, not revolutionaries, were wanted.

Hoar most actively served the New England Woman's Suffrage Association in the years 1868–1881, during which time he wrote several of its most widely distributed pamphlets, urged Republican state conventions to adopt resolutions in behalf of woman suffrage in municipal elections, and secured the appointment in the United States Senate of a standing committee on woman's rights.[1] Hoar

[1] "Woman's Rights and The Public Welfare" (Boston, 1869), G. F. Hoar, "Woman Suffrage Essential to a True Republic" (Boston, 1873), G. F. Hoar, "Woman's Co-operation Essential to Pure Politics" (Boston, 1877), pamphlets, Hoar Papers; *Congressional Record*, 45th Cong., 3d sess., 1084 (7 February 1879); Thomas Wentworth Higginson to Hoar, 19 February 1869, Elizabeth Cady Stanton to Hoar, 11 January 1872, 12 January 1882, Lucy Stone to Hoar, 30 January 1872, 24 June 1876, 23 July 1877, Susan B. Anthony to Hoar, 9 February 1879, Helen M. Cooke to Hoar, 17 February 1879, Obediah Wheelock to Hoar, 14 January 1882, Hoar Papers.

repeatedly proclaimed his belief that there was no distinction between the sexes in the capacity to "love the country, select its servants, and appreciate its necessities." The political participation of women would serve not only the cause of republican equality but the promotion of political virtue. Woman, by her very nature pure and high-minded, was the natural opponent of corruption. Hoar's conception of woman was chivalric. He had worshipped his mother, been greatly impressed by the intellectual strength of his boyhood teacher, Mrs. Sarah Ripley of Concord, and had found in the constant praise of both his wives a source of comfort and a confirmation of their wisdom.

There was, however, another, less emphasized argument supporting the claims of justice and reform. If the Massachusetts Republican party took the lead in supporting the political rights of women, these advocates of virtue would enlist in the ranks of the Republican party and so serve as a proper counterweight to the Irish immigrants flocking to the ranks of the Massachusetts Democracy. Hoar agreed with Henry B. Blackwell, editor of the the *Woman's Journal* and president of the New England Woman's Suffrage Association, that one advanced the security of the Republican party as well as the cause of righteousness by identifying that party with the woman's rights movement.[2]

It was possibly the failure of the cause of woman suffrage to serve as a party rallying ground—indeed, its tendency by the 1880's to create dissension in state conventions—that caused Hoar to participate less actively in the movement as the decade of the 1880's wore on.[3] He still subscribed to its principles, and addressed the convention of the New England Association as late as 1891, but he ceased to advocate resolutions in its behalf by the Republican state convention.[4] Increasingly he expressed the belief that

---

[2] *See,* for example, Blackwell to Hoar, 22 May 1872, 28 July 1876, Hoar Papers.

[3] In the Republican National Convention of 1876, Hoar had worked to persuade the platform committee to grant an audience to a delegation of woman suffragists and allow them the privilege of seats on the convention floor. By the time of the convention of 1884, Hoar was advising that nothing would be gained by dispatching a delegation from the Woman Suffrage Association to Chicago.

[4] G. F. Hoar, "Women and The State," 24 September 1891, pamphlet, Hoar Papers.

legislative action should follow rather than accompany the work of education.[5]

The course of Hoar's interest in labor reform followed a similar pattern, but here he looked, at least for a time, to legislative instruments and the intervention of the federal government. Throughout his political career Hoar identified the prosperity of America with the expansion of its manufactures, but he never subscribed to the doctrines of Social Darwinism. He was a broad constructionist who believed that government could serve to protect the liberties of the individual and advance the proper claims of various economic interests. As government could provide tariff protection for the manufacturer and subsidies for the railroad, so it could concern itself with the needs and hours of labor.

During his brief service in the Massachusetts General Court in the 1850's, Hoar had tried to introduce a statewide ten-hour law, and the expansion of the industrial labor force in succeeding decades persuaded him that the condition and grievances of labor represented a problem deserving of study by the national government. He would not admit that America possessed permanent class divisions as did the nations of Europe, but various pressures inspired Hoar to give increasing attention to the problems of industrial labor in the 1870's.

An appreciation of the potential political power of the mechanics of Massachusetts supplemented a humanitarian concern for their welfare. In Massachusetts a labor party emerged in the late 1860's and early '70's. While it never achieved significant organizational form or success, it threw a mild scare into the ranks of the dominant Republicans. Hoar advocated planks in the Republican state platform respectful of the needs and grievances of the industrial laborer, and took pains to reply promptly to those of his constituents who expressed doubt that the Republican party had the interests of the workingman at heart. Labor unions, he wrote, were the natural product of industrial expansion and he was prepared to acknowledge the right of the American workingman to strike for a fairer share of the profits created by his labor. The

[5] *See* Hoar to Lucy Stone, 14 August 1889, Hoar Papers. This letter provides the best illustration of the tempered views of Hoar's later years.

strike weapon, however, should only be used as a last resort, and union members must neither damage property nor coerce their fellow workers. Economic prosperity was, of course, the surest guarantee of improved conditions and labor should in consequence support the Republican party and its policy of protection. There was no truth in the charge that the Republican party favored the rich and powerful.[6]

Ambition as well as political realities and the calls of conscience served to stimulate Hoar's interest in the rights of labor. For most of his eight years in the House of Representatives he served on the Committee on Education and Labor. Desirous of increased recognition in congressional and party councils, he saw in committee leadership the path to prominence. As the most active member of the committee he would seek to establish a national labor commission authorized to study and evaluate the conditions of industrial labor in America.

In the summer of 1871 Hoar had toured England, and had taken the opportunity to collect pamphlet material on British labor conditions and trade unions. Events across the channel, however, provided more dramatic illustration than did the resources of the British Museum. The formation and collapse of the Paris Commune fascinated Hoar. He sent his wife a running analysis of the fate and prospects of the unhappy French. He could feel little sympathy with the doctrines of "the Paris communists," but much sympathy for the plight of the long-neglected French workingman. The assumptions and goals of the Internationale (the International Association of Workingmen) were not unreasonable. As best he could determine they were four in number:

---

[6] Cf. James Water to Hoar, 2 October 1869; John Wells to Hoar, 19 September 1871; Horace N. Day, Vice-President of the National Labor Union, to Hoar, 14 December 1871; William J. Jessup, President, Workingmen's Assembly, State of New York, to Hoar, 1 April 1872; and, particularly, correspondence between Ira Steward and Hoar, 18–31 August 1871, Hoar Papers. Steward would later emerge as the leading socialist orator of Boston; in the 1870's he took upon himself the role of keeper of Hoar's conscience respecting the rights of Labor. He expressed his faith in Hoar's honesty, but feared the influence of Hoar's party colleagues: "Wealth has taken possession of the Republican party as fully as ever Slavery dominated the old Democratic organization." Steward to Hoar, 18 August 1871, Hoar Papers.

1st, That there is a relation existing among the laboring men of differing countries stronger than that which attaches them to their respective sovereigns; 2nd, That they will not permit their rulers any longer to use them as instruments for making war on each other, or for lowering wages by using the working-men of different countries to undersell each other; 3rd, That they will take all means to throw light on the conditions of the working classes every where, by gathering accurate and thorough statistical information; 4th, That education at the public charge is to be insisted on as the right of every man, and as the indispensible condition of a remedy for existing evils.

It was unfortunate that the movement had attracted "many violent and visionary persons." By attacking the law itself these men endangered the very basis of all social relationships. The French Republicans had indeed been pushed by the forces of the Right into actions desperate and unwise. The object lesson for the rest of the world was to grant economic justice to the working classes before they became desperate. "I hope our Republican statesmen will take warning in time and not leave our working men to take their lessons in political economy from Wendell Phillips. If they do we may in lesser degree repeat the experience of France."[7]

Hoar's prescription was less bold than his diagnosis. The preventive remedies he offered were confined to investigation and publicity. Back in Washington, he offered on behalf of the Committee on Education and Labor a bill "to provide for the appointment of a commission on the subject of the wages and hours of labor and the division of profits between labor and capital in the United States."

After affording the House a description of his recent travels and observations, Hoar proceeded to explain the bill's necessity. Surely conditions of labor here were far better than those abroad, but here too there were grievances and it was particularly important

[7] Hoar to Ruth A. Hoar, 5 June, 6 June, 25 June, 13 August, 1871; Hoar to unidentified correspondent, 30 January 1872, Hoar Papers. Hoar viewed the Boston reformer, Wendell Phillips as undoubtedly adle-pated and probably a socialist.

to heed the cries of protest in a country where the laboring classes "are the State itself." Many solid members of the laboring classes, not only "agitators and malcontents," were beginning to insist that under the existing arrangements of governmental taxation and finance, labor failed to obtain "its due and proper share." He was not prepared to estimate the degree of justice in these complaints, but if wrongs there were, the cure was obvious: knowledge of the facts. "Just as in regard to many of the diseases which beset the human frame, the cure is not medicine but light. Let them be brought into the sunlight and the sick will get well."

The sunlight of careful study and statistical compilation would demand but a modest expenditure of federal funds and was owed the judgment of the laboring men. With information would come understanding and so corrective legislative action if such proved necessary:

> So far as I am concerned, I welcome the investigation as cheerfully, if its results shall be to show that in all the measures to which I have given my assent there has been error, as if it shall be the reverse. This is a question whether the daily life of millions of Americans can be made better. It is a question too high for party, too sacred to be mingled with the petty schemes or the petty ambitions of mere politicians.[8]

Hoar's proposal for the establishment of a labor commission finally passed the House, but it failed by a narrow majority in the Senate. During the decade of the seventies he tried twice again to secure the appointment of a "permanent board, to whose attention every complaint of labor and every question of the need of new legislation might be brought," but on each occasion the Senate raised objection. It was not until 1884 that the Senate consented to the establishment of a federal Bureau of Labor Statistics, and then it did so largely at the behest of northern manufacturers eager to show that the conditions of the American laborer were superior to those of his European counterpart.

Hoar would consider himself a friend of labor throughout his career, and was receiving the praise and confidences of the head

[8] *Congressional Globe*, 42d Cong., 2d sess., 102–103 (13 December 1871).

of the "National Eight-Hour Delegation" as late as 1882.[9] By the 1880's, however, Hoar expressed a growing reluctance to recognize class divisions, as those divisions became more apparent. Hoar spoke less of the grievances of labor as he became more suspicious of the power of alien doctrines and the tactics of organized labor. He never ceased to believe that labor had a right to organize, but he became increasingly convinced that it had no right to call for the union shop or to become infected with the foreign ideologies of socialism, syndicalism, and worse. The congressman who bemoaned the failure of Grant to support his labor commission bill would some two decades later lead the Senate in a denunciation of General Coxey and his ragged army.

In the Grant years education and labor provided the fields most congenial to Hoar's efforts as a reformer, but he exhibited as well a mild sympathy for the temperance movement and a sincere if intermittent interest in federal railroad regulation.[10] More complex but of longer duration was his interest in one final area of reform, and this of distinct influence in the demarcation of divisions within the Republican party: civil service reform.

In the 1870's Hoar was recognized as a man opposed to government by patronage, and by contemporary and comparative standards the recognition was just. There is no denying the fact that at the very time Hoar was expressing his disgust at the machine tactics of Ben Butler and Roscoe Conkling he was consulting with his friends on the disposition of post offices and the appointment of federal census takers.[11] There is a legitimate distinction to be drawn, however. A few key offices in the state Hoar was determined to redeem from "the Butler crowd," but it cannot be said that he enjoyed the distribution of patronage, sought to create a personal machine, or ever consciously swapped political office for

[9] J. G. Wills to Hoar, 15 October 1881, 10 January 1882, Hoar Papers.

[10] Hoar delivered a short speech in 1874 in behalf of the unsuccessful McCrary Bill advocating federal supervision of the charges and practices of railroads engaged in interstate commerce. *Congressional Record*, 43d Cong., 1st sess., 2415–2417; 2459–2462 (24, 25 March 1874).

[11] *See*, for example, Thomas Russell to Hoar, 8 February 1869, W. R. Hooper to Hoar, 15 April 1870, W. W. Rice to Hoar, 1 May 1870, Hoar Papers; Hoar to Governor William Claflin, 24 May 1869, Claflin Papers, Rutherford B. Hayes Library.

political support.[12] By the end of Grant's first term Hoar was convinced of the inefficiency of an unrestricted patronage system and its potential for personal and public corruption. It would be Hoar's growing opposition to the demands for unlimited prerogative by the senatorial oligarchy that would gradually define his position as an opponent of the Stalwart faction of the Republican party.

The Stalwart Republicans dominated Congress and the Republican party during the Grant years, especially after 1870. They embraced the larger share of the old Radical Republicans—who no longer existed as a distinct political grouping by the early seventies—and a majority of the party professionals who now began to dominate the state delegations in Congress. The Stalwart leaders were the Republican chieftains in various states of the Middle West and Northeast who utilized their local organizations to obtain seats in the United States Senate and their senatorial power to retain mastery at home. The most prominent and powerful were Roscoe Conkling of New York, Simon Cameron of Pennsylvania, Zachariah Chandler of Michigan, Oliver Morton of Indiana, and John Logan of Illinois. These men were without a political philosophy, but they possessed a distinct political creed. Bleakly summarized that creed ran as follows: The purpose of politics is the attainment of political power; political power is best expressed in the establishment and growth of personal political machines; political machines are created and maintained by the disposal of offices and the winning of elections.

The Stalwart leaders were not personally corrupt, but they accepted as essential to the political process a spoils system inherently susceptible to corruption. While they would not pilfer from the public treasury, they saw nothing wrong with the purchase of votes or the purchase of political support by means of federal legislative favors. They have sometimes been called, "toadies of business," but this must be qualified. By no means were all the Stalwarts conscious admirers of the new captains of industry, nor were they particularly aware of the changing patterns of power within the

---

[12] *See* Hoar to Charles Sumner, 15 March 1869, Misc. Papers, New York Public Library; and Hoar to Secretary of the Treasury George S. Boutwell, 8 February 1872, Hoar Papers.

American economy. They were usually men almost completely consumed by the preoccupations of politics. The Stalwarts could and would be used by certain particular business interests not because they were sycophants but because they were myopically concerned with the preservation of personal political power. If in practice they often "ran interference" for particularly business interests desirous of public lands and public subsidies, they did so not from any conscious desire to influence the rate of industrial expansion but because they saw in the conciliation of various pressure groups the best path to undisturbed control of political appointments and favors.

The Stalwart leaders, though primarily interested in the preservation of their state machines, demanded place and power in the national government by way of political protection. They sought especially to dominate the Senate, the branch of the federal government empowered to approve or reject presidential nominations for federal office. Through the agency of the Senate they would seek to control the national administration and party. A recent student of the United States Senate in the post-Civil War generation has denied that there was any effective party control in Congress in the Grant years. He asserts that "bills were usually enacted without party superintendence" and "questions of party influence rarely intruded into substantive discussions."[13] Such a judgment denies the effective strength of the Stalwart Republicans by exaggerating their aims. They were interested not in "substantive discussions" but in controlling patronage, not in "bills" but in offices. Their organization of the Senate was less efficient than that of Aldrich, Allison, and company two decades later, but their desire to rule that body was quite as strong. They sought to rule the Senate in order to control the Grant Administration and so the Republican party.

Grant, a strange admixture of bewilderment and stubbornness, proved to be a malleable instrument in the hands of the Stalwart leaders. They persuaded him that they provided his chief

[13] David Jay Rothman, *Politics and Power: The United States Senate 1869–1901* (Cambridge, Mass.: Harvard University Press, 1966), 76. Rothman's study is without doubt the most penetrating analysis to date of the Senate in the postwar generation.

support, and that their enemies were his. Stalwart Republicanism —with its emphases on strict party regularity and the politics of spoilsmanship—became identified with the administrations and years of Ulysses S. Grant. And this fact made life difficult for such men as Congressman Hoar, who abhorred equally political disloyalty and political corruption. For the eight years of his congressional service in the House of Representatives, Hoar remained outwardly loyal to Grant while increasingly distrustful of "Grantism." The relations of Hoar with Grant and with "Grantism" are worth tracing in some detail. Not only do they illustrate the evolution of new factional divisions within the party but also the twisted course of those Republicans who while refusing to bolt in 1872 would openly contest the power of the Stalwarts in the Republican Convention of 1876.

Ulysses S. Grant and George F. Hoar were most dissimilar men; Hoar's inherited goals of "high thinking and simple living" were not those of Grant. When they first met, however, in the spring of 1869, it was under the most pleasant circumstances. Grant had more or less accidentally hit upon the name of Ebenezer Rockwood Hoar for the post of Attorney General in his cabinet, and Hoar was delighted with his brother's selection. He suffered through a few agonizing days when it appeared that Grant's offer of the Treasury Department to George S. Boutwell, former governor of Massachusetts, might necessitate the withdrawal of Rockwood's name, but Grant stubbornly ignored the proprieties of geographic balance and, in Hoar's words, was "a trump all through."[14] He informed his wife to give no heed to rumors that the appointment was "but a temporary one" and that Grant meant to fill it subsequently to greater political advantage.[15]

---

[14] Hoar to Ruth A. Hoar, 10 March 1869, Hoar Papers. *See,* also, Hoar to Ruth A. Hoar, 28 February, 4 March 1869; E. Rockwood Hoar to Hoar, 8 March 1869, Hoar Papers.

[15] Hoar to Ruth A. Hoar, 13 March 1869. The Governor of Massachusetts offered George Hoar the seat on the Massachusetts Supreme Court left vacant by Rockwood's cabinet appointment. The new congressman wrote his wife: "It was a great temptation, but I did not feel that I could properly subject my district to a new canvass for a candidate for Congress." Hoar to Ruth A. Hoar, 13 March 1869, Hoar Papers. The "temptation" was real but not great. Five years earlier he would have immediately accepted, but in 1869 he was ready to seek achievement in a political rather than judicial capacity.

In the late spring of 1869, Grant toured Massachusetts and briefly visited Worcester and the wide veranda of Hoar's house on Oak Avenue. Some months later he acknowledged a memorandum from the Worcester congressman upholding presidential independence and advocating the repeal of the Tenure-of-Office Act, and in the winter of 1870 Grant had cause to be pleased with Hoar's defense of his administration from charges of extravagance and reckless expenditure.[16] Certainly through the winter of 1870, Hoar's relations with Grant were without blame or blemish. And then occurred the first test: Rockwood Hoar was dismissed from the cabinet. Grant was persuaded by such political advisers as Roscoe Conkling and Benjamin Butler that his Attorney General was a political liability. Grant's first design was to elevate Rockwood Hoar to a seat on the Supreme Court, but these same advisers—angered by the Attorney General's refusal to consult their wishes in the selection of judges for some newly created circuit courts—refused to cooperate. The nomination of Rockwood Hoar to the Supreme Court was rejected by the Senate in what was the first clear display of Stalwart strength and cohesion. Grant did not contest the decision of the Senate but shortly afterwards curtly demanded the resignation of the Attorney General.

It was a severe test for the party loyalty of both brothers, but neither appears to have considered the possibility of public protest. George Hoar was, however, a firm believer in the virtues of his brother. He remained loyal to Grant, but the eager cordiality of his earliest references to the President now disappears. If the President was forgiven for the sake of the party and its policies, his treatment of Rockwood was perhaps never forgotten.[17]

[16] E. R. Hoar to Hoar, 14 November 1869, J. E. Tucker to Hoar, 5 February 1870, Hoar Papers; *Congressional Globe*, 41st Cong., 2d sess., 955–958 (1 February 1870).

[17] Later in life Hoar took great pains in correspondence with friends and newspapers to put the chief blame for his brother's political injury upon "certain selfish Senators" and not upon Grant, but took yet greater pains to defend the conduct and honor of his brother, especially against the charge of "packing" the Supreme Court prior to the second Legal Tender Case. *See*, for example, Hoar to Charles Francis Adams Jr., 22 February 1895, Hoar to Charles Bradley, 3 June, 9 June 1898, Hoar Papers; G. F. Hoar, "The charge against President Grant and Attorney-General Hoar of packing the Supreme Court of the United States, to secure the reversal of the Legal-Tender Decision by the appointment of Judges Bradley and Strong, refuted" (Worcester, 1896), pamphlet, Hoar Papers.

While Grant continued to be accorded loyalty as party chieftain, Hoar was by 1871–72 increasingly suspicious of certain Stalwart leaders influential with the Grant administration. One way to remain loyal to the king was to attribute all blame for royal misdeeds to his courtiers. Of these courtiers the most obnoxious in Hoar's eyes was Representative Benjamin F. Butler. The open battle between Butler and the Hoar brothers for control of the Republican party of Massachusetts would await Grant's second term, but it was an open secret in 1870 that Butler had used his influence with certain Stalwart senators to deny Rockwood Hoar a seat on the Supreme Court and surely no secret in Massachusetts that George Hoar had labored in the Republican state convention of 1871 to thwart the desires of Butler for the gubernatorial nomination.

The last year of Grant's first administration saw Hoar receive scores of letters from Harvard classmates and other self-proclaimed members of "the educated and better sort" denouncing the low moral plane of the national administration.[18] Hoar's approval of their views was obviously expected. Hoar replied most cautiously. The Liberal Republican movement had been founded; already there were rumors of a Republican bolt in the forthcoming election. Hoar had no intention, whatever his suspicions of evil advisers, to support or encourage secession. Independence was to be displayed by participation in moral reform movements and by efforts to guide one's party in the ways of righteousness, not by party disloyalty nor collaboration with the Democratic enemy.

In retrospect one can see that the Liberal Republican movement was but the first of several political protests directed against the character and pace of social and economic change in the postwar period. The Liberal Republican movement was the earliest and in some ways the most inchoate and negative, but it assumes its true significance only when placed within a pattern of political protest embracing such seemingly diverse efforts as those associated with

---

[18] He also received from the Governor of Massachusetts a copy of a resolution of the General Court condemning "the policy of bartering the public lands of the nation to Corporations as an injurious innovation upon the time honored policy of the Government." W. B. Washburn to Hoar, 3 April 1872, Hoar Papers.

the Greenbackers, the Mugwumps, the Anti-Monopolists, and the Populists. For all their differences, these movements would entertain a common fear of the consequences of the postwar economic revolution and a sense of nostalgia for the supposed stabilities of a half-remembered past.

Finding its origin in the specialized quarrels of the Republican party in Missouri, the Liberal Republican movement represented by 1872 a national expression of concern with the morals of the Grant administration and the political influence of certain corporate interests. The more blatant examples of scandal within the administration and Congress had yet to receive full publicity, but by 1872 such Republican figures as Carl Schurz, Charles Sumner, Charles Francis Adams, and Lyman Trumbull already suspected the worst. Jay Gould's gold conspiracy had given the warning, rumors were spreading of corruption in the War and Treasury departments, and the end of the year saw the beginnings of the long and tangled investigation of Crédit Mobilier. Republican editors such as Samuel Bowles and Horace White were already identifying the Stalwarts and castigating their willingness to accord special privileges to mining, timber, and railroad companies in the public domain.

The basis of the Liberal Republican movement was suspicion: suspicion of Grant, of the Stalwarts, of the disturbing effects of economic expansion and social change. None of the original Liberal Republican dissenters, and few of their supporters in the election of 1872, were economic reformers. They were not concerned with the conditions of labor, or with city slums and farm mortgages, but they did usually entertain a sense of disgruntlement with the nouveaux riches. They possessed a half-articulated fear of the disturbing effects of the new industrial wealth on accustomed patterns of society and politics.

But if social and economic change helps explain the inspiration of the Liberal Republican movement, its recommendations were almost exclusively political. Political purity was its chief demand and solution. Away with nepotism, croneyism, special favors, machine politics. Let merit and honesty rule and every office-holder be cast in the mould of Washington, or at least Madison, and there would be no need to fear false policies. With corruption abolished, sectional harmony would succeed the peculations and acerbations of carpetbag rule in the South; capitalism would continue to expand but be safely divorced from politics; and the country, reunited and purified, would reclaim its old morality and stability.

It was all a bit vague but nonetheless earnest. Men like Schurz, Adams, Trumbull, George W. Julian, and Gideon Welles were perhaps indefinite about causes and prescriptions, but they were positive in their dislikes. They disliked Stalwart politics and the spoils system; they disliked continued military intervention in the South; they disliked Grant. On such specific economic issues as monetary inflation and high protective tariffs they exhibited internal differences of opinion—although a majority opposed both —but on opposition to Grant and Grantism there was unity.

The limited, somewhat patrician, and rather negative approach of the Liberal Republicans made doubtful the longevity of their movement, but in 1872 opposition within the Republican Party to Grantism proved sufficient to inspire a third party convention and the nomination of a presidential ticket. Although this ticket would receive the endorsement of the Democratic Convention, its composition was that rare thing, an historically verifiable error. The Liberal Republicans would nominate Horace Greeley for the presidency and B. Gratz Brown as his running mate, and by doing so would unite Northern eccentricity and antebellum democracy. For Republicans such as George Hoar, anxious to remain true to party and conscience both, the selection of Greeley was an unexpected boon.[19] Hoar would in all probability have refused to bolt the party had the Liberal Republicans nominated Adams or Trumbull; indeed he had determined by the summer of 1872 to do what once he had believed he should never do, reject and repudiate the counsels of Charles Sumner. But surely he was grateful that in the battle for "honorable allegiance to party" he was given the easy target of Horace Greeley.

There would be many campaigners in the election of 1872 more influential than Hoar but few whose contribution was more in-

---

[19] Hoar had considered resigning from Congress at the end of his second congressional term, but was persuaded that the threat of party division demanded that men of principle must stay in the fight lest "the Conkling crowd" capture the party and the Democrats, the nation. Hoar to Ruth A. Hoar, 25 May 1872; T. L. Nelson to Hoar, 5 June 1872; James G. Blaine to Hoar, 10 August 1872. Hoar Papers.

teresting. His speeches would reflect the goals and arguments of those Republicans who while entertaining certain of the same suspicions as the bolting Liberals saw in party regularity the path of political duty and achievement.

Repudiation of party allegiance, argued Hoar, was justifiable on only two grounds: desertion by the party of the principles upon which it was founded; its nomination of a man of evil character. In the present election there was no reason for any man to desert the Party of Union and Liberty. The Republican candidate, whatever the faults of a few of his friends, was a worthy and honorable man, and the party he represented remained constant to its principles of equal rights and justice for all. The Republican dissidents were but the tools and instruments of the Democratic party, a party that had yet to renounce the evil doctrines of its past or accept the just consequences of its defeat at Appomattox.

This was the underlying theme and argument of Hoar's many campaign efforts in the late summer and fall of 1872. Those efforts reached their climax in a much publicized speech commemorating the organization of the "Grant and Wilson Club of Worcester." On this occasion Hoar met head-on what was for most members of the old Free Soil element of the Massachusetts Republican party the major difficulty: how to explain their support of Grant while continuing to honor the man who stood forth as Grant's most bitter personal enemy, Charles Sumner.

Hoar began his speech by reminding his listeners of the six points of the Chicago platform of 1868—equal rights and equal suffrage; honest payment of the public debt; reduction of taxation; economy of administration; encouragement of the new immigrant; and amnesty towards the defeated—and proclaimed Grant the honest advocate of each and every point. Charges that the General was uninterested in the plight of the Negro or in the welfare of labor were completely false; charges of personal impropriety of conduct were based on malice and not evidence. Hoar proceeded to a scornful description of the personal vagaries and fluctuating opinions of Horace Greeley, and then, abruptly, his speech changed direction. He paused and stepping to the very edge of the platform, uttered the sentences that hushed a cheering mob to silence: "I do not forget that in all this I am compelled to differ with one with whom for my whole political life hitherto it has been my pleasure to agree on all questions of national policy . . . I cannot name in public the name of Charles Sumner and words of eulogy not spring, unbidden, to the lips . . . But we cannot give up our judgment even to his . . . Mr. Sumner in recent speech and letters has done a great wrong to the President, has done a great wrong to you, and a greater wrong than all to himself."

Temperamental differences and unfortunate misunderstandings were most probably responsible for Sumner's estrangement from Grant and his recent attack upon the latter's candidacy, but whatever the explanation the charges of their former chieftain must be answered and repudiated. Mr. Sumner slandered honest men when he declared that the Republican National Convention that renominated Grant had been "composed of delegates chosen largely under the influence of office holders, who assembled to sustain what is known as Grantism." He had no right to accuse the Massachusetts Republicans who refused to follow him of "placing a man above principles"; nor any cause to declare them possessed of a "hatred for the South." "All that the vanquished complain of has been done with Mr. Sumner's full approbation. The only expressions of hate come from those with whom he is now acting." Let Sumner show willingness to be reconciled to Grant and let the rebels of the South pledge honest friendship to the North, and the party and nation would be united in honor and forever.[20]

Hoar's speech gained much praise throughout New England. His reputation as an opponent of Butler and a long-time disciple of Sumner gave his defense of party regularity a significance beyond the power of the party hack. The reaction of an old Free Soiler from Blackstone, Massachusetts was typical: "To feel that in supporting Grant one must needs part company with Sumner & Trumbull & Schurz . . . whom we have been accustomed to

[20] "Address of Hon. Geo. F. Hoar, August 13, 1872, Published by the Grant and Wilson Club of Worcester," pamphlet, Hoar Papers. The emotional strain Hoar experienced in challenging Sumner is indicated by his great gratification when in the winter of 1873 Sumner called upon him in Washington and indicated a willingness to resume their old relationship. Hoar to Ruth A. Hoar, 5 December 1872; 15 January 1873, Hoar Papers.

regard as lights & leaders of the Republican party has been to me a source of constant trouble. Your speech has cleared up things better than any dozen things I have read . . . With entire confidence in your candor to state things as you see & understand them you have, besides steadying me in my waverings, steadied others, I am sure."[21]

Although the Liberal Republicans attracted some support in Massachusetts, party defections were far fewer in 1872 than would be the case with the Mugwump revolt twelve years later. The fact that Greeley and not Charles Francis Adams headed the coalition ticket partially explains the unwillingness of many men of conscience to vent their disappointment with Grant in party rebellion, but of greater influence was the fact that the Civil War was but seven years over and the Grand Old Party still stood in the eyes of many Massachusetts Republicans as the party of the great crusade. Such men as Moorfield Storey and the younger William Lloyd Garrison, who in 1884 would damn Hoar for favoring Blaine over Cleveland, were in 1872 in complete agreement with Hoar's position and quick to praise the "salutary influence" of his campaign speeches.[22] Together they cheered the defeat of Greeley and the Liberal Republican movement.

The admiration expressed by Hoar for Grant and his administration during the campaign of 1872 would decline appreciably during the next four years. Two factors in particular brought Hoar into open opposition to the Stalwart supporters of Grant: Butlerism in Massachusetts and continued corruption in Washington.

In 1873 General Benjamin F. Butler made his first all-out effort to capture control of the Republican caucus and party in Massachusetts. During the previous four years he had gained increasing influence over Grant and over Grant's appointments in Massachusetts, but within the state he had been checked by what he considered the Old Guard: Senators Sumner and Wilson,

---

[21] A. A. Putnam to Hoar, 15 August 1872. *See*, too, Dwight Foster to Hoar, 15 August 1872; W. Townsend to Hoar, 22 August 1872; S. S. Zundike to Hoar, 23 August 1872, Hoar Papers.

[22] *See* Scrapbook, 1872 (2 September), Papers of Moorfield Storey, Library of Congress; Garrison to Hoar, 10 September 1872, Hoar Papers.

Representative Henry L. Dawes, former Governors Claflin and Bullock, William B. Washburn, John M. Forbes, and the Hoar brothers. He was now confident that he had built up sufficient support among the recipients of his patronage to gain victory and the Republican gubernatorial nomination.

It was the Boston merchant and railroad builder, John Murray Forbes who laid the initial strategy for Butler's defeat in 1873. Several months before the Republican state convention was to meet, Forbes was calling for secret meetings of "sound men" to organize against Butler's efforts to control the caucus, and urging Hoar to see Grant and have a showdown respecting the administration's support for Butler: "The only way to settle anything with Grant is to go to him face to face & set down & fix a quest. *Yes* or *No*—Letters I think light his cigars! I fear he considers Ben Butler *the* representative of his party in Mass."[23]

Forbes and others engineered a meeting of Republican leaders in Boston early in August which issued a call to the people of Massachusetts to repudiate the gubernatorial ambitions of General Butler. Butler considered that the Hoar brothers were primarily responsible for this proclamation and published an open letter in which he castigated his opponents generally and denounced with particular bitterness the motives of George F. Hoar. Hoar now dropped all pretense of neutrality. In a widely distributed "Reply to General Butler" he attacked the person, morals, and character of Grant's powerful lieutenant. Its conclusion is illustrative of its tone and argument:

> Gen. Butler's real grief arises from the opposition he is encountering in his plan to get possession of the government of Massachusetts by a fraud on the Republican voters . . . It would be hard to find a leading supporter of General Butler who will say that he deems him honest, truthful, disinterested, or incapable of using power to gratify both his ambition and his revenge . . .
>
> In his entire life General Butler has done . . . but two things well. He out-blackguarded a New York mob in 1864, and with a United States army at his back, he kept down a rebel city in

[23] Forbes to Hoar, 9 July 1873, Hoar Papers.

1862. Massachusetts is not likely soon to stand in need of either of these processes . . . The history of all his other attempts may be comprised in three words—*Swagger, quarrel, failure.*[24]

Butler was not slow to respond. Invading the enemy's home territory he addressed a large public meeting in Worcester, where he alluded pointedly to Hoar's absence from the battlefield of the Great War and accused him of shameless hypocrisy. The latter charge was inspired by Hoar's decision to draw his portion of the retroactive salary increase awarded all congressmen by the short-lived Salary Grab Act of 1872 and then donate the money to the Worcester Free Institute for Industrial Science. Butler proudly proclaimed his support of the Salary Act and declared he had used his share "to buy meat," whereas Hoar had used his to appear virtuous before his constituents and "to buy votes."[25]

Addressing virtually the same audience a week later, Hoar defended the logic of donating the tainted salary money to the benefit of his tax-burdened constituents, rather than returning it to the Treasury, and moved to the attack with a blistering denunciation of Butler and his "machine." On this occasion, corruption was awarded the symbol of an octopus, with Butler its head. As Worcester had led the great battles against Slavery and Rebellion, so now it would not falter in the third great struggle of this generation, "the battle with corruption."[26] Hoar's friends believed that such forthright attacks upon Butler were largely responsible for turning the tide. At the Republican state convention in October, Butler was defeated and Governor William B. Washburn renominated.

[24] *Worcester Evening Gazette,* 7 August 1873. This "Reply" was widely acclaimed by the enemies of Butler throughout New England. Congressman Henry L. Dawes and Senator Justin S. Morrill agreed that Hoar had seized Butler "by the throat and given him such a shaking as few of the tribe ever get." H. L. Dawes to Hoar, 17 August 1873; Justin S. Morrill to Hoar, 18 August 1873, Hoar Papers.

[25] A Butler paper in Newburyport, Massachusetts, rhetorically inquired: "Who is Geo. F. Hoar? He is the present representative in Congress of the Eighth Congressional District of this state, or rather the representative of certain large wire concerns and other manufacturers carried on in that district . . . A curious blending of the cute Yankee and the Puritan, in all those respects which most revolt liberal and enlightened minds . . . The Holy Willie of our political life, he is what he is by lineal descent." *Newburyport Daily Herald,* 25 August 1873.

[26] Worcester *Daily Spy,* 4 September 1873.

Thwarted in Massachusetts, Butler increased his efforts in Washington to control an ever larger share of federal patronage. His success strained Hoar's determination to make no public criticism of Grant, and led Hoar and his friends to attempt at times to fight Butler by methods not unlike his own.[27] On one occasion they secured and published a "confession" from the unfriendly brother of the new Collector of the Port of Boston; subsequently, they sought to obtain records from the War Department that would prove that Butler had been guilty of swindling during his wartime occupation of New Orleans.[28] Butler became for Hoar the symbol of all evil. Butler's influence upon Grant he found inexplicable. As Grant's second administration wore on that influence appeared to demonstrate the widening extent of corruption in the national government.

As evidence accumulated of scandal in official circles, Hoar determined to help save his party by encouraging his colleagues to take the lead in exposing corruption within the ranks.[29] It was both a moral duty and a political necessity for the Republicans to seize the initiative in investigating Crédit Mobilier and the other scandals that cast a lengthening shadow over the Grant administration. Hoar did not attempt to analyze the causes for the decline in political morality in Washington; he was anxious, indeed, to attribute it to the criminal weakness of a few men—blemished apples in an otherwise healthy barrel. He failed to see the decline in public morality as part of the broader picture of postwar inflation and social dislocation. Certainly he failed to see any connec-

---

[27] William W. Rice, soon to be Hoar's brother-in-law, forwarded several long letters in 1874–75, in which he detailed the declining popularity of Grant among "honest Republicans" in Massachusetts. Butler's ability to secure the Boston collectorship for one of his henchmen was the particular grievance. Rice warned that henceforth in Massachusetts: "We couple Butler and Grant together—It seems no longer possible to separate them." Rice to Hoar, 1 March, 7 March 1874, Hoar Papers.

[28] See *Boston Herald*, 3 October 1874; Hoar to Ruth A. Hoar, 18 December 1874, C. O. Thompson to Hoar, 24 February 1874, George N. McCrary, Secretary of War, to Hoar, 28 October 1878, Hoar Papers.

[29] Hoar's kinsman, the distinguished lawyer William M. Evarts expressed the discouragement felt by many when he wrote: "I confess to feeling a profound conviction that the Republican Party is running out [of] most of its claims upon any body but its office-holders." Evarts to Hoar, 10 April 1873, Hoar Papers.

tion between misconduct in Washington and the Tweed Ring in New York City. The latter was of Democratic origin and marked by unexampled evil.

The Tweed Ring, like the Grant scandals, served to illustrate the political danger of monetary inflation. Official salaries, low before the war, were often markedly inadequate in a postwar world characterized by rising prices and heightened social emulation. For public figures who wished to run with the New Rich the course was increasingly uphill. Indeed, the Salary Grab Act of 1872, though blameworthy in form, was a highly defensible measure. Public opinion demanded its recall, however, and for the public official without private means it was often a question of whether to scrimp or to barter the influence of office for legal retainers and favorable stock options.[30]

A classic example of such exchange was arranged by the Massachusetts congressman Oakes Ames in behalf of Crédit Mobilier, the mirror image of the Union Pacific. The Union Pacific, heavily subsidized by the federal government in behalf of the general welfare, reached Promontory Point and bankruptcy at about the same time. Its major stockholders had bled it white in their generous concern for a construction company, Crédit Mobilier, owned by these same stockholders. In an effort to avoid exposure these men had sought through the agency of Ames to dull the curiosity of Congress by distributing shares of stock in Crédit Mobilier among some of the more influential congressmen—these men to have the chance to buy now and pay later with anticipated dividends virtually guaranteed to cover the purchase cost.

Rumors of the troubles of the Union Pacific and suspicions respecting the involvement of certain congressmen were abroad in Washington by the winter of 1872, but it was not until after the election of that year that Congress finally authorized a full-scale investigation, and then only under the sharp urging of the Democratic opposition and such troubled Republicans as Luke Poland, Samuel Shellabarger, and George Hoar. Actually two separate investigations were underway in the House of Representatives by

[30] Hoar chose to scrimp and lived in two rooms of a Washington boarding house, where he cursed the flies and missed the cuisine of New England.

February 1873: that headed by Poland, directed to examine the relations between Crédit Mobilier and certain congressmen; that headed by Jeremiah Wilson of Indiana, directed to examine the management of the Union Pacific and the relations between the railroad and the United States government. The Poland committee received the greater attention, but the efforts of the Wilson committee are in retrospect the more instructive. Its report represented a sincere if limited attempt to comprehend the problem of the relations of the state and those businesses possessed of a public interest. The most hard-working member of that committee and the chief author of its final report was George Hoar.

The gist of the report lay in its declaration that the Union Pacific, by accepting and then misusing a federal subsidy, had rendered itself liable to federal regulation, and the national government could require its reform and reorganization. Its argument was best summarized in a letter to the *New York Tribune*, which Hoar possibly wrote and certainly approved:

> The United States advanced means to the Company to build the road under certain conditions and for the public benefit, and to secure the repayment of the loan at maturity the Government took a lien upon the property. It now appears that the conditions of the grant have not been fulfilled, and that the directors of the road, or a governing Ring of them, have fraudulently converted to their own use the resources which Congress set apart as endowment for the corporation and a capital for its future business. In other words, they have unlawfully depreciated the value of the security pledged to the United States, and the Government is entitled to interfere for the protection of its own interests.[31]

[31] *New York Tribune*, 29 January 1873. *See*, too, clippings and handwritten memoranda in file, "Re Railroads, 1873–1879," Hoar Papers. Hoar's interest in the Union Pacific and its tortured relations with the United States government continued into the 1880's. He continued to believe that the government could "compel the railroad . . . to perform the conditions of the act of endowment," but, influenced by a long correspondence with Charles Francis Adams Jr., expressed a growing concern for the legal rights and financial problems of the company officers.

An interesting and revisionist account of the Union Pacific's activities, profits, and congressional relations will be found in Robert William Fogel, *The Union Pacific Railroad: A Case in Premature Enterprise* (Baltimore: Johns Hopkins Press, 1960).

Hoar's hope that the political impact of corruption could be erased by means of public investigation proved illusory. Not only did Crédit Mobilier continue to provide a source of Democratic propaganda but so, too, did the activities of agents in the Treasury and War departments and the continued obtuseness of Grant. In a mood of personal discouragement, Hoar seriously thought of retiring from public life with the completion of his third congressional term. Unlike a rather half-hearted effort two years earlier, that of July 1874 was in earnest. His bank account was low and his faith in Republican virtue momentarily shaken. He informed his constituents that he planned to withdraw from Congress at the end of his current term. Neither his supporters nor the party managers would hear of it. If he did not run, the seat would be lost to the Democrats; to withdraw at so critical a moment would be cowardly. Hoar reconsidered, delivered a series of campaign speeches in behalf of his party and its "glorious 14-year history of progress," and was re-elected, though by a reduced majority.[32]

The fortunes of the Democratic party revived in 1874. Reaping political profit from government scandal and economic depression, the Democrats captured the House of Representatives, and it appeared that the defamed party of secession would soon be restored to power and the White House. Hoar's fourth term would be an unhappy one, made more so by his efforts to censure and expel Grant's Secretary of War, William W. Belknap.

General Belknap, the better to support an extravagant wife, arranged to receive a share of the fees of an appointee of the War Department possessed of lucrative rights to supply certain Indians on the Fort Sill reservation. The story broke with dramatic force in the early days of March 1876. In the words of Henry L. Dawes, "the news of the discovery of a terrible crime in Belknap . . . in its fulness and blackness, and disgusting detail . . . fell like a dark pall upon the nation. No event since the assassination of Lincoln caused such universal gloom." It appeared that the Grant administration "was doomed."[33]

[32] Samuel May to Hoar, 3 September 1874, Hoar Papers; Hoar to Peter C. Bacon *et al.*, *Boston Journal*, 7 September 1874; Washington Townsend to Hoar, 6 November 1874, Hoar Papers.

[33] Occasional Diary of H. L. Dawes, 1852–1876, Dawes Papers, Library of Congress.

After a short but tangled discussion the House voted to impeach the Secretary and requested the Senate to institute trial. The discussion in the House did not concern the guilt of Belknap— which was obvious to the most partisan—but centered about a technical if significant point. Shortly before the House began the proceedings of impeachment, Grant had received and accepted Belknap's resignation. This action raised the question: Is an officer who has left office still subject to proceedings of impeachment and trial? The Democrats insisted he was; the Republicans were divided. After expressing some initial doubts, Hoar decided that the House possessed full constitutional authority to proceed with the articles of impeachment. On March 2, 1876 the House voted to indict the former Secretary, and Hoar was appointed to serve as one of seven House managers to prosecute the impeachment before the Senate.

With dilligence and a heavy heart Hoar labored in the closing days of March to prepare for the Senate trial. It had been a "hideous winter." The Belknap affair appeared the very symbol of the errors of the administration and the misdeeds of the Stalwarts, and the danger they posed to the power and popularity of the Republican party.[34] The damage would be lessened, however, if only the Republican senators would unitedly denounce the guilt of Belknap.

Hoar's speech before the tribunal of the Senate had two aims: to impress the Senate with the horror felt by the Constitutional Fathers for the crime of bribery, and to persuade the Senate that it was the intent of the Constitution not only to force the corrupt from public office but forever after to forbid them a share in the public confidence.

It was true that the clause of the Constitution referring to the tenure of office-holders said only that the guilty "shall be removed from office on impeachment and conviction," but an earlier clause had determined that the Senate was to possess the full common law power of impeachment; i.e., the right not only to declare a man removed from office but disqualified "to hold and enjoy any office of trust and profit under the United States." It must be obvious

---

[34] Hoar to Ruth A. Hoar, 2 March, 5 March, 12 March, 26 March 1876, Hoar Papers.

that removal would in many cases be an insufficient remedy as compared with perpetual disqualification from holding office. If the dangerous political crime of bribery was to be limited to the punishment of removal, then an office-holder could obviously escape all punishment by resigning after the discovery of his misconduct. The present case was a clear example. Was General Belknap to escape judgment on the technicality that he had resigned prior to the inauguration of impeachment proceedings in the House? Surely it was now out of the power of the Senate to remove him from office, but he must not escape the judgment of perpetual disqualification.

Hoar appealed to the sensibilities and apprehensions of the Republican majority. They must show the public that the scandals of recent years were but an evil growth on the body politic and the Republican party would excise that growth without fear or favor. True loyalty to the party could best be exhibited by a refusal to be dissuaded from the path of duty by the deceptive appeals of political friendship. In a final preroration Hoar listed the scandals of the past and demanded the conviction of Belknap as a pledge to the future:

> My own public life has been a very brief and insignificant one... But in that brief period I have seen five judges of a high court of the United States driven from office by threats of impeachment for corruption or maladministration . . . I have seen the chairman of the Committee on Military Affairs in the House . . . rise in his place and demand the expulsion of four of his associates for making sale of their official privilege of selecting the youths to be educated at our great military school. When the greatest railroad of the world, binding together the continent and uniting the two great seas which wash our shores, was finished, I have seen our national triumph and exultation turned to bitterness and shame by the unanimous reports of three committees of Congress . . . that every step of that mighty enterprise had been taken in fraud. I have heard in highest places the shameless doctrine avowed by men grown old in public office that the true way by which power should be gained in the Republic is to bribe the people with the offices created for their service . . .

These things have passed into history. [When the] Macauley who writes the annals of our time will record them with his inexorable pen [let him] . . . close the chapter by narrating how these things were detected, reformed, and punished by constitutional processes which the wisdom of our fathers devised for us, and the virtue and purity of the people found their vindication in the justice of the Senate.[35]

Hoar's speech better served his conscience than his cause. The Senate Republicans refused to exhibit the unity he demanded. After a long and interrupted trial, Belknap was acquitted—the House indictment failing to receive the necessary two-thirds majority. The Belknap scandal would provide heavy ammunition for the Democrats in the fall elections, as Hoar had feared. Indeed, the Democrats would seize upon Hoar's preroration and would distribute it broadcast as a handy compilation of Republican crimes and misdemeanors.

In an effort to assure the redemption of past evils and the continued rule of the Republican party, Hoar determined to politick to secure the defeat of Roscoe Conkling and the Stalwarts in the national Republican convention.

By the summer of 1876 Hoar had come to view Roscoe Conkling as the epitome of the Ultra Stalwarts and the threat they posed to the success and good name of the Republican party. It was perhaps Conkling's manner as well as methods that made him appear to Hoar as the most objectionable of the Stalwarts. Conkling was a handsome man who held a high opinion of himself and a low opinion of mankind. The product of Utica, New York, and middle-class respectability, he gained early success as a lawyer and orator and by the 1860's was the acknowledged if not undisputed boss of the state Republican party in New York. He had great talent for creating a political machine and greater talent for endangering it by displays of personal pique and vindictiveness. Arrogant without disguise, he had many toadies and no friends, a fact which bothered him not at all. He sought only to be admired for his physique

---

[35] *Congressional Record*, 44th Cong., 1st sess., *Proceedings of the Senate: Trial of W. W. Belknap*, 63 (6 May 1876).

and feared for his political power. In Conkling's view, politics was a game, but a serious one. Each state was seen as a fiefdom, controlled by a lord-boss who provided offices and protection in return for the fealty and support of his vassal-henchmen. In American politics as in medieval France, the ultimate concern was personal preservation.

Conkling's brand of partisan *Realpolitik* was increasingly distasteful to such Republicans as Hoar. Politics, they felt, should be the source of accomplishment as well as office. When Roscoe Conkling began to refer scornfully to the "snivel service reformers," Hoar's suspicions of the spoils system were confirmed. The Conkling crowd must not control the Republican party nor choose its nominee in the crucial election ahead.

Speaker James G. Blaine and Attorney General Benjamin Bristow appeared to be the most likely instruments for thwarting Conkling and his friends at the Cincinnati convention. Hoar was in correspondence with admirers of both men in the spring of 1876, but between the two he definitely favored Bristow. Blaine's opposition to Conkling was judged to represent a conflict of personalities rather than principles. In any case, Massachusetts should send to the convention a delegation uninstructed and free to swing its weight in the most advantageous manner—first to thwart the designs of Conkling and then to select among the anti-Conkling candidates the man best able to make the party of sound doctrines once again the party of pure politics. Secretly Hoar hugged the thought that it might be possible in the convention to arrange the nomination of his friend, William A. Wheeler of New York. Wheeler possessed a moral character equal to that of Bristow and a personality potentially more popular.

Hoar's hopes and efforts respecting the decision of the Cincinnati convention are of significance as they reflect not only the division of the Republican party occasioned by the clumsiness and arrogance of the Stalwarts but also the division that existed among the opponents of the Stalwarts. Some, such as Hoar, were prepared to support any candidate not identified with the Conkling faction, and while convinced that the Stalwarts must be defeated were equally convinced that the battle must be waged within the confines of the party. Others—some of them returning emigrés from the Liberal Republican movement—were determined to force a reformer upon the convention and were prepared to stir up popular pressure outside the party to effect that end. The decision of the Republican convention in 1876 kept the latter group within the party, but they were, in effect, already political independents. Those who thought as Hoar did would provide the core of what later became the Half-Breed faction of the Republican party— party regulars who disliked both the narrow partisanship of the Stalwarts and the political self-righteousness of the Independents.

The situation in Massachusetts represented a microcosm of the party as a whole. If in Massachusetts there was no single Stalwart boss, there were Ben Butler and Senator George S. Boutwell— quite different types but both strong supporters of the Grant administration. Then there were the Blaine men, such as Charles Devens; the Bristow men, suspicious of Blaine but prepared to accept him in a pinch; and, finally, Republicans like Thomas Wentworth Higginson and Moorfield Storey, who proclaimed their increasing readiness to discard all party affiliation unless the Republican nominee was spotless and to their liking. Hoar, by now one of the dominant figures in the state party, worried over the likelihood of another bolt and the danger of a convention deadlock.[36]

The month of May saw Hoar attempting to diminish friction between the Blaine and Bristow forces by honoring both men at a dinner at the Wormley Hotel, and accepting a position as one of Massachusetts' delegates-at-large to the convention scheduled to open on 14 June. Before it would open events occurred to hurt the chances of both Blaine and Bristow and accentuate factional division within the party. In the last weeks of May, Blaine's suspicious associations with the Little Rock and Fort Smith Railway became the subject of investigation and the talk of Washington. Though Blaine took the floor of the House on 5 June to offer a flamboyant defense, his chance for the Republican nomination was badly damaged.[37] Some of the most reform-minded and

---

[36] *See* Hoar's confidential letter to his relative, J. Evarts Greene, 6 March 1876, Hoar Papers. Also Ellis H. Roberts to Hoar, 27 May 1876, Hoar Papers.

[37] *See* James G. Blaine Papers, I, Library of Congress (particularly the certificate of J. S. Black and Matt H. Carpenter, 2 June 1876); Diary of James A. Garfield, 27 May, 5 June, 8 June 1876, Garfield Papers, Box 3, Library of Congress.

zealous of the Bristow boosters openly denounced Blaine, and though Hoar refused to attend their preconvention conferences, he was now certain it would be a serious mistake for the Republicans to nominate Blaine.[38] He could not believe that Blaine was guilty of any illegal act, but his dishonest acquaintances and lack of prudence rendered him justly vulnerable. As for Bristow, his enemies appeared to outnumber his friends. It appeared increasingly doubtful whether the angered Blaine men would ever lend Bristow their support. Hoar looked eagerly but unsuccessfully for signs of a Wheeler boom.

Developments at the Cincinnati convention cast little credit on Hoar's skill as political prophet, but, in the odd way of politics, they worked to his personal advantage. He did not seriously consider Rutherford B. Hayes prior to the convention and would not vote for him prior to the decisive ballot, but the choice of Hayes would assist Hoar in securing a seat in the Senate, where he would be for four years the confidant of the Hayes administration.

On the first six ballots at Cincinnati, Hoar and a majority of the Massachusetts delegation voted for Bristow and had the limited satisfaction of seeing that gentleman's total inch forward from 111 to 126. On each ballot Blaine led with around 300 votes; Conkling and Oliver Morton had about a hundred each; Hayes and a half-dozen other "favorite sons" trailed behind. All efforts by John M. Forbes and the Hoar brothers to stimulate further interest in Bristow were unavailing. The Blaine forces stood firm; the Bristow candidacy appeared dead. It was at this point that certain of the Stalwarts panicked. Don Cameron of Pennsylvania and Conkling suddenly became convinced that Blaine, their declared personal enemy, was certain to win unless they broke the deadlock by throwing their state delegations to a third candidate. In one of the more inexplicable decisions of politics they chose to

[38] *See* Henry Blanchard to Hoar, 10 May 1876; Bellamy Storer to Hoar, 1 June 1876, Hoar Papers. When Blaine suffered a sun stroke as he was about to attend church on Sunday, 11 June 1876—three days before the convention was to open—one Bristow man telegraphed E. Rockwood Hoar: "We feel that providence has taken Blaine entirely out of the question." E. Farnsworth to E. R. Hoar, 13 June 1876, Hoar Papers. For a more sympathetic view of Blaine's stroke and swift recovery *see* Diary of James A. Garfield, 11 June, 16 June 1876, Garfield Papers, Box 3, Library of Congress; and Henry L. Dawes to Electa S. Dawes, 14 June, 18 June 1876, Dawes Papers, Box 14, Library of Congress.

toss them to Rutherford B. Hayes, governor of Ohio and a pro-claimed advocate of civil service reform. It was a pyrrhic victory but their immediate objective was obtained; Blaine was defeated. When the Bristow forces saw the Stalwarts about to receive credit for breaking the deadlock, they hastily caucused and decided to throw their votes to Hayes. Hayes was nominated on the seventh ballot, and a highly confused Hoar declared himself content with the result. He was even more content when his friend and Conkling's New York enemy, William Wheeler received the vice-presidential nomination.[39]

Hoar's satisfaction grew as he studied the views of Hayes and the style of his Republicanism over the next few weeks. There was reason for satisfaction. Hayes' style of Republicanism was very similar to that of Hoar—both might be classed as early Half-Breeds. Hoar saw in Hayes a man who would purify the politics of the party while sustaining its principles; a man who would combine civil service reform and governmental economy with continued concern for the protection of domestic manufactures and the soundness of the currency. Better days were ahead for his party and himself; only a disputed election and a strange and potentially dangerous compromise obstructed the way.

---

[39] The day after Hayes's selection Hoar wrote his wife that it was "not a nomination to arouse great enthusiasm but respectable and safe." Two days later he declared the nomination "better than any that was proposed except Bristow or Wheeler." As for Wheeler's vice-presidential nomination, it was a source of balm as well as congratulation. It gave the lie to those who charged the Massachusetts delegation with wasting its influence and failing the candidacy of Bristow. Hoar to Ruth A. Hoar, 17 June, 19 June, 20 June, 22 June 1876; William A. Wheeler to Hoar, 24 June 1876, Hoar Papers.

# 3

## The Hayes Interlude

Never were Stalwart tactics more ingenious or prevalent than during the campaign of 1876 and its immediate aftermath, and never would victory taste more bitter. The Stalwarts brought political amorality to perfection in behalf of a candidate they would soon despise.

The congressional elections of 1874 had shown that American two-party politics were back to normal. The unnatural predominance of the Democrats in the 1850's and then of the Republicans in the dozen years after Fort Sumter were to be succeeded by a period of twenty years when the outstanding feature of national elections was the evenness of party strength—a fact of considerable importance in explaining the reluctance of either major party to welcome political innovation. The Republican managers in 1876 were little interested in scanning the far political horizon, but they were well aware that they presently faced a hard, uphill struggle. The odds-makers predicted a victory for the Democrats and their candidate, Governor Samuel Tilden of New York. The Panic of 1873 had initiated a serious depression, the political onus of which would bear heaviest on the party in power. The well-advertised

Grant scandals, the overthrow of the "carpetbag governments" in all the southern states but three, the desertion to the Democratic party of some of the Liberal Republicans of '72, the alleged reform-mindedness of the Democratic candidate—these and other factors appeared to many observers to guarantee a Democratic victory. These observers underestimated the Stalwart managers of the Hayes campaign, especially Zachariah Chandler, chairman of the National Committee. Money and oratory were his initial weapons; when these proved insufficient, others were available.

Zach Chandler, perhaps the most intelligent of all the Stalwart chieftains, found the Hayes campaign a source of many frustrations. The political sensitivities of the Republican candidate were a constant irritant and he cursed the Hayes Republicans of Ohio as men quick to beg political funds from the National Committee but too lazy to put the screws on political friends and office-holders. Certain Stalwart reliables threatened to "fly the track" if offices were not pledged; Negro leaders such as Frederick Douglass demanded reassurance and attention; former contributors proved reluctant to invest in what appeared a losing cause; in the South the remaining carpetbag governments were fast losing control, and their Republican officials were deeply discouraged.[1] A letter from one of Chandler's Indiana lieutenants, written in the closing days of the campaign, expressed the anxiety as well as the methods of the Stalwart managers:

> [The Democrats] seem to think they have nothing to do but let the polls open . . . I could not do otherwise than yield to the judgement of our best men, and go to work.
>
> I have the apportionment of funds made out, and have sent my runners to all distant localities. I want to be cautious and discreet, and yet beleive [*sic*] *ten* more could be judiciously and

[1] Z. Chandler to R. B. Hayes, 12 September 1876; R. G. Ingersoll to Z. Chandler, 25 September 1876; Frederick Douglass to Z. Chandler, 19 August 1876; Patrick N. Tynn to Z. Chandler, 1 November 1876, Zachariah Chandler Papers, VI, Library of Congress. When Chandler unsuccessfully requested Hoar to spend three weeks campaigning in the South, he had warned: "Our friends in the South must have the moral support of prominent Northern Republicans . . . or they cannot make the canvass with reasonable hope of success." Z. Chandler to Hoar, September 2, 1876. Hoar Papers.

profitably expended. I have so telegraphed in cipher to Jay Gould asking him to consult you . . . Not a dollar will go for anything *but use next Tuesday*. So far as it is now distributed, it is in the hands of men who don't steal . . .

I have adopted the plan of using most of the *funds* where we have the election boards, and a large floating population. In strong Democratic counties, we will use enough to insure a full poll of the vote and to pay broad shouldered fellows to stand at the polls.[2]

On the evening of 7 November it appeared that broad shoulders had not provided sufficient insurance; Democratic dollars and runners had apparently gained the prize for Tilden. And then, in the oft-told tale, the editor of the *New York Times* saw light in the darkness. If Florida, South Carolina, and Louisiana, three states under slipping carpetbag rule which were apparently going for Tilden, could be claimed by the Republicans, the "victorious" Tilden would have only 184 electoral votes and his opponent, 185.

It is still not certain which candidate and party was the true choice of the majority of eligible voters in these three states, but the papers of Zachariah Chandler and of the New Hampshire senator, William E. Chandler, leave no doubt that it was the intention of the National Republican Committee to persuade the election boards of those states to declare for Hayes by whatever means necessary.[3] Their justification was a sincere belief that thousands of Republican Negroes had been either prevented from voting or coerced to vote the Democratic ticket under threats of economic coercion and physical abuse. They determined to correct this wrong by persuading the Republican-controlled canvassing

[2] Patrick N. Tynn to Z. Chandler, 1 November 1876, Zachariah Chandler Papers, VI, Library of Congress.

[3] Among the more explicit communications in the weeks immediately following the election are those by the anxious carpetbag governors, M. L. Stearns of Florida, Daniel H. Chamberlain of South Carolina, and William P. Kellogg of Louisiana. *See*, especially, M. L. Stearns to Z. Chandler, 9 November 1876, Zachariah Chandler Papers, VI, Library of Congress; T. W. Osborne to M. L. Stearns, 9 November 1876, D. H. Chamberlain to W. E. Chandler, 15 November 1876, W. E. Chandler to W. P. Kellogg, 13 January 1877, W. E. Chandler, "The Hayes-Tilden canvass in 1876" (typed memorandum), Papers of William E. Chandler, vol. 43, Library of Congress.

boards of South Carolina, Florida, and Louisiana to invalidate, in those counties where Democratic coercion had been most evident, a sufficient number of Tilden ballots—by whatever pretext or device—to assure Republican success. If two wrongs failed to make a right, at least the last executed could help elect a president.

In the mind of Zachariah Chandler there was no occasion for either fear or half-measures: "The official count of the state of South Carolina shows that the state has gone for Hayes and Wheeler and we hope to have the same good news from Florida and Louisiana . . . If the Southern Rebels have not had fighting enough let them try it again. They can have all they want on short notice."[4] Southern election officials were assured of place and protection if their Democratic neighbors proved intolerant, and timid agents, frightened by thoughts of subsequent investigation, were removed to posts distant from the Democratic House of Representatives.[5]

The end justified all means, and the end appeared accomplished when the election boards of all three states certified a Republican majority of the total of "accepted ballots" and declared the Republican slate of electors legally chosen. In all these states, however, the Democratic electors refused to be read out of the election in so summary a fashion and submitted to Washington their names and ballots as representative of the legal will of Louisiana, Florida, and South Carolina. One of the most corrupt of presidential elections now achieved its status and title of the Disputed Election. Whether it deserves the further title of the Stolen Election depends on one's assessment of the Electoral Commission, an institutional innovation for which George F. Hoar as much as any man deserved the credit and the blame.

Hoar arrived in Washington on 4 December 1876 for the second session of the Forty-fourth Congress, privately pessimistic concerning Hayes's chances and sincerely worried over the prospect of

[4] Z. Chandler to James C. Courray, 20 November 1876, Zachariah Chandler Papers, VI, Library of Congress.

[5] John Sherman to D. A. Weber and James E. Anderson, 20 November 1876 (copy), William S. Dodge to W. E. Chandler, 19 December 1876, W. E. Chandler to George William Curtis, 5 January 1877, Papers of William E. Chandler, vol. 43, Library of Congress; Jay Gould to Z. Chandler, 30 November 1876, Papers of Zachariah Chandler, VI, Library of Congress.

armed resistance by the supporters of Tilden should they be defeated by means they considered illegal.[6] He determined to try with such friends in the House as George W. McCrary of Iowa to fashion an arrangement that would accord Hayes the greatest possible chance of success while denying the supporters of Tilden proper pretext for filibuster, slander, or rebellion.

Hoar was one of the seven House members appointed to a joint committee empowered to consider ways and means of settling the disputed election returns. After looking in vain for constitutional precedents, the joint committee began gradually to settle upon a scheme whereby Congress would establish a special, extraconstitutional commission to determine the rightful presidential electors of those states submitting conflicting returns—its decision to be final unless rejected by *both* the Republican Senate and the Democratic House.[7] Agreement upon the idea of a commission was more easily reached than an understanding respecting its composition. There would be members selected from the Senate, the House, and the Supreme Court, but how selected and how many? Various schemes of selection by lot were rejected, and the joint committee finally proposed a commission to be composed of five senators, five representatives, and five Supreme Court justices —the Senate to choose by party caucus and individual roll call three Republican members and two Democrats; the House to select three Democratic members and two Republicans; four justices of the Supreme Court to be identified in the enabling statute and these empowered to select a fifth from the membership of the Court. With the third week of January, the joint committee recommended the compromise device of the Electoral Commission to Senate, House, and public. It met criticism but final acceptance from all three bodies.

It was members of Hoar's own party who were the harshest initial critics of the Electoral Commission plan. Republicans as

<hr>

[6] Hoar to Ruth A. Hoar, 5 December 1876, Hoar Papers.

[7] James A. Garfield to Hoar, 29 December 1876; manila envelope marked, "Electoral Commission," Hoar Papers. The latter contains handwritten drafts attributed to Representative George McCrary, to whom Hoar allowed chief credit for fashioning the final version. *See* Hoar to Rutherford B. Hayes, 2 March 1877, Hayes Papers, Rutherford B. Hayes Library.

diverse as Jay Gould, the railroad speculator, and Adin Thayer, "the honest boss" of Worcester County, expressed their distrust for the plan, and a majority of the Stalwart Republicans would have none of it.[8] The latter took the position that the Constitution gave the presiding officer of the Senate full and unassisted authority to settle all disputes respecting the tally of electoral ballots. A deadlock, with Grant continuing in the White House, or a count by the presiding officer of the Republican Senate; such was the only option that most of the Stalwart Republicans were prepared to offer the Democratic opposition.

Hoar offered in the House the most effective speech in behalf of the Electoral Commission bill, analyzing the constitutional impropriety of letting the presiding officer of the Senate assume the right of Congress to determine electoral contests, describing the dangers of deadlock, and urging the necessity of achieving a solution that a majority of both parties and sections would accept as fair. He denounced the suggestion that the Electoral Commission was but a complicated device for deciding the presidency by lot. Even if one were to allow that the members drawn from House and Senate might be subject to "bias arising from old political opinions," surely the Supreme Court judges would be so conditioned by training and so mindful of posterity that they would not exhibit party division—and this was as true of the four whose names were enumerated in the bill as of the fifth they would select.[9]

When Hoar delivered this speech, two things had already occurred: (1) The Senate had approved the Electoral Commission bill by a sizeable margin, almost all the Democratic senators and a majority of the Republicans voting for it; and (2) Justice David Davis, a man of independent political leanings, whom all had thought the most likely justice to be selected for the fifth judicial seat on the commission, was elected to the Senate by the Illinois legislature and in consequence declared himself ineligible to serve

---

[8] Jay Gould to Zachariah Chandler, 17 January 1877, Zachariah Chandler Papers, VII, Library of Congress; Adin Thayer to Hoar, 21 January 1877, Hoar Papers. The Massachusetts General Court, however, passed a resolution approving the Electoral Commission bill by an overwhelming majority. Stephen M. Allen to Hoar, January 26, 1877, Hoar Papers.

[9] *Congressional Record*, 44th Cong., 2d sess., 940–942 (25 January 1877).

on the commission. The latter development, assuring as it did that the fifth judge would be a man of Republican background, should supposedly have defeated the Electoral Commission bill in the Democratic House—the Republicans voting for it, the Democratic majority against it. It proved otherwise. Almost all of the Democratic members of the House voted for it and secured its enactment; a majority of the Republican congressmen—including James Garfield and certain of Hayes's closest friends—voted against it.[10] In short, a majority of the Republican senators voted for the commission arrangement when it seemed likely that the fifteenth member would be an Independent with Democratic leanings; a majority of the Republican representatives voted against the commission plan after it was apparent that three of the judges would be Republicans. For this paradox there is no complete explanation but rather a significant probability: the Electoral Commission plan authored by Edmunds, McCrary, and Hoar was not a partisan trick nor was it a part of either the so-called "Bargain" or the broader "Compromise" of 1877. Its operation would facilitate both, but the bill itself was neither a product of conspiracy nor a conscious instrument for sectional economic development. It was, as Hoar had told the House, a bipartisan emergency arrangement "for determining that most vital of all questions, the title to executive power . . . under circumstances of special difficulty." The commission plan was designed to give each party the hope that their candidate could win and so have a free and clear title to the presidency. Those who voted for it were those most alarmed by the constitutional crisis of the disputed election. Hoar's efforts as a member of the joint committee were not primarily motivated by partisanship. His votes as a member of the Electoral Commission, however, are more liable to the charge.

Once the commission bill passed, the Republicans, like the Democrats, determined to fill the party complement with their best men and to secure a battery of eloquent lawyers to argue the party's case. From the Senate, the Republicans selected Edmunds of Vermont, Morton of Indiana, and Frelinghuysen of New Jersey; from

[10] *See* Diary of James A. Garfield, 18 January, 20 January 1877, Garfield Papers, Box 3, Library of Congress.

the House, James Garfield and George F. Hoar.[11] With unaccustomed unity Zachariah Chandler, Levi P. Morton of New York, and John Murray Forbes of Boston raised money for the Republican counsel, and General Lew Wallace consented to serve with others for a fee of two thousand dollars.[12]

The party's "case," which would be argued by Wallace and other Republican counsel before the sympathetic if narrow Republican majority of the commission was very simple and quite opposed to traditional Republican doctrine. Its constitutional bias was that of states' rights; its thesis, that each state, not Congress, had the right to determine who were its proper presidential electors. The Electoral Commission, serving as but the agent of Congress, had no power to go behind the returns but was constitutionally bound to accept the decision of the state, or, more exactly, the decision of that agency of the state empowered by its constitution and laws to certify the election result.

This was the argument of the Republican counsel and it was the argument proclaimed by Hoar as he prepared to cast his first vote, in behalf of the Hayes slate of electors from the state of Florida. It was a position expressed with clarity and inspired by partisanship. Previously Hoar's stand had been that of the broad constructionist, the man who would empower the national government to secure the political and educational rights of American citizenship. Having two years earlier been willing to go behind the returns and investigate fraud and corruption in the election of a Louisiana governor, it was primarily party loyalty that now persuaded Hoar to stand forth as the defender of the authority and certificates of the Republican election boards of Louisiana, South Carolina, and Florida. This fact was emphasized when the disputed returns from Oregon came before the commission, which sat in judicial dignity in the old Court chamber of the Capitol.

Oregon had undoubtedly gone Republican, but one of its three Republican electors proved to be constitutionally ineligible to

---

[11] *Ibid.*, 27 January, 30 January 1877.

[12] Levi P. Morton to Z. Chandler, 29 January 1877; J. M. Forbes to Z. Chandler, [?] January 1877, Zachariah Chandler Papers, VII, Library of Congress.

serve. The Oregon Democrats had thereupon proclaimed a Democratic elector automatically elevated to the vacancy; the Republicans had insisted that the two eligible Republican electors were empowered to fill the state quota. The state secretary, a Republican, certified the names of three Republicans; the Oregon governor, a Democrat, forwarded to Washington a mixed slate. Here the commission majority did go behind the returns, at least to the point of determining for themselves which was the legal certifying agency in the state of Oregon. It was determined that the laws of Oregon gave the secretary of state the authority "to make the canvass and record it" and the governor's function was only that of a filing clerk. The decisions of the commission majority in accepting the returns filed by the carpetbag governors of Florida, Louisiana, and South Carolina and rejecting that filed by the Democratic governor of Oregon were not directly contradictory but they exhibited a marked degree of flexibility.

Hoar's votes in the sessions of the commission were partisan in orientation but they were given with a clear conscience. Not only did he fear that a decision by the commission to go behind the returns would dangerously prolong the constitutional crisis, but he was certain in his own mind that "the will of the people" in all four states demanded the recognition of the Republican electors.[13] This conviction he would express and defend now and later, and never more succinctly than in his autobiography:

> There was no question or pretense in any quarter that the will of the people of Oregon was not given due effect by the judgment of the Electoral Commission.
>
> I do not believe that there are any considerable number of intelligent persons in the country, now that the excitement of the time has gone by, who doubt that the will of the people of South Carolina and Florida and Louisiana was carried into effect by the judgment of the Commission, and that their judgment baffled an unscrupulous conspiracy to deprive the ma-

[13] *See* "Draft Biography of H. L. Dawes by Anna L. Dawes," Chapter VI, 31–32, Dawes Papers, Container #39, Library of Congress.

jorities in those states of their lawful rights in the election because those majorities were made up largely of negroes.[14]

When the commission on the last day of February 1877 completed its labors by voting in behalf of the Hayes electors of South Carolina, and again by a vote of 8 to 7, Hoar was relieved, disappointed, and anxious. He was relieved that the commission had upheld the Republican position at all points and accorded Hayes the essential twenty electoral votes; disappointed that the judicial members had divided along party lines and so lessened the strength of the commission's decision; anxious that the Democrats might filibuster and prevent Congress from completing the count by inaugural day. Seemingly uninformed of any "bargain" between the friends of Hayes and certain Democratic congressmen, nor privy to the broader if more informal arrangements of the "Compromise of 1877," Hoar was both surprised and grateful when the Democratic speaker of the House, Samuel J. Randall, squashed the obstructionist efforts of certain northern Democrats and the House at 4:15 in the morning of the second of March completed the count, approved a resolution affirming the election of Hayes, and declared the troubled history of the Forty-fourth Congress at an end.[15]

Though not a participant, Hoar must at some point have become aware of the rumors circulating about Washington by late February of the "Wormley conference"—where friends of Hayes met with certain southern Democrats and offered pledges that the

[14] G. F. Hoar, *Autobiography of Seventy Years* (N.Y., 1903), I, 374. *See*, too, Hoar to S. D. Pinkerton, 5 July 1904, Hoar Papers. Not only did Hoar consider his service on the commission one of the most valuable services he ever rendered the American public—a framed and autographed composite picture of the members of the commission hung in the downstairs hall of his Worcester home from 1878 until his death—but he appointed himself the custodian of the reputation of its Republican members. Charges by Abraham Hewitt and others that Justice Bradley had been persuaded to change his vote always incited heated and lengthy denials. *See.* especially, William Jordan to Hoar, 17 March 1877; Hoar to Charles Bradley, 9 June 1898; Hoar to Joseph M. Rogers, 11 February, 25 April 1904, Hoar Papers.

[15] *See* Diary of James A. Garfield, 1 March 1877, Garfield Papers, Box 3, Library of Congress. Garfield's diary for the month of February 1877 offers the best contemporary description of the arrangements and hearings of the Electoral Commission.

last of the federal troops would be withdrawn from the South if the southern Democrats accepted the predictable decision of the Electoral Commission. Actually there were several meetings at the Wormley Hotel in the month of February, not merely the single dramatic session of historic fable, but recent research has in any case largely exploded their significance.[16] Professor C. Vann Woodward has proven that the alleged bargain of February 1877 was but a minor feature of a far-broader agreement, one arranged over a period of many weeks and featuring the economic interests of certain railroad promoters and southern business men as well as the political needs of the Hayes Republicans and Southern Redeemers.[17] Ex-Whig elements in the South saw in a temporary combination with certain Northern capitalists and Republicans a more likely path to economic revival than appeared probable with a national administration controlled by Tilden Democrats, and so consented to the election of Hayes. A victory for the Anglo-Saxon tradition of orderly compromise was secured through the instrumentalities of racial distrust and economic ambition. The Compromise of 1877 was in fact, however informal its nature and incomplete its fulfillment, not only an arrangement for the election of a president and the future "redemption" of three southern states, but a half-conscious effort to work out a new distribution of party power and a new balance between the rival claims of sectional capitalists.[18]

Though Hoar played no part in the correspondence and discussions that fashioned this broader compromise, the electoral count bill had helped facilitate it, and Hoar would be among the first to endorse the intentions of President Hayes to inaugurate the New Departure. He would give that endorsement as the junior senator from Massachusetts.

[16] *See* Diary of James A. Garfield, 26 February 1877, Garfield Papers, Box 3, Library of Congress. In his diary Garfield took care to explain that he attended the meeting of 26 February only at the invitation of Representative Stanley Matthews, where "suspecting that a compact of some kind was meditated" and "former consultations" had been held, he warned the assembled against any arrangements "that would be or appear to be a political bargain."

[17] C. Vann Woodward, *Reunion and Reaction* (Boston: Little, Brown, 1951), especially 208–246.

[18] Roy Nichols, *Stakes of Power* (New York: Hill and Wang, 1961), 217–229.

In June 1876 Hoar had announced to his Worcester constituents that he would not be a candidate for a fifth congressional term. He refused to reconsider his decision and informed his wife that his public life was over and his political ambitions fully satisfied.[19] He believed the former to be true; the latter was pure self-deception. By August 1876 Hoar had his eyes fixed on the senatorial seat of George S. Boutwell. He considered his chances negligible, however, and he was determined not to risk his political purity with a personal campaign or open canvass.[20] Fortunately there were in Massachusetts sources of support that would satisfy his ambition without endangering his principles.

The senatorial candidacy of George Hoar found support from a fairly wide political spectrum in Massachusetts: the old Free Soil element represented by former Governor William Claflin; politically conscious young lawyers such as John D. Long and Hoar's former law student, Colonel John D. Washburn; anti-Butler Republican professionals such as Adin Thayer; Republican businessmen-politicians, represented by Alanson W. Beard; self-declared political Independents, such as Moorfield Storey. For varying reasons these men would see political advantages in the elevation of Hoar to the Senate. For some his election would represent a reassertion of the old faith of the Republican party; for others it would represent a defeat for the Stalwarts; and for still others it would represent an opportunity to deliver a blow to a despised personal enemy, Ben Butler.[21] It was possibly to Ben Butler more than any man that Hoar would owe his initial election to the United States Senate. It was the proclaimed animosity of Butler as much as any act of his own that marked Hoar as "the reform candidate"; it was the endorsement of Butler, more than any act of his own, that marked Boutwell as a Stalwart and a man

---

[19] Hoar to John D. Washburn, 2 July 1876; Hoar to Ruth A. Hoar, 2 July 1876, Hoar Papers.

[20] As late as December 1876, Hoar informed his wife that Boutwell would be re-elected and that perhaps "it would be for the best." Hoar to Ruth A. Hoar, 5 December 1876, Hoar Papers.

[21] Hoar to William Claflin, 13 October 1876, William Claflin Papers, Rutherford B. Hayes Library; I. W. Potter to Hoar, 10 May 1876, John D. Washburn to Hoar, 30 June 1876, Adin Thayer to Hoar, 22 December 1876, Hoar Papers.

tainted with "the bad and mischievous element in the Republican party."[22]

George Boutwell had enjoyed a distinguished and erratic political career. Originally a Democrat he had been one of the first of the Massachusetts Democrats to swing into the Free Soil ranks, and in consequence had enjoyed election to the governor's chair in 1851 and to Congress in 1863. He had served as Secretary of the Treasury in Grant's first administration, neither participating in corruption nor seemingly desirous of discovering it, and then had succeeded Henry Wilson in the United States Senate, in March 1873, when Wilson was elevated to the vice-presidency. Boutwell's abbreviated senatorial term would expire in March 1877 and his re-election or replacement would be determined by the Massachusetts General Court in January.

Massachusetts had a tradition of retaining her senators for several terms and as late as the spring of 1876 few observers doubted Boutwell's re-election. Eighteen hundred and seventy-six was a poor year for the Grant administration, however, and for those associated with it in the public mind, and by the late summer groups were organizing within the Republican party of Massachusetts determined to defeat Boutwell and so express their displeasure with Grant and with Butler. Boutwell had incurred the displeasure of some by voting to acquit Secretary Belknap and the anger of others by his association with the Stalwarts in the Cincinnati convention. Not a Stalwart in his political morals, Boutwell was a man of stronger feelings than intelligence, and one of his strongest feelings was that of loyalty. In his loyalty to Grant, he refused to convict Belknap, to support Bristow, or to fight the influence of Butler with the Grant administration. The last was his greatest sin in the eyes of a growing number of Massachusetts Republicans and Independents.

One man could have probably saved Boutwell: Henry L. Dawes of Pittsfield, elected to the United States Senate two years previously. Dawes, a rather enigmatic figure, was a charter Republican with a public reputation for conservative good sense and rock-

[22] *New York Daily Tribune,* 20 January 1877.

ribbed honesty. So far as his own interests were concerned he was highly opportunistic, and in the bitter senatorial contest of January 1877 he played both sides of the fence. Through the agency of his daughter he informed Hoar as early as August 1876 that he looked forward to greeting Hoar as a fellow senator, but Dawes' closest political adviser, Edward R. Tinker would offer advice to the Boutwell forces during the long days of balloting in the General Court.[23] Dawes probably wished to see Boutwell unseated but was reluctant to declare his preference in case the latter was to remain his senatorial colleague. The only certainty is that Dawes refused openly to endorse Boutwell and lend Boutwell his aura of taciturn and total respectability. Failing to receive this, Boutwell could rely only on the clumsy and distant support of the Grant administration and the two-edged support of the Butler machine. Against the skilled, careful organization of Thayer and Washburn, this proved insufficient.

As reported in the press "Col. Washburn took the job of organizing inside the Legislature while Mr. Thayer worked quietly at the Hoar headquarters in the Tremont House." Washburn divided the Hoar supporters in the legislature into county committees that were instructed to make a thorough canvass of the members from their respective counties "and report faithfully every morning at headquarters" to Mr. Thayer.[24] Their efforts, in conjunction with the editorial pressures exerted by the *Boston Advertiser* and *Herald*, secured converts and victory. After three days and seven ballots, Hoar gained the necessary majority of both houses of the General Court.

The senator-elect had remained in Washington, determinedly ignorant of the labors of his friends. The latter were now warmly thanked and they replied with long letters, describing the struggle and apportioning praise with a liberal hand.[25] More interesting, however, were the reactions of the Massachusetts press and the

[23] Ruth A. Hoar to Hoar, 1 August 1876; Hoar to Ruth A. Hoar, 2 August, 10 August 1876; Adin Thayer to Hoar, 21 August 1877, Hoar Papers.

[24] Unidentified clipping of 21 January 1877, Pamphlet Box, "Jan., 1877," Hoar Papers.

[25] *See*, especially, Adin Thayer to Hoar, 21 January 1877; John D. Washburn to Hoar, 14 January 1877. Hoar Papers.

Massachusetts Independents. The *Boston Herald* and *Advertiser* proclaimed his election a "victory for the best wing of the Republican party" and a defeat for "the power of the lobby of federal office-holders"; the *Globe* and the *Post* were convinced that Hoar's election would help restore the lost prestige of Massachusetts in the Senate. A more balanced appraisal was offered by Samuel Bowles, editor of the *Springfield Republican:*

> The election of Geo. F. Hoar . . . is a step in advance. It represents party elevation and emancipation. Mr. Hoar has not the Senatorial temper and impartiality, it must be confessed, but he has in high degree the Senatorial moral and intellect. If he is one-sided and partisan and provincial, it is the one-sidedness and partisanship and provincialism of a great, strong, independent and honest nature—such as Massachusetts has furnished and honored before.[26]

Bowles's judgment was echoed by Hoar's Harvard classmate, Professor Charles Eliot Norton, self-acknowledged "apostle of beauty" and a political Independent. Norton thought Hoar a shade illiberal and too ready to revive the sectional animosities of the past, but he was certain that for Hoar as himself good politics was to be defined in terms of purity and principle. "To all of us who have the honor of Massachusetts at heart," he informed his classmate, "your election is a matter of heartiest satisfaction." Less than three weeks later, however, Norton felt compelled to chide Hoar for the latter's commendation of the defeated Boutwell. This was judged a "bad sign" and Hoar was warned: "We look to you to maintain Puritan traditions of uprightness & intelligence."[27]

As with many of the initial Half-Breeds, Hoar was often caught between the partisan intolerance of the Stalwarts and the intolerant moralism of the Independents. The Hayes administration found itself in a similar position, and it found no one more sympathetic than the new senator from Massachusetts. Hoar becomes in the Hayes years, for the first time, a figure of national political im-

[26] Excerpts from the *Worcester Evening Gazette*, 15 January 1877. *See*, too, George S. Merriam, *The Life and Times of Samuel Bowles* (N.Y., 1885), II, 277.

[27] Norton to Hoar, 25 January, 14 February 1877, Hoar Papers. *See*, too, William Everett to Hoar, 21 January 1877, Hoar Papers.

portance. With his senatorial victory he gained in Massachusetts the right to share political power with Henry L. Dawes; with the confidence granted him by Rutherford B. Hayes he gained the opportunity to help fashion the policies of the national administration.[28]

The Hayes administration would be a source of derision for many Democrats and of contention for numerous Republicans, but in Hoar's opinion it was "a brilliant administration." There was no administration earlier or later he found more congenial to his own brand of Republicanism. Empathy was shown in two ways: in his relations with Hayes on matters of patronage; in the support he offered administration policies concerning the South, the currency, and the civil service.

From the beginning of his administration, Hayes saw in Massachusetts a potential source of support and determined to include a Massachusetts man in his cabinet. Hoar was equally determined that the claims of his old law partner, the Civil War hero, Charles Devens, be acknowledged. His sense of political propriety forbade him, however, to cajole or demand. His recommendation was offered in terms respectful of presidential independence. Recommendations so cast were most pleasing to Hayes. Not only was Devens soon informed of his selection as Attorney General, but Hayes would subsequently consider Hoar the soundest Massachusetts man in Washington. He would ask Hoar's advice respecting the appointment of William M. Evarts as Secretary of State, accord quick acceptance to Hoar's recommendations concerning the claims of various deserving Massachusetts veterans, and accept more slowly Hoar's choices for the more important federal offices in Boston.[29]

[28] As earlier that power had been wielded by the forces of Henry Wilson and Boutwell and later would be by Henry Cabot Lodge, so in the years, 1877–1893 the Hoar-Dawes group predominated through its lieutenants, Adin Thayer, Alanson Beard, and Edward Tinker.

[29] Charles Devens Jr. to Hoar, 6 March 1877, Hoar Papers; Hoar to R. B. Hayes, 8 March 1877, 16 July 1879, 15 January, 26 January, 25 June 1880, Hayes Papers, Rutherford B. Hayes Library; Hoar to Commissioner, Bureau of Pensions, 6 July 1878, Hoar Papers. Hoar was offered the post of minister to England in 1879, which he declined. W. M. Evarts to Hoar, 4 August, 5 December 1879; Alexander Bullock to Hoar, 8 December 1879; "Diary Ledger of G. F. Hoar, December 1, 1879–May 7, 1880," Hoar Papers.

Hoar's influence with the Hayes administration was suspected early, and he was the recipient of hundreds of letters from self-seeking constituents. He was selective in forwarding their claims. Usually he tried to make a distinction between referral and recommendation; always he took pains to inform the officer in question that he had no intention to trespass upon the independence or efficiency of his department. Hoar, indeed, had little desire to create a personal machine. The paradox of his position and that of the Hayes Administration was that righteous efforts to rid the Republican party of the taint of Stalwart politics apparently made it necessary to force the dismissal of one's enemies and promote the claims of one's friends. Civil servants should be protected in their tenure of office, Hoar believed, but only after Butler men had been removed and replaced by Republicans respected for personal character and capacity. Hoar was not unaware of the seeming ambiguity of a civil service reformer demanding the removal of office holders on the score of their factional affiliation. In a letter to John Murray Forbes, he wrote:

> Your telegram reached me just as the Senate was about to vote on Odell [of the Boston Appraiser's Office]. I had never heard of him before. I could therefore say nothing except that he is a Butler man which is hardly a reason to assign to the Senate. *Our* way of thinking prohibits us from making the claim that appointments or confirmations shall turn on the mere wish of the Senator. Our friends at home must therefore supply us with some material when the question of appointing or confirming these Butlerite officers comes up hereafter.[30]

It was wrong to use patronage to build a personal machine; it was necessary to use patronage to place certain key federal offices in Massachusetts in the hands of men sympathetic to "the Cincinnati Platform and present Administration." Applicants for the job of census taker should be respectfully referred to the Census Bureau in Washington, but more aggressive tactics were in order when it came to replacing one of Butler's lieutenants as Collector

[30] Hoar to J. M. Forbes, 16 March 1877, Hoar Papers. *See*, too, Hoar to Forbes, 10 May 1877, Hoar Papers; Hoar to Forbes, 30 May 1877, G. F. Hoar Papers, Rutherford B. Hayes Library.

of the Port of Boston. Alanson W. Beard was hand-picked by Hoar and a long and successful campaign waged to secure his appointment to the Custom House.[31]

Hoar had occasion in the years 1878–1879 to be rather dismayed at the political vigor exerted by the new Collector in cleaning house, but the displeasure of Butler was good evidence that purity was in the ascendant, and the subsequent desertion by Butler to the Democratic party, cause for relief.[32] In the future all enemies would be "in front of us," and there would be constructed in Massachusetts a Republican organization known for its opposition to political servility and constant in its devotion to the state's federal senators.[33] Principle would triumph over all, even paradox.

If Hoar found the appointment policy of Hayes generally satisfactory, he considered the new tone in the White House positively delightful. Unlike his more sophisticated cousin, William M. Evarts —who groaned over official state dinners "where the water flowed like champagne"—Hoar had nothing but respect for the prohibitionist principles and social simplicity of "Lemonade Lucy" Hayes. He found the anxious gravity and moralistic speech of her husband as satisfactory as his opposition to fiat money.[34] Hoar's confidence was returned in full measure. Hayes declared himself "highly gratified" when Hoar persuaded the Massachusetts Republican convention in 1877 to bestow a blanket approval on the

[31] The Battle of the Custom House was waged from April 1877 through 18 March 1878. Typical campaign memoranda are the following: A. W. Beard to Hoar, 14 April 1877, 13 January 1878; William Cogswell to Hoar, 4 October 1877; A. W. Beard to Adin Thayer, 6 January 1878; Adin Thayer to Hoar, 14 January 1878; J. M. Forbes to Hoar, 19 January 1878, Hoar Papers. *See,* too, Parker C. Chandler to H. L. Dawes, [?] January 1878, W. A. Simmons to H. L. Dawes, 18 January, 25 January 1878, A. W. Beard to Dawes, 24 January 1878, H. L. Dawes Papers, Library of Congress; G. F. Hoar to R. B. Hayes, 18 February, 23 February 1878 and 23 February 1878 (#2), Hayes Papers, Rutherford B. Hayes Library. Hoar would always regard the Boston collectorship and the offices of Boston District Attorney, Postmaster, and Port Assessor as essentially political appointments. These offices must be held by men sympathetic to the policies of the federal administration.

[32] *See* A. Beard to Hoar, 6 May 1878; 28 February 1879, Hoar Papers; and the excellent article by William B. Mallam, "Butlerism in Massachusetts," *New England Quarterly.* 33 (June 1960), 186–206.

[33] Hoar to H. L. Dawes, 28 August 1878, H. L. Dawes Papers, Library of Congress; Hoar to William Claflin, 20 November 1878, William Claflin Papers, Rutherford B. Hayes Library.

[34] *See* Hoar to Hayes, 21 August 1877, 28 June 1879; Hayes to Hoar, 2 July 1879, Hayes Papers, Rutherford B. Hayes Library.

policies of the new administration. The President could only hope that other states would follow the lead of Massachusetts and give to the nation leaders possessed of "the character of the persons taking part in politics there."[35]

Hayes's satisfaction with Hoar's performance before the Republican convention in Worcester, 19 September 1877 was indicative of more than personal cordiality. It was indicative of Hayes's apprehensive concern for the public reception accorded the New Departure. In retrospect, Hayes's controversial effort to formulate a new southern policy for the Republican party stands forth as the most significant feature of his administration; surely it was the policy which most absorbed Hoar's attention. With conscious effort, Hoar declared himself in the years 1877–1878 a "statesman of reconciliation."

The New Departure was a policy of "reunion and reaction." An effort would be made to restore harmony between the sections by refraining from further federal intervention in behalf of the southern Negro and southern Republican. It was a policy suggested by the Liberal Republicans of 1872, indicated by the Republican platform of 1876, and encouraged by the particular difficulties of Hayes's position. Though probably never fully cognizant of the compromise arrangements that made possible his inauguration, Hayes was well aware of the fact that the House of Representatives continued under Democratic control, and that northern opinion appeared increasingly wearied with the long aftermath of Reconstruction and increasingly apathetic toward the cause of Negro rights.[36] After some backing and filling, Hayes on the twenty-fourth of April ordered the last of the federal troops

[35] Worcester *Daily Spy*, 20 September 1877; *Knoxville Dispatch*, [?] September 1877, as quoted in the *Boston Journal*, 25 September 1877. In December 1878, Hayes twice tried to persuade Hoar to enter his cabinet, and when unsuccessful expressed disappointment and regard in equal measure. Hoar to Ruth A. Hoar, 11 December, 13 December 1878; C. P. Searle to Hoar, 26 March 1879, Hoar Papers.

[36] One of the more penetrating and concise evaluations of this apathy and its causation will be found in James W. McPherson's *The Struggle for Equality: Abolitionists and the Negro in the Civil War and Reconstruction* (Princeton, N.J.: Princeton University Press, 1964), 430–431:

The freedom and equality of the Negro was based in part on the idealistic traditions of the abolitionist movement, but in greater part on the military and political exigencies of war and reconstruction. The North's conversion to eman-

withdrawn from the South and offered no interference when there quickly followed the collapse of the last two carpetbag governments at Columbia and New Orleans. Making a virtue of necessity, he declared that the withdrawal of the troops was symbolic of a new policy. The national government would seek to heal the scars of war by cultivating the good will of the southern whites—allowing them a fair share of national economic benefits and political honors —while relying upon their leaders to respect the rights of the Negro. The nation and Republican party should advance old goals by new tactics. Efforts to support carpetbag governments by force of federal arms and to protect Negro rights by means of federally supported Republican organizations must give way to a policy of sectional trust and constitutional restraint.

The New Departure facilitated the return of Bourbon democracy to control of southern politics, accelerated the decline of the Republican party in the South, and encouraged the disfranchisement of the southern Negro. Such were not, however, its intentions. Though his policy was as much the result of external pressures as personal conviction, Hayes sincerely believed that by reconciling the southern whites to the intentions of the national administration it might be possible to build a strong biracial Republican party in the South and so better insure equality of opportunity for the Negro. A policy of sectional conciliation need mean neither the sacrifice of southern Republicans nor southern Negroes, declared Hayes, and George F. Hoar proclaimed his agreement at the Republican state convention in Worcester.

Well aware that many charter Republicans in Massachusetts were critical of the public dismissal of Radical Reconstruction, Hoar sought to persuade his fellow delegates of its propriety and wisdom. The President had been subject to severe criticism in three particulars: "He has refused to use the military forces to maintain the governments of Chamberlain in South Carolina and Packard

---

cipation and equal rights was primarily a conversion of expediency rather than one of conviction . . . A policy based on "military necessity" may be abandoned when the necessity disappears, and this is what happened in the 1870's. It became expedient for northern political and business interests to conciliate southern whites, and an end to federal enforcement of Negro equality in the South was the price of conciliation. The mass of northern people had never loved the Negro, were tired of the "everlasting negro question," and were glad to see the end of it.

in Louisiana; he has appointed a Southern Democrat, formerly a high officer in the Confederate army, to a seat in his Cabinet; he has manifested in his personal and official bearing a spirit of friendliness and confidence toward the Southern whites." In each particular criticism was unjustified.

It was true that the withdrawal of troops from Columbia and New Orleans had facilitated the overthrow of Republican state governments there, but the President was virtually forced to withdraw the troops because the Democratic House had in the previous Congress blocked appropriations for the army. What is more, the President saw the danger and futility of continued military intervention. He had not abandoned force just because force for the time being was impossible; rather he had determined "to meet in a spirit of confidence and friendship the assurances of prominent Southern men, of a desire on their part to support in good faith, hereafter, the results of the war and the whole amended Constitution." To declare now that the time for conciliation had come implied no repudiation of the righteous Republican efforts of the past. The war had been fought to bring the South "not to your feet, but only to your side." This was understood by that gallant Civil War veteran, General Rutherford B. Hayes and so he welcomed to his cabinet the former Confederate, David M. Key and offered to the southern whites his friendship and assistance. There could be no permanent national prosperity without Southern prosperity; there could be no permanent protection of the rights of the southern Negro without the cooperation of the southern whites. The American people would not renounce their duty toward the colored population of the South, but they would see that the time for exercising extraordinary executive power was past and the time for accepting the pledges of the Southern leaders was at hand.[37]

[37] Hon. G. F. Hoar, "The Republican Party in Massachusetts" (pamphlet), Hoar Papers; Worcester *Daily Spy*, 20 September 1877. In publicly proclaiming his support for the New Departure, Hoar effectively if half-consciously seized the lead of the Massachusetts Republican Party from his colleague, Henry L. Dawes. Dawes' some-time adviser, Samuel Bowles, editor of the *Springfield Republican*, had urged Dawes to issue a statement prior to the state convention, but Dawes held back with habitual caution and expressed his support only later and less forcefully. *See* Bowles to Dawes, 26 August 1877, H. L. Dawes Papers, Box #23, Library of Congress; Bowles to Henry M. Spofford, [n.d.], Merriam, *Life and Times of Samuel Bowles*, II, 430.

Hoar's address was the subject of certain veiled sneers by the Democratic press—who contrasted his present "conservatism" with his Radical speeches of the past—but the state convention adopted a platform parroting his views at all points.[38] Those views were surely at variance with his stern warnings during the election of 1872 to beware the unrepentent southern supporters of Horace Greeley, but his conversion was neither sudden nor imitative. Over the past two years Hoar had become disillusioned with the success of Radical Reconstruction. Service on a subcommittee investigating electoral frauds in Louisiana in the winter of 1875 had encouraged disillusionment. That investigation, by revealing numerous instances of corruption and factional bickering, and displaying the antagonism of the business community of New Orleans for the Republican state government, gave him reason to doubt the stability of the Southern Republican organizations under existing policies and conditions. Sympathy for the circumscribed liberty of the President and growing disenchantment with the fruits of force combined to persuade Hoar to accept the states' rights features of the New Departure and declare that policy consistent with Republican principles.[39]

Hoar and Hayes both felt that education offered the best permanent guarantee for proper observance of the Civil War amendments in the South. Through the agency of the common school the Negro would gain moral elevation and general respect, and the re-educated southern white would be made aware of the wastefulness of racial suspicion and prejudice. Whereas Hoar had earlier advocated a program of national support of primary education as a supplement to federal intervention in behalf of the rights of the southern Negro, he now apparently saw it as a substitute to such intervention. To the members of a Young Men's Independent Republican Club in Massachusetts he wrote:

[38] *See* the *Boston Post.* 20 September 1877.

[39] Although Hoar was not, as noted earlier, a participant in the correspondence and conversations that formed the Compromise of 1877, he was aware of the obligation owed by Hayes to the southern Democrats who had refused to filibuster against the final report of the Electoral Commission. Hoar instructed his Massachusetts constituents to accept in good faith "the pledges of these same men respecting obedience to the amended Constitution." Interview, *Boston Globe*, 5 September 1877.

The experience of General Grant's administration, and the nature of Republican government itself, satisfy us that the rights of no class of citizens can be long preserved in any State against a minority who are their superiors in education, courage and physical power by the mere application of force from without . . . I have long been of the opinion that they will never be secured until institutions of universal learning like our own shall be established throughout the whole country, and that every recourse, both of private liberality and national power, should be strained to effect that result.[40]

Though both sincere and carefully rationalized, Hoar's new role as a proponent of sectional harmony was neither uniformly praised nor of long duration. One of the most caustic of his critics was James G. Blaine. While presenting Congress with a statue of Maine's first governor, Blaine had taken occasion to offer various insulting references to the tyrannical conduct of Massachusetts in the years when Maine was its province—possibly inspired by the failure of Massachusetts to support him in the convention of 1876. Hoar leaped to the defense of his state. Blaine then turned on Hoar and somewhat irrelevantly accused him of being "a person prepared to do every possible thing to bring about a reconciliation between the two sections of the country" and a man forgetful of the duty owed the southern Negro by the Republican party. Hoar hotly denied the charge, but its sting remained.[41] More disagreeable than the attacks of Blaine, however, was the dismal failure of the southern Republican party in the congressional elections of 1878. The electoral failure of the New Departure inspired fresh doubts respecting its justice and wisdom. By the spring of 1879 Hoar was no longer convinced of either.[42]

Various events were responsible for Hoar's short tenure as a leading apostle of sectional reconciliation and accord. Among the more obvious were the campaign victories of the Democrats in

[40] Hoar to Young Men's Independent Republican Club of Melrose, Massachusetts, 19 January 1878, Hoar Papers.

[41] *Congressional Record*, 45th Cong., 2d sess., 458–459 (22 January 1878); *Boston Advertiser*, 23 January 1878; *Ohio State Journal*, January 26, 1878.

[42] See *Congressional Record*, 45th Cong., 3d sess., 1022–1025 (5 February 1879).

1878, the failure of the southern whites to join the Republican party, the continued intimidation of Negro voters in the South, and the conduct of the southern Bourbons in Congress. In combination they inspired a revived suspicion of southern democracy and a renewed insistence on the injustice of racial discrimination.

Suspicion of southern democracy was reflected in a demand that the "unrepentent" Jefferson Davis be explicitly excluded from a bill granting pensions to veterans of the Mexican War and, more relevantly, in a speech denouncing the obstructionist tactics of the Democratic leadership in the House of Representatives.[43] Hoar's renewed battle for Negro equality was reflected both in his call for greater Negro representation at West Point and in his opposition to suggestions that there be established an annual quota of Negro cadets. The latter would be discriminatory. The cure was not to establish an artificial ratio, but to make assignments "absolutely forgetful" of differences of race and to remember "that every human soul is equal in political and personal rights to every other human soul."[44] That conviction also found expression in Hoar's encouragement of the efforts of General Thomas M. Conway to assist the emigration and resettlement of "oppressed freedmen desirous of leaving the South."[45]

Never at any time did Hoar publicly criticize the southern policy of Hayes but after the spring of 1879 he was no longer its spokesman. Perhaps the clearest indication of Hoar's disenchantment with the New Departure came with his speech before the Republican state convention at Worcester, 16 September 1879. On the very platform where two years before he had demanded faith in the word and pledges of the statesmen of the South, he was to be heard denouncing those who had "usurped" the governments of Louisiana, Mississippi, and South Carolina and rendered ineffective the right of Negro suffrage:

[43] *Congressional Record,* 45th Cong., 3d sess., 2225–2227 (1 March 1879); 46th Cong., 1st sess., 64–68 (25 March 1879). *See,* too, Hoar's defense of the character and senatorial seat of William P. Kellogg, the last of the carpetbag senators, *Congressional Record,* 46th Cong., 2d sess., 3164–3166 (10 May 1880).

[44] *Congressional Record,* 46th Cong., 2d sess., 2858 (29 April 1880). *See,* too, Charles W. Walker to Hoar, 10 April 1880, Hoar Papers.

[45] Hoar to John M. Forbes, Henry P. Riddle, and Adin Thayer, 28 May 1879; General Thomas M. Conway to Hoar, 24 June 1879, Hoar Papers.

The time requires fair warnings and plain truths. If our brethren at the South will show us any way to promote their moral or material prosperity, no one of their own representatives will pursue it with more eagerness or desire than ours. We will help build their schoolhouses; we will help revive their commerce; we will help improve their rivers and harbors and cover their land with railroads. But for their sake, as well as our own, we will not permit them to wipe out the results of the war, or to trample under their heels either our own constitutional rights or those of our Republican fellow-citizens.[46]

If Hoar's support of Hayes' Southern policy sharply diminished as time went on, his faith in the fiscal wisdom of the administration and its Secretary of the Treasury John Sherman grew steadily. Hoar was a "hard money man" throughout his public career, an advocate of a specie currency. He had accepted the issue of greenback dollars during the Civil War years, and never doubted the constitutional right of the national government to declare them legal tender, but they were to be justified as a wartime, emergency measure. His personal sentiments were rather like the simplistic notions of the Loco Focos of Andy Jackson's day; he could not help but feel there was something at least potentially dishonest in giving a workingman a piece of paper for a hard day's labor.

In the Grant administration, Hoar had voted consistently in favor of contracting the greenbacks and advocated a policy whereby the greenback dollar would be declared redeemable in gold—and so, in effect, hard money. Paradoxically, however, he voted against the Specie Resumption Act of 1875, which provided for the full redeemability of greenbacks in gold as of 1 January 1879. Though he would later proclaim this act one of the greatest accomplishments of the Republican party, he was at the time of its passage disappointed that it did not enforce its support of hard money with a provision for the gradual retirement of all greenback dollars. Without such a provision he suspected that it would

---

[46] Worcester *Daily Spy*, 17 September 1879 (four-page supplement); *Boston Journal*, 17 September 1879.

prove ineffectual or indeed an instrument for future inflation of the currency.[47]

It would be deceptively easy to categorize Hoar's opposition to greenbacks and monetary inflation as the automatic response of a politician-spokesman of the business community. On several counts this would be an oversimplification. Hoar, though strongly convinced of the national value of the business community, was no political puppet for any group or class.[48] In addition, the term "business community" is more an historian's convenience than an historical reality; there were many and differing groups of businessmen with different and often conflicting aims. Finally, in Massachusetts as elsewhere the issue of monetary inflation could and did cut across class lines. By no means were all "friends of the people" spokesmen for an expanding and unbacked paper currency; nor were all manufacturers, investors, and mercantile men supporters of a hard money policy. Hoar's correspondents reflected a considerable diversity of views. Alvin Cooke, one-time candidate of the Massachusetts Labor party, believed that the suspension of specie payments had been "a great misfortune to the laborer" and of benefit only to "capitalists, speculators and moneyed institutions"; while W. H. Bailey, a self-determined "average man," informed Hoar that unless the Republican party adopted a more flexible monetary policy, the common people would flock to the inflationist standard of Ben Butler. In similar fashion, though virtually all of Hoar's correspondents from the financial district of Boston praised his hard-money stand, the manufacturers of Massachusetts were divided in opinion. Philip L. Moen, president of Worcester's largest factory, demanded an honest dollar backed by gold for the salvation of the creditor class, but a Mr. Fullam, manufacturer of boots and shoes, favored more greenbacks—declaring the manufacturing

[47] The Specie Resumption Act of 1875 was a compromise measure and not an unconditional victory for the advocates of hard money. *See* Irwin Unger, *The Greenback Era: A Social and Political History of American Finance, 1865–1879* (Princeton, N.J.: Princeton University Press, 1965), 255–263.

[48] Despite the pressure of various Massachusetts insurance firms, Hoar would advocate that the surplus funds of the Geneva Award be distributed among the victims of British depredation, not their underwriters. *Congressional Record*, 46th Cong., 2d sess., 1218–1222 (1 March 1880).

community in need of an expanded currency as well as a sound one.[49]

As the Greenbacker movement took political shape in the mid-seventies, Hoar's opposition to "rag money" grew, and when his old enemy Butler came out in 1878 in favor of fiat paper money, opposition became dedication. He lauded the continued firmness of Hayes and Sherman and the latter's efforts to build up the gold reserve of the Treasury so that resumption would be formally inaugurated on schedule. There was no reason to compromise with those who wished to repeal the law providing for payment of Civil War bonds in gold, to tamper with the notes of the proven national banking system, or to inflate the currency with new issues of unbacked paper dollars. America was to be congratulated that Hayes had never been infected by the "Ohio craze" as had, unfortunately, too many Republicans of the Middle West.

The Democrats, in Hoar's opinion, were not to be trusted on financial questions, and in the congressional elections of 1878 his great fear was that the Greenbacker party would fuse with the Democrats. That third party had made relatively little progress in Massachusetts—where its agrarian character had limited appeal for the factory hands—but the depression of the seventies still lingered on, and Hoar felt obliged to spur the Massachusetts Republicans to a major effort against the Greenback heresy. The lines of battle were laid down in a full dress speech at Worcester's Mechanics Hall, 21 September 1878.

The currency question was proclaimed the major issue before the nation, and Hoar offered his audience a capsule history of the inflationary dangers that always accompanied an unchecked issue of paper money. Fiat money would always fast depreciate in value whatever its monetary description. All reputable students of political economy agreed that there were inexorable laws of value,

[49] Alvin Cook to Levi Barker, 25 October 1870; W. H. Bailey to Hoar, 21 September 1878; Philip L. Moen to Hoar, 16 January 1878; L. Fullam to Hoar, 26 January 1878, Hoar Papers. Representative correspondents from the financial district of State Street, Boston were John M. Forbes, Thomas Jefferson Coolidge, H. P. Kidder, William Gray, and William Endicott Jr. These men now supplemented such older correspondents as Philip Moen as Hoar's friends and advisers. Though heedful of their opinion, Hoar at no time was willing to act as their senatorial messenger. *See* Hoar to Forbes, 1 February 1879, Hoar Papers.

not to be changed by government lawmakers or engravers: "We take gold and silver for money because they are the things which in their nature vary in value least, but we do not make or change value by law." Specie currency had inherent value and was the only sound monetary medium, except in conditions of extreme national emergency. The chief evil of "rag currency," however, was not that it flew in the face of historical experience and economic theory; its chief evil was the mischief it would wreck upon the wages of the workingman, the savings of the honest widow, the stability of commercial exchange. The very people Ben Butler claimed to represent would be most hurt if his views were supported in Massachusetts and adopted by the nation. The dictates of self-preservation as well as common honesty should prevent the people of Massachusetts from falling prey to the folly of further experiment with irredeemable paper currency. And if only Massachusetts held firm "the returning sense of the people" would bring the other states into line and allow the country to proceed on a "career of prosperity, of wealth and of glory."[50]

The defeat of Butler in the gubernatorial election of 1878, the formal resumption of specie payments in January 1879, and the gradual return of industrial prosperity in the last years of Hayes's administration were in Hoar's view highly satisfactory and closely associated events. The return of prosperity was to be credited to the operation of natural economic laws of supply and demand, which had been allowed to function unhampered by fiscal irresponsibility.

Hoar's antagonism to irredeemable paper was more pronounced than his opposition to another instrument for monetary inflation, Silver. As a congressman he had voted in 1873 for the law dropping silver from the coinage list, but he did so in simple recognition of the fact that the then overweight silver dollar had not circulated for many years. It would be this law, of course, that in the years of Hayes's administration would be referred to by silver miners and monetary inflationists as the "Crime of '73," the evil product of an international gold conspiracy.

[50] *Boston Herald*, 21 September 1878 (special supplement).

The "crime" was surely ex post facto; for it was not until the latter half of the seventies that silver production increased to an extent sufficient to drive the value of silver below its old coinage ratio to gold of 16 to 1.[51] By 1878 a silver dollar coined at the old ratio would be worth, in terms of gold, only about 97 cents, and so would serve as an instrument of monetary inflation. Consequently, spokesmen for agrarian debtors began gradually to switch their allegiance from greenbacks to silver and to call for the recoinage of silver. Spokesmen for silver miners desirous of a new market for their product joined the cry.

When Representative Richard Bland from the silver mining state of Missouri first introduced his bill for a return to "free and unlimited coinage of silver dollars," Hoar was suspicious but also somewhat bewildered. He did not have the instinctive aversion to silver that he had for irredeemable greenbacks; silver was specie and possessed of inherent value. A self-taught student of political economy who sought to combine certain of the natural economic laws of Adam Smith with a firm belief in the protectionist theories of Matthew Carey, Hoar's tools of economic analysis were simple and few.[52] Nor did historical precedent appear to offer much guidance—had not the great Alexander Hamilton favored coinage of both gold and silver? Several conferences with Secretary Sherman, however, convinced Hoar that a large addition to the cur-

[51] For a somewhat contrary view, *see* Allen Weinstein, "Was There a 'Crime of 1873'?: The Case of the Demonetized Dollar," *Journal of American History*, 54 (September 1967), 307–326. Professor Weinstein believes that while there was no "conspiracy" there was "gold-standard malice aforethought" by certain of the act's authors and advocates.

[52] The conscientious Hoar was aware of his deficiences as a student of economics, and spent part of the summer of 1878 collecting material on fiscal policy and theory. The previous November he had lamented to his wife: "I have not given to the financial questions before the country the study which they demand of me if I would discharge my duties faithfully and intelligently. I ought to have the whole summer at my command and abandon the practice of law altogether, if I would succeed as a Senator." Hoar to Ruth A. Hoar, 17 November 1877, Hoar Papers.

Hoar was obliged to supplement his senatorial salary by taking selected legal cases during the congressional vacations—often in behalf of the Worcester & Nashua Rr. Company and in informal partnership with his brother Rockwood. His fees in the 1870's averaged less than four thousand dollars a year and represented about one third of his annual income. Cash Books, Hoar Papers.

rency of underweight silver dollars would penalize wage-earners and creditors alike.[53] But fraud was in some measure relative. While there could be no compromise with the Greenbackers, there might be with "Silver Dick" Bland. The recoinage of silver dollars if specifically limited would be judged unfortunate but not dishonest.

It was Hoar's colleague Henry Dawes who took the lead, with Senator William Allison of Iowa, in fighting the Bland bill when it passed the House and reached the Senate. That bill was allowed to pass the Senate only after it had been modified to provide for the coinage of from two to four million dollars worth of silver per annum. Hoar voted for the revised version of what came to be known as the Bland-Allison Act, persuaded that some compromise was necessary with the silver forces, and then turned around and heartily cheered Hayes's veto of the measure.[54] He voted against the motion to override the veto, but was not greatly disturbed when the Bland-Allison Act became law. The Greenbacker movement was the financial heresy to be feared; the recoinage of silver, only a modest misdemeanor. Silver coinage was to be limited by law and he had received the assurances of Secretary Sherman that the underweight silver dollars would be backed by gold.[55]

The position of the Hayes administration on civil service reform was surely less consistent than its policies respecting the South or the currency, but it was Hayes's verbal support of this reform, more than any other single issue, that helped to characterize his administration for friend and foe alike. No other stand was more excoriated by the Stalwarts or more praised by George F. Hoar.

[53] Hoar also received tutorial assistance from a former colleague in the House, Washington Townsend of Pennsylvania, who forwarded a long analysis of the declining worth of silver in relation to gold and a yet longer analysis of the economic errors of the Bland coinage bill. Townsend to Hoar, 7 November 1877, Hoar Papers.

[54] Senators Dawes and Justin Morrill had at one point doubted Hayes's firmness of will on the money question. See Morrill to Dawes, 22 June 1877, H. L. Dawes Papers, Box 23, Library of Congress.

[55] In December 1879 there was a quiet meeting of certain "eastern Senators" where Hoar proposed concerted action "to suspend coinage of silver." He was soon convinced by Sherman, however, that the Bland-Allison Act would not endanger the Treasury's gold reserve. See Diary Ledger, 1 December 1879—7 May 1880, Hoar Papers.

Hayes, like Hoar, was sincerely interested in improving the honesty and morals of the civil service, but both men were uncertain as to the proper instrument for effecting reform. Hayes placed chief reliance on a vague order to the members of his cabinet, and Hoar appeared hopeful that public opinion alone would effect the cure.[56] Hoar did not call at this time for an active and funded civil service commission. Merit he demanded, but merit ratings smacked too much of federal bureaucracy. Some prohibitory legislation might prove necessary but it was not by law that reform in the public service could best be attained. "It must be effected by the great power of public sentiment."[57] Hoar was, in general, suspicious of legislative reformation of political institutions. In an article describing his service in the House of Representatives and the evolution there of various parliamentary abuses, he concluded with the declaration: "I do not believe in radical changes in the institutions of the state, contrived by *doctrinaires*. The practice of the House of Representatives is a growth, not a scheme."[58] His attitude was that of a man who sought to combine the faith of Jefferson with the cautionary strictures of Burke. Optimistically certain of liberty's expanding future, he was equally convinced that institutional change was a slow and historically consistent process.

Hoar was disappointed when Hayes's limited resistance to the patronage demands of Conkling and others failed to effect a moral revolution in the public service, but he assured Hayes that his administration marked a crucial turning point. He had shown that party loyalty need not be perverted to spoilsmanship. If standards of honesty and capacity in the civil service were still short of those demanded by the Founding Fathers, at least a beginning had been made and the Republicans had displayed to the country an administration concerned not with the rewards of political power but the efficiency of the public service.

Hoar overrated the accomplishment of the Hayes administration and its identification with civil service reform, but this exaggeration

[56] For an indication of the limited compliance accorded Hayes's cabinet instructions, *see* John Sherman to Blaine, 2 July 1879, Blaine Papers, I, Library of Congress.

[57] *Boston Globe*, 5 September 1877.

[58] G. F. Hoar, "The Conduct of Business in Congress," *North American Review*, 128 (February 1879), 133.

was characteristic of all factions of the party. Perhaps the outstanding feature of the Hayes administration from the standpoint of the history of the Republican party is that it was a Republican administration heartily disliked by a majority of the party's leaders in Congress. Surely the Stalwart politicos held Hayes often in contempt and always in distrust.

Hayes like Hoar was an original Half-Breed. The term "Half-Breed Republican" is frequently identified with the factional divisions of the Republican party in New York state and confined to the enemies of Roscoe Conkling and the supporters of James G. Blaine. Such identification erroneously limits the significance and duration of the Half-Breed tradition in the post-Civil War history of the Republican party. The Half-Breed Republicans would never operate as a disciplined bloc, but by the late 1870's there were in Washington Republican politicians seeking to establish a new center among the factional divisions of their party. These men were the original Half-Breeds.

Party regulars, the Half-Breeds were neither political independents nor political spoilsmen. They damned party bolters—convinced that only in party allegiance lay the opportunity for power and achievement—and distrusted the deification of personal loyalty characteristic of the Stalwarts. The political amateur who would demand the immediate application of his own set of doctrinaire principles was to be scorned; the spoilsman who saw politics as but a game was to be superseded. The political style of the Half-Breeds was less personal and more intelligent than that of the Stalwarts. They believed in party as an instrument for fashioning legislative policy as well as Democratic defeat. If they lacked a distinctive political philosophy, they possessed definite political goals. Identifying the future of the country with its industrial strength, they were concerned to maintain social harmony while encouraging economic growth. They desired the expansion of foreign trade, the protection and diversification of industry, a stable currency, and an improved standard of living for a politically content urban labor force. Most Half-Breeds were aware that the changing economic patterns of America raised new political issues—the lobbyist, the nature of the civil service, the power of the railroads—that deserved attention and possible national intervention. Later some would express an erratic suspicion of trusts and monopolies, but in the late 1870's they saw the corporation as a symbol of economic expansion and so of national progress. Favoring corporate growth, they pictured their alliance with business as an alliance of equals—partners in the economic and social progress of America.

By the middle of Hayes's administration certain politicians were already representative of the goals and prejudices of Half-Breed Republicanism. Not James G. Blaine—who at this point represented a particular wing of the Stalwarts and became a Half-Breed only with the campaign of 1880—but men like Hayes, Hoar, George Edmunds, William Wheeler, Stanley Matthews, Henry Blair, William Evarts, George McCrary, Henry Dawes, and John Sherman.[59] These men were not all of a piece; Hoar was perhaps more optimistic in his ameliorism than most, more ready to use the national authority to promote certain selected reforms. They are all to be distinguished, however, from both the Stalwart and Liberal-Independent factions of their party. This distinction can of course be exaggerated—in comparison with the ideological divisions of French politics it was indeed modest—but in Washington it was increasingly recognized in the late seventies. And the Half-Breed tradition would outlast the life of its earliest spokesmen. As a separate faction within the Republican party the Half-Breeds are distinguishable only in the period, 1878–1890, but the hopes and limitations of George F. Hoar and other Half-Breeds would be reflected later in certain of the aspirations and contradictions of the Roosevelt Progressives.

The initial skirmishes between the Stalwarts and the early Half-Breeds centered about the presidential figure of Rutherford B. Hayes. Few men of modest bearing have had the opportunity to be so hated. Not only did he remain "His Fraudulency" to many Democrats, but such Stalwarts as John Logan, Roscoe Conkling,

[59] For confirmation of this judgment of Blaine *see* his correspondence for 1875–1879, Blaine Papers, I, Library of Congress. James Garfield and Justin Morrill may be classified as Half-Breeds by the Republican Convention of 1880, if not before. *See* Diary of James A. Garfield for the years, 1878–1880, Garfield Papers, Boxes 4, 5; and Morrill Papers, XXIX, Library of Congress.

and the Camerons of Pennsylvania despised him. They viewed him as a man trying to ingratiate himself with southern Democrats, Independents, and reformers and threatening to wreck the organization of the Republican party in the process. If he didn't know that the distribution of offices in payment of political debts was essential, he was a fool; if he did know and still talked of civil service reform, he was a hypocrite.

The Stalwarts determined to retain control of the Republican National Committee and succeeded.[60] Zachariah Chandler had retired to his demesne of Michigan, but he was continuously consulted by his Stalwart friends who lamented the absence from Washington of his "counsel & good Judgment in these days of 'reform.'" There could be no cooperation of the Grant men— true Republicans—with Hayes. If Hayes and his friends had been honest there might be some hope, but "as they are not honest it is false to the party to have its members believe they are."[61] The Blaine wing of the Stalwarts was less dedicated in its opposition to Hayes than that led by Conkling and Don Cameron. Blaine's disciple Eugene Hale indeed attempted at times to reduce Stalwart suspicion and to persuade the President to adopt the "conciliatory" patronage policy of Grant. Occasionally such efforts appeared about to succeed, but ill-feeling always triumphed.[62]

[60] *See,* for example, W. E. Chandler to Zachariah Chandler, 23 July 1877, Zachariah Chandler Papers, VII, Library of Congress; W. E. Chandler to Blaine, 13 December 1879, Blaine Papers, I, Library of Congress.

[61] W. B. Allison to Z. Chandler, 17 December 1877; W. E. Chandler to Z. Chandler, 26 February 1878, Zachariah Chandler Papers, VII, Library of Congress.

[62] Hale wrote Zachariah Chandler, October 28, 1877 (Zachariah Chandler Papers, VII, Library of Congress):

> I dined with the President last night & had a long full talk with him alone afterwards over the whole situation, telling him very fully what I understand to be the main cause of the disaffected feeling of our people, 'ie' the fear that he and his administration are trying to make something out of the Democratic Party, and are abandoning our own organization. Some late events have given him some light on this . . . & it is quite evident that the civil service order to officials, will be hereafter interpreted so that all mischief will be taken out of it.

A fortnight later, however, Hoar informed his wife that Conkling's anger with the President continued unabated, and that a majority of the Senate Republicans might attempt a public repudiation of Hayes on the Senate floor. Hoar to Ruth A. Hoar, 10 November 1877, Hoar Papers.

Republican division would be briefly patched over in the spring of 1879 under the pressures of Democratic victory and aggression, but by the year's end the Half-Breed Republicans were increasingly convinced that plans must be laid for a decisive defeat of Stalwart arrogance in the next presidential convention. To block the Stalwarts was a party duty; to prevent the nomination of Grant, a clear necessity.

The battle over the Republican nomination in 1880 represented a climactic round in the struggle between the Stalwarts and the Half-Breeds. The nomination of Garfield would mark a clear victory for the Half-Breeds and a personal triumph for George F. Hoar. In his opinion no convention had appeared to threaten greater trouble for the party; few had ended in a nomination more prudent or more gratifying.

Hoar's intention in the spring of 1880, as four years earlier, was to see that Massachusetts sent to the Republican convention a delegation formally uninstructed and carefully selected. He wished to antagonize neither the Grant men nor the Blaine men in Massachusetts while making concerted efforts to see that a majority of the Massachusetts delegation favored neither Grant nor Blaine. The Massachusetts delegation should husband its strength behind a favorite son from New England while watching for the opportunity to promote the cause of some prominent Half-Breed as the compromise choice of the convention. The over-all strategy was early determined but there was considerable confusion over tactics.

Some of Hoar's closest political friends in Massachusetts made moves to start a boom for John Sherman in the months preceding the Massachusetts state convention, but Hoar discouraged their efforts.[63] Though he admired the performance of Sherman in the Treasury Department, Hoar believed that an active Sherman boom would incite the Grant and Blaine men in Massachusetts to increased effort. Sherman, moreover, had been too long in politics to be without enemies and though very worthy was also very dull. By April Hoar had determined to promote Senator George F. Edmunds of Vermont as the nominal candidate who should hold

[63] Adin Thayer to Hoar, 27 February 1880; Parker C. Chandler to Hoar, 12 April 1880, Hoar Papers.

the Massachusetts delegation together in the early ballots at the national convention. There should be no formal instruction of the Massachusetts delegates, but they should be men prepared to stand by the honest Edmunds until an opportunity arose to switch the support of Massachusetts to a more politically available Half-Breed.

These plans were disclosed but gradually. To Theodore Bates, a young Worcester corset manufacturer with political ambitions, Hoar wrote simply of the need to "send men to Chicago with no labels about their necks," but to his relative Evarts Greene, Hoar requested that his personal substitute at the state convention be "some one who favors Edmunds."[64] Events at the Massachusetts state convention in late April went according to plan. The delegates-at-large, headed by Hoar, were all Edmunds men. The convention endorsed Edmunds candidacy, but declared the delegates at liberty to promote the cause of true Republicanism as conscience and conditions dictated.

The month of May was occupied with rumors concerning the suspected designs of Stalwart Don Cameron, chairman of the National Committee, and with deliberations concerning the respective strength of various Republicans who might break the anticipated deadlock between Grant and Blaine. George Hoar briefly considered Hamilton Fish and Frederick Frelinghuysen, had second thoughts about Sherman, wondered out loud if there was any possibility of renominating Hayes, and expressed his admiration for James Garfield.[65] But by the time he left Worcester for Chicago Hoar had failed to produce the name of any candidate likely to stampede the convention, the majority of whose delegates would be pledged either to redeem the reputation of Blaine or to revive the presidency of Grant.

The Republican convention of 1880 provided a sequence of defeats for the Stalwart Ultras, and in the rather surprised figure of Senator Hoar they met their first obstruction. It was the intention of Don Cameron and the Grant faction to arrange the machin-

---

[64] Hoar to T. C. Bates, 4 April 1880, Hoar Papers; Hoar to J. Evarts Greene, 9 April 1880, Misc. Papers, New York Public Library.

[65] Hoar to Samuel Hoar, 13 May 1880; E. Rockwood Hoar to Hoar, 18 May 1880, Hoar Papers.

ery of the convention so that one of their number would be elected as convention chairman and instructed to enforce the unit rule. The unit rule would require that a state cast all of its votes for the candidate who was the choice of a majority of the delegation. If enforced it would virtually have ensured the selection of Grant on the first ballot. Grant was the choice of Conkling, Logan, Cameron and so of a majority of the delegations of New York, Illinois, and Pennsylvania, but there were some sixty-three members of those three delegations who preferred Blaine or some other candidate. Under the unit rule the votes of all would be counted for Grant; if each delegate was allowed to cast an independent ballot, they would not. As chairman of the National Committee, Cameron was determined to open the convention, enforce the unit rule in the selection of the temporary chairman, and thereby pave the way for Grant's nomination on the first ballot. Secrecy was not a Stalwart virtue, however, and their intentions were widely advertised by the time the convention opened. The Blaine forces and the Half-Breeds determined to make an all-out fight on the issue of the unit rule and threatened to depose Cameron from the national committee if he insisted on installing a Stalwart toady as convention chairman. Cameron finally backed down, and the Blaine forces and the Half-Breeds seized upon Hoar as a figure whose honesty and integrity would be recognized by all sides. Honesty and integrity were hardly the qualities Cameron and Conkling desired in the convention chair, but with reluctance they agreed, first to seat Hoar as temporary chairman and then as permanent chairman of the convention.[66]

Though parliamentarily correct at all times, Hoar as presiding officer did not pretend to impartiality. He considered that the unit rule proposal was a direct insult to the independence of a delegate and his voice quavered with pleasure as he announced that the resolution advocating its adoption had failed to pass. Throughout the convention, Hoar sharply separated in his own mind his tasks as chairman and his responsibilities as the leader of the Massachusetts delegation, and in the latter capacity he continued when off the rostrum to worry, to caucus, and to center his hopes in-

[66] *See* Diary of James A. Garfield, 1 June 1880, Garfield Papers, Box 5, Library of Congress.

creasingly upon the figure of John Sherman's floor manager, Representative James Abram Garfield. Garfield's efforts in behalf of the civil rights plank were worthy of his Massachusetts ancestry; his speech in behalf of Sherman vastly better than Conkling's grandiloquent nomination of Grant. By the third day of the convention Hoar had personally decided that Garfield was to be preferred above all other available candidates—and it was no secret to the Half-Breed delegates that Garfield was available.

When on the sixth day of the convention the Wisconsin delegation suddenly threw its sixteen votes to Garfield, the Garfield boom had begun and Hoar soon had the opportunity to use his gavel in its behalf. Garfield felt obliged as Sherman's manager to deny the action of Wisconsin—though on several previous ballots he had not objected when receiving the vote of two Pennsylvania delegates. He demanded recognition of the chairman and speaking to "a question of order," began his protest: "No man has a right, without the consent of the person voted for, to announce that person's name, and vote for him, in this convention." Banging his gavel a single time, Hoar cut him short: "The gentleman from Ohio is not stating a question of order. He will resume his seat. No person having received a majority of the votes cast, another ballot will be taken. The Clerk will call the roll."[67]

In later years, Hoar would recount and relish that moment often, and take increasing credit for thwarting Garfield's modesty and securing his nomination: "I interrupted him in the middle of his sentence. I was terribly afraid that he would say something that would make his nomination impossible, or his acceptance impossible, if it were made. I do not believe it ever happened before that anybody who attempted to decline the Presidency of the United States was to be prevented by a point of order."[68]

Hoar and Massachusetts were deserving of credit, but the crucial role was not theirs but Blaine's. The inflexible loyalty of the Blaine forces on the first thirty-four ballots prevented Grant from gaining

[67] *Official Proceedings of the National Republican Conventions of 1868, 1872, 1876 and 1880* (Minneapolis, 1903), 622.

[68] G. F. Hoar, *Autobiography of Seventy Years*, I, 396–397; Hoar to J. W. Tucker, 8 June 1895, Hoar Papers.

the nomination during the first three days of balloting, and it was Blaine votes which finally secured the nomination for Garfield on the thirty-sixth ballot. If it was the independence of the Half-Breed delegations that made the Garfield candidacy possible, it was Blaine votes that powered it to victory.[69] Garfield knew this as well as Blaine, and the process had begun whereby Blaine would be within a year's time a leader of the Republican Half-Breeds.

The Grant forces were awarded the nomination of Conkling's friend, Chester A. Arthur as the vice-presidential nominee. Hoar's brother considered Arthur's nomination an act of spitefulness on Conkling's part—"a mere plagiarism from that Roman Emperor who made his horse consul."[70] The Massachusetts delegation voted against the New York Stalwart, but in point of fact the nomination represented another defeat for Conkling. He had scorned the peace offering and was angry with Arthur when the latter accepted the place against his advice.

For the Half-Breeds, generally, the choice of Arthur for second place seemed a very modest concession in behalf of nominal party unity. Their mood was one of relief and self-congratulation. Upon his return from Chicago, Hoar spoke to a cheering throng at Worcester and acclaimed the defeat of the unit rule, the rescue of the two-term tradition, and the choice of Garfield—a man who combined the military valor of Grant, the financial wisdom of Sherman, and the oratorical powers of Blaine.[71] Garfield was informed that his nomination was "the strongest possible for our latitude," and the nominee was soon the object of a steady stream of advice. John Murray Forbes was suggested for the post of national chairman, and upon his refusal Garfield was urged to select Eugene Hale, an honest man who would help to bring the Blaine forces solidly behind the ticket. Garfield's letter of acceptance should be delayed until the Democrats disclosed their platform,

[69] The Massachusetts delegation did not give Garfield any votes until the thirty-sixth and decisive ballot, when he received all but four. Previously the majority of the Massachusetts delegation had voted for Edmunds through the twenty-eighth ballot and for John Sherman on the twenty-ninth through the thirty-fifth.

[70] E. Rockwood Hoar to Hoar, 10 June 1880, Hoar Papers.

[71] *Worcester Evening Gazette*, 15 June 1880. *See*, too, Hoar's speech at Faneuil Hall, 30 June 1880 as reported in the *Boston Evening Transcript*, 1 July 1880.

and when it was submitted should lay great stress on "the era of business prosperity now opening" and his intention not to disturb business "by radical changes of policy."[72]

Blaine's wholehearted campaign effort in behalf of Garfield convinced Hoar that whatever their past differences, Blaine was an honest patriot. Hoar was ready to welcome Blaine as a fellow Half-Breed, and Blaine was quite prepared to move from the outmoded posture of the Stalwart and swing his followers in line behind Garfield. Indeed the success of the Half-Breeds in the presidential election of 1880 lay not only in the victory of Garfield over General Winfield Hancock, but also in the fact that they shortly gained what previously they had lacked, a strong leader.

For the Republican party the 1880's would be the decade of Blaine. The dominant faction was that of the Half-Breeds; the Stalwart Republicans fade into the background and with them the politics of spoils. The transition begun in the Hayes administration is completed under Blaine's leadership in the 1880's, and the Republican party becomes a party identified with the needs and ambitions of the New Industrialism.

---

[72] G. F. Hoar to Garfield, 20 June, 22 June 1880, Garfield Papers, vol. 77, Library of Congress. *See,* too, J. M. Forbes to Garfield, 10 June 1880; Garfield to J. M. Forbes, 20 June 1880, *ibid.*

# 4

## *The Eighties: Years of the Half-Breeds*

The inauguration of Garfield marked the completion of Hoar's twelfth year in Washington. He was now fifty-four and had already assumed the appearance of a young-looking old man, an appearance he would retain until his death in 1904. When he had first appeared in Washington, his hair, sandy in color, was worn in long sideburns, and his erect carriage and slender figure had made him seem taller than his height of 5′9″. Twelve years later, his hair was white and his face and figure had filled out until he looked rather like Dickens's Mr. Pickwick. The clothes he had worn in the 1860's—a full broadcloth suit with standing collar, loose black bow tie, and gold stickpin—now made him appear old-fashioned in appearance. His light blue eyes were framed in gold-rimmed spectacles, earlier attempts to cultivate a mustache had been long forgotten, and his face was clean-shaven, pink-cheeked, and very round. A few years later a lady visitor in the Senate gallery would point to Hoar and inquire, "Who is that clean looking man?"[1]

[1] C. Oakle, "Noted Senators: How They Look and How They Dress," *Golden Argosy.* 11 August 1888, Scrap Book, Personal #3, Hoar Papers.

Had Hoar overheard, he would have been pleased and certain that she referred to his principles as well as his person.

If Hoar aged early in physical appearance, he compensated by the continued possession of what he called, "a New England constitution." Except for periodic discomfort with his eyes he suffered remarkably little illness until after his seventy-fifth year. In the spring of 1881 he no longer addressed his wife as "Carrisima Pussycatta"—she was now usually "my dear little woman"—but he felt hale, hearty, and full of confidence for the new administration and the state of the union. Asking his wife to forward from Worcester his dumbbells for morning calisthenics, he prepared to do battle for the renewed hopes and promise of the Republican party. Hoar confidently predicted an eight-year reign for Garfield and a predominant position for those Republicans identified with high protection, civil service reform, federal aid for internal improvements, and distaste for Roscoe Conkling.[2] His optimism was not lessened when reports circulated that he would be offered the first place in the cabinet. In point of fact Garfield had of necessity to offer the State Department to Blaine, but the rumor alone appeared to augur well for the nature and direction of party leadership.[3]

Hoar was pleased with Blaine's selection. He had periodically admired Blaine's political skill and personal charm and was ready to welcome him now to the ranks of the anti-Stalwarts. The other cabinet appointments were well made and Garfield's declared intention to select Horace Gray for the next Supreme Court vacancy was a matter of personal pride and satisfaction for Hoar.[4]

[2] Hoar to Garfield, 8 November 1880 (two letters), Papers of James Garfield, Library of Congress; Garfield to Hoar, 8 November 1880, J. M. Forbes to Hoar, 11 November 1880, Hoar Papers.

[3] L. S. Howlett to Hoar, 8 November 1880; Hoar to Ruth A. Hoar, 20 December 1880, Hoar Papers. In the letter to his wife Hoar wrote: "Mr. Dawes made to me in behalf of the [Massachusetts] delegation the proposal to present my name to Gen. Garfield for Secretary of State. They think the situation such that he would be not unlikely to make the appointment." An appreciation that he lacked the temperament of a successful diplomat, together with a distaste for the hospitality and costs associated with the position, led Hoar to discourage the idea.

[4] Gray, Chief Justice of the Supreme Judicial Court of Massachusetts, was Hoar's Harvard Law School classmate and life-long friend. He would be appointed to the United States Supreme Court by President Arthur, shortly after Garfield's assassination. Governor John D. Long was prepared to offer Hoar the post of chief justice of the state court upon Gray's elevation, but Hoar refused. E. Rockwood Hoar to

Hoar's initial hopes respecting the likelihood that Conkling and the bosses would be quietly and tactfully isolated were soon shattered by the Robertson Affair. But shortly before that factional struggle began, Hoar had thrown himself into a far happier battle in defense of Senator William Mahone of Virginia.

William Mahone was an able egocentric and a Virginia "Readjuster," a rebel from the conservative leadership of the Virginia Democratic party. With the aid of Republican votes he had defeated the regular Democratic candidate and presented himself to the United States Senate as an Independent Democrat. In the eyes of Senator Ben Hill of Georgia he was a traitor to the saving solidarity of party, race, and section; as seen by Hoar, Mahone was the herald of a bright new morn—or at least an entering wedge in an all too solid South. On 14 March 1881, Hill excoriated Mahone's declared intention to vote with the hair-thin Republican majority and so enable the Republicans to organize the Senate. Hoar leaped to Mahone's defense. The political independence that he had found so discreditable in the Liberal Republicans of 1872 was now pronounced worthy of protection against the lash of partisan fury. The tirade and threats of the Senator from Georgia were an insult to the Senate.[5]

Hoar hoped that the Mahone movement was the first of many in the states of the South. White men in Mississippi and South Carolina as well as Virginia were "chafing under the terrible yoke which they have borne."[6] Perhaps the New Departure was not the failure he had feared. The division of the southern whites could serve to promote the political rights of the southern Negro. In the Senate he made a conscious effort to cultivate Mahone, and at that gentleman's request Hoar met with members of the Republican State Executive Committee of Virginia to encourage and coordinate their fund-raising efforts.[7]

As late as the fall of 1885 Hoar would attempt to interest Boston money in the campaigns of the Readjusters, but by then he had

---

Hoar, 8 January, 30 January 1881; Edmund H. Burnett to Hoar, 21 December 1881, Hoar Papers.

[5] *Congressional Record.* 47th Cong., special sess. of Senate, 26 (14 March 1881).

[6] Hoar to J. M. Forbes, 19 March 1881, Hoar Papers.

[7] Mahone to Hoar, 3 October 1881, Hoar Papers. *See,* too, Diary of James A. Garfield, 29 April 1881, Garfield Papers, Box 5, Library of Congress; Garfield to Henry L. Dawes, 2 May 1881, Dawes Papers, Box #25, Library of Congress.

become convinced that the movement was the result of special conditions in Virginia and offered little hope for a two-party South or for the southern Negro.[8] By the end of Mahone's single term in the Senate, Hoar was convinced that only a strong federal elections bill offered hope for a healthy Republican party in the South.

In the struggle over Mahone and the organization of the Senate at the beginning of Garfield's administration, the Republican senators stood united and harmonious. Yet almost concurrently, they were at each other's throats as another skirmish was fought in the battle between the Half-Breeds and Stalwarts. The specific issue was whether Garfield would be allowed to appoint W. H. Robertson, a political enemy of Roscoe Conkling, as collector for the port of New York.[9] The more general issues were: the independence of the executive, the strength of the alliance between the Garfield administration and the supporters of Blaine, and the control and direction of the Republican party.

Hoar was among the first to place the battle over Robertson's confirmation within the context of party leadership.[10] The Stalwarts had been defeated in Cincinnati in 1876, only subsequently to frustrate the friends and administration of Hayes; they had been defeated in Chicago in 1880 and must be prevented from playing their obstructionist game once more. He was aware, however, that to outsiders the struggle seemed but a petty quarrel over the distribution of offices in a single state and the concentration of the Senate upon this quarrel, foolish and wasteful. Aware that public explanations would further widen party division, Hoar released his frustration by long letters to the most trusted of his supporters in Worcester and a stern word of correction to his son: "The contest which you think is a fight as to whom the little offices should be meted out to is one as important in principle and likely

[8] Warren Miller to Hoar, 7 September 1885; Mahone to Hoar, 30 September 1885; Chauncey I. Filley to Hoar, 10 December 1885; Hoar to Ruth A. Hoar, 15 November 1886, Hoar Papers.

[9] For Garfield's motivation and Blaine's influence, *see* Diary of James A. Garfield, 22 March, 23 March 1881, Garfield Papers, Box 5, Library of Congress.

[10] Hoar and Dawes had been among the first senators to consult with Garfield on the situation in New York, and they approved Garfield's decision to inform the Senate "that the vote on R's confirmation was a test of friendship or hostility to the administration." *See* Diary of James A. Garfield, 10 March, 11 March, 2 April, 3 May 1881, Garfield Papers, Box 5, Library of Congress.

to be as serious in result as has ever taken place since the beginning of the Government."[11]

Hoar's initial certainty that Conkling had "lost his ascendancy" began to falter as the weeks went on and certain New England correspondents exhibited an unfortunate willingness to blame the personal ambitions of Blaine for the administration's sorry beginnings.[12] It was with a sense of relief that he saw Conkling cut short the long and bitter struggle by committing one of the more dramatic stupidities of American politics. With oratorical gestures, Conkling resigned his Senate seat in protest against the nomination of Robertson. The junior senator from New York, Thomas C. Platt dutifully followed. Conkling's design was to storm back to Albany, be swiftly re-elected, and then, his complete control over the Republican party in New York officially confirmed, return to Washington and a humbled Garfield. Hoar suspected that Conkling would find re-election difficult and that Conkling's foolish display of arrogance would redound to the benefit of the Half-Breed leaders.[13] He agreed with his old friend William Claflin that "the people will endure ill nature even to ugliness but not stupidity."[14]

With Conkling's departure from Washington, Hoar's confidence in the future of the Garfield administration returned. He could wish that Blaine would exert his predominating influence more tactfully, but he was certain that the country would soon appreciate the strength of character beneath the bearded facade and hesitating manner of his good friend Garfield. With Garfield recognized as captain and Blaine his trusted first mate, the administration would soon inaugurate a program that would revive and expand the old national faith of the party. The Garfield years

---

[11] Hoar to Rockwood Hoar, 12 April 1881, Hoar Papers.

[12] E. Rockwood Hoar to Hoar, 4 April 1881, Hoar Papers; Hon. Gilman Marston to H. L. Dawes, 8 May 1881, Dawes Papers, Box #35, Library of Congress.

[13] W. H. Robertson happily informed Senator Dawes that "the reelection of Conkling and Platt is absolutely impossible . . . No one will be elected who is not friendly to the Administration of Genl. Garfield." Robertson to Dawes, 25 May 1881, Dawes Papers, Box #25, Library of Congress. *See*, too, Garfield to W. H. Robertson, 22 May 1881 (copy), Dawes Papers, Box #25, Library of Congress; H. L. Dawes, "Garfield and Conkling," *Century Illustrated Monthly*, 47 (January 1894), 341–344.

[14] Claflin to Hoar, 19 May 1881, Hoar Papers. *See*, too, Francis Haviland to Hoar, 26 February 1882; E. Rockwood Hoar to Hoar, 28 February 1882, Hoar Papers.

would witness renewed insistance on honest elections in all sections, federal encouragement of foreign exports and internal improvements, and the stimulation of an industrial prosperity that would assure social harmony as it improved the standards of labor.

With the explosion of two bullets in Washington's Union Depot, 2 July 1881, the dream vanished. During the agonizing weeks and months that followed, as Garfield struggled to avoid martyrdom and all public business was virtually suspended, Hoar experienced a growing certainty that he and the nation were about to be cheated. With the death of Garfield on the nineteenth of September and the accession of Chester A. Arthur, theft appeared consummated. Chet Arthur, one of the New York Stalwart gang, a friend of Conkling! The Republicans seemed doomed to struggle through a third Grant administration and without the compensation of a military hero. Republican popularity, purity, and progress must suffer; the Half-Breeds be driven from the field. Hoar's widely quoted eulogy of Garfield was not only an expression of personal loss but an expression of despair by a Half-Breed lieutenant.[15]

The Half-Breeds were not dislodged, however, during the three-year reign of Arthur, only occasionally threatened and often provoked. The Stalwart politicos received a share of patronage but only a minority share. Arthur became, indeed, something of an eleventh-hour Half-Breed. Blaine was soon out of the State Department, but his successor, Frederick Frelinghuysen was no Stalwart, and Blaine in retirement remained the most popular of Republican leaders. The failure of Arthur to play the role of a Stalwart puppet was the final blow; by the mid-eighties, the Stalwart Republicans as a cohesive faction had faded and dissolved.

Hoar, however, never recognized Arthur's conversion. He considered Arthur's break with Conkling the result of political expediency and fear, and his administration quite unsatisfactory. Hoar's difficulties with his party in Massachusetts explain in fair part his distaste for Arthur. Certain of Arthur's Massachusetts

[15] G. F. Hoar, "Eulogy upon the Life, Character and Public Services of James Abram Garfield . . . delivered by Hon. George F. Hoar, at the invitation of the City Council of the City of Worcester, Mass. in Mechanics Hall . . . December 30, 1881" (Worcester 1882).

appointments were judged deplorable and his interference in Hoar's re-election contest, outrageous.

Acting on the recommendations of George Boutwell and Secretary of the Navy William E. Chandler, Arthur decided to replace Alanson Beard as collector of the port of Boston and appoint Roland Worthington, editor of the *Boston Traveller*. Hoar and Dawes strongly protested Arthur's intention, convinced that Boutwell was attempting to re-form the Grant men of old into a new threat to their control of the Massachusetts Republican party. Indeed, they suspected, incorrectly, that Boutwell might be in league with Ben Butler, now the predominant figure of the Massachusetts Democrats. Their protests and a concerted campaign by their friends to persuade Arthur to reverse his decision were to no avail. Worthington, a recognized party enemy, was nominated late in March 1882, and Hoar and Dawes never forgave nor forgot.[16] They did not attempt to exercise the weapon of senatorial courtesy—their protests against its use by Conkling denied them the right—but they remained bitterly aggrieved.

The supporters of Hoar and Dawes in Massachusetts found 1882 a difficult year. Not only was the Boston Customs House turned over to a party enemy but there was a minor uprising in the Republican state caucus in June and certain middle-aged Turks led by F. L. Burden, W. E. Barrett, and Henry Cabot Lodge rejected the gubernatorial candidate of the Hoar-Dawes forces, Representative William W. Crapo, and selected Robert R. Bishop. Bishop was then defeated in November by the Democratic candidate, none other than the ultimate nemesis, Benjamin F. Butler. Though Hoar consoled Dawes with the assurance that they were personally blameless for this "great calamity and disgrace," the thought of Butler in the commencement procession at Harvard would haunt Hoar for the next seven months.[17]

There was a more immediate disaster to contemplate, however. Could the shattered Republican forces be reorganized in time to assure Hoar's re-election by the Massachusetts General Court in

[16] *See* Dawes to Hoar, 8 January 1882, J. M. Forbes to Hoar, 3 January, 23 January 1882. William Claflin to Hoar, 30 January 1882, Hoar Papers; Alanson Beard to Dawes, 20 March 1882, Dawes Papers, Box #26, Library of Congress.

[17] Hoar to Dawes, 8 November 1882, Dawes Papers, Box #26, Library of Congress.

January 1883, or would "the Stalwarts and others who have sympathized with Butler and his ways in the past" seek an alliance with the Democrats to defeat him and unhorse the Massachusetts Half-Breeds?[18] Hoar received many reports of the secret machinations of "your Republican enemies," and, though determined to stand above the battleground of political maneuver, he was deeply worried. He was convinced that his defeat would widen the breach within the state party and diminish its salutary influence upon the national organization. Hoar would not campaign in his own behalf, but he alerted his friends to the dangers at hand and expected them to utilize all honorable means to overcome them.[19] Among these dangers, he allowed, was the very real possibility that Arthur would actively intervene in the Massachusetts senatorial election in opposition to the incumbent.

Arthur had no love for the suspicious and stiff-necked Hoar and undoubtedly desired his defeat. His intervention, however, was limited to a few rather bumbling efforts by Secretary of the Navy Chandler in conjunction with Roland Worthington, and probably did Hoar little harm.[20] The weakness of the anti-Hoar forces lay in the fact that the man selected to unseat Hoar was John Davis Long, himself something of a Half-Breed and genteel reformer and a man whose strong desire for fame and a seat in the Senate was matched by an equally strong set of inhibitions. It is quite possible that if Long had engaged in active bargaining with Ben Butler he might have gained election by the General Court. An emissary of the new governor suggested that Barkis was more than willing to enter upon negotiations. Long declined. He was willing to conspire with friends, but an alliance with Butler was repugnant.[21]

Senator Dawes worked zealously in Hoar's behalf, as did many others. Dawes ordered his lieutenants to emphasize the importance

---

[18] Hoar to Dawes, 8 November 1882, *ibid.*

[19] *See* Hoar to Dawes, 10 November 1882, *ibid.*

[20] Leon B. Richardson, *William E. Chandler: Republican* (New York: Dodd, Mead, 1940), 342. *See,* too, W. W. Clapp to Hoar, 7 January 1883, W. W. Clapp Papers, Houghton Library, Harvard University. Clapp was editor of the *Boston Journal* and a staunch supporter of Hoar.

[21] Margaret Long, ed., *The Journal of John D. Long* (Rindge, N.H.: R. R. Smith, 1956), 137; 164. *See,* too, *Boston Evening Traveller,* 3 January 1887.

of Hoar's re-election for "the Manufacturing Interests of New England" and for the strength and purity of the Massachusetts delegation in Washington.[22] W. W. Clapp promoted Hoar's cause in the editorial pages of the *Boston Journal*; while Adin Thayer, John D. Washburn, Edward Tinker, and Theodore C. Bates set up shop at Parker's Hotel and saw each doubtful legislator in turn. With almost anticlimactic ease, Hoar was re-elected on the third ballot, January 18, 1883.[23]

Hoar's relief was matched by a justifiable pride. He had within the past five months cast two votes that had brought cries of anguish from some of his more timid supporters. In August 1882, he had voted to override Arthur's popular veto of a river and harbor bill and then, but a few days before the General Court was to convene, he had risked the displeasure of the Grand Army of the Republic by voting to restore General Fitz John Porter to his old army rank and perquisites. Porter, in the minds of many veterans, had disgraced himself at the second battle of Bull Run, and his cause was highly unpopular with soldier-politicos and lobbyists for the G.A.R. Hoar would take care to offer the public a speedy defense of both votes, but in each instance he had scorned suggestions that he retreat or abstain. As Long had hungered for Hoar's senatorial office but would not bargain with Butler, so Hoar was anxious to remain in Washington but would not vote against his conscience. One man's virtue denied him the prize, the other's allowed him to accept it with a pleased sense of righteousness.

Hoar received no letter of congratulation from Arthur, but from Rutherford B. Hayes and James G. Blaine came praise and commendation.[24] That both men saw fit to congratulate the party

[22] *See* William B. Wood to Dawes, 15 January 1883, Dawes Papers, Box #26, Library of Congress. According to the later recollections of Dawes's devoted daughter, Anna: "[My father's] considerate and amiable temper . . . enabled him to get on with Mr. Hoar better than some of their colleagues . . . Moreover Mr. Dawes and Mr. Hoar both knew that the candidacy of Gov. Long was a part of a settled plan to oust the Old Guard in Massa't and put in new men." "Draft Biography of H. L. Dawes" by Anna L. Dawes, chap. 6, pp. 13–15, Dawes Papers, Box #39, Library of Congress.

[23] Theodore C. Bates to Hoar, 21 January 1883, Hoar Papers.

[24] *See* Hoar to Hayes, 25 January 1883, Hayes Papers, Rutherford B. Hayes Library; Hoar to Rockwood Hoar, 19 January 1883, Hoar Papers.

as well as Hoar bore witness that the Half-Breeds had not been dislodged by the accession of Arthur, merely disturbed.

Those policies of the Arthur years most indicative of this fact concerned the reform of the civil service and the relations of government and business. The Pendleton Act highlighted the first; the issues of internal improvements and the tariff illustrated the last.

The Civil Service Act of 16 January 1883 was in a very real sense Garfield's posthumous legacy to American legislative history. Surely in Hoar's case, Garfield's assassination by a crazed office seeker persuaded him to accept a more centralized system for civil service reform. His was no sudden conversion, however, as was the case with Arthur. Hoar's interest in civil service reform, as already noted, stretched back at least to the early seventies. He had been disturbed by the way in which the Tenure-of-Office Act encouraged senatorial Stalwarts to form political liveried companies and had wanted Grant to demand its complete repeal; he had delivered a strong reform speech in the campaign of 1876 and had cheered the civil service order of Hayes. By September 1881, he was prepared to preside at a Boston meeting where Representative George Pendleton of Ohio discussed his plans for a bipartisan civil service commission empowered to administer examinations to candidates for the "nonpolitical" offices of the federal bureaucracy.[25] Hoar had once declared that such a commission smacked too much of British practice and posed a potential danger if staffed by the corrupt or the doctrinaire. The assassination of Garfield, by dramatizing the necessity of reform, diminished his fears. Previously he had advocated less partisanship in the appointment of clerical, postal, and revenue officers; now he demanded it:

> There is no legitimate connection whatever between sound political principles and the transmission and distribution of mails, the survey of public lands, the collection of internal revenues or duties on imports ... any more than between

[25] *See The Nation* 28 September 1876; Dorman B. Eaton to Hoar, 25 March 1881, Moorfield Storey to Hoar, 26 September 1881, Hoar Papers; Hoar to H. L. Dawes, 24 August 1881, Dawes Papers, Box #25, Library of Congress.

sound opinions and service in the army or navy. A partisan civil service, substituting personal for public ends in political activities, in the end degrades party.

The tendency . . . to make of the public officers a compact and disciplined cohort for the service of the person to whose influence their appointment is due . . . is wholly vicious . . . To cure [this evil] demands the combined and sincere efforts of both political parties.[26]

In the interim between the death of Garfield and the passage of the Pendleton Act (September 1881–January 1883), there were to be seen three differing opinions among the civil service reformers: there were those who wished the reform to be limited and provisional in character and completely divorced from the influence of the executive; those who accepted the concept of a presidentially appointed commission and were willing to see the merit system extended through the lower ranks of the federal bureaucracy; and those who wished to transform that bureaucracy into a genuine civil service, British-style. The latter group was strong within various municipal reform clubs, but had few supporters in Congress. There, Hoar was to be found with the second group; his colleague Dawes, with the first.

The position of Henry L. Dawes on any issue of reform was never too lucid and in the fall of 1882 his ability to speak in behalf of reform while obstructing reformers achieved near perfection. Dawes abhorred political discomfort as much as political corruption. He desired to do good without antagonizing any significant source of support. Sincerely desirous of seeing the quality of the civil service improved, his distaste for Chet Arthur made him suspicious of a presidentially appointed commission. The clamor of political Independents for immediate passage of the Pendleton bill inspired a fear that it might prove detrimental to party organization. He introduced his own civil service bill, a restricted and congressionally oriented measure, partly to frustrate the Pendleton bill, partly from a conviction that it was politically safer.

[26] G. F. Hoar, "The Appointing Power," *North American Review.* 133 (November 1881), 464–476.

If Dawes expected Hoar to follow his lead, he was soon disappointed. Hoar had determined not only to support the Pendleton bill in the Senate but to work in its behalf. Hoar informed the Senate that there were but two objections that might be raised to the bill: insufficient limitation on the removal of office holders who were competent and honest; the novelty and expense of the commission form of administration. He insisted that the first objection was rendered irrelevant by the fact that appointing officials would have little incentive to remove the competent as they would have no control over their replacement—at least for the enumerated positions. As for the second objection, a certain degree of centralized control was necessary for the proper establishment and maintenance of the merit system. Let his colleagues seize the moment and pass the Pendleton bill and the present session of Congress would receive "a conspicuous place" in the political history of the country.[27]

The Pendleton Act did not mark the lame-duck Republican Congress that passed it as conspicuous in the political history of the country. It placed only a minority of federal offices on the enumerated list—appointment to which would be by competitive examination under rules prescribed by the three-man Civil Service Commission. There was no wholesale conversion of the federal bureaucracy into a tenured, professional civil service. The principle of nonpolitical selection had been established, however, and it was a principle of basic importance to a nation whose bureaucracy was in another generation to experience geometric increase. Certain of the consequences of civil service reform were neither beneficial nor expected, but with the passage of the Pendleton Act there was a perceptible if modest improvement in the moral climate of Washington.[28]

The most significant contribution Hoar made to the long-term improvement of the federal service he made in 1886 in behalf of

---

[27] *Congressional Record,* 47th Cong., 2d sess., 353–354; 607–608 (16, 23 December 1882). *See,* too, Dorman B. Eaton to Hoar, 9 December 1882; Arthur Hobart to Hoar, 13 January 1883, Hoar Papers.

[28] *See* Ari Hoogenboom, *Outlawing the Spoils* (Urbana: University of Illinois Press, 1961), 217–267, for an able analysis of the provisions and limited impact of the Pendleton Act.

the independence of the executive. He had long called for the repeal of the remaining provisions of the Tenure-of-Office Act, but several of his party colleagues, suffering anachronistic memories of Andrew Johnson, had refused to agree that the Senate should formally surrender all control over the power of the President to remove officials within the executive department. Hoar was convinced that until the constitutional rights of the President in this connection were clearly reaffirmed, there would remain the danger of future editions of the degrading struggles fought by Hayes and Garfield with Roscoe Conkling. The return of the Democrats to power in the election of 1884 gave him the opportunity to push through a full repeal of the old and obnoxious measure.

Hoar led the fight, and at the cost of considerable criticism. John Sherman denounced the repeal bill of 1886 and warned Hoar that he was working against the interests of both party and Senate.[29] As he would on several subsequent occasions, Hoar proclaimed his partisan loyalty while speaking against the wishes of a majority of his party's politicians. In a speech describing the initial passage of the bill and its subsequent evil effects, Hoar took care to castigate both Johnson and Cleveland, while supporting the initial claims of the one and the present needs of the other.[30] Only three Republicans voted with Hoar in the Senate, but their votes were sufficient to ensure passage.

As Cleveland's assistance was not acknowledged in December 1886, so some four years earlier Arthur's support of the Pendleton Act was judged of doubtful sincerity and little use. It is probable that Hoar would have been more generous if he had not already tangled with Arthur on two issues respecting the relations of government and business: federal appropriations for internal improvements and the protective tariff. That Arthur, the former Stalwart, cast himself in each case in the role of the reformer was an additional irritant.

Perhaps no single act of Arthur's received more acclaim at the time nor more praise by historians subsequently than his veto of

[29] John Sherman to Hoar, 16 December 1886, Hoar Papers.
[30] *Congressional Record*, 49th Cong., 2d sess., 137; 140–142 (14 December 1886).

the river and harbor bill of 1882. Arthur has been pictured as an overweight David who stood forth to do battle against the evil forces of the pork-barrel and lobby. The River and Harbor Act of 1882 has usually been described as an extravagant example of political jobbery, designed to serve only the political interests of various district congressmen. This was the burden of Arthur's veto message, and most historians have accepted the validity of its judgments. Hoar did not. He suspected Arthur's motives and considered the act a wise and proper measure for the economy of the country and the manufacturers of Massachusetts.

Hoar had been absent from Congress when the river and harbor bill initially passed Congress and so was not recorded in its favor. When Arthur's veto message of July met with almost unanimous support by the Massachusetts press, including such Half-Breed papers as the *Boston Journal* and Worcester *Daily Spy* Hoar was advised by various political supporters not to risk unpopularity by voting to override that veto. Hoar rejected their advice. No single decision of his life—until his vote against the Treaty of Paris, February 1899—proved more immediately unpopular. The *Springfield Republican* declared Hoar in disgrace; Charles Eliot Norton in a commencement address at a female seminary bewailed the decay of public virtue and took Hoar for his example.

Norton's equal in his conviction of personal righteousness, Hoar was too politically shrewd not to see that attack was the best defense. Mindless of a steaming heat wave, he locked himself in his Worcester library and began a study of committee reports and the recommendations of government engineers for five years past. He emerged with one of the shortest and most effective papers he ever wrote, an eight-page Letter to the People of Massachusetts. Its purpose was twofold: to analyze in detail the specific appropriations itemized in the River and Harbor Act; to prove that such internal improvement measures were deserving of support for "grave, honest, sound, Republican, Massachusetts reasons."

The measure was not extravagant. Figured on a per capita basis its cost was far less than the internal improvement measures once so eloquently defended by Massachusetts' own Daniel Webster. Items attacked as narrowly local would develop waterways to serve the nation's river and harbor system in the same manner that spur lines served its great railways. It was to the interest of the country and Massachusetts that a national system of waterways be developed and expanded. Only in this way would there be effective competition between rail and water transportation, reducing freight rates and improving the position of Massachusetts manufactures. But there were still broader considerations. In America centrifugal forces were strong; there were too few things that drew the hearts of the people to the nation as compared to those that centered their affections upon their state or locality. Internal improvements, by expanding domestic commerce between the sections, would not only aid the national economy but foster a greater sense of national unity. The measure was as wise in its ultimate consequences as it was prudent in its immediate costs. Whatever the people felt now in the heat of carefully manipulated emotion, their sober second thought must commend this act to their support.[31]

Though Hoar never gave his suspicion public expression, he was convinced that both Roscoe Conkling and Jay Gould were behind the torrent of abuse that met the river and harbor bill. Conkling wished to make trouble for his old senatorial enemies; Gould did not wish to see his railroad interests checked by the competition of improved water transportation.[32] His friends believed it wiser to emphasize Hoar's courage than his suspicions. They gave his public letter wide publicity and applauded his bold defense.[33]

The River and Harbor Act exacerbated relations between Arthur and the Half-Breed leaders in the Senate, the very opposite of Arthur's intentions. Arthur had vetoed the bill in an effort to rid himself of the stigma of past Stalwart association and to show the business community that he favored economical government. Hoar suspected Arthur's veto to be dictated by Conkling, when in

[31] G. F. Hoar, "The River and Harbor Bill: An Analysis, Letter To the People of Massachusetts," 12 August 1882, pamphlet, Hoar Papers.
[32] Hoar to Dawes, 25 September 1882, Dawes Papers, Box #26, Library of Congress.
[33] W. W. Clapp to Hoar, 7 August 1882, William Claflin to Hoar, 14 August 1882, Hoar Papers; Hoar to Dawes, 16 August 1882, Dawes Papers, Box #26, Library of Congress; Hoar to William Claflin, 1 September 1882, William Claflin Papers, Rutherford B. Hayes Library.

fact it was a bid to gain leadership of the Half-Breeds. Arthur's choice of battleground was ill-chosen, however, and undeserving of the praise accorded it then or later. The River and Harbor Act of 1882 might well have been trimmed, but its defeat would not have served the national interest.[34]

On another issue respecting the relations of the government and the economy, it is far from certain that Hoar spoke for the national interest, but on no issue was he more convinced that he did. When Arthur proposed that Congress modestly revise the tariff and reduce certain customs duties, Hoar believed the recommendation endangered not only the manufacturers of tin plate but a great Republican principle.

Hoar was a firm believer in the economic wisdom of a high protective tariff from the day he first voted to the day he died. Associating the rapid growth of Worcester and other New England industrial cities with the beneficial operation of the tariff, he was convinced that the superior living standards of the laborers of Worcester and the nation were attributable to the protection of domestic industry. A protected market was an expanding market. In the eyes of most New England manufacturers, Hoar was "sound" on the tariff question.

Once again, however, it would be misleading to categorize Hoar as the spokesman of industry. Tariff bills were long and complicated matters; by no means did all New England manufacturers agree upon the details and rates of various schedules and duties. If Hoar sympathized verbally with the desires of all manufacturer-correspondents, he best served those who agreed with his own high protectionist principles. When he had received simultaneous complaints from a stove manufacturer that higher duties on steel would increase his raw material costs and from Washburn, Moen & Company that technological innovations in England made in-

---

[34] The river and harbor bill of 1884 was similar in its costs and projects and passed Congress with little comment. Hoar made extensive preparations in its defense, and compiled long tables describing the relative costs of river and harbor improvement in England, France, and the United States. Hoar to Chief of Engineers, U.S. Army, 11 May 1883, Hoar to Joseph Ninno, Jr., 23 May 1883, Hoar Papers; *Congressional Record*, 48th Cong., 1st sess., 5841–5848 (1 July 1884).

adequate the current duties on imported steel, Hoar voted for higher duties.[35] There were times when his vote was cast for the lower duty on particular schedules, but these occasions were relatively rare and usually concerned materials unsuited to the geography of America.

Upon the accession of Garfield, Hoar had hoped to see Congress pass a new and higher tariff bill that balanced in coherent fashion as many interests as possible under the guiding principle of ample protection. By the early 1880's, however, men of capital were even less united on the tariff issue than they had been in earlier decades. A good majority of manufacturers still favored it, but by no means all merchants, investors, and railroad men. In Massachusetts, for example, such State Street figures as John Murray Forbes and William Endicott Jr. now came out for selective tariff revision— in a downward direction. While Greenbackers had threatened, they had hugged tight to the leadership of Hoar and Dawes, but now they exhibited increasing restlessness on the tariff issue. It was largely in answer to the complaints of such men that President Arthur recommended the establishment of a tariff investigating commission and endorsed its proposal for limited tariff revision late in 1882. Congress, suggested Arthur, should review the tariff to determine whether it was not possible to reduce this source of federal taxation and so lessen the Treasury surplus and encourage economy.

Hoar responded coldly to the President's invitation. He had voted for the tariff commission once he was convinced that its members would be friendly to the basic principles of protection.[36] Its studies might advise Congress of any particular iniquities in the existing schedules and its existence might avert hasty and ill-considered special tariff bills, but he cautioned against radical

[35] Buck Brothers to Hoar, 11 October, 4 December 1869; Ethan Allen & Company to Hoar, 26 January 1870; J. D. E. Jones to Hoar, 28 January 1870; P. L. Moen to Hoar, 19 April 1870; T. K. Earle & Company to Hoar, 7 May 1870; Hoar to Ruth A. Hoar, 25 June 1870, Hoar Papers.

[36] Hoar had corresponded in April 1880 with John L. Hayes of the National Association of Wool Manufacturers, who informed him that the industrial associations were increasingly inclined to favor such a commission. Hayes to Hoar, 13 April 1880, Hoar Papers.

reduction, especially against the egregious folly of an across-the-board cut.[37]

The final result of Arthur's recommendation was the Mongrel Tariff of March 1883, the product of legislative logrolling and intramural antagonism between House and Senate. It reduced some duties and raised others in no discernible or logical pattern. Neither the protectionists nor the tariff reformers applauded it. Hoar voted for both the Senate and conference versions but thought it inferior to its predecessor; J. M. Forbes and William Endicott expressed undiluted disapproval. Forbes forwarded to Hoar a warning from Endicott that if the Republicans did not take the initiative, the Democrats "will come to the front as the champions of reduced taxation." The tariff should not be a party question; it was a business question. The times called for economy and moderate protection—sufficient to prevent "damage to existing interests."[38]

Hoar was dismayed and puzzled by the increasing division of eastern men of capital respecting the tariff. When Forbes joined the Mugwumps in the election of 1884, Hoar declared that Forbes's wavering stand on the tariff should have served to warn his friends. When still other businessmen later found merit in Cleveland's tariff message of 1887, Hoar deplored the spread of "infection." Time and again during the Cleveland years, Hoar would bewail the clumsiness of Arthur while excoriating the "free trade notions" of the Democrats. If only Arthur had supported protection as a true Half-Breed, then the Republicans might have passed a tariff bill in 1883 so logical and popular that the Democrats would have been denied the opportunity for mischief.

For most of the eighties, Hoar was displeased with the direction and calibre of presidential leadership. That of Arthur was clumsy;

[37] *Congressional Record,* 47th Cong., 1st sess., 6463–6466 (25 July 1882).

[38] William Endicott, Jr., to Forbes, [?] December 1883; Forbes to Hoar, 16 December, 17 December 1883, Hoar Papers. Forbes and Endicott entertained the notion, common among tariff reformers, that a reduction of tariff rates would automatically reduce the Treasury surplus. In fact, such a reduction was more likely to inspire an increase in the quantity of taxable imports sufficient to compensate for the lower per-item assessment. The correlation of the surplus and the tariff was a source of continuous misunderstanding for both sides in the tariff debate.

that of Cleveland, mischievous. Not only did neither man properly appreciate the necessary association between the protective tariff and economic growth, but more generally neither paid sufficient attention to the needs and relations of capital and labor. Hoar's vision in the latter respect was limited if not astigmatic, but he was one of the first of the Half-Breed leaders to sense the social dangers inherent in the nation's rapid economic growth and to favor their legislative investigation. He served with other Half-Breeds as a slender bridge between the interventionist tradition of a Whig past and a Progressive future.

Hoar would have the government concern itself with the problems of industrial growth not from a desire to promote economic equality but in an effort to promote social harmony. While enjoying industrial acceleration America must maintain the sense of community that he imagined to be characteristic of its past. Ideally he would have had American industry cast in the mould of the modest-sized corporation typical of Worcester and have allowed the American laborer and capitalist to possess but a single interest, as had the harness maker and his three helpers in Concord days. America in the 1880's, however, seemed to have outgrown Concord, and it was necessary for the government to attempt to recapture the old harmonies by expressions of carefully modulated legislative concern.

Primarily that concern should be directed to industry—cautioning it against abuses and so promoting its growth and social acceptance—but the conditions of labor were also a proper and constitutional subject for national investigation. The American workingman would best be assisted by the continued development of our great economic resources under the beneficial stimulus of the tariff, but his lot might also be improved by means of union organization and legislative encouragement. The latter, however, must never promote class division or dissension. In a letter to the future magazine publisher, S. S. McClure, Hoar gave a revealing summary of his hopes and fears respecting labor organization and labor legislation. McClure had implied that Hoar thought too little of the rights of Labor and too constantly of the interests of business; Hoar declared the accusation quite unfounded:

For thirty five years I have been in favor of reducing the hours devoted to labor by our workmen to a space which will leave them in command of a reasonable time in each day for leisure, recreation, rest and self improvement. So much, at least, the wonderful powers of machinery, the employment of the new and vast forces now in the service of man ought to accomplish for the workman . . .

[But] I look with infinite regret upon every thing which shall tend to array the workmen of this country together as a class, opposed to any other class, or accustom them to think of themselves as interested in the welfare of any portion of the State less than the whole. Their interest cannot be separated from that of capital . . .

Especially short sighted and suicidal will be any policy on the part of the workmen which is unjust to other men or interferes with that absolute freedom which is the birthright of all.[39]

The complaints of labor leaders against Hoar and other Republican leaders were not directed primarily to their failure to pass labor legislation, but rather to the supposed favoritism the Half-Breeds exhibited toward the interests of big business. Though he would have denied the charge, Hoar's votes in the Senate were on balance highly favorable to the interests of capital. Hoar identified the progress of America with its industrial transformation. The actions of government should promote those objects designed to realize the economic potential of the nation and avoid those measures that would harm the economy by destroying the confidence of business. The nation's creditors should be protected by national bankruptcy legislation; the nation's inventors given the

[39] Hoar to S. S. McClure, 20 August 1886, Hoar Papers. Equally indicative of the attitude of the Half-Breeds respecting Labor is the speech written by James G. Blaine in 1886 for a presumably inarticulate Republican gubernatorial candidate. The citizens of Maine were informed that the Republican party of that state recognized the right of labor to combine but would allow neither the combination of labor nor the combination of capital "to interfere with the just and legal rights of others." Government should seek to promote the friendly cooperation of capital and labor, and to this end might provide "an impartial system of arbitration," make "the existing statute which defines ten hours a day's work absolute & mandatory" for all industries, and pass a child labor law. Blaine Papers, III, Library of Congress.

incentive of exclusive patents; the interests of investors carefully considered in any regulations of the railroads, and this for the public interest. Labor could not prosper if capital did not; the public interest could not be served if the legitimate interests of business were denied.

Hoar was not a victim of the Spencerian doctrine of Social Darwinism; it took too little notice of the power of a United States senator to do good. He did believe, however, in social evolution, and saw the man of capital, though occasionally a danger to political purity, as a vital instrument for national progress. When engaged in defending his bankruptcy bill against the charge that it was unfair to the "great community of debtors," Hoar was stung into offering what was a virtual eulogy of these agents of progress:

> The leading merchants and manufacturers of this country are not a set of sharks and Shylocks . . . They are men who will compare favorably with any class of men on the face of the earth . . . there is in the present or past ages no chivalry that has shown more generosity than the class of men who have been successful, East and West, North and South, in the business and trade of the American Republic. They built our railroads, they covered the sea with our commerce, they made our flag favored the world over, created the wealth and prosperity of America . . . These men are permeated through and through with the American spirit, with the American character, with the American traits, and one great part and characteristic of that character is generosity, kindness, and fellow-feeling for the poor.[40]

A Massachusetts senator sacrificed neither his independence nor his principles by acknowledging the interests and requests of the manufacturers, merchants, and investors of the Commonwealth.

The phrase "conflict of interests" had not been coined in the 1880's, but Hoar appreciated its existence and dangers and was highly solicitous of his own reputation for integrity. He carefully distinguished the legitimate attentions a politician owed to his

[40] *Congressional Record*, 49th Cong., 1st sess., 4887 (25 May 1886).

industrial constituents and self-seeking acts of favoritism. Many saw nothing wrong with a congressman maintaining close association with various industries whose interests were directly affected by congressional legislation, but Hoar did not agree. Misuse of official position was most improper and—what was almost as bad—quite imprudent. Hoar informed the attorney of Worcester's largest industry that he would happily forward his arguments to the Attorney General, but he could not serve as its counsel before the relevant departments in Washington; he secured for the inventor of a new type of carpet loom a special examination, but would not consent to pressure officials at the Patent Bureau in his behalf.[41]

Perhaps Hoar's most suspicious action in a long public career was his decision in 1885 to serve briefly as counsel for the American Bell Telephone Company, then engaged in fighting for its government patents and monopoly rights. Hoar did not appear in its behalf before any government agency, but he did consent to accept a check for three hundred dollars for "advice received."[42] Far more typical, however, of his personal standards of conduct was his refusal to accept stock from a Massachusetts Telegraph Company in return for nominal service upon its board of directors:

> I am satisfied that I cannot with propriety accept the offer. It is quite probable that questions may come up in Congress in dealing with which I should find it a serious embarrassment to hold the office of director of an important telegraph company . . . I do not think that it would or should be of much of a guaranty for the honest or able management of the concern, or of the value of its stock or bonds, if it were known to the public that I received such bonds as I had without paying for them in money, and that my judgment as to the confidence to be placed in the enterprise was biassed by the fact that I was to receive a large salary.[43]

[41] *See* J. H. Dewey to Hoar, 28 March 1882; Hoar to Henry M. Teller, 12 July 1884; Hoar to A. Livermore, 11 September 1884, Hoar Papers.

[42] W. H. Forbes to E. Rockwood Hoar, 24 June 1885; W. H. Forbes to G. F. Hoar, 8 July 1885, Hoar Papers.

[43] Hoar to J. C. Prince, 6 October 1885, Hoar Papers.

Hoar invested very modestly in certain insurance and railroad companies, but the only intimate connection he entertained with what might be called big business was in the capacity of counsel. Among Hoar's legal clients during his senatorial years were the Worcester and Nashua Railroad and the Boston and Albany Railroad. For both he served in association with his brother E. Rockwood Hoar, who carried the burden of court appearance.[44] Having deplored the unfortunate connection of James G. Blaine and the Little Rock and Fort Smith Railroad, Hoar made careful distinction between the roles of senator and legal consultant. The latter occupation was necessary for the education of his son, but it was never to interfere with his public duties or influence his public decisions. Quite possibly one reason for Hoar's long if wavering interest in federal railroad regulation was that it stood witness to his refusal to allow pecuniary considerations to undermine his senatorial independence.

Hoar had no doubt as to the authority of the federal government to regulate interstate railroad traffic under the commerce clause of the Constitution, but he was less certain as to means and methods. Initially he appeared to favor a federal railroad commission that would have only investigatory powers. The operations and accounts of the major railroads must be open to the public scrutiny, stock-watering and illegal rebates should be prohibited, but any attempt by the federal government to prescribe the contractual arrangements between the railroads and their freighters or to regulate railroad rates would probably fail. The laws of trade, of supply and demand, must form the chief reliance of the public respecting the good conduct of the railroads.[45]

By 1886 Hoar would be prepared to allow a federal railroad commission certain regulatory as well as investigatory powers. His conversion was due in part to the labors of his fellow Republican, Shelby M. Cullom of Illinois, chief spokesman in the Senate for the necessity of railroad regulation. Cullom had kept Hoar fully informed of the progress of the committee hearings he conducted

[44] *See* William Aspinwall to Hoar, 14 September 1886; E. Rockwood Hoar to Hoar, 5 October, 10 December 1886; Hoar to Edward R. Brown, 4 February 1889, Hoar Papers.

[45] *Congressional Record*, 48th Cong., 2d sess., 689; 750 (14, 16 January 1885).

about the country in the spring of 1885, and a year later conferred with his older colleague on the legislative significance of the Supreme Court decision in Wabash, St. Louis and Pacific *v.* Illinois.[46] In the latter case, the Court, backtracking from its decisions in the early Granger Cases, decided that the regulatory authority of a state was primarily limited to intrastate railroad traffic. It was now clear that effective regulation of the major railroads could only be provided by the federal government.

In his autobiography written many years later, Senator Cullom would declare that Hoar opposed the Interstate Commerce Act that Cullom, with Democratic assistance, piloted through the Senate early in 1887, and that Hoar opposed it "because he thought it would injuriously affect his locality, although he knew very well it would be of inestimable benefit to the country as a whole."[47] Cullom's memory was unfair to fact and to Hoar. When the Interstate Commerce Act received its first full-dress debate in the Senate in the spring of 1886, Hoar declared his approval of all its provisions with the exception of Section 4. Section 4 prohibited geographic discrimination by the railroads—forbidding a railroad to charge more for a short haul than a long haul and requiring that freight charges correspond to travel mileage. Hoar believed the prohibition unwise. Under certain circumstances a railroad could freight bulk goods more easily and cheaply for a long distance than a short one. The short-haul prohibition would restrict the necessary competitive freedom of the long-distance operator, and possibly work to the disadvantage of such embarkation ports as Boston. The other portions of the bill received Hoar's approbation, and he was one of a large majority of senators that voted in favor of the bill when first it passed the Senate on 12 May 1886.[48]

Cullom and Hoar came to loggerheads only when the interstate commerce commission bill returned to the Senate after its revision by the conference committee of House and Senate. Hoar had expected that committee to knock out Section 4 and was highly displeased to see it had not. Addressing the Senate on 14 January

---

[46] Cullom to Hoar, 27 April 1885; James H. McKenney to Hoar, 31 August 1886, Hoar Papers.

[47] Shelby Cullom, *Fifty Years of Public Service* (Chicago, 1911), 211.

[48] *Congressional Record*, 49th Cong., 1st sess., 4227–4228; 4423 (6, 12 May 1886).

1887, Hoar reiterated his objection to the short-haul provision, while restating his belief in the necessity of a federal commission and documenting his long interest in the national supervision and encouragement of all forms of industrial transportation.[49] Cullom insisted that Hoar was attacking provisions in the conference report that he had earlier approved and that his objection to Section 4 was inspired by his concern for the shipping interests of Massachusetts.[50] Hoar was undoubtedly influenced by the opposition of certain mercantile interests in Boston to parts of the interstate commerce bill, but his stand was consistent with his general attitude respecting the relationship of government and business. Government could properly investigate the operations of business, but it should avoid too direct involvement in the contractual relations of businessmen and their customers. As was often the case in the economic analyses of Half-Breed leaders, the distinction was more neat than practical, but it was the distinction of a sincere man trying to meet the problems of a new economic era while only dimly perceiving its outlines. It was on the basis of such distinction that Hoar rose before the final roll call to declare his approval of a federal commission and to cast his vote, with the Senate minority, against the Interstate Commerce Act.

The Massachusetts railroad promoter, John Murray Forbes, approved Hoar's vote but disagreed with him respecting the necessity of any kind of federal railroad regulation.[51] Forbes, however, was no longer listened to by Hoar with the respect that once he had commanded. They had fallen out over the tariff of 1883, and, more important, Forbes had bolted the party in the election of 1884. That election was for Hoar the most trying event of the decade of the eighties. It was also the most crucial for the party he served. It witnessed an example of treason within the ranks that would affect the confidence and quality of Republican leadership for the remainder of the decade.

In the Republican convention of 1884, Hoar attempted to keep the Massachusetts delegation behind the nominal candidacy of George Edmunds of Vermont in an effort to frustrate both the

[49] *Congressional Record*, 49th Cong., 1st sess., 634–641; 660; 664 (14 January 1887).
[50] Cullom, *Fifty Years of Public Service*. 213; 324.
[51] J. M. Forbes to Hoar, 28 January 1887, Hoar Papers.

supporters of President Arthur and those of James G. Blaine.[52] This tactic had worked four years before when he had sought to prevent the nomination of either Grant or Blaine, but it failed miserably in 1884. In the interim several changes had occurred.

The relationship of Blaine and Hoar had changed. By 1884 Blaine was recognized by Hoar as a fellow Half-Breed, and in consequence his opposition to Blaine's candidacy was no longer an expression of ideological or factional division but only of political prudence. Hoar, with Edmunds, Justin Morrill, William Evarts, and other Half-Breeds did not oppose the nomination of Blaine in 1884 because they suspected his present politics but because they doubted his probable election. Blaine's Stalwart past would be an embarrassment. The limited nature of Hoar's objections to Blaine's candidacy would mitigate against both the clarity and the success of preconvention maneuvers.

Those maneuvers were additionally frustrated by one very obvious fact: the only man who could defeat Blaine in the Republican convention was Arthur, and Hoar could not abide the thought of another four years of Chet Arthur.[53] A majority of the Republican leaders in Massachusetts shared Hoar's dilemma. Henry Cabot Lodge, chairman of the Republican state committee; Governor George D. Robinson, who had rescued the gubernatorial office from Ben Butler; and John D. Long were equally determined that the Republicans not fight the presidential election of 1884 under the handicap of either Blaine or Arthur. A man must be chosen whose past record would need no defense or apology.[54]

Blaine's swift nomination by the Republican convention was a disappointment and a surprise. Unlike Lodge and several other members of the Massachusetts delegation, however, Hoar never for a moment contemplated bolting the party. Searching for con-

---

[52] *See* George William Curtis to Hoar, 19 March 1884; J. Evarts Greene to Hoar, 12 April 1883; E. Rockwood Hoar to Hoar, 7 May 1884, Hoar Papers.

[53] To the editor of the *Boston Journal,* Hoar wrote: "The materials for an attack on [Arthur] . . . are fearful if they are put together, as they will be if he is a candidate." The Massachusetts delegation at Chicago should "refuse to take the responsibility of choosing between evils." Hoar to W. W. Clapp, 16 May 1884, W. W. Clapp Papers, Houghton Library, Harvard University.

[54] *See* Lodge to Hoar, 27 May 1884, Hoar Papers.

solation, he declared the Republican platform was the best since the days of Lincoln. The planks on civil rights in the South, civil service reform, and the protective tariff were exemplary, and if that calling for the exclusion of Chinese labor was both unfortunate and false to the faith, those alluding to the hours of labor and the regulation of corporations were satisfying illustrations of the progressive spirit of the Republican party. The best issues, however, were the old issues, and presented with the task of supporting a candidate of clouded reputation, Hoar had every intention of concentrating upon them.

In Hoar's opinion, the Republican candidate had occasionally displayed in the past a dulled sense of public ethics, but he was not a crook. The affair of the Mulligan letters had shown Blaine to be liable to the charge of imprudence not corruption. He had not sold his influence as Speaker of the House to the Little Rock and Fort Smith Railway, but most unwisely he had so mixed his public position and personal affairs as to give credence to such a charge. When asked many years later by the editor of the *American Historical Review* to review a biography of Blaine, Hoar, while refusing, took opportunity to summarize his judgment of Blaine and his critics. He entertained identical opinions during the campaign of 1884: "I don't believe that he was ever corrupt or ever offered to be corrupted. I think the construction, which was put upon the Mulligan letters by his antagonists, was not only harsh but savage . . . But I should be constrained to say also that in the matter of propriety of personal conduct, Mr. Blaine made some grievous errors."[55]

Hoar's estimate, though kind, was not necessarily incorrect. Perhaps on two occasions Blaine knowingly used his political influence to bolster his income, but he was hardly the political Benedict Arnold that was depicted in the pages of *The Nation* and *Harper's Weekly*. There is an element of mystery in the career of James G. Blaine, but it resides not in his financial dealings but in

[55] Hoar to J. Franklin Jameson, 10 August 1895, Hoar Papers. *See,* too, Hoar to Charles Francis Adams, Jr., 15 February 1895, Hoar Papers. During the campaign of 1884, Hoar devoted but a single speech to a detailed analysis and refutation of the specific charges leveled against Blaine. A lengthy report of this speech will be found in the *Boston Sunday Herald,* 24 August 1884.

his political popularity. He was without doubt the most prominent figure in the Republican party throughout the 1880's, even though he spent a large part of the decade sulking in semiretirement. Idolized by many as "the truest Republican," he was the author of none of the acts or principles extolled in the Republican platform of 1884. Not until his second tour of duty as Secretary of State would he accomplish anything of lasting historical significance; yet by the election of 1884 Blaine had exerted an almost charismatic effect over his followers for more than a decade.[56]

But if there were Republicans who idolized Blaine, there were others to whom he was anathema. Many of these determined to bolt the Republican party in disgust over his nomination. They were the Mugwumps.

As is true of any political faction, the Mugwumps of 1884 had their individual differences of aim and inspiration, but they possessed certain common denominators. Patrician in temperament, they were social conservatives, depressed by the excesses of the nouveau riche and disenchanted with the possibilities of racial equality. Almost without exception they entertained an instinctive dislike for the institutionalization of party organization and leadership, and they preferred yesterday to today. They were constantly comparing the compromises of the present with the supposed virtues and meaningful direction of the past. As Geoffrey Blodgett has observed of the Boston brand of Mugwump: "Their talents were guided by an awesome legacy, the New England of Thoreau and Emerson, of Parker, Whittier, and Sumner. To this inheritance they sought to restore political viability . . . Mugwumpery was above all an escape from party. By breaking fixed rules of political behavior, the Mugwumps hoped to change them, and so recapture for men some of the potency that the party had absorbed for itself."[57]

---

[56] *See*, for example, the letters from the impressionable young John Hay to Blaine, 27 January, 26 May, 17 June 1876, Blaine Papers, I, Library of Congress. Also, W. E. Chandler to Mrs. J. G. Blaine, 18 July 1881; S. B. Elkins to Blaine, 9 December 1888, Blaine Papers, II; III, Library of Congress.

[57] Geoffrey T. Blodgett, "The Mind of the Boston Mugwump," *Mississippi Valley Historical Review*, 68 (March 1962), 615, 629.

Boston and New York were the centers of Mugwumpery, and of the many articulate Mugwumps in those cities perhaps none was more typical than the Boston corporation lawyer, Moorfield Storey. With his fellow Mugwumps, Storey shared a strong sense of moral certitude and a conviction that the way to solve current problems was to bring to bear the principles of abstract justice he had learned in his youth. With his fellow Mugwumps, Storey possessed a rather clouded view of the causation of those problems but a very personal concern that they be solved. Party was far less important than principle and conscience. To endorse Blaine was to desert the faith of the Fathers. To defeat Blaine was presumably to insure a revival of the politics of principle, where the better sort would again play a vital role in the shaping of the national destiny.[58]

The most superficial description of the Mugwump creed makes obvious one fact: George Frisbie Hoar shared a great deal of the social background and political moralism of the Mugwumps. And in the election of 1884 there would be no supporter of the Republican candidate who excoriated the Mugwumps more bitterly than did Hoar. It has been said that none can quarrel more angrily than cousins. The election of 1884 proved that none could quarrel more bitterly than fellow claimants to the mantle of Sumner.

Hoar considered the Mugwumps to be traitors to tradition as well as party. Those who were sincere were foolish, those who were using the facade of political independence to cover their animosity towards tariff protection and Negro rights were positively wicked. They were all the more to blame as they came from the ranks of educated men. Harvard, once the home of heroes, was now but a Mugwump hermitage, immune from reality. Its faculty was composed of men who were blind to the essential role of party in a democratic republic.

The Mugwumps struck back with the unforgivable weapon: the historical record. Was there any relationship, they asked, be-

---

[58] *See* the letter of Storey's friend, George Crocker to Hoar, 13 August 1885, Hoar Papers. Also, Scrap Book #1, Moorfield Storey Papers, Library of Congress; M. A. De Wolfe Howe, *Portrait of an Independent: Moorfield Storey, 1845–1929* (Boston: Houghton Mifflin, 1932), 4–5.

tween the current object of Mr. Hoar's praises and the man he had opposed in the Republican conventions of 1876, 1880, and that of last June? Could Mr. Hoar continue to praise the independent spirit of the Free Soil bolters of '48 and concurrently bow down to the graven image of party regularity? Were the Mugwump critics of Mr. Blaine guilty of slander when they uttered words almost identical with those used by Mr. Hoar during his famous speech at the Belknap Trial? "The true significance of Blaine's candidacy," declared *The Nation* "is that it represents the final stage of the disease, the ravages of which in the body politic Senator Hoar graphically described eight years ago . . . [Has] this disease . . . infected some of the doctors?"[59]

Attacks by the "dudes" and "Pharisees" of New York City were disagreeable to Hoar, and those of various Mugwump members of the mercantile society of Boston even more so, but the defectors over whom he truly mourned were men who had been his fellow warriors in antislavery days, like Thomas Wentworth Higginson. At least during the early stages of the campaign, he tried to persuade them back to righteousness:

> My dear Colonel Higginson:
> I wonder what there is in the atmosphere about Cambridge that makes everybody who looks through it incapable of seeing anything in its true proportions . . . You do not belong with President Eliot and his absurd associates who are doing so much to spoil our youth for American citizenship and who look with absolute indifference on the murder of American citizens at the polls on account of their opinions and the overthrow of the constitution by the suppression of the rights of fair election in great States, while they are filled with indignation at the removal or appointment of a clerk for opinions' sake.[60]

Higginson was not to be persuaded, nor were Hoar's nephews, Samuel and Sherman Hoar. No single aspect of the campaign of

[59] *The Nation,* 14 August 1884. *See,* too, "open letter" of Mr. Verdant Green to Hoar, 19 September 1884, Scrap Book #1, Moorfield Storey Papers, Library of Congress.

[60] Hoar to Higginson, 4 July 1884, Hoar Papers.

1884 was more provoking than this invasion of Mugwumpery into the very bosom of his family. Hoar was far more disturbed than was his brother, the father of the young defectors. Rockwood Hoar's reaction to the Mugwump movement was one of half-amused resignation, an attitude typified by his remark: "I have no objection to the Mugwumps going out, but they need not slam the door after them."[61] George Hoar considered his brother's tolerance misplaced and was certain that ill-informed dilettantes on the Harvard faculty were largely responsible for the corruption of his nephews. Indeed, it appeared at times that Hoar believed Blaine to be running against President Charles Eliot as well as Grover Cleveland and was as anxious for the defeat of the one as the other.[62]

Hoar's anxieties were connected but not equal. Hoar's bitter antagonism for Eliot and the Mugwumps was the product of his overriding desire to defeat the Democratic enemy. He convinced himself that Cleveland was the willing captive of the southern Bourbons and that his election would threaten the Civil War amendments, the currency, and the policy of protection. Blaine must be supported for the Republicans must retain the presidency.

During the campaign Hoar received a flood of requests to appear and speak at rallies throughout the New England states. He frequently took the stump in Blaine's behalf, but his most praised effort was embodied in a letter, not a speech. Hoar's "Answer to Mr. Schurz" was one of the most quoted of all Republican campaign documents in the fall of 1884.

[61] Moorfield Storey; Edward W. Emerson, *Ebenezer Rockwood Hoar: A Memoir* (Boston, 1911), 268–269.

[62] When congratulating President Daniel Coit Gilman of Johns Hopkins for his Phi Beta Kappa Address at Harvard in June 1886, Hoar took the opportunity to unburden his soul on the invasion of politics by the gowned amateur. Hoar to Gilman, 25 July 1886, Hoar Papers:

I have sometimes thought that the most unscholarly utterances we have on current politics come from scholars, the most unscientific judgments come from men of science, the most thorough blackguards are the educated gentlemen . . . I think these gentlemen forget that the scholar's political judgments are only of value when he has applied the methods, the thoroughness, the patience, the self-command, of scholarship to politics.

No Republican defector in 1884 was more celebrated or articulate than Carl Schurz, and at Brooklyn in early August he had delivered what his fellow Mugwumps considered a mighty blow in a speech denouncing the character and record of James G. Blaine. The Republican National Committee sought a man of unspotted reputation to answer Schurz and the choice fell to Hoar. The assignment was willingly accepted. Hoar judged Schurz's influence with the German-American community to be both mischievous and dangerous and he decided to cast his answer in the form of a letter to a wavering and perplexed German-American lad—hastily discovered by the Republican National Committee.

With fatherly concern Hoar told his young friend to beware of false slurs upon party loyalty. It appeared very noble and independent to damn party loyalty as narrow partisanship, but party association in republican America was quite a different thing than in monarchical Europe. In America one's party was the indispensable instrument by which free men executed their will. It was "an instrument itself possessing intelligence, judgment, conscience." For a party to serve its essential purpose, it was necessary that it be more than a loose conglomeration of individuals each free to go his own way without concern for the wishes of the majority:

> A majority of that party must necessarily determine its plan of battle, and the commander under whom it will fight. When you separate yourself from the party whose principles and purposes are yours, you effectually abandon those principles and purposes.

Only an extreme partisan would deny there were men of good will among the Democrats and Mugwumps, but, in the main, the honesty, purity, education, and strength of the nation was to be found in the Republican party. It was with Republican men and Republican principles that his young friend belonged and must remain.[63]

[63] "Senator Hoar's Answer to Carl Schurz's Brooklyn Address of Aug. 5th, 1884: A Statesman Against A Many-Sided Politician," pamphlet, Hoar Papers. Hoar's letter was dated 21 August 1884 and was first published in the Boston papers on 26 August 1884. *See*, too, Scrap Book #1, Papers of Moorfield Storey, Library of Congress.

In this letter, Hoar made no direct allusion to the famous exposé of the *Buffalo Evening Telegraph* with its charge that Cleveland had in his younger days fathered an illegitimate child, the product of a brief liaison with a widow named Maria Halpin. Although insisting that the Republican party viewed public and private morality as one and indivisible, Hoar considered it demeaning to his argument to engage in personal accusations. Just before the publication of his letter to Schurz, he had addressed a Republican rally in Shrewsbury and had felt obliged to reprove the scandal-hungry members of his audience. When he had suggested that Cleveland's brief and unsatisfactory record as governor of New York was all that was known of him, a voice from the audience had cackled, "No it ain't." After "much laughter" was recorded, Hoar had restored order with the stern declaration, "Well, it is all you know which I propose to discuss."[64]

A man of delicate, even prudish, sensibilities, Hoar never told a dirty story in his life and disapproved of those who did. However, in the heat of political battle, his resolution to avoid discussion of Cleveland's private life gradually weakened. As the Mugwumps and Democrats stepped up their attack on Blaine, Hoar began to make indirect allusions to Cleveland's sexual past. In a speech at Malden, he warmly praised the Sons of Ireland for their contribution to the construction of the nation's railroad system, and concluded his eulogy with the observation: "They are a race famous for their industry . . . and famous, as some presidential candidates may learn to their sorrow, for their love of chastity."[65]

The Blaine campaign was from the beginning a defensive affair, and finally a losing cause. Hoar's own efforts were almost irrelevant. Despite the noise of the Boston Mugwumps, Blaine was never in danger of losing Massachusetts, but New York, not

---

[64] *Boston Sunday Herald*, 24 August 1884.

[65] Scrap Book #1, Papers of Moorfield Storey, Library of Congress. The extent to which some Republicans were prepared to go in blackening Cleveland and his Mugwump supporters is indicated by a Republican handbill in the Hoar Papers attacking the Mugwump minister, Henry Ward Beecher. Beecher was supposed to have declared: "If all the men in the State who have broken the seventh commandment would vote for Cleveland we would elect him," and this was twisted to mean that Beecher had both convicted himself and "villified" the moral character of all the "Fathers and sons of America."

Massachusetts, would determine the election. In that state a number of factors worked against Blaine: the third ticket of the Prohibitionists; Conkling's continuing influence in Oneida County; the weather on election day; and the Reverend Samuel Burchard's ricochet slander of the Democrats as the party of "Rum, Romanism, and Rebellion."[66] New York went to Cleveland by a slim plurality of 1,000 votes and with it went the election.

Hoar's reaction was not only one of partisan disappointment but of personal bitterness. The nomination of Blaine had been a mistake, but northern Mugwumps and Bourbon illegality were to blame for the election result, not the indiscreet and slandered Blaine. The Mugwumps had divided the educated class in the East and wasted its influence by their vicious attacks on those who had remained loyal "to the principles and the party that once all of our kind was glad to honor."[67]

Defeat strengthened Hoar's sectional and political antipathies.[68] He had periodically doubted the wisdom of Arthur's policy of granting patronage to Democratic Independents in the South. Now he was certain that the Republicans could never unseat the southern Bourbons nor do justice to the Negro by self-conscious efforts at sectional harmony or fragile alliances with individual

[66] In what stands as one of the more extreme misjudgments of American politics, Hoar was certain that the visit by a delegation of Protestant ministers to Blaine at his New York City hotel had been a stroke of great skill. To a Worcester audience at the conclusion of the campaign, Hoar declared: "I confess I have been profoundly touched by the account of the visit to Mr. Blaine of the clergymen at New York. In that sublime spectacle, the piety and the patriotism of America seemed to be laying their hands in benediction on the head of our candidate. Can we not safely follow where these men lead?" (Rough draft, Hoar Papers.)

[67] Hoar to Henry Cabot Lodge, 18 November 1884, Lodge Papers, Massachusetts Historical Society. Also, Lodge to Hoar, 18 November 1884; John D. Long to Hoar, 24 September 1884, Hoar Papers. Hoar became convinced—in later years—that the Democrats had stolen the election by stuffing ballots and juggling returns in New York City. For a refutation of his suspicions *see* William Gorham Rice and Francis Lynde Stetson, "Was New York's Vote Stolen," *North American Review*, 199 (January 1914) 79–92; David S. Muzzey, *James G. Blaine: A Political Idol of Other Days* (New York: Dodd, Mead, 1934), 308, 323.

[68] Hoar never forgave the Mugwumps for their treachery in 1884, and the efforts of certain of those gentlemen to persuade Hoar to initiate an effort to welcome them back into the Republican fold were summarily rejected. *See* George G. Crocker to Hoar, 13 August 1885; Hoar to William Lloyd Garrison, Jr., 2 March 1887, Hoar Papers.

malcontents. The belief of certain northern Republicans that the tariff issue would split the Solid South if only the Republican party ceased to talk of Negro rights was both foolish and false. The South must be forced to recognize the rights of its Republicans and the votes of its Negroes. Hoar's speech to the Commonwealth Club some six weeks after the election bore witness to his determination to associate the Republican party once again with a pre-eminent concern for Negro suffrage and honest elections in the South. He would not introduce a federal elections bill until 1890, when once again the Republicans had gained control in Washington, but he had already determined to do just this when he addressed the Commonwealth Club. Let the Mugwumps bray at those who refused to be "modern" and appease the southern whites. As for for him, his mission henceforth was clear: "I think that to secure upon this continent the spirit of equality . . . and to leave to the future a system of laws, institutions, and administration under which . . . millions of men will represent the black race in the manhood and citizenship of this republic—is a cause to which . . . we may not disdain to renew our vows and to consecrate whatever may be left to us of service."[69]

One small but real source of comfort to Hoar on Inauguration Day, 1885, was that not only was "that hippopotamus Cleveland" to be sworn in, but so, too, was his cousin William M. Evarts as the newly elected senator from New York. Evarts' election offered evidence of the sharp decline of Conkling's organization in New York state, and of the gradual disappearance of the Stalwart faction of the Republican party.[70] Though their presidential candidate had suffered defeat, the Half-Breeds were more firmly in

[69] Boston *Commonwealth*, 3 January 1885. Hoar's speech was delivered on 27 December 1884. In a letter to a congregational minister, Hoar likened political conditions in the South to those in Czarist Russia: "If the thirty million of the colored race who within fifty years will inhabit the states of the South are to be a race of peasants, denied their practical and equal share in the government by such processes as have prevailed in recent years, the republic itself cannot continue. The Russian 'despotism tempered by assassination' is quite as desirable as republicanism tempered by both assassination and fraud" (Hoar to the Reverend Joseph Cook, January 31, 1885, Flavius Josephus Cook Papers, Duke University Libraries).

[70] Hoar to Evarts, 21 January 1885, Papers of William M. Evarts, vol. 32, Library of Congress.

control of the Republican party than ever before. Hoar was aware of this fact, but in his more pessimistic moments doubted its relevance. Of what value was the eclipse of Conkling when the Democrats controlled the national administration?

Grover Cleveland's first administration did not aspire to revolution in either domestic or foreign policies, but Hoar felt obliged frequently to sound the notes of alarm. These were intended primarily to warn Cleveland not to play the role of a southern puppet, but they also served to allow Hoar to retain his franchise as a Republican regular while promoting certain measures opposed by his more partisan colleagues.

On the issue of civil service reform and appointment policies, Hoar had little reason to quarrel with Cleveland. Both men, in fact, were strong advocates of civil service reform in theory and modest exponents of merit appointment in practice. Their basic similarity did not, however, prevent Hoar from entertaining near constant suspicion of Cleveland as one false to the Pendleton Act. In a long Senate speech he assailed Cleveland for retreating from his promise not to pervert public offices into political weapons, and he insisted that the President's effort simultaneously to serve God and the Democratic party was of benefit only to the latter.[71] Hoar believed that Cleveland's appointees in the customs houses were selected on the ground that they would undervalue imports and so defeat the principles of protection, and he both damned Cleveland for not appointing more Negroes to office and suspected that the few who were chosen were but political dupes.[72] Actually he had far less to complain of than either the doctrinaire Mugwumps, who were displeased that Cleveland surrendered to patronage demands at all, or various hungry Democratic politicians, who were angered that the President surrendered so grudgingly.[73]

[71] *Congressional Record,* 49th Cong., 1st sess., 2706–2709 (24 March 1886).

[72] Herbert Radclyffe, Secretary, Home Market Club of Boston, to Hoar, 19 April 1888; Frederick Douglass to Hoar, 15 December 1886, Hoar Papers.

[73] Hoar was obliged at one point to declare his gratitude for the reappointment of his old friend, General Pickett as postmaster of Worcester. Hoar to Postmaster General W. J. Villas, 18 February 1887 (copy); Hoar to Cleveland, 21 February 1887, Papers of Grover Cleveland, Library of Congress. *See,* too, Hoar to Cleveland, 26 January 1888, *ibid.*

It was really only on two counts that Hoar entertained strong grievance against the Cleveland administration, but these were in his mind of so great an importance that they served to justify its general damnation. In Hoar's eyes, the Cleveland administration sought to wreck the principle of protection, while it was oblivious to the needs of the southern Negro.

Cleveland devoted his State of the Union message of 1887 to the need for revision of the protective tariff system. His advocacy of customs duties that would but compensate for the higher labor costs of the American manufacturer was judged by Hoar to be a declaration of war against American industry. Hoar was one with his party colleagues in denouncing the Mills tariff bill, which passed the Democratic House in June 1888, and he was among the leading architects of the Republican strategy in the Senate to dump the Mills bill, fashion a high tariff substitute, and then bottle the latter in committee while awaiting the next election.[74]

With the Democrats in control of the House and the Republicans of the Senate there was no chance in the years 1887–1888 for a general revision of the tariff in either direction. There did appear some likelihood, however, that Cleveland might be able to modify the protective system in behalf of improved relations with Britain and Canada. Secretary of State Thomas F. Bayard signed with Canada a limited reciprocity treaty, whereby the rights of Americans to fish in Canadian waters were acknowledged in exchange for certain American concessions including the free entry of Canadian fish in American markets. The fishing towns of Massachusetts were angered and Hoar jumped to their defense. When the treaty was submitted to the Senate, Hoar made it a point of virtual dedication to defeat it. He offered on 10 July 1888 a four and one-half hour speech, tracing in detail the complex history of the North Atlantic fisheries from the French and Indian Wars to the negotiations of Bayard. He sought to prove with endless examples that confirmation of the treaty would mean the destruction of the fishing towns of New England—cradles of the merchant

[74] Herbert Radclyffe to Hoar, 25 July 1888; Henry Cabot Lodge to Hoar, 14 August 1888, Hoar Papers. *See*, too, Scrap Book, Personal, #3, Hoar Papers.

marine and navy—and concluded with broadside aspersions on the motives and feeble diplomacy of the Cleveland administration.[75] He considered this speech to be his greatest effort in the Senate to date. It was, in fact, a wonderful combination of honest belief and partisan blindness—a combination characteristic of Hoar's general reaction to Grover Cleveland.

The presence of a Democrat in the White House allowed Hoar to criticize the national government's unconcern with Negro civil rights far more vigorously than when President Arthur had engaged in his lazy flirtation with the southern Independents. As chairman of the Committee on Elections and Privilege, Hoar promoted a long investigation of political corruption and lynching in Washington County, Texas; as a member of the Judiciary Committee, he reported a bill for national inquests of reported Negro massacres in Louisiana and South Carolina, and in each instance the failure of the Democratic members to cooperate was laid squarely at the door of Cleveland.[76] It was surprising and discreditable that many northern businessmen, fearful of disturbing their southern investments, were ready to ignore and indeed share the administration's complicity in these "political murders." The "new doughfaces" did not appreciate that once the southern Bourbons had finished destroying human rights they would start attacking the rights of property. If ever the Bourbons controlled Congress they would reveal themselves as enemies of the nation's credit as well as its honor.[77]

Fortunately the veterans of the Union Army were more quick to appreciate and denounce the Bourbon flavor of Cleveland's administration. Previously Hoar had been quietly suspicious of the demands of the G.A.R.; now he joined its lobbyists in denouncing Cleveland's veto of the dependent pension bill and delighted them by introducing a bill in the Senate which called for a small pension for *all* "bona fide veterans" of the Union Army.[78]

[75] *Congressional Record*, 50th Cong., 1st sess., 6042–6065 (10 July 1885).

[76] *See* Mrs. F. A. Palmer to Hoar, 3 August 1886; "A Negro Citizen," of Washington County, Texas, to Hoar, 27 January 1887; Hoar to Republican Club of South Framingham, 22 June 1887, Scrap Book, Personal, #3, Hoar Papers.

[77] Hoar to William E. Chandler, 11 July 1887, W. E. Chandler Papers, vol. 75, Library of Congress.

[78] *Congressional Record*, 50th Cong., 1st sess., 566 (19 January 1888). *See*, too, Hoar to Robert A. Stuart, 18 April 1888, Hoar Papers.

Cleveland's veterans policy offered Hoar the occasion for patriotic bombast, but on two major issues alone did they differ: the protection of industry and the protection of the Negro. On many other aspects of public policy their views were most similar. They were both hard money men; both wished to see the national government economical and honest; both sought to promote the general welfare of the nation's businessmen while avoiding favors to special interests. Hoar had to admit that the policies of Secretary of the Treasury Daniel Manning were remarkably sound, for a Democrat, and he was grudgingly aware that the success of his efforts to repeal the Tenure-of-Office Act and push through Congress his presidential succession bill and his electoral count bill was largely due to the influence of Cleveland.

The presidential succession bill was the result of Hoar's long-standing conviction that the existing system of presidential succession posed a danger to the proper continuity of government policy. Rather than have the Speaker of the House stand next in line to the Vice President, it would be better to have the succession fall to the Cabinet officers in order of their rank—the Secretary of State, the Secretary of the Treasury, and so on. The Speaker might be associated with the party in opposition to a deceased or disabled President; the Secretary of State would never be. Moreover, American history showed that the Secretaries of State were more likely to be men of broad views and experience; the Speaker of the House might owe his position primarily to the constant devotion of a single-district constituency. It was Hoar's initial purpose to include in his bill a provision specifying the form and manner for determining when the President or Vice President could be removed for disability, but finding most of his Republican colleagues disinterested he unfortunately did not press this feature.[79] Hoar's presidential succession bill was enacted in January 1886, largely as the result of Democratic support. It provided in many ways a more intelligent arrangement than that authorized by the law of 1947 which repealed it. John Sherman, ever suspicious of constitutional innovation, thought the bill a "dangerous concession to our adversaries."[80]

[79] *Congressional Record*, 49th Cong., 1st sess., 180–183, 220–221 (15, 16 December 1885).
[80] John Sherman to Hoar, 16 December 1886, Hoar Papers.

Sherman offered a similar reaction to the electoral count bill, which Hoar piloted through Congress at the same time. Hoar was determined to clarify the procedures connected with the casting and counting of electoral ballots in order that the nation might never again witness the dangerous indecision of January–February 1877. The principle of his bill was that which had supported his argument in behalf of the Hayes electors when a member of the Electoral Commission: the right of the legal certifying officers of a state to determine its properly chosen electors and the duty of Congress to accept their decision.[81] Again the Democrats, with Cleveland's approval, provided the votes necessary for passage. Aware of this fact, Hoar soon felt obliged to make a highly partisan address in which he declared that Cleveland alternately cowered before the Bourbons and the British with disgraceful regularity.

Surely in Hoar's eyes, Cleveland suffered a severe handicap; he was a Democrat. However similar the amalgam of reform views and conservative fears shared by both men; however like the views of Eastern Democrats and Half-Breed Republicans, Cleveland must remain an enemy. Hoar desired a Republican Half-Breed administration, and in the election of 1888 he saw in Benjamin Harrison a likely instrument to defeat Cleveland and provide a true successor to the lamented Garfield.

It was not until the last forty-eight hours of the Republican Convention at Chicago that Hoar became convinced that Harrison was the chosen instrument of victory, but months earlier he had begun to inform his followers in Massachusetts of the crucial nature of the coming election and the general strategy to be followed. In February 1888 he had addressed the party membership by means of a letter to the editor of the *Boston Advertiser:*

It is not a personal question that is involved in the next election. It is a contest of opinions, principles, purposes. I trust the Republicans of Massachusetts will send men to Chicago who, whatever may be their attachment to individuals, will feel at

---

[81] *Congressional Record,* 49th Cong., 1st sess., 816–817, 1019–1026 (21 January 1886; 1 February 1886).

liberty to go for the candidate who . . . shall seem surest to be elected . . .

It is time we had in this country an administration and a legislature with the will and the capacity to enable this country to resume its march of progress which has been interrupted since 1874 . . . Our country has had two drivers quite long enough. For 14 years nothing has been done by way of legislation in this country to which both parties have not consented. The country will either serve God or Baal . . . honest elections or Southern practice.[82]

Hoar would again head the Massachusetts delegation and again he wished that delegation to be uninstructed by the state convention. Hoar saw the leading candidates for the Republican nomination as John Sherman, Walter Q. Gresham, Benjamin Harrison, William B. Allison, and Blaine—and ranked them, on the score of personal preference, in that order. Despite his praise of Blaine after the latter's defeat in 1884, Hoar did not wish the burden of his candidacy again and was quick to believe and to emphasize that gentleman's vague declination. By late May Hoar had struck upon a candidate whom he thought might be more politically available than any of the front runners, General Phil Sheridan. The Sheridan boom was a brief one, however, and by June Hoar was prepared to support John Sherman, convinced by the secretary of the Boston Home Market Club that Gresham was unsound on the policy of protection.[83]

The Republicans assembled at Chicago on 21 June, and Hoar informed his wife that he saw in prospect a long, hot, and "odious" week. With nineteen candidates formally in the field, it was obvious that the selection would not be easy and a lengthy deadlock most probable. Hoar led the Massachusetts delegation in voting for John Sherman on the first few ballots, but was constantly circling about the convention hoping to discover some arrangement that might bring matters to a quick and harmonious conclusion.

[82] *Boston Daily Advertiser*, 23 February 1888.
[83] A. W. Beard to Hoar, 14 May 1888; E. Rockwood Hoar to Hoar, 18 May, 18 June 1888; George B. Loring to Hoar, 28 May 1888; Herbert Radclyffe to Hoar, 5 June 1888; Hoar to Ruth A. Hoar, 30 May, 8 June 1888, Hoar Papers.

At one point he wired his kinsman, Sherman to ask if he would step aside for a dark horse, William McKinley—and found Sherman reluctant. Soon after, he caucused with a group of William Allison's supporters and discovered that the Iowan was anathema to Senator Chauncey Depew of New York. Finally, after long consultation with the able industrial lobbyist, James S. Clarkson, Hoar decided that Harrison's nomination was the best of those possible. Hoar agreed to see all the eastern delegations, and Clarkson began to tackle those from the West, informing them that the bandwagon was about to roll and not to be behind-hand. "What is old man Hoar up to," inquired Matt Quay. Quay found out in time to deliver the votes of Pennsylvania to Harrison on the eighth and final ballot.[84]

Hoar forwarded "expressions of hearty gratification" to the nominee. With his congratulations he enclosed a lengthy note from a correspondent solicitous that Harrison's letter of acceptance start the campaign on the proper note. Harrison should denounce contract laborers imported from Italy, this would please the Irish; he should speak of the sad decline of our ship-building industry, this would please the merchants; he should promise improved mail service to South and Central America, this would please the Spanish voters of New York City; he should emphasize the tariff as the guardian of the workingman's wages, this would please the workingmen and their employers alike.[85] Harrison was a better politician than either Hoar or his correspondent, and it is doubtful if the advice was needed. Harrison would direct his own campaign and he would direct it with a keen appreciation that the contest would be close and that it would be decided in the "swing states" of Indiana, New York, and New Jersey.

These states had determined the last two elections—as they would this—for they were among the few states possessing major

---

[84] Hoar to Ruth A. Hoar, 20 June, 22 June 1888, Hoar Papers; John Sherman to Hoar, 23 June 1888 (telegram) John Sherman Papers, Library of Congress; Leland L. Sage, *William Boyd Allison: A Study in Practical Politics* (Iowa City: State Historical Society of Iowa, 1956), 226–227.

[85] Hoar to Harrison, 19 July 1888; Nathaniel McKay to Hoar, 13 July 1888, Papers of Benjamin Harrison, vol. 33, Library of Congress.

party organizations of roughly equal strength.[86] The post-Civil War generation was not the era of unexampled Republican ascendancy—with interruptions by Cleveland—that is sometimes depicted. Republican domination of the national government ended in 1874, and between that date and 1888 the Democrats controlled the House for twelve years and shared effective control of the Senate for six. Harrison and his advisers were now determined to gain control of both branches of Congress as well as the presidency and to do this they must concentrate upon the "swing states" of the industrial East. In those states, and so in the national campaign, the tariff issue seemed to offer the best chance of success.

Hoar agreed, but he was unwilling to emphasize the protection of industry at the expense of the protection of the Negro—as he suspected was the intention of Matt Quay, the national campaign chairman, and other political barometers of Big Business. The horrors of free trade and Bourbon crime should be proclaimed alike. In Massachusetts, however, there appeared to be far greater interest in the tariff issue than the Fifteenth Amendment. When the Boston Mugwumps began to defend the economic arguments of Cleveland, Hoar was driven to acknowledge the immediate primacy of the tariff.

It was Hoar's habit at the beginning of a campaign to block out his stump talk on short square pieces of note paper, jotting down major headings, statistical support, and anecdotal references, and writing out in full the final peroration. This basic speech he would alter to match the location and audience but the list of points seldom varied in number or in order. The memoranda of his stump speech of 1888 saw Hoar make the following points respecting the tariff: The arguments of the tariff reformers found

[86] Between the years 1876–1894 there was a marked stability in the sectional pattern of electoral returns. New England and the Upper Mississippi Valley were Republican country and the southern and border states, strongly Democratic. "Doubtful states" were consequently the object of special interest for the national committee of both parties. George Mayer, *The Republican Party, 1854–1964* (New York: Oxford University Press, 1964), 171–172. *See*, too, Carl N. Degler, "American Political Parties and the Rise of the City: An Interpretation," *Journal of American History,* 51 (June 1964), 41–59; Samuel P. Hays, *The Response to Industrialism, 1885–1914* (Chicago: University of Chicago Press, 1957), 143.

their logical conclusion in the free trade doctrines of Calhoun; the destruction of the protective system would necessitate heavy federal excise taxes and would be followed by lower wages for all and unemployment for many; the policy of protection by expanding production and stimulating competition would continually cheapen the cost of all basic articles of consumption; the primary purpose of the tariff was not to protect the profits of business but the living standard of Americans of all classes and sections.[87]

Hoar's stump speech, though emphasizing the tariff, made several references to the obligation owed the Negro by party and nation. In a chapter he contributed to a campaign textbook, he proclaimed his confidence that the Republicans would not rest until "the ballot-box is as sacred as the American hearth."[88] But as the campaign reached its climax the dangers of a Democratic victory took precedence over discussions of moral duty. The old mission remained, but first "the hangman from Buffalo" must be removed and his evil Mugwump allies must be humiliated. It was Hoar's opinion that in the latter task he made a major contribution with his "Harvard speech."

Certain Mugwump members of the Harvard faculty had addressed a tariff reform meeting at Tremont Temple, at which they had praised the political courage and economic wisdom of Cleveland. This goaded several hundred Harvard undergraduates to form the Harvard Republican Club and to counterattack with a giant rally. All alumni high in Republican circles were asked to speak, and Hoar was appointed to give the major address. As he advanced to the podium, draped in its crimson folds, he received the college cheer, three times repeated. Properly inspired, Hoar proceeded to castigate those who would drag the fair name of Harvard in the mire of free trade, electoral fraud, and mugwumpery. Alma Mater was not in politics but surely her politics were Republican. Picture the heroes of Harvard, her scholars, statesmen, patriot-soldiers stepping from their portraits on election

[87] Memoranda, Speech of 1888, Pamphlet Box, Hoar Papers. *See,* too, Hoar's speech at "Faneuil Hall meeting of Boston workingmen," October 1888, Scrap Book, Personal, #3, Hoar Papers.

[88] John D. Long, ed., *The Republican Party: Its History, Principles, And Policies* (New York, 1888), 343.

day. Two men knock and seek their favor. The portly figure they shun—Madam Boylston hides her face; the laureled soldiers sneer and ask for his Civil War substitute. But to the other, who modestly hangs back, they call: "Come up here stainless citizen, great lawyer, excellent senator, gallant soldier, come up here patriot, president. You are admitted to all the degrees ad eundem, honoris causa. We claim the right to speak to-night for Harvard. Harvard welcomes you to her company and crowns you with her crown."[89]

The Cambridge Mugwumps were perhaps discomforted but they possessed in any case no electoral votes. Those of New York, New Jersey, and Indiana went to Harrison and with them the election of 1888. By a rather narrow margin the Republicans would also enjoy a majority of both houses of Congress. Hoar was ecstatic and wired Harrison: "Mass. is full of thankfulness to God who hath won us the victory."[90] He did not acknowledge the respective efforts of Matt Quay, Sackville-West, or the organized "floaters" of Indiana. At a victory dinner in Boston, Hoar announced that "Americanism has come back to America." The nation was now assured of "a loyal Supreme Court, an honest census in 1890, honest elections, and no more disrespect for the American flag and Massachusetts fishermen."[91]

Harrison was more cautious and restrained in his jubilation. In a letter to Hoar acknowledging a copy of his Harvard speech, Harrison declared that he was well aware of the difficulties and perplexities that "are lying in ambush along my path."[92] The chief of those perplexities had been illustrated by the wavering emphasis of Hoar's campaign speeches between the poles of tariff protection and Negro rights. Would the Harrison administration accept the advice of the American Iron and Steel Association and forget the Negro question, and by emphasizing the issues of the tariff and prosperity seek favor with the businessmen of the South? Or would that administration take advantage of the Republican majorities

[89] "Harvard Republican Meeting, November 2, 1888" (Cambridge, 1889), 30–38, pamphlet, Hoar Papers.

[90] Hoar to Harrison, 9 November 1888, Papers of Benjamin Harrison, vol. 46, Library of Congress. *See,* too, Hoar to Harrison, 22 November 1888, *ibid.*

[91] Home Market Club Dinner, 15 November 1888, Scrap Book, Personal, #3, Hoar Papers.

[92] Harrison to Hoar, 26 November 1888, Hoar Papers.

in Congress to establish a national education system, pass a federal election law, and make good the pledges of the Fourteenth and Fifteenth Amendments?[93] That would be the central question of the Harrison years. It was a question never squarely faced, and so the southern Negro was sacrificed once again and to little political advantage for the Republican party.

[93] Governor Joseph B. Foraker of Ohio, a latter-day Radical Republican, wrote Hoar shortly after the election: "The tariff was a fortunate question for us, but the question of a free ballot and a fair count has so much of patriotism, Christianity, and human rights involved that the people of this country are determined to have it settled." Foraker to Hoar, 24 November 1888, Hoar Papers.

# 5

*The Harrison Years:*
*Protection and Sacrifice*

Benjamin Harrison was a man of mediocre abilities who enjoyed but a single term as president. The years of his presidency, however, provide a significant checkpoint in the postwar transformation of the Republican party. They witness the last stand of such older leaders as James G. Blaine and William E. Chandler, and the rising prominence of such new men as Nelson Aldrich, William McKinley, and John Coit Spooner. They illustrate the increasing efficiency and institutionalization of party organization, and the increasing authority of corporate power in the shaping of the party's policies and direction. Above all, they mark the final defeat of the old aims of Radical Republicanism and the increasing determination of national policy in accordance with the tug and pull of sectional economic interests. The Harrison years reached their natural climax when the effort of George Frisbie Hoar to repledge the party's allegiance to the cause of Negro suffrage fell victim to the economic dissatisfaction of western silver kings and the economic demands of eastern industrialists.

Three pieces of legislation of the year 1890 may serve, in their relationship and disposition, to illustrate the increasing predominance of economic interests in the determination of the policies and leadership of the Republican party. The Sherman Silver Purchase Act passed and gave the western silver interests partial satisfaction. The McKinley Tariff Act passed and gave eastern industry, with a few significant exceptions, all that it desired. The federal elections bill failed to pass, a sacrifice to the demands of sectional harmony, economic profit, and monetary inflation. The tangled story of these three measures describes the direction of the Republican party in the years of Harrison. It illustrates as well the ambivalent position of George Frisbie Hoar: the conscience-ridden partisan who sought to honor the moral pledges of the past while acknowledging the material demands of the present.

Shortly after Harrison's inauguration, Hoar, as chairman of the Committee on Privileges and Elections, began to study the question of a new national election law. Considerations of justice and policy combined to convince him that the time had come to reassert the right of the Negro voter in the South to national protection.[1] Initially, Hoar had in mind a scheme providing for separate registration rolls and election dates for federal elections. When he broached this idea in December 1889, however, it met with little enthusiasm on the score of the duplication of effort and costs that would be involved. By the spring of 1890 Hoar and the new senator from Wisconsin, John Coit Spooner, had in cooperation drafted a more sophisticated measure, the key parts of which provided for supervision of state registration and election procedures by federal court-appointed officers from both major parties. This draft would embody the heart of the famed "force bill" of 1890.

From the start, Hoar was fully conscious of the controversial nature of the bill. Before he formally introduced it, he saw every Republican senator and secured his opinion. A large majority

---

[1] Now as earlier, Hoar's concern for the southern Negro was not unmixed in motive or without a tone of noblesse oblige, but neither was it insincere. Not a social equalitarian, Hoar had perhaps as little prejudice against color as any man in national politics. There was no federal senator more often praised by northern Negroes in the Harrison Years than G. F. Hoar. *See* Hoar to Sherman Jackson, 15 April 1892; J. Gordon Street to Hoar, 1 May 1892, Hoar Papers. Jackson was a Negro student whom Hoar helped send through Amherst College.

expressed their approval.[2] Encouraged by this deceptive display of Republican unity, Hoar introduced on 24 April Senate Bill 3652 "to amend and supplement the election laws of the United States and to provide for more efficient enforcement of such laws." Senator James L. Pugh of Alabama gave warning that the Senate minority would resist it by every parliamentary method "allowed by the Constitution."[3] Before the Democrats would be granted the opportunity, however, Hoar's bill became the object of brief dissension between the Republican majorities of Senate and House. The House had appointed a special committee charged with bringing in an elections bill, and the members of the committee, which was headed by Henry Cabot Lodge, insisted that the lower house be allowed the right to originate any bill that proposed to revise the election of its own membership. Largely through the instrumentality of a newspaperman and lobbyist, John P. Davenport, a compromise was worked out: Hoar would hold back his bill in the Senate committee and grant the House bill the right of way; in return, Lodge would modify his own draft in conformity with the Senate proposal.[4]

The Lodge bill passed the House by a straight party vote in the early days of July 1890, and was subsequently sent to the Senate.[5] It closely followed the main lines of the Hoar-Spooner bill, but attempted to broaden its reform provisions with sections on the selection of juries and other matters. Hoar's committee quickly struck out these latter sections and lessened the penalties provided. Debate over the Sherman Antitrust Act now intervened, and it was not until 7 August 1890 that Hoar was able to report to the Senate his revised draft of the House elections bill. His report concluded with the declaration, "I am directed to say that the minority of the committee dissent from the favorable recommendation."[6]

The word "dissent" inadequately described the determination of Senator Arthur Pue Gorman, of Maryland, and his Democratic

[2] *See* memorandum of "Opinions as to bill before its Introduction," Pamphlet Box, 1890, Hoar Papers.

[3] *Congressional Record*, 51st Cong., 1st sess., 3760.

[4] John P. Davenport to Hoar, 27 April 1890, Hoar Papers.

[5] *Congressional Record*, 51st Cong., 1st sess., 6940–6941.

[6] *Ibid.*, 8277–8278.

colleagues to denounce and defeat a measure which they insisted would destroy the sovereign rights of the states, pervert the federal judiciary, and bring strife, bloodshed and dictatorship in its train. Like its Reconstruction counterpart, this was that thing of evil name and memories, a "force bill."

Was it? In sum, the bill sought to deter the intimidation and corruption of voters in congressional elections by permitting the presence of national party officials and the arbitration of the federal circuit courts. Upon the petition of one hundred or more citizens in a congressional district, a circuit court was empowered to appoint federal supervisors (on a bipartisan basis) to watch and report registration and election procedures. In case of dispute concerning any election certificate, the judge of the circuit court in question was empowered to determine whose name would be submitted to the House as the candidate-elect. The federal circuit court was also empowered to initiate investigation against persons charged with election bribery, intimidation, and fraud—such persons to be convicted upon the judgment of a jury drawn from the district.

Although pointed primarily at the South, the bill would be applicable to all congressional districts throughout the country. Its central feature was to make the federal circuit courts, rather than the state governors and state certifying boards, the arbiter of congressional election procedures and returns. That this would bring the federal judiciary more directly into politics was undeniable, as was the fact that the judges of the federal circuit courts of 1890 were mostly Republican appointees. The measure did not, however, embody any provision for the use of federal troops or marshals, and it did not immediately affect the election of any state or local official. It was hardly a nonpartisan measure, but only by the most strained etymology was it a force bill. So it was labeled, however, by its opponents.

The opposition of the Bourbon Democrats did not surprise Hoar and the advocates of the bill, but they failed to anticipate the threat posed by another administration measure, which for certain Republicans held a far higher priority, the McKinley tariff bill, or the threat posed by the Silver Republicans of the West, men conciliated but not appeased by the Sherman Silver Purchase Act. The federal elections bill was fated to become entangled with sectional demands for currency expansion and tariff protection.

The Bland-Allison Silver Act of 1878 only whetted the appetite of the representatives of debtor agrarians and silver kings. Between 1878 and Harrison's inauguration both agricultural prices and the market value of silver had continued to fall; corn sold at thirteen cents a bushel, the market ratio of gold and silver was now 22 to 1. Debtors and miners demanded that the Harrison Congress provide for the Treasury purchase of the entire production of the silver mines of the West—and in the process so increase the volume of money and the velocity of its circulation that crop prices would rise and debt burdens shrink. Several silver bills had been introduced into the Senate by the spring of 1890, and the first of several paradoxes was that it was the most radical of these measures that received the Senate's assent.

It is customary to think of the Senate as the more conservative of the two houses of Congress throughout the post-Civil War generation, but in 1890 it possessed no disciplinarian of the quality of Czar Reed of the House and it did possess a bloc of eighteen Silver senators—their number recently enlarged by the admission of several states from the Great Plains. The House had approved a bill designed to increase silver purchase but not silver coinage. In the Senate, Preston Plumb of Kansas tacked on an amendment which made the bill virtually a free coinage measure. It was passed by a vote of 42–25 on 17 June. In the opinion of George Frisbie Hoar, who had sought unsuccessfully to limit its provisions and then voted against it, it was a most dangerous bill. He was quite prepared to see some expansion of the currency and was not opposed to a continuation of silver coinage, but until all the great commercial nations of the world could jointly agree upon a fixed ratio for gold and silver, such coinage should be as restricted as politically feasible.[7] His party colleagues assured him that Reed would never let the measure pass the House, and their confidence was justified. The House defeated the Senate bill, 152–135, and a conference committee was appointed. There John Sherman played his accustomed role as the mediator of eastern fears and western demands, and a compromise bill, the Sherman Silver Purchase Act, was the result. It passed both houses by 14 July 1890. The vote of the Sen-

[7] *Ibid.*, 6183 (17 June 1890). *See,* too, Hoar to Nathaniel P. Hill, November 4, 1891, Hoar Papers.

ate was strictly on party lines, all Republicans, including Hoar, voting in its favor.

In the final analysis the Sherman Silver Purchase Act was not the result of any Mephistophelean bargain but the product of careful confusion. On the surface it was an inflationary measure. It authorized the Treasury to purchase monthly four and a half million ounces of silver bullion. This silver was to be paid for with treasury certificates of full legal tender, and these certificates were, in turn, redeemable in gold or silver coin at the discretion of the Secretary of the Treasury. As the western silver mines produced little more than four and a half million ounces a month and as silver dollars were to be coined at the overvalued ratio of 16 to 1, the act appeared designed to offer full satisfaction to the silver miners and the advocates of monetary inflation. On three counts, its concessions were far more restricted than was initially apparent: (1) under the old Bland-Allison Act, purchases had been made in dollar terms and as the price of silver had fallen, the same number of gold dollars had bought more and more silver. Under the new act there would be a fixed limit to the amount of silver purchased and if the market price of silver fell so would the expenditure of the Treasury; (2) under the new law, the Secretary was obliged to coin the purchased silver into silver dollars only when in his opinion coinage was necessary for the redemption of the silver certificates; (3) the new law reaffirmed the Treasury's purpose to back silver dollars with gold and maintain the fictional parity of gold and silver dollars. Despite the torrent of abuse it would receive three years later, during the battle over its repeal, the Sherman Act of 1890 was only slightly more inflationary than the existing Bland-Allison Act and distinctly less costly to the United States Treasury.

This was half-appreciated by many senators at the time of its passage and helps explain both why it did not satisfy the senators from the Mountain States nor distress such men as Mark Hanna.[8] By no means were a majority of eastern capitalists in arms against the Sherman bill. They did believe, however, that the Silverites

[8] *See* Mark Hanna to John Sherman, 10 December 1890, Papers of John Sherman, Library of Congress. *See*, too, John P. Townsend, President, Knickerbocker Trust Company, to Sherman, 13 December 1890, William P. St. John to Sherman, 17 December 1890, *ibid.*, and George F. Edmunds to Hoar, 28 July 1890, Hoar Papers.

should now shut up. But in both country and Senate that was just what the spokesmen for silver had no intention of doing. The Sherman Silver Purchase Act was barely passed before Senators Stewart and Teller were already planning to introduce another silver bill. Their efforts would materially help to prevent passage of the federal elections bill, though not before the latter had been delayed and damaged by a third measure, the McKinley Tariff Act.

In the campaign of 1888, National Committee Chairman Matt Quay and his fellow solicitors had promised their manufacturer prospects that the election of Harrison would assure ample protection for one and all. From the beginning of Harrison's term there was strong pressure on the relevant committees in House and Senate to make good that promise. Hoar was himself in favor of a new and higher tariff act, and one of the lesser ironies of the legislative history of the year 1890 was that in his struggle for federal supervision of southern elections, Hoar would find himself arrayed against the supporters of a tariff bill that he considered both necessary and wise.

The tariff measure began to take shape in the House Committee of Ways and Means, under the direction of its new chairman, Congressman William McKinley of Ohio. As with every tariff measure of the post-Civil War years, it proved easier to make promises than to arrange duties to the satisfaction of all domestic producers. And as in every tariff measure of the post-Civil War period, the prime struggle was not between protectionists and tariff reformers but involved the conflicting interests of domestic producers who wished protection for raw materials or semi-finished goods and those others who sought only the protection of finished manufacturers.[9]

William McKinley's solution was to assure industrial justice by raising rates all around. There were, of course, a few exceptions.

[9] *See,* for example, A. W. Beard to Hoar, 22 May 1890, H. C. Lodge to Hoar, 24 May 1890, pamphlet folders, "Massachusetts Tariff Matters" and "Massachusetts Matters, Tariff: Carpet Wool, Chocolate, Bronze Powder," Hoar Papers; Papers of Nelson Aldrich, Box 26, Library of Congress for months of May–June 1890; Papers of John Sherman, Library of Congress for months of June–July 1890.

Sugar was put on the free list, and domestic sugar growers compensated with special bounties, and duties were lowered on certain other raw materials that lacked a strong lobby or the prospect of large-scale domestic production. The bill that passed the House on 21 May 1890, by a vote of 164–142, was unquestionably, however, an example of high protectionism. In an effort to attract the support of agrarian representatives its schedules included a majority of the country's commercial crops, and certain of its industrial duties were prohibitory by design.

In the Senate the McKinley bill was sent to the Finance Committee and after a good deal of bickering and some minor revisions that committee reported it out to the Senate in mid-July. When after three weeks time it had made no further progress in the upper chamber, Matt Quay, conscious of his obligation to the Pennsylvania iron and steel industry, became alarmed. He saw old Granny Hoar and his elections bill as the chief obstacle to the passage of the tariff act prior to the forthcoming congressional elections. And so the long if fluctuating antagonism between the national protection of industry and the national protection of the Negro reached its climax, and the federal elections bill shortly received the first of three separate but associated defeats.

On 18 August 1890 Quay demanded recognition and introduced a resolution designed to assure that in the scramble of administration measures the tariff would be accorded top priority. Proposing in effect a change in the rules of the Senate, Quay enumerated five measures upon which the Senate was to concentrate prior to a September adjournment—the tariff or revenue bill headed the list, the elections bill was conspicuous by its absence.[10]

Hoar compared the resolution and designs of Quay to those of the benighted Whigs who had approved the Compromise of 1850. The spirit of the Free Soilers of old must rise to smite the crafty and the timid; he would serve as its instrument. On 19 August he offered a two-part substitute for the Quay resolution—proposing certain temporary limitations upon debate in the Senate and a

[10] *Congressional Record,* 51st Cong., 1st sess., 8724. It was generally accepted among the rumormongers of Washington that Quay had secretly conferred with Democratic Senator Gorman and the two were contemplating a temporary alliance whereby the Quay resolution would pass, the McKinley tariff bill be assured passage, and the elections bill be quietly interred. *See* Hoar to D. W. Farquhar, August 12, 1890, Hoar Papers.

definite timetable for the discussion and vote upon the elections bill. At ten o'clock the next morning, before a packed Senate, he delivered a dramatic plea in behalf of his substitute resolution and the elections bill.

The tariff and other parts of the administration's program bespoke economic wisdom, Hoar declared, but the federal elections bill was of the greatest importance for it reclaimed the conscience of party and nation. The elections bill concerned the very nature and purpose of representative government. It sought to assure the exercise of majority rule and to thwart all who would destroy the Constitution by means of electoral "fraud, intimidation, and bribery." The crucial question was at whose will ultimately did one hold his rights as an American citizen? At the will of the nation, surely, and just as certainly was every American entitled to evoke the power of the United States for the protection of the rights and benefits of that citizenship. This bill was in no sense a vindictive measure; its avowed enemy was not the old Confederacy, but the unconstitutional usurpation of government control by an illegal minority. "There was never a more senseless utterance than to call that a force bill which transfers the settlement of a great public question from the shotgun to the court."

Hoar directed the last minutes of his speech to his party colleagues. He reminded them of the pledges of Republican conventions and candidates to work for "fair and honest elections" in every section of the land, and declared his conviction that the postponement of the elections bill, as provided in the Quay resolution, would mean its probable interment. Could any Republican take satisfaction in the passage of the tariff, if it was secured at the cost of the historic principles of the party? "No man . . . will question the sincerity of my devotion to the protective system . . . but I shall take little satisfaction [in the new tariff bill] if it is to be the price of the dishonor of my country or the broken pledges of my party."[11]

Quay, little affected by Hoar's oratory, was determined to exclude the federal elections bill from consideration during the current session, push through the tariff bill, and secure an early adjournment. Hoar was equally determined that the Senate Republicans give precedence to the elections bill and promise to work

[11] *Congressional Record,* 51st Cong., 1st sess., 8842–8848.

for a change of the Senate rules that would neutralize Democratic obstruction.[12] It appeared likely that continuing division within the Republican ranks would deny passage to either bill prior to the forthcoming congressional elections. The prospect of those elections dictated an effort at compromise.

On the evening following Hoar's speech, the Senate Republicans caucused by special invitation at the house of Senator James Mc-Millan, and after several hours of heated discussion reached an agreement. The tariff bill would be given the highest priority and all would labor to secure its enactment within two weeks time. Four other bills, relatively noncontroversial, would be pushed toward passage, and a speedy adjournment would then follow. At the beginning of the next session of Congress, the Republicans would agree "to take up for consideration . . . the Federal elections bill, and to keep it before the Senate, to the exclusion of other legislative business, until it is disposed of by a vote."

Hoar had consented to withdraw his demands that the federal elections bill be enacted and in operation before the November elections, and to accept a four-months postponement. In return he had demanded a written pledge that at the next session the elections bill be granted undisputed priority. This pledge he drew up in his own hand, and when it had received the signature of every Republican senator but one, he had obtained a clear majority of the Senate membership and a seemingly certain guarantee of the bill's subsequent enactment.[13]

Hoar declared himself fully satisfied. Victory was postponed but assured. He happily followed the lead of Senator Aldrich through-

[12] "Webb," the Washington correspondent of the *Boston Journal*, praised Hoar's efforts as an expression of an "older and purer Republicanism." Quay was labeled the leader of the "trade-and-dicker faction" of the party, a man ready to forego the opportunity to advance the cause of the Negro in order that he might more quickly accomplish the desires of those special interests to whom he was beholden. *Boston Journal*, 21 August 1890.

[13] This document survives today among Senator Hoar's papers encased in two envelopes, the last of which is marked, "Senators Agreement as to Election Bill & proposed change of rule." Hoar circulated it among the thirty-five caucus participants on the morning of 22 August, and then through the agency of Senators Spooner and Eugene Hale sent copies to the seven Republican senators currently absent from Washington. Six of these returned their copies signed, two "with emphasis"; only the maverick senator from South Dakota, Richard F. Pettigrew, raised objection. Pamphlet Box, Personal, 1890, Hoar Papers. *See*, too, *New York Tribune*, 23 August 1890.

out the series of votes concerning the tariff bill, voting for Senate passage on 10 September and final passage of the conference version on 30 September. The McKinley Tariff enacted and the Senate recessed, Hoar returned to Worcester and impatiently awaited the second session of the Fifty-first Congress. The controversy over silver had presumably been compromised with the Sherman Act, the tariff had passed, now the federal elections bill must be enacted. George Frisbie Hoar saw the climax of his public career at hand.

With the beginning of December the Congress reconvened, and on December 2 Hoar moved that the Senate proceed with consideration of the elections bill. Almost immediately a skillful, if faintly disguised, filibuster was begun by the Democratic opposition. Led by Gorman of Maryland, George Gray of Delaware, and Matthew C. Butler of South Carolina, the Democratic opposition exhibited an unwavering determination to prevent the Republican majority from changing the rules of the Senate or passing the elections bill.[14] By careful prearrangement, members of the Democratic minority

[14] One editorial can stand for many in evidence of the bitterness of southern reaction and the central role granted Hoar by the southern press. For the *Louisville Courier-Journal*, Hoar was an "irresponsible troublemaker" and his bill a shameless effort to revive the hatreds of the Civil War and bring dishonor to every southern hearth and home:

Old Dame Partington, with specs on nose and broomstick in hand, sweeping back the waves of the Atlantic Ocean, cuts a respectable figure by the side of this senile Senator, with his little Force bill, which is going to regenerate the world, by making the average black man the superior of the average white man . . . He may be fairly described as a cross between a grind-stone and an encyclopedia. The fairy-god-mother who stood over his cradle gave him everything except good nature, good sense, and good looks. He is a man of the most equal temper, for he is mad all the time . . . His hatred of the South is so great that he fancies it honest . . .

Yet this is the leader whose spreading Bloody Shirt the Red Republicans in Congress are about to rally. . . . This is the tin soldier who is to assemble forces in the desolate camps and to re-organize the coffee-coolers for a grand and final assault. This is the wooden nut-meg, which . . . is to steer the Gory Old Party through the Red Sea of Federal intervention to the uplands of tariff robbery and agrarian rapine.

*Courier-Journal*, 11 December 1890, Scrap Book, Personal, #3 (1887–1893), Hoar Papers.

engaged in endless digressions and oratorical diversions and utilized every parliamentary device that could be remembered or invented.[15] The Republicans, anxious to terminate debate as soon as possible, remained grimly silent. By common consent their voice was expressed by Hoar, the measure's floor manager. Hoar resolved to restrict his efforts to short rejoinders, but was finally stung by the taunts of his opponents to prepare a major speech that took the greater part of two days to deliver and that allowed the filibustering southerners a welcome respite.

Hoar's speech of 29–30 December stands as illustration of the anxious determination and mixed motives of the most active supporters of the elections bill. Throughout that long and somewhat rambling address runs the theme of "redemption"—redeeming the pledge of the Republican party to the Negro; redeeming the sadly twisted ideals and program of the Reconstruction decade; redeeming the destiny of the Republican party as a great centralizing force, leading all parts of the nation toward the goals of economic expansion and moral progress:

> If this bill shall be adopted and prove effectual it will be the last of the great measures which have in them any thing of legal restraint which the changes in our Constitution have made necessary. Another measure, which I had fondly hoped would precede, must follow. That is a measure to secure for every child on American soil the education which shall fit him for citizenship . . . When these two things are brought to pass the ideal Republic will have become real.
>
> The struggle for this bill is a struggle for the last step toward establishing a doctrine to which the American people are pledged by their history, their Constitution, their opinions, and their interests.

He recited again and at length the "incontestable proof" of the constitutionality of the measure, its moderate nature, its historic precedents and concluded with an imprecation and a plea:

[15] Senator Gorman served as the chief Democratic strategist. John Lambert, *Arthur Pue Gorman* (Baton Rouge: Louisiana State University Press, 1953), 154–156.

[It is said] that these two races can not live together except on the terms that one shall command and the other obey. That proposition I deny. They can live together, neither, as a race, commanding, neither, as a race, obeying. They can live together obeying nothing but the law, framed by lawmakers whom every citizen shall have his equal share in choosing . . .

The error . . . of the South, in dealing with this problem, is in their assumption that race hatred is the dominant passion of the human soul; that it is stronger than love of country, stronger than the principle of equality, stronger than Christianity, stronger than justice . . .

If the Democratic party of the South had shown one-tenth of the energy in raising up and fitting for citizenship their colored fellow-citizen . . . that they had put into . . . contrivances like the new Mississippi constitution, the two races would to-day be dwelling together under the flag in freedom and in honor, in peace, in prosperity, and in mutual regard. You have tried everything else, try justice.[16]

With no end to the Democratic filibuster in sight, a mood of discouragement and mounting impatience was noticeable within the Republican majority. Sensing this, Hoar had given warning on Christmas Eve that he would seek to impose cloture if the obstructionists did not relent, and he pleaded on several occasions with his colleagues not to allow other issues, especially further discussion respecting the volume and composition of the national currency, to interfere with their pledged duty to concentrate upon the elections bill. The major source of danger he saw, too late, lay within the ranks of the silver senators.

In the last days of December Senators William M. Stewart of Nevada and Henry Moore Teller of Colorado announced that they were not satisfied with the Sherman Silver Purchase Act and declared their conviction that the defeat of the Republican party in the recent congressional elections represented a popular demand for further silver legislation. When they received no satisfaction from the managers of the elections bill, the Silver Republicans made temporary alliance with the Democrats, and on

[16] *Congressional Record,* 51st Cong., 2d sess., 853–862; 864–874.

5 January 1891, succeeded in squeezing through the Senate a resolution that temporarily set aside the elections bill in order that a new coin and currency measure might be considered.

The success of the Stewart-Teller maneuver surprised and enraged the managers of the federal elections bill. John Coit Spooner declared that an "exceedingly disgusting combination" of "the confederates under alleged Republican leadership" had succeeded in sidetracking the elections bill. Hoar's stout and tranquil exterior only partially concealed his chagrin. A dozen years later he would write of Stewart and his cohorts in prose starched with anger: "I never have known by what process of reasoning they reconciled their action with their word."[17]

The maneuver of the silver bloc delivered a most damaging blow to the elections bill. It did not, however, secure the enactment of additional silver legislation. Stewart's coinage bill passed the Senate on 14 January but was predictably buried in the House.

Senators Hoar, Spooner, and Aldrich then made their last successful effort in behalf of the elections bill. A motion was introduced on 16 January to make that bill once again the order of business. It passed only with the tie-breaking vote of Vice-President Levi P. Morton. Hoar expressed satisfaction, but the narrowness of the victory showed that the strength of his forces had already peaked.[18] The proponents of the elections bill would subsequently attempt to defy tradition and impose cloture. This attempt unsuccessful, their final defeat quickly followed.

It was only with reluctance that Hoar and Nelson Aldrich, the acting majority leader in the Senate, sought to force termination of debate. They realized that the opponents of the elections bill could now pose as the defenders of senatorial liberty—and they did.

The quiet Maryland drawl of Senator Gorman wept long and dramatically; nor did he rely on oratory alone. In the words of his sympathetic biographer, "It was at this juncture that the ceaseless opposition of the Democratic minority achieved the peak of

---

[17] Spooner to Governor W. D. Hoard, 11 January 1891, Papers of John Coit Spooner, Library of Congress; G. F. Hoar, *Autobiography of Seventy Years*, II, 156.

[18] *See* the analysis of John J. Davenport in his letter to W. E. Chandler, 8 January 1891, Papers of W. E. Chandler, Library of Congress.

perfection."[19] Stultifying orations alternated with childish games of hide-and-seek with the sergeant at arms as the Democrats sought to increase the exasperation and further erode the unity of the Republican majority. Aldrich's attempt to amend the rules of the Senate in order to render ineffective the Democratic filibuster was met in turn by a filibuster of increasing ingenuity.

Aldrich and Hoar were driven to seek the aid of Vice-President Morton, who was persuaded to rule that Aldrich might demand immediate consideration of his resolution to make cloture the main order of business. On Saturday, 24 January, in a noisy and angry chamber, Aldrich made his final effort. He asked the unanimous consent of his fellow senators to terminate debate by any one of four means. A chorus of voices growled objection to each proposal in turn. Cloture and the elections bill having been thwarted, they would now be permanently shelved. The end was predictable; its abruptness was surprising and its manner anticlimatic.

Shortly after noon on Monday, 26 January, John T. Morgan of Alabama gained the floor of the Senate and began a rather desultory tirade. After an hour he was interrupted by the junior Republican senator from Colorado, Edward O. Wolcott: "If the Senator from Alabama will yield to me, I move that the Senate proceed to the consideration of the bill . . . making an apportionment of Representatives in Congress among the several States under the Eleventh Census." Morgan expressed gratification at the interruption. After a brief parliamentary squabble, the reapportionment bill became the order of business, by a vote of 35–34. The elections bill had received its final defeat.[20] Postponed in behalf of tariff legislation, crippled by the controversy over silver, damaged by its association with cloture, the federal elections bill of 1890–1891 suffered the final humiliation of being sacrificed to a bill to which neither party had pledged its opposition nor its honor.

The contest over the elections bill had various implications and consequences for the Republican party. Most obviously, the defeat of the bill, and particularly the manner in which it was defeated, demonstrated the increasing political authority of economic

[19] Lambert, *Gorman*, 160.
[20] *Congressional Record*, 51st Cong., 2d sess., 1738, 1740.

groups. Certainly the motives of the bill's supporters were not exclusively idealistic nor those of its Republican opponents unremittingly selfish, but the contest was in part a struggle between human rights and economic interests and the latter proved the stronger.

Hoar and other of the more ardent supporters of the elections bill undoubtedly hoped that with the Republicans divided on such issues as silver and tariff reciprocity, the issue of "fair elections in the South" could serve as a means to party harmony and success.[21] The point to be made, however, is not that these men were partially motivated by partisan considerations—for surely they were— but that they were motivated, too, by a strong sense of the duty they and their party owed the southern Negro. The motivation of those Republicans who initially were reluctant to grant priority to the elections bill and later helped to derail and defeat it were equally mixed, but in all cases they may be characterized by a pronounced apathy toward the civil rights of the Negro. The Silver Republicans saw the Negro problem as one of little importance to their section, and inferior in significance to the needs of their constituents and contributors. Other Republican senators viewed the elections bill as likely to create sectional strife and so harmful to business, especially to northern investment in the expanding industrial economy of the South. And still others, such as Senators Preston Plumb and John J. Ingalls of Kansas, viewed the issue of Negro rights as irrelevant to their chief concern, the agricultural depression and the threat of the Northwest Alliance.[22]

Any analysis of Republican defection must include the barely concealed tension between generations within the Republican ranks. The elections bill was clearly associated with Harrison, Hoar, William Chandler, and Sherman; and certain more youthful

[21] *See* Hoar to Henry L. Dawes, 9 November 1890, Hoar Papers.

[22] Typical statements indicative of these considerations will be found in the following letters: J. H. Purnell to Matthew S. Quay, [?] November 1890 (copy); C. L. Poorman to John Sherman, 12 December 1890; George Wallace to Sherman, 29 December 1890, John Sherman Papers, Library of Congress; George W. Crosby to Hoar, 9 December 1890; William E. Barrett to Hoar, 28 January 1891, Hoar Papers. *See*, too, *Philadelphia Evening Telegraph,* 11 December 1890; Fred A. Wellborn, "The Influence of the Silver-Republican Senators, 1889–1891," *Mississippi Valley Historical Review,* 14 (1927–1928), 462–480.

Republicans saw it as an illustration of the desire of their seniors to cling to old and outmoded issues. Consequently there emerged the interesting paradox that some of the more self-consciously "modern" members of the party expressed little interest in what was one of the most significant legislative innovations proposed during the decade of the 1890's.[23]

In another but connected sense the contest over the elections bill represented a delayed postscript to the tangled and bitter history of the Reconstruction decade. It witnessed the last explosion of sectional anger and bitterness in the post-Civil War generation, as it represented its last effort in behalf of equal political rights for the American Negro. The next fifteen years would see the continued revision of southern state constitutions, the continued decline of the Republican party in the South, and the perfection of legalized and compulsory Jim Crow segregation. With the defeat of the elections bill, the Republican party and Congress virtually abdicated the field of civil rights legislation. The political role of the Negro in the South was, of course, a declining one before the elections bill was ever introduced, and there is no certainty that the passage of the bill would have markedly altered that development. What does seem certain, however, is that the defeat of the elections bill made clear the apathy of large parts of the North for the cause of Negro civil rights and thereby accelerated the evolution of Jim Crow in the South.

For a time such charter Republicans as Hoar refused to recognize the finality of the decision of January 1891. Three months after that decision Hoar wrote, in unconscious imitation of the words of Charles Sumner, "The question will not down. Nothing is settled that is not right." But soon there came the reluctant admission of defeat. By the mid-nineties, a discouraged Hoar was advising the Negro to "cultivate the virtues of integrity, industry, frugality, chastity" while quietly awaiting a better day. He would never accept, however, the necessity of Negro disfranchisement and segregation. At one point he was ready to believe that it might be well for illiterate Negroes voluntarily to forego their political

[23] Hoar's friend Albert Clarke at one point had felt compelled to warn Hoar that certain Bostonians were referring to him as "an ante-diluvian." Clarke to Hoar, 21 December 1890, Hoar Papers. *See, too, Boston Herald, 9 January 1891.*

rights for the sake of their more educated brothers, but he denounced the suggestion of Julian Hawthorne that the Fifteenth Amendment be repealed for the sake of racial harmony and he considered the "back to Africa" proposals of Senator John Morgan both ridiculous and evil. He died convinced that the "Grandfather Clause" was unconstitutional, that Congress had full authority to pass a national antilynching law, and that Jim Crow represented a "practical re-establishment of slavery in everything but name."[24]

In Hoar's own public career the contest over the elections bill marked a definite turning point. That contest represented his greatest effort to that time to lead the Senate and determine the direction of his party. Subsequently he would continue ably to represent the interests of New England and would retain the dutiful respect of his colleagues, but it would increasingly be the industrialists-in-politics such as Aldrich and Hanna or young lawyer-orators such as Spooner and Beveridge who would shape the policies of the Senate majority. Hoar's most publicized labors were still ahead of him—those associated with his opposition to jingoism and imperialism in the days of McKinley—but those labors would see him represent the principles of the Fathers, not the majority of the Senate or party. With the McKinley administration, the policies of the party would increasingly be determined in the White House and disclosed in the Senate by a small coterie of administration supporters, and Hoar was not of their number. With the nineties the evolution of big business—the power it exerted and the problems it raised—would increasingly dominate the political scene, and Hoar was never comfortable in dealing either with the trusts or with trust-busting.

[24] G. F. Hoar, "The Fate of the Election Bill," *Forum*, 11 (April, 1891), 135–136; Hoar to Nathan Appleton, 23 January 1892; Hoar to Albert Clarke, 5 December 1894; John E. Bruce to Hoar, 20 February 1895, 25 December 1898; Hoar to John E. Bruce, 25 February 1895 (copy); Hoar to R. R. Wright, President, Georgia State Industrial College, 22 January 1897; Hoar to the Reverend Louis H. Taylor, 30 November 1898; Hoar to Caroline M. Putnam, 19 May 1900; Hoar to Henry B. Blackwell, 14 September 1901; Hoar to Julia Ward Howe, 22 April 1902, Hoar Papers; *The Nation*, 52 (29 January 1891), 81; G. F. Hoar, "Party Government in the United States," *International Monthly*, II (September 1900), 425–427; Vincent P. DeSantis, *Republicans Face the Southern Question: The New Departure Years, 1877–1897* (Baltimore: Johns Hopkins Press, 1959), 204–221; Stanley Hirshson, *Farewell to the Bloody Shirt: Northern Republicans and the Southern Negro, 1877–1893* (Bloomington: Indiana University Press, 1962), 234–252.

That discomfort was the product of uncertainty, not myopia. Forever conscious of the duties of a public man, Hoar gave the problem of the trusts long and laborious study, sensing earlier than many its economic and political importance.[25] But he never solved the implicit contradiction between the glorification of economic growth and the fear of industrial combination. The prosperity of the moderately large corporation, such as those identified with the development of Worcester, he cherished; the Standard Oil Trust he suspected of being disloyal to the American system of free enterprise. But how to encourage the one, while restricting the other? The answer was not easy.[26] For a time he thought it had been discovered in the Harrison Years with the passage of the Sherman Antitrust Act.

Considering that the Sherman Antitrust Act has received so little praise, it is surprising that there has been such a vigorous contest over its title of authorship. There is no question that on 4 December 1889, John Sherman introduced in the Senate a bill "to declare unlawful trusts and combinations in restraint of trade and production," but the credit for the subsequent reconstruction and passage of the measure has been attributed to several senators. Hoar's claims were most fully set forth in a letter he wrote many years later to a younger colleague whom he held in but limited esteem, Senator Joseph B. Foraker of Ohio. Foraker had written an article on the role of Ohio in the Senate in which he attributed all credit for the Sherman Antitrust Act to John Sherman, and Hoar determined to set the record straight:

My Dear Senator:

We all know Mr. Sherman's great wisdom, especially when he had to deal with questions of finance, in which he was at home. But he was quite in the habit of introducing bills, especially at

[25] By the late 1880's many of Hoar's business correspondents were complaining of "the avaricious trusts." *See*, for example, L. J. Campbell to Hoar, 17 September 1888; Pamphlet Box, "Re Trusts, 1884—," Hoar Papers.

[26] By the end of 1888 Hoar was already prepared to approve a federal antimonopoly measure, but believed it must be drafted with the greatest care. He agreed with a friend who wrote: "The draftsman is in need of the peculiar skill of the hunter who in shooting at the animal dimly seen in the fog is expected to hit it if it was a deer and miss it if it was a calf." Thomas M. Cooley to Hoar, 12 January 1889, Hoar Papers.

the beginning of a session of Congress, which were sent to him by other people, or the scheme of which was proposed in the newspapers, without giving them much consideration, and very often without supporting them afterward himself . . .

The Anti-Trust bill which he introduced in 1890, was considered too radical by the Committee to whom it was referred— the Committee on Finance—who amended it, undertaking to deal with the matter in a very different manner. To that I moved an amendment on the floor of the Senate, and the bill was finally referred to the Judiciary Committee. We struggled with the question there, and at last I proposed to the Committee the present law . . . That was objected to very strongly by several members, but finally they agreed to it . . .

The bill was then reported back to the Senate and, after discussion, passed the Senate. The House disagreed to it, and proposed some amendments, and the bill went to Conference. Mr. Edmunds, Chairman of the Committee, and I who was the author of the measure as it was reported, were made the Senate Conferees, as is usual in such cases. The Conference Committee of the two Houses disagreed, and a new Conference was appointed. We, however, were appointed again on the new Conference. The House yielded, and the measure became a law.[27]

There would appear to be little profit in reviewing in detail the counter claims offered by the supporters of Senators Sherman, Evarts, and Edmunds.[28] Sherman surely provided the initial and somewhat fortuitous impetus, but his bill was rewritten, not revised, in the Judiciary Committee. There the chief figures were

[27] Hoar to Foraker, 27 June 1903, Papers of Joseph B. Foraker, Cincinnati Historical Society.

[28] Indicative of an abundant literature are the following: Joseph B. Foraker, *Notes of a Busy Life* (Cincinnati: Stewart & Kidd, 1916), II, 160–167; Winfield S. Kerr, *John Sherman: His Life and Public Services* (Boston, 1908), II, 199–207; John D. Clark, *The Federal Trust Policy* (Baltimore: Johns Hopkins Press, 1931), 52–56; Fred Shannon, *Economic History of the People of the United States* (New York: Macmillan Company, 1934), 509; Marvin H. Bumphrey, *Authorship of the Sherman Antitrust Law* (Cincinnati, 1912), 3–10; Hans B. Thorelli, *The Federal Antitrust Policy: Origination of an American Tradition* (Baltimore: Johns Hopkins Press, 1955), 197–214.

Edmunds and Hoar. They should share the praise or blame in equal portion. If one attempts a textual criticism of the act, it is possible to trace a majority of its specific phraseology to Edmunds, but if one seeks to discover the inspiration for certain of its more important features and changes, it is impossible to separate their labors. The measure that passed, after long struggle, on 2 July 1890, was in fact the Edmunds-Hoar Antitrust Act. But more important than the question of its title is that of its intended purpose. Was the act purposely weak and ineffective? Was it designed to pacify popular antipathies while leaving the trusts carefully undisturbed?

Its chief section was its first, prohibiting "every contract, combination in the form of trust or otherwise, or conspiracy, in restraint of trade or commerce among the several States, or with foreign nations." In the Judiciary Committee it had been decided not to attempt to define a "combination" or "trust," not to include intrastate commerce, and not to widen the prohibition to include combinations in restraint of production as well as trade. Some writers have seen in this careful delimitation a positive conspiracy on the part of the Judiciary Committee.[29]

An analysis of Hoar's role reveals no conspiracy, only caution. Hoar was keenly aware of the fact that Congress was engaged in a pioneer operation of public regulation and anxious that it not do more than seemed immediately necessary. What he primarily desired was a piece of legislation that would make clear the authority of the federal judiciary to enforce the old common-law prohibition against illegal combinations in restraint of trade.[30] His legal training, his admiration for the historic contribution of the judiciary, and his agreement with the majority philosophy of the Supreme Court as it was then composed, combined to persuade him that it was safer to put the real but elusive problem of the trusts in the hands of the courts. The same considerations made him

[29] Matthew Josephson, *The Politicos, 1865–1896* (New York: Harcourt, Brace, 1938), 458–459; Clarence Stern, *Republican Heyday: Republicanism Through the McKinley Years* (Ann Arbor: privately printed, 1962), 18, 54.

[30] Hoar explained in the Senate: "We have affirmed the old doctrine of the common law in regard to all interstate and international commercial transactions, and have clothed the United States courts with authority to enforce that doctrine by injunction." *Congressional Record*, 51st Cong., 1st sess., 3146–3147, 3152 (8 April 1890).

equally determined that the measure be constitutional; specifically, that it find clear justification in the commerce clause of the Constitution. It was on that ground that he doubted the wisdom of including within the act's enumerated prohibitions intrastate trade or combinations in restraint of production.[31]

In one sense, the approach of Hoar and Edmunds was conservative; they were fearful of hampering industrial expansion and sought to go slowly. Yet their approach may be likened to the position of Theodore Roosevelt in a later decade. As would Roosevelt, they viewed the danger of trusts as a selective matter and considered the conduct and not the size of a trust to be the true source of danger. When in the 1890's they determined to build their anti-trust act around the term, "in restraint of trade," they expected the courts to interpret that phrase "as a technical term in the English law," intended to prohibit only those combinations "improperly in restraint of trade . . . such combinations as [were] contrary to public policy."[32]

It was a point of view judged unsatisfactory by Henry Demerest Lloyd and other of the early Muckrakers, but it was adopted by the federal judiciary during the administration of William Howard Taft. It was a position that represented the ambivalent attitude of the Half-Breeds toward the political and economic power of big business; it was not a position that represented a conscious intent to deceive and defraud the public.

Matthew Josephson has done historical accuracy a disservice by implying the contrary. In his influential study of politics in the Gilded Age, Josephson indicted both the act and its authors:

> One provision [of the Antitrust Act] attempting to define Trusts and combinations, written by Edmunds and Hoar, furnished . . . "guide-boards for persons desiring to evade the law." In after years these eminent lawyers and constitutionalists, Hoar and Edmunds, both pursued a most lucrative practice of advis-

[31] In Hoar's opinion the fact that an article was the subject of transportation gave Congress no constitutional authority to consider all dealings in that article as interstate commerce. *See* the *Congressional Record,* 51st Cong., 1st sess., 4559–4560 (12 May 1890).

[32] *See* Hoar to Joseph B. Foraker, 28 May 1903 (copy), Hoar Papers; Hoar to Foraker, 27 June 1903, Papers of Joseph B. Foraker, Cincinnati Historical Society.

ing combinations, pools, and Trusts exactly when their contractual arrangements were valid and would be upheld by the courts and when they contravened statutory prohibitions.[33]

The charge is both indirect and false.

While the Sherman Act was being fashioned, Hoar refused to answer any queries from Massachusetts businessmen about its probable provisions. After the passage of the act he explained those provisions to several manufacturer correspondents, but only with the firm of Washburn and Moen of Worcester does Hoar appear to have offered specific advice on their probable liability under the new act.[34] Such advice could in any case be no more than an estimate of the more likely directions of future judicial interpretations. One of the reasons, indeed, why Hoar had sought to leave the implementation of the act to the judiciary, and not to an executive commission, was his belief that the federal judiciary stood above the pressures of special interests and industrial lobbys.

If Hoar is not liable to the charge of corruption, neither can he be properly accused of a desire to advance the fortunes of business at the expense of industrial justice and the American workingman.[35] George Frisbie Hoar wished justice to be done, and he did not wish to rock the boat. If only labor would be sensible and industrialists not too greedy, he was sure that industrial expansion would lead to a better life for all Americans. Convinced that the great majority of manufacturers were good and farsighted men, he desired to protect them from labor agitators and selfish monopolists alike. Government regulation was not in itself either unconstitutional or unscientific, but it was potentially disturbing to the natural operations of free enterprise capitalism. Hoar was prepared to sponsor national legislation that would discourage the

[33] Josephson, *The Politicos*, 459. Josephson gives as reference a page in Foraker's *Notes of a Busy Life* which offers neither documentation or support.

[34] Charles F. Washburn to Hoar, 7 August, 14 August 1891, Hoar Papers.

[35] Hoar favored a provision in the antitrust bill expressly exempting labor unions from its scope. His failure to protest more vigorously the deletion of such a provision in the final draft was the result primarily of a mistaken conviction that the federal judiciary would assume such an exemption. *Congressional Record*, 51st Cong., 1st sess., 2728–2729 (27 March 1890). *See*, too, Thorelli, *The Federal Antitrust Policy*, 197, 527.

illegal activities of the few who would abuse the rightful freedom of the many, but such legislation must be drafted with caution lest the curse exceed the cure. In the final analysis, it was better to do too little; it was much more easily corrected.[36]

Many of the genteel reformers of the early 1890's entertained a high respect for Hoar. Though occasionally he disappointed them by his insistence on party regularity, they agreed that his politics were pure if partisan. Wharton Barker, a Philadelphia patrician who enjoyed a mild preoccupation with reform causes, offered the opinion that Hoar and Justin Morrill were "almost the only men now in public life" who viewed public questions from the standpoint of "the interests of the people."[37] Such men as Barker and Morrill believed with Hoar that a portion of the heritage of the Republican party was a conviction of the relevance of morals to politics. They believed as well that while the heritage of the party was adaptable to the needs of an expanding economy, it must never be denied.

It was in this light that Hoar had viewed his fight for the federal elections bill of 1890. The history of that struggle had seemed to show that neither the party nor the Senate was prepared to reclaim the principles of Sumner. The administration of Harrison, for which Hoar had held such high hopes, was by its end a source of disappointment. The election of 1892 and the return of Cleveland were seen as positive indignities.

[36] *See* handwritten copy of Hoar's speech before the Commercial Club of Boston, 28 April 1893, Hoar Papers.

[37] Wharton Barker to Hoar, 28 May 1891, Hoar Papers.

# 6

*Suspicion and Tolerance:*
*Cleveland's Second Administration*

For George Frisbie Hoar and his party the years of Grover Cleveland's second administration were an unhappy time. It was a period destined to be succeeded by an era of Republican unity and popularity, but that was not easily foretold. Hoar saw the Cleveland years, especially those preceding the Republican congressional victories of 1894, as a time of increasing Republican disunity over the old issues of silver and the tariff, disturbing public agitation over the newer problems of the trusts and "the money power," and mad movements in behalf of Populism, Socialism, and the popular election of federal senators. In these years he exhibited on occasion a partisanship as narrow as that in the days of Andrew Johnson; at other points he attacked nativism and religious prejudice with an independence remindful of his labors in behalf of the Free Soilers of Kansas, but at all times he considered himself and his party deeply aggrieved.

This sense of grievance found expression in a renewed and heightened antipathy for the Mugwumps. These eastern intellectuals actually deserved little credit for Cleveland's victory in 1892, but Hoar believed that they were largely responsible for confusing the voter and bringing discredit upon the party system. There had been a time when all respectable young men of the North had understood that the Republican party was the party of progress and high principle, and then these articulate recreants had come along with their cant of voting the man and not the party, and had falsified the meaning of political independence while sowing confusion and Republican defeat.[1] The epitome of the Mugwumps in Hoar's view was E. L. Godkin, editor of the *New York Post*, and the month of June 1895 witnessed a correspondence between them of illustrative if exaggerated bitterness.

Hoar had taken the opportunity during a Decoration Day address to denounce those of his countrymen who found their pleasure in suspecting the motives of all public men and to declare at one point: "One of our best beloved men of letters gives his woeful picture of the degradation of American politics and then dedicates his book to the most unscrupulous liar connected with the American press." When Godkin stiffly requested an identification of the culprits, Hoar was quick to satisfy his curiousity:

> Sir, I meant Mr. Lowell by the phrase "one of our best beloved men of letters." By "the most unscrupulous liar connected with the American press," I mean you.

The New York reformer replied in kind:

> Sir, I wrote to you for the purpose of securing under your own hand, evidence of the depths of blackguardism, and absurdity,

[1] In a letter to his friend Dorman B. Eaton, Hoar wrote:

The man who doesn't belong to a party, that is, who doesn't unite with other men who agree with him in desiring to accomplish useful public ends, by proper organization and combined effort, is always useless and commonly mischievous. The most mischievous person that I know of in politics, is the man who says he votes for the best man without regard for party. However abominable may have been the Conklings, the Butlers and Tom Platts, they have done less mischief than these worthy and amiable men, in my opinion. . . . Party government is the government of principles. Any other government is the government of men.

Hoar to Eaton, 25 April 1895, Hoar Papers. This letter was not sent, perhaps because on rereading it Hoar determined he had been too hard not on the Mugwumps but on Tom Platt.

which a modern Senator can reach. The blackguardism is perhaps explained by the character of a good many of your colleagues, with whom you pass a large part of the year. The absurdity is your own . . . I don't think you are worth disgust. The worst charge that can be made against you is silliness, and of this you have been long suspected.[2]

Perhaps only the principled can really hate; surely the articulate do so most colorfully. The occasion for the quarrel was unimportant; what it reflected was a strong sense of frustration on both sides. Godkin was bitter because the Cleveland administration had failed the cause of reform; Hoar was bitter because the Democrats controlled the executive and the times were sadly out of joint.[3]

A younger Republican who entertained identical sentiments toward the Mugwumps generally and Mr. Godkin in particular was Theodore Roosevelt. Roosevelt before long would view Hoar as a disgrace to the Republican party but during the first half of the 1890's he saw Hoar as the Cicero of the Senate and was happy to join him in belaboring the independents.[4] Each man proclaimed his own high standard of political morality and independence, but

[2] Godkin to Hoar, 31 May 1895; Hoar to Godkin, 3 June 1895; Godkin to Hoar, 5 June 1895, Hoar Papers. Hoar's letter was returned to him by Godkin. Scribbled on its margin are the words, "Returned to an old blackguard," and scribbled on its back, in Hoar's hand, the sentence: "This letter was returned to me Nov. 11th '97, more than two years after its date."

Some years later Hoar would bitterly but unavailingly protest an effort on the part of various Harvard Alumni to honor Godkin with a testimonial dinner.

[3] Hoar's partisan distrust for Cleveland was not uninterrupted, however. He felt obliged on one occasion to praise his appointment of Richard Olney as Secretary of State and to thank Cleveland for retaining his old friend and relation, J. Evarts Greene, as postmaster at Worcester. Hoar to Richard Olney, 8 June 1895; Grover Cleveland to Hoar, 14 January 1897, Hoar Papers; Hoar to Grover Cleveland, 15 January 1897, Papers of Grover Cleveland, Series II, Library of Congress.

Cleveland is supposed to have once said of Hoar: "The recording angel is going to have a rough time of it with that old fellow. He has done so many good things and said so many spiteful things that I shouldn't know how to deal with him." Cited in M. A. DeWolfe Howe, ed., *Later Years of the Saturday Club, 1870–1920* (Boston: Houghton Mifflin Company, 1927), 136.

[4] *See* Roosevelt to Nelson Aldrich, 21 October 1895, Papers of Nelson Aldrich, Library of Congress; Roosevelt to Hoar, 21 April 1896, Hoar Papers. Roosevelt also agreed with Hoar that Cleveland entertained a strong prejudice against Negro office-holders and was an enemy of true civil service reform. *See* Roosevelt to Hoar, 8 December 1894, Hoar Papers.

they were equally intolerant of the man who in a "snarling spirit of indiscriminate detraction" denounced party loyalty and made a fetish of "flocking by himself."[5]

The increasingly dogmatic and petulant tone to be noted in Hoar's letters and speeches during the years of Cleveland's second administration was not inspired alone by the Mugwumps and their imagined evil influence. The hard times following the Panic of 1893, Republican division, and the personality and prose of Grover Cleveland all combined to lessen his pleasure in public service. Removed from the chairmanship of the Judiciary Committee in March 1893, when the Democrats organized the Senate, Hoar found himself relegated to an office in the basement of the Capitol. This indignity did nothing to improve his spirits and, according to one Washington journalist, Hoar and Senators Frye, Higgins, and Chandler in their adjoining and gloomy basement rooms held frequent "conclaves in which Cleveland was handled without gloves."[6] There they agreed that the President was almost exclusively responsible for the Panic of 1893, and there they agreed that in a time of economic and political depression the highest duty for a Republican lay in a course of patriotic obstruction.[7] Such obstruction, however, must be selective. In those instances where Cleveland was prepared to oppose the dangerous Populist influence among the southern and western members of his party, he might be supported after a little verbal drubbing; at other points, he should furnish the target of attack. The debates over the repeal of the Sherman Silver Purchase Act and the Wilson Tariff bill would provide illustration.

The Sherman Silver Purchase Act had not reversed the decline in the commercial price of silver but in conjunction with the generous appropriation measures of the Harrison years it had an appreciable effect upon the Treasury surplus and the gold reserve. When Cleveland had entered office the gold reserve in the Treasury had fallen to a point but slightly above the level of $100,000,-000, the figure that had come to be regarded, for no good reason,

---

[5] *See* Hoar's speech to the Brooklyn Institute of Arts and Sciences, 30 September 1897, Scrap Book VI (1897), Hoar Papers.

[6] *Statesman,* 21 December 1893, as cited in Leon Burr Richardson, *William E. Chandler: Republican* (New York: Dodd, Mead, 1940), 459.

[7] *See* Hoar to Ruth A. Hoar, 11 August 1893, 10 June, 16 June 1894, Hoar Papers.

as the figure of minimum safety necessary to the maintenance of the gold standard. Pressured by European creditors (themselves the victims of depression conditions), and fearful lest the Treasury soon be forced to suspend specie payments, American investors began to convert their silver certificates to gold. The resulting decline in the gold reserve appeared to justify their initial fears. The Panic of 1893 that followed had more basic causes but it was precipitated by the apprehensions of the investing community respecting the level of the gold reserve. That panic in turn increased the run on gold. The purchase clause of the silver act of 1890 was seized upon as the symbol of all threats to fiscal safety. Among the first to accept this oversimplification was Grover Cleveland.

To the displeasure of many Democrats from the South and West and the anger of the small band of Populist representatives, Cleveland called Congress into special session and demanded the immediate repeal of the Sherman Silver Purchase Act of 1890. For Republican advocates of sound money, Cleveland's stance as savior of the currency was almost equally provoking. Hoar spent weeks in preparing a speech that would attempt to show America why it must accept the recommendation of the President and grant him no credit.

Hoar's Senate speech of 15 August, 1893 had four separate aims, all sincerely held, all self-contradictory: (1) he wished to conciliate the bimetallist western Republicans while soothing the fears of eastern capitalists; (2) he wished to damn Cleveland and express implicit agreement with Cleveland's analysis of the dangers facing the gold reserve; (3) he wished to demonstrate that he and other Senate Republicans had been correct in 1890 to vote for the Silver Purchase Act and were now required by duty to vote for its repeal; (4) he wished to prove himself a bimetallist in the tradition of Alexander Hamilton and to show that there must be an end to further silver coinage.[8] It could not have been an easy speech to

---

[8] Hoar went to infinite pains to prove that the Sherman Act had represented a great improvement over the Bland-Allison Act and that those who voted for it in 1890 should be viewed as the financial saviors of the nation even while they voted now to repeal it. He introduced long tables designed to show that the Bland Act was more costly to the Treasury and to the nation's credit than was the Sherman Act. *Congressional Record*, 53d Cong., 1st sess., 346 (1 August 1893). *See*, too, typed memorandum, "The Bland Bill and The Sherman Law Compared," Hoar Papers, and the *Boston Journal*, 1 August 1893.

write, nor is it a very interesting speech to read. It goes far to prove, however, that Hoar was apprehensive of further sectional division within the Republican party, suspected that gold monometallism would have the long-term effect of restricting the currency and depressing prices, and feared above all things silver monometallism, which he was certain would lead to financial chaos and economic decline. One paragraph may serve in illustration of his conclusion that all true bimetallists must vote against silver:

> Believing with Hamilton that the bimetallic standard is that upon which alone this country can permanently and safely rest, and believing also, with Hamilton, that whenever the two metals separate the standard must be conformed to the more valuable, I am in favor of at once putting a stop to the purchase of silver for coinage. Otherwise it seems to me clear that our gold will take its departure, and we shall be left in that most wretched of conditions, a nation with a single monometallic standard composed of an inferior metal, constantly fluctuating and rapidly degenerating.[9]

The various reactions this speech inspired among Hoar's correspondents help perhaps to explain certain of its contradictions. Those who welcomed his demands for repeal showed little sympathy with his defense of the original act; those who sympathized with his concern over currency restriction were unmoved by his depiction of the horrors of monetary devaluation. H. G. Curtis of State Street, Boston, was impatient with all talk of international cooperation in behalf of bimetallism and demanded exclusive concentration upon the cessation of silver purchase. The Clothing Manufacturers Association and the head of the Boston Stock Exchange agreed. "Honest Republicans" of Eldorado, Kansas and Aspen, Colorado, however, declared that his defense of traditional bimetallism should have been followed by a demand for continued silver coinage as the only means of reversing the present strangulation of credit. And the secretaries of the People's Party Club of Massachusetts and the "Central Labor Union of Boston and Vicin-

---

[9] *Congressional Record*, 53d Cong., 1st sess., 343 (15 April 1893).

ity" cautioned Hoar to "take heed of the interest of the producing classes as well as those of the banking and money power."[10]

In the Senate there was equal diversity of opinion, and the silver bloc made a desperate effort to kill the repeal bill by means of parliamentary obstruction. Only after obstruction had run its course, all compromise efforts had failed, and the silver issue had effected further division in the ranks of both parties did the repeal bill pass.[11] It had been a sorry wrangle and an important one. It made probable the failure of tariff reform and Grover Cleveland's second administration; it served to strengthen the allegiance of certain groups within the East and within the Republican party to the gold standard. It was only now that gold assumed for a majority of eastern investors, bankers, and manufacturers the character of fiscal sanctity. In the process, Hoar, once viewed as conservative on the money question, would become in some eyes, barely dependable.

Accompanying the repeal act was a resolution calling for continuing efforts in behalf of the restoration of silver coinage by means of international agreement. If many senators viewed this as only eyewash, Hoar was not among them. Until the passage of the Gold Standard Act of 1900 Hoar would label himself an "international bimetallist." He believed that as it had been possible in the past for most commercial nations to maintain both gold and silver

[10] Hoar to H. G. Curtis, 18 August 1893; Resolution of The Clothing Manufacturers Association, 12 October 1893; Charles Head to Hoar and H. C. Lodge, 11 October 1893; Hoar to T. B. Murdock, 11 September 1893; Hoar to T. B. Murdock, 11 September 1893; Hoar to Mrs. E. M. Ross, 23 August 1893; W. R. Conway to Hoar, 22 August 1893; Henry Abrahams to Hoar, 7 October 1893, Hoar Papers. *See*, too, Hoar to Louis Curtis, 19 August 1893; Hoar to Jonathan A. Lane, 23 August 1893; Representative J. H. Walker to Hoar, 25 October 1893; Henry B. Blackwell to Hoar, 1 December 1893, 24 January 1894, Hoar Papers.

[11] Before the repeal bill finally passed, Hoar had become almost as irritated with certain of its advocates as with its enemies. He wrote a friend in Boston:

The Eastern press and, to a large extent, the business men of the East have treated the question intolerantly, dogmatically and, in some instances, ignorantly. They will reap the fruit of their mistake in spite of the victory, and this single question will greatly increase the political power of what is Socialism in this country, under which all interests which depend on a sound, safe and certain dollar will suffer.

Hoar to Franklin Brown, 27 October 1893, Hoar Papers.

as monetary mediums it should be now. If only all major trading countries cooperated, they should be able to find some means whereby the coinage ratio of these two metals would always reflect their respective true worth and an international standard of value be established, measurable in both gold and silver. He was far from clear just how this might be arranged, but he was certain that such an arrangement would be best for the long-term interests of monetary stability and for the short-term needs of Republican unity. Hoar quietly supported the efforts of Francis A. Walker and his Committee for the Promotion of International Bimetallism; cabled encouragement to an international bimetallic conference that opened and failed in London in the spring of 1894; and urged the Republican platform makers in 1896 to avoid dogmatic or exclusive subscription to the gold standard.[12]

Once Hoar determined for himself what were "sound Republican policies," he would alter them only with difficulty and often not at all. "Bimetallism when possible," protection of Negro suffrage, suspicion of Bourbon democracy, high protection: these were not only policies but principles, and principles were not subject to reconsideration. Such loyalty to the past was criticized on occasion, but when the issue was a Democratic tariff—especially one so liable to criticism as the Wilson-Gorman tariff of 1894—rigidity was judged more excusable; indeed, for many Republicans, positively essential.

[12] Francis A. Walker to Hoar, 15 January 1894, Hoar to Walker, 2 February 1894, Hoar Papers; *Congressional Record*, 54th Cong., 1st sess., 2158–2159 (26 February 1896); Hoar to Lodge, [?] June 1896 (cable), Henry Cabot Lodge Papers, Massachusetts Historical Society.

Hoar was in England in June–July 1896, seeking rest and a cure for iritis, and took the opportunity to try, unsuccessfully, to obtain from Arthur James Balfour a public letter promising British "sympathy" for American efforts to revive bimetallism. Hoar also now began a long correspondence with the English bimetallist and determined friend of the great, Moreton Frewen. Their correspondence reveals that for Hoar, as for William E. Chandler and others, international bimetallism was not a hypocritical dodge designed to appease the West, as has often been alleged, but the product of sincere conviction. The following letters are representative: Hoar to Moreton Frewen, 7 June, 23 June, 21 July, 11 August, 28 November 1896; 19 January 1897, Moreton Frewen Papers, Box 15, Library of Congress; Frewen to Hoar, 23 July, 24 July, 15 August 1896, Hoar Papers. *See*, too, Hoar to Arthur James Balfour, 22 June 1896 (copy), Hoar Papers; W. E. Chandler to Edward O. Wolcott, 14 June, 21 June, 27 June, 6 July 1897; Wolcott to Chandler, 11 June 1897; Memorandum "Sent to Sen. Allison by W. E. Chandler," 4 July 1897 (copy), Papers of W. E. Chandler, vols. 112, 113, Library of Congress.

Grover Cleveland returned to the presidency in 1893 with his natural conservatism strengthened, but with a continued determination to reform the tariff. He would probably have done well to have proposed tariff revision to the Fifty-third Congress before dividing his party over the issue of silver repeal. By the 1890's, however, the Democratic party was already divided over the tariff issue. Especially in the Senate was it clear that protectionism cut across party lines. Refusing to recognize this, Cleveland demanded that the Democratic majorities of House and Senate make good the pledge of the party platform. In the House, the protectionists among both parties were unable to prevent passage of a tariff bill providing for an appreciable reduction of import duties, but in the Senate the industrial lobbyists were more successful. And in the Senate George Frisbie Hoar had the opportunity to play the role he was so quick to damn, the role of a member of the minority determined to obstruct and delay.

There is little profit in detailing each barb and motion offered by Hoar in the long and frustrating Senate debate over the Wilson tariff bill, but his major speeches of 8 May and 12 June deserve brief mention. They saw Hoar offer not only a bitter criticism of the sectional anomalies of the original bill and its many Senate amendments but also a major counterattack. Old arguments and new, the arguments of industrial diversification, home markets, and the standard of wages, were offered in what was Hoar's mea culpa for protection.

A protective tariff, Hoar proclaimed, was as valid for the 1890's as it had been when championed by Henry Clay. It was true that now America was a great industrial nation and few of its manufactures were of infant proportions, but this happy circumstance was the result in large part of the intelligent tariff legislation of the past thirty-three years and Congress had now the duty to defend that which it had encouraged. He remained convinced that the effect of the tariff was to lower consumer prices, by means of increased domestic competition, but this fact did not lessen the present necessity of tariff barriers. Protection was not a stage on the road to international free trade. It was an eternal principle so long as Americans wished to retain for American labor the American market. The wage level in the United States must be forever higher than its European counterpart. Without continued tariff aid the

American manufacturer—whatever his superior initiative and machinery—could compete with the sweated labor of Europe only by reducing wages and thereby diminishing the economic comfort and moral improvement of the American labor force.[13] Nor was it the factory worker alone who benefited from the tariff. Farmers and professional men must see their stake in industrial prosperity and the close identification of industrial prosperity with the tariff.

Hoar accompanied his defense of protection with a biting attack on the insincerity of Democratic professions respecting the public value of tariff reduction. The Wilson bill as revised by Senator Gorman and his allies was not a free trade measure, not a revenue tariff, but a monstrosity. It was a tariff for the protection of the products of the South and the protection of the seats of a few northern Democratic congressmen. It denied protection to northern lumber, woolens, and labor, and lavished it upon southern rice, coal, and sugar. This mongrel measure was nothing less than an effort by the Bourbon democracy to gain revenge for Appomattox. He was well aware that after the last shameful trade had been made and the last miserable amendment added that the Democratic majority—"this coalition between the aristocrat and the Populist"—would ram the illogical and dangerous measure through the Senate, but let them not think they would escape the wrath of the people nor the judgment of history:

> [This bill makes] war on property, on frugality, on honest labor, on honest, moderate earnings. . . . Its warfare is upon the savings bank, upon the life insurance, upon the yeoman, upon the farm, and upon the workman in the mill. The power which is behind it may seem to secure for itself a brief victory; but the men who are wielding it know well that it is doomed.[14]

[13] Hoar made great point throughout the debate of the desire of the workingmen of New England that its representatives defeat the Democratic effort at tariff revision, and actively encouraged memorials and petitions by labor groups. *See* the *Congressional Record*, 53d Cong., 2d sess., 481 (3 January 1894); John H. Lorimer, Central Labor Union, Worcester, to Hoar, 29 January 1894; Hoar to Edward Fitzwilliam, 12 January 1894, Hoar Papers.

[14] *Congressional Record*, 53d Cong., 2d sess., 4474–4486, 6149–6154 (8 May 1894, 12 June 1894). *See*, too, memorandum, "Menagerie of High Protective Free Traders," Hoar to Edward L. Pierce, 14 February 1894; Hoar to the Reverend George H. Johnson, 23 February 1894, Hoar to J. C. Ayer, 6 March 1894, Hoar Papers; Worcester *Spy*, 12 September 1894.

There was a certain illogic in Hoar's attempt simultaneously to damn Populist influence and Democratic protection of the sugar trust, but his opposition, if partisan, was not necessarily erroneous. The Wilson-Gorman Tariff as finally passed by Congress was an unsatisfactory measure in the eyes of Cleveland as well as Hoar. Though its average level of duties was lower than that of the McKinley Act—reducing that level from 49 percent to 39 percent of the total value of dutiable imports—its chief result was to maintain the existing protective system, increase its internal inconsistencies, and deny the Democratic claim to tariff reform. The peppery Populist Ignatius Donnelly, in an editorial addressed to Hoar, damned both parties as enemies of tariff reform:

> If Hoar [were] a statesman . . . he would have said: "Our democratic brethren and ourselves have been humbugging the people of this country for half a century, with the pretense that there were two sides to the question of duties on imports from foreign countries . . . The democrats are now in power and everyone can see there is no free trade [in their bill] . . . The only differences between the two parties are as to matters of petty detail."
>
> But Hoar thinks too much of his nut-megs to make any such speech as that . . . He is simply exposing the democratic fraud for the purpose of maintaining the republican fraud. It is a clamorous contention between cheats.[15]

In Massachusetts, Hoar met criticism less caustic but more worrisome. During the long Senate battle he received resolutions from the Massachusetts Reform Club demanding an end to obstruction and a speedy disposition of the tariff bill, but those resolutions had been dismissed when they were seen to contain the names of few important manufacturers and many Mugwumps.[16] More disturbing were the letters of business men who, having cheered the obstructionist efforts of their federal senators, now expressed querulous complaint that they had not been more influential in fashioning the bill's provisions. Most of these corre-

[15] *The Representative* (Journal of the State Farmers Alliance, Minnesota), 30 May 1894, Hoar Papers.
[16] Hoar to Andrew Fiske, 10 May 1894, Hoar Papers.

spondents agreed that free trade was false in principle, but some favored reciprocity with Canada and many believed that the competitive position of New England might have been improved by placing coal, hides, and wool on the free list. Hoar and his new senatorial colleague, Henry Cabot Lodge, answered their complaints with tactful severity. Their critics must understand that for the principle of protection to be applied at all, it must be applied equitably:

> To have free trade for some articles and protection for others cannot be sustained . . . by any argument either of justice or political economy. If we are to ask protection for the products of New England manufactures, we have no right to refuse that protection to the products of any other part of the country. It is impossible to take the position that every thing that goes into one of our factories should go in free and every thing which comes out of it should have a protective duty. Protection as a system is both wise and defensible; but protection as a preference, as exemplified in the existing bill, is utterly wrong.[17]

One feature of the Wilson-Gorman Act elicited unwonted unity among the manufacturers of Massachusetts. They unanimously opposed its income-tax amendment. In retrospect that tax was exceedingly modest. It embodied, however, the principle of all income tax legislation: the support of government expenditure by assessment apportioned to annual earnings. Although he had not opposed a similar measure during the Civil War, Hoar, grown more conservative in a year that saw the spread of Populism and industrial warfare, labeled the amendment socialistic. Not only was the tax dangerous in principle, but it would prove inequitable in practice. It would subject the savings accounts and beneficiary societies of the hard-working citizens of Massachusetts to spoliation while allowing the landed squire of the South to escape taxation; it would grant the government inquisitorial powers to investigate the concerns of private citizens and make public their business secrets; it would help to perpetuate the internal revenue system and inspire further antagonism between classes and between sections.

[17] H. C. Lodge to Alfred M. Whiting, 26 July 1894 (copy); Hoar to W. C. Courtts, 21 May 1894; Hoar to Sylvester Cunningham, 16 June 1894, Hoar Papers.

In the state elections of 1894 Hoar expressed sympathy with the manufacturers of Massachusetts in their opposition to the tax and the "incomprehensible blanks for returns," and the next year congratulated them on the Supreme Court decision that declared the income tax unconstitutional. Privately he thought the argument of the Supreme Court majority too general and inclusive, but that the tax in question was odious, sectional, and clumsy he sincerely believed.[18]

Hoar's views respecting the income tax were closely associated with his conviction that Populist denunciations of the "money trust" were false and inflammatory and that the labor marches of 1894, such as that led by General Jacob Coxey, were misguided and dangerous.

Populist clamor against "the money power" increased in volume as the agricultural depression intensified with the contraction of credit following the Panic of 1893. Angered by repeal of the Sherman Silver Act and Secretary Carlisle's expensive bond sales to J. P. Morgan and Company, western voices rose in number to denounce the Wall Street monopolists and eastern Shylocks who dictated government policy and robbed the producing masses. Hoar's reaction to their charges was unsympathetic but ambivalent. On occasion he scoffed at the very notion of a money trust; at other times, he recognized the political and social problem posed by great concentrations of economic power but emphasized the need of caution in any effort of regulation.

His first reaction was to imply that the Populists and their allies were attacking a straw man:

> The so much abused money power, so far as I understand it, consists, in this country, of men who are loaning money to Westerners at 5%, when their own bankers and speculators demand 10% or 12% . . . I do not myself think that these men . . . have in the slightest degree . . . attempted to interfere with our financial system.
>
> . . . The idea that there are men in New York, Boston, and other centers, who can at any time throw the whole business of

[18] *Congressional Record*, 53d Cong., 2d sess., 5589–5592, 6778–6779 (1 June 1894, 23 June 1894); Selwyn Z. Bowman to Hoar, 14 February 1895; draft of "Campaign Speech, 1895," Hoar Papers.

the country into confusion, and who make enormous fortunes by bringing on hard times and good times, at their pleasure . . . is an absurd and mischievous delusion.[19]

As depression conditions spread throughout the country, however, and agitation and discontent increased, Hoar was persuaded that these charges required a more reasoned rebuttal. Such a rebuttal he offered in a series of campaign speeches in the summer of 1895, and then in a great summary effort at Clark University in 1897.

Talk of a sinister conspiracy of Wall Street bankers whose greed determined the course of the economy was quite unjustified, but the evolution of our economy had created two very real dangers: "the evil of an unequal and unjust division of wealth; the destruction of honest, individual industry by giant monopolies." These matters were rightfully subject to the power of the law, but their investigation should be disciplined by a cautious concern for the rights of property and the needs of economic growth. Great fortunes honestly made were not the proper object of legislative inquiry, but only those that were the clear result of illegal chicanery. It was not even monopoly, per se, that was evil—if by monopoly one simply meant the transaction of business by "one or a few great instruments, rather than many." After all, the railroad was a great monopoly and the experience of the past generation had taught America that "a regulated and controlled monopoly does the carrying trade of the country better than an unregulated competition." The enemy of free enterprise was not great size but dishonest practice:

> It is, in my judgment, the duty of the people to prevent by a use of all the legislative and judicial forces of the Government the crushing out of weak or individual competition in any kind of business by . . . combined competition. On the other hand, we cannot prevent, and it is not for the public interest to prevent, the building up of a large business by reducing the price to the people by the economies which can be practiced alone by conducting businesses on a large scale . . . All that you can do is to

[19] Hoar to C. L. Glynn, 13 September 1893; Hoar to F. R. Cordlay, 15 September 1893, Hoar Papers.

see that they do not menace or corrupt legislation; that they do not use their wealth as a political influence; and that they shall not be permitted to crush out any rivalry by dishonest expedients.[20]

By the criteria of a later day Hoar's approach to the associated problems of combination and monopoly was conservative and cautious. Judged in relation to the Republican party of the 1890's, however, he stood to the left of center. If he associated the protection of corporate property with the values of America, for many of his colleagues they were identical. The relative liberalism of Hoar's position was recognized by the grandfather of the Muckrakers, Henry Demerest Lloyd:

> Dear Sir,
> I read your admirable address On Trusts . . . with great pleasure and profit. You are one of the few statesmen of ours who always stand for the state . . . There is one point in this matter on which I would beg the privilege of submitting one or two considerations for a revision of your expressed opinion. It is as to the alleged cheapening [of costs] . . . by the Oil Trust.[21]

Jacob Coxey never felt the need to write to Hoar; undoubtedly if he had, his estimate of the latter's statesmanship would have been considerably lower. When Coxey and his fellow marchers finally straggled into Washington on May Day, 1894—demanding that the government directly intervene against the depression by means of work projects and monetary inflation—they received no more sympathy from Hoar than from Grover Cleveland. It was the senator's opinion that "demonstration of masses of the people has no lawful place; only the formally elected representatives of the people can speak for the sovereign will."[22]

[20] Clark University Speech, 19 July 1897, Scrap Book #6 (1897), Hoar Papers. *See*, too, draft of "Speech to be delivered at the Boston Music Hall, July, 1895," Hoar Papers. Hoar informed one correspondent that he saw no objection to the election to Congress of officers of large banking and business interests. They could serve the people while informing Congress with their special knowledge. Hoar to Theodore B. Hapgood, 22 March 1894, Hoar Papers.

[21] H. D. Lloyd to Hoar, 7 August 1897, Hoar Papers.

[22] *The Nation*, 3 May 1894.

Before Hoar saw fit to lecture Coxey, however, he had already engaged in target practice with one of the more eccentric of Bostonians, Morrison I. Swift. Coxey's army was not the product of Massilon, Ohio, alone; it had contingents and supporters from many other regions, including the Boston Common.

It was on the Boston Common on Sunday, 15 April 1894, that Swift, a self-proclaimed man of the people, addressed a mass meeting and passed about a petititon. This petition was in the form of a letter to Senator Hoar, demanding that he and the Congress take immediate responsibility for ending the depression and be prepared to welcome Coxey's army, including the detachment from Boston, when it arrived in Washington. Hoar offered his reply in the form of a public letter. It was utterly impossible for the government to become the employer of the unemployed. The Constitution and the example of classical Rome both forbade it. Once the government moved into the realm of providing bread and circuses, parties and demagogues would soon attempt to outbid one another and republican government in America would be at an end. Surely everyone had the constitutional right to petition the government, however unwise their specific proposals might be, but that petition should not be made in such a manner as to incite violence or disrupt orderly political processes. Anarchists might find cover within an army of marching petitioners and use the resulting disturbance for their own purposes, and any man sincerely interested in the welfare of the American laborer could do him no worse service than to introduce socialism or anarchism into this nation. Despite the occasional vicissitudes of its economy, capitalist America was still the best hope of the poor and needy.[23]

Hoar's prediction that dangerous consequences would attend Coxey's expedition was moderation itself when compared to those of some of his more agitated correspondents. Public buildings would be burned to the ground, Washington shut off from the country, and Capitol Hill drenched in blood—or so prophesied certain Bostonians. "Have you not a right to imprison those leaders before they arrive in Washington," asked one counterrevolu-

[23] Swift to Hoar, 15 April 1894; Hoar to Swift, 22 April 1894 (copy), Hoar Papers.

tionary, "and put those under them in Penitentiarys and Work Houses."[24]

Conservative apprehensions proved needless. Coxey and his followers—among them, his wife Lucille and his son Legal Tender—arrived in Washington only to be rebuffed by Cleveland and Congress alike. Coxey was arrested for violating a no trespassing ordinance as he attempted to make his way to the steps of the Capitol, and his tired "revolutionaries" subsequently concentrated on how best to get back home. In the Senate, Hoar denounced the effort of the marchers to dictate the policies of sixty-five million American citizens and their lawfully chosen representatives, but he saved his chief scorn for the Populist senators who lent encouragement to Coxey's army. When Senator William V. Allen of Nebraska and Senator William M. Stewart of Nevada called for a repeal of the act regulating the use of the Capitol grounds, under which Coxey had been prosecuted, Hoar denounced both their motion and their motives. Coxey had known of the regulation in question; like the antiriot laws of every state and territory, it was necessary and proper. Mob assemblies offered a perfect opportunity for misguided fanatics, anarchists, and assassins, and so must always be subject to regulation. He for one would not bid for popularity at the expense of the public safety.

The conclusion of his address was admiringly described by a Washington reporter:

> "It is needless for me," said Mr. Hoar, drawing his finger up and looking about the chamber, his eyes pausing when they reached Mr. Allen and Mr. Stewart, "to declare that I sympathize with all my fellows in distress. I sympathize with them a great deal more than some of those who always prate of sympathy for the downtrodden in order to advance their disgraceful political ambitions."
>
> The Senate burst into ringing applause at this utterance . . . Mr. Hoar closed with an impressive declaration that the Senate would stand on its constitutional rights, and it would not be

[24] "A Concerned Citizen" to Hoar, 17 April 1894, Hoar Papers.

frightened into doing what was not best for the country by any mob demonstration, or by declarations, whether they came from the camp of Coxey or the seat of war from Nevada.[25]

Hoar's remarks were the subject of general praise by the eastern press. There were, of course, a few dissenting notes. A young resident of Holyoke, Massachusetts, member of the new Socialist Labor party, criticized Hoar's declaration that "the Government has no right to support the people; the people should support the Government." Wasn't the Government established for the sole purpose of managing the business of the country in the interest of the people? Then let the Government perform its duty.[26]

Morrison Swift reacted in similar fashion, but Swift was a rather special kind of socialist, and one that Hoar could better understand. When Swift finally managed to bring a small Boston delegation to Washington, weeks after the main body of Coxey's army had decamped, Hoar granted them an interview and informed his wife: "They seemed very harmless and had very much the same theories that Mr. Alcott and the Brook Farm people deluded themselves with in my boyhood." Utopianism might well be misguided, but having been baptized in Concord it was not dangerous.[27]

The labor marches and industrial warfare of 1894 caused many easterners to turn against labor unions as well as labor violence. Hoar was tempted to take the same path but resisted. He had little sympathy for Eugene Debs or the Pullman strikers, but rather than renounce his earlier support of labor combination he limited his criticism to the tactics and personal ambition of various union leaders. He also began to entertain vague thoughts of how labor unions might be morally elevated by the inclusion within their ranks of professional men and civic-minded women.

[25] Newspaper clippings, 10 May 1894, Scrap Book #4 (1894), Hoar Papers; *Congressional Record*, 53d Cong., 2d sess., 4570 (10 May 1894).

[26] Adam Ramage to Hoar, 13 May 1894, Hoar Papers.

[27] Hoar to Ruth A. Hoar, 28 May 1894, Hoar Papers. When Swift returned to Boston he held a "mass rally for the unemployed" in Faneuil Hall, and circulated a petition proclaiming that as no member of Congress possessed any understanding of the depression and its causes, all should resign. Copy of petition, "Let Congress Resign!", Hoar Papers.

The Pullman strikers were "misguided and deluded men" who had done mischief to their country and "much greater mischief to themselves." Their violent tactics were fruitless as well as wrong. They struck not only against George Pullman but against the American people, the greatest labor organization of all. It was this organization in the final analysis that must determine "what laws shall regulate labor and capital, the limits of collection and accumulation of property, and how many drones may live in the hive." It was not for a few men in Chicago to settle these questions.[28] .

In Hoar's eyes the Pullman strike exemplified a very real danger: the infection of the American labor movement by foreign doctrines. One way to counter this trend might be to have members of the white-collared class infiltrate the unions. "Let people who will study the question from a humane point join the Unions, making it their business to see justice done, keeping the Unions out of false positions, but throwing all their strength into helping them where they are right." Such infiltrators could, for example, sympathize with the seamstresses of New York in their struggle against the sweating system of the New York City clothiers, while explaining to them that any adjustment of wage scales by means of strike action could only be impermanent. Wages must ultimately be determined "by economic conditions which neither the working women nor their friends can much affect."[29]

It was not easy to remain at one and the same time convinced that the soul of America lay within the noble breast of the working man and the strength of the American economy lay in the growth of the industrial corporation. But Hoar tried very hard. The promise of America was so great, he believed that there was no reason for labor violence or corporate greed; neither could be more than a temporary phenomenon. The American capitalist system was essentially fair and equitable.

Hoar always considered himself a liberal-minded man and in measure he was. It was on moral rather than economic issues,

[28] See copy of Hoar's address at opening of Clark University Summer School, 16 July 1894, Hoar Papers.
[29] Hoar to Mrs. Josephine Shaw Lowell, 10 October 1894, Hoar Papers.

however, that his liberalism was most certain; for it was when he spoke in behalf of moral improvement or against discrimination that he found it most easy to apply the principles of the past to the problems of the present. This was evident at many points during the 1890's, but never more unmistakably than in the battle he waged against the American Protective Association in Massachusetts in the years 1894–1895.

The resurgence of nativist fears and religious bigotry that inspired the growth of the American Protective Association in Massachusetts and other northern states in the early 1890's was not the product of sudden hysteria. Not only can its roots be traced back to the Know-Nothing movement of the 1850's and earlier, but one can see indications in the decades of the 1870's and 1880's of a growing suspicion of the diversity imposed on American society by mass immigration. The self-acknowledged "old stock" and the older and more fundamental Protestant churches felt challenged and threatened by the social changes they attributed to the immigrant, and, especially, to the Catholic immigrant. This growing sense of unease fed old fears about the power of the papacy and Catholic clergy and old suspicions respecting the loyalty of Catholics to the constitutional separation of church and state. In Massachusetts these fears and suspicions were increasingly directed against the growth of parochial schools. The Common School—the glory of Puritan New England—must be defended, and in the process the continued political, economic, and educational leadership of an older America be assured. By the fall of 1888 Hoar was already receiving printed petitions from vaguely organized groups of "true Americans," requesting congressional legislation to protect "our common schools against the aggressions of a religious sect which has of late given palpable evidence of a purpose to war upon them."[30]

These incipient members of the APA movement would from the beginning entertain strong doubts of Hoar's reliability; for Hoar had indicated on several occasions his belief that the true way to promote a "love of New England liberty and New England traditions" among the Irish Catholics of Massachusetts was to praise

[30] Memorial, unsigned, from Brookline, Massachusetts, Pamphlet Box (1888), Hoar Papers.

every sign of its existence. He frequently quoted John Boyle O'Reilly's ode to Plymouth Rock, commended the nonsectarian charity of St. Anthony's Society in Worcester, and compared the heroes of the Irish Home Rule Movement to the patriots of Lexington and Concord.[31] Such expressions brought forth the charge that "Mr. O'Hoar" was pandering to the Irish Catholic vote. He was not. What Hoar wished indeed was not too unlike the desire of his critics. Where they, however, would try to limit the opportunities of those who were not Sons of the Puritans, Hoar would try to transform the Boston Irishman into a Puritan through praise and encouragement. He had no desire to change their religion— that was persecution—but, unconsciously perhaps, he wished them to become Congregational Catholics. Hoar himself disliked parochial education on the ground that it was potentially antagonistic to the desired unity and harmony of the Old Commonwealth, but where he differed from his critics during the A.P.A. fight, as earlier, was in his firm conviction that religious proscription was both tyrannous and self-defeating. It could only make realities of the fears that inspired it; it could only prove false to the traditions it pretended to uphold.[32]

By the fall of 1893 the American Protective Association had begun to assume organizational form. Composed of secret societies, it sought to proscribe the election of Catholics to public office and their employment as teachers in the public schools. To secure those aims it made a concerted effort to gain control of the machinery of the Republican party in Massachusetts and some dozen other states.[33] Hoar was among the first to sense the threat the A.P.A. posed to the principles and reputation of his party, and before another year had past he had reason to be more certain of that threat. Aware of Hoar's lack of sympathy with their aims, the

[31] *See*, for example, Archbishop John Ireland to Hoar, 19 February 1891; Hoar to C. O'Connell Galvin, 29 March 1893, Hoar Papers.

[32] Hoar was also convinced that the increasing strength of secularism in American society dictated ecumenical cooperation, hopefully under Unitarian leadership. *See* Hoar's address, "The Harmony of Christian Faith," to the Unitarian Conference at Saratoga, 25 September 1894, draft, Hoar Papers.

[33] The best study of the A.P.A. as a national movement is Donald L. Kinzer, *An Episode in Anti-Catholicism: The American Protective Association* (Seattle: University of Washington Press, 1964).

A.P.A. faction at a party caucus held in Worcester in September 1894 thought it time to serve warning. Hoar was not granted the accustomed courtesy of election as a district delegate to the state party convention.[34] By December Hoar was informing his one-time ally in the elections bill struggle, John C. Spooner: "We are having a considerable contest with the organization known as 'A.P.A.'s' . . . and shall probably have a great deal more difficulty with them."[35]

Hoar bided his time, however, before making a public denunciation of the A.P.A. If he was awaiting a call to arms by his junior colleague, Henry Cabot Lodge, Massachusetts Governor Frederic T. Greenhalge, or any of the leading Republicans of state or nation, he must have been disappointed. Discreet silence was the almost universal response of these gentlemen. Exaggerating and fearing the retaliatory power of the A.P.A. membership, they evidently hoped that if only the secret order was ignored it might evaporate. After considerable deliberation, Hoar decided that the course of safety and honor demanded that the aims of the A.P.A. be brought into the open and denounced. As Charles Sumner had faced down the Know-Nothings in 1856–1857, so he would now take the lead in persuading his state and party to oppose these latter-day nativists. A letter from an irate Orangeman, the owner-manager of the T. C. Evans Advertising Agency of Boston, gave Hoar the opportunity he sought.

In a speech at Clark University, Hoar had deplored the attempt to revive between men of different faiths the "animosities and feelings of the dark ages." Evans leaped to the attack. In a long and virulent letter he accused Hoar of wishing to see the Protestants adopt the Confessional and rang every change on the old theme of the political enslavement of the Catholic laity to the orders of their priests and pope. A good Romanist could not be a good American, so all Romanists should be excluded from offices of public trust in the schools as in the state.

Hoar's reply was released to the papers in the form of a public letter on 13 August 1895. Despite its length it was reprinted in full

[34] *Taunton Evening Herald,* 22 September 1894; *New York Times,* 1 October 1894. *See,* too, William Claflin to Hoar, 21 September 1894, Hoar Papers.

[35] Hoar to Spooner, 3 December 1894, John Coit Spooner Papers, Library of Congress.

by over a score of papers across the country. It remains the single most eloquent contemporary criticism of the tactics and probable consequences of the A.P.A. hysteria. Its final paragraphs are typical of its argument and language:

> Your method would overthrow the common school system, would overthrow the republican party, and would end by massing together the Catholic voters, as proscription always does mass men together, to increase and strengthen that political power which you profess so much to dread ... The time has come to throw down the walls between Christians ...
>
> The American spirit, the spirit of the age, the spirit of liberty, the spirit of equality, especially what Roger Williams called soul liberty, is able to maintain herself in a fair field and in a free contest against all comers. Do not compel her to fight in a cellar. Do not compel her to breathe the damp malarial atmosphere of dark places. Especially let no member of the republican party, the last child of freedom, lend his aid to such an effort. The atmosphere of the Republic is the air of the mountain top and the sunlight and the open field. Her emblem is the eagle and not the bat.[36]

The reaction to Hoar's letter was immediate and varied. Evans himself found Hoar's letter aggressive and misleading; while an anonymous "Irish-American" informed him that "Our Holy Mother Church does not need heretical protestant apologists." There were other criticisms from other correspondents, but a majority rallied to his support. Indeed, his letter initiated a perceptible counterrevolution to the movement and power of the A.P.A. Such journals as *The Nation, The Independent,* and the *New York Times* applauded Hoar's courage; John Hay forwarded congratulations from Washington; and the champion of the "social gospel," Washington Gladden pronounced the A.P.A. unchristian as well as unpatriotic. Ministerial correspondents were somewhat divided in opinion, but the old Abolitionists stood together. Thomas Wentworth Higginson, Archie Chandler, Edward Atkin-

---

[36] Hoar to T. C. Evans, 5 August 1895, for release, 13 August 1895 (copy), Hoar Papers.

son were united in admiration. Atkinson declared that Hoar's letter almost persuaded him to return to the Republican fold.[37]

Of all the letters Hoar received, none was more buoyant in its praise or prose than that from the President's Office of the Police Department, City of New York:

> My dear Senator Hoar,
>
> I am too busy to get away from here for anything not of the utmost importance; but there is one fight that I esteem more important than that in which I am at present engaged. If I could be of the least assistance to you in your battle with the A.P.A., I will esteem it a favor to have you call upon me. I will write or speak at any time or in any place you think best.
>
> I wish that a few more of our big public men had your pluck in tackling the issue. I suppose I cannot be of any service in the fight, but if I can be I shall esteem it a favor if you will call on me. It is the fight of all others I should care to be in!
>
> Yours sincerely,<br>Theodore Roosevelt[38]

The A.P.A. movement gradually melted away after 1895; its chief consequence, a sharpened social difference between Catholics and non-Catholics in the smaller towns of the East and Middle West. Probably it had little effect either in stimulating or delaying the spread of parochial education. Hoar's role in the decline of the A.P.A. can, of course, be easily exaggerated. His letter to Evans was more a precipitant of that decline than its cause. Nonetheless

---

[37] T. C. Evans to Hoar, 13 August, 29 August 1895; M. C. Russell to T. C. Evans, 31 August 1895; "Irish-American" to Hoar, [?] August 1895; "Friend of Liberty" to Hoar, 13 August 1895, Hoar Papers; *The Nation*, 22 August 1895; *The Independent*, 22 August 1895; *New York Times*, 18 August 1895; John Hay to Hoar, 14 August 1895; G. S. Minot (quoting Washington Gladden) to Hoar, 14 August 1895; T. W. Higginson to Hoar, 18 August 1895; Archie Chandler to Hoar, 17 August 1895; Edward Atkinson to Hoar, 15 August 1895, Hoar Papers. *See*, too, Kinzer, *An Episode in Anti-Catholicism*, 185–189.

[38] Roosevelt to Hoar, 15 August 1895, Special Collection, Hoar Papers. Hoar had earlier applauded Roosevelt's fight against the saloon in New York City to Roosevelt's great delight. Roosevelt to Hoar, 18 July 1895, Hoar Papers; Roosevelt to H. C. Lodge, 20 July 1895, Elting Morison, ed., *Letters of Theodore Roosevelt* (Cambridge: Harvard University Press, 1951), I, 469.

it remains true that no major Republican figure had publicly denounced the A.P.A. prior to that letter. It is similarly easy to exaggerate the singleness of Hoar's purpose. Surely he was concerned with the future as well as the honor of his party. Though little worried about his own political future—he was easily re-elected to the Senate in 1895—he was well aware that for his party to confine its appeal to the more narrowminded Protestant Yankee would spell disaster. It remains true, however, that Hoar's opposition to religious proscription was primarily the result of a sincere commitment to an ideological abstraction. Hoar's battle with the A.P.A must be seen as but one chapter in a life-long concern to support "the eternal principles" of the Declaration of Independence. In his eyes, the words of that document were neither literary gloss nor the propaganda of anxious revolutionaries. They were a safe and proper guide for the legislators of America. Legislative policy was never safer, more truly conservative, than when it adhered to the faith of the Fathers. God *had* created all men free and equal. It was piety not politics that inspired Hoar to oppose discrimination: against the Negro, the Indian, the Chinese immigrant, or the Boston Irishman.[39]

[39] Hoar's scorn for those who would deny the faith was perhaps never better expressed than during his long and unsuccessful battle in the early 1880's to oppose legislation that would prohibit further Chinese immigration to America. In his view, Chinese exclusion represented nothing less than the legalization of racial discrimination, and his opposition was constant if unavailing. He opposed the initial exclusion bill of 1880; denounced the twenty-year suspension law of 1882; voted against the Sino-American Treaty of 1886, which prohibited the immigration of Chinese coolie labor; and, finally, in 1902 was the sole senator to cast his vote against the law continuing the "temporary" suspension of Chinese immigration. When burned in effigy in Nevada in 1882 because of his defense of the Chinese, he declared himself singularly honored.

Though there were China Traders in Boston, there were few if any Chinese voters in Massachusetts and Hoar's stand aroused more criticism than praise. In the 1890's it was sharply criticized both by Boston Brahmins about to form the "Immigration Restriction League" and by the Boston cigarmarkers' union, determined not to suffer the competition of the economical Chinaman. Hoar's consistent opposition to immigration restriction was inspired by principle not politics. And the same might well be said of his more limited efforts in behalf of fair treatment for the American Indian. His plans for "Indian reform" were those of the Anglo-Saxon convinced that the Indian would be happier if transformed into a yeoman-farmer, but they were inspired by the same sense of right and duty that underlay his opposition to Chinese exclusion and Catholic proscription.

George Frisbie Hoar's interest in political and economic reform declined as he grew older; his devotion to certain principles of personal and public morality only grew stronger. Hoar would not personally accept this distinction between institutional and moral reforms, but he unconsciously applied it, and never more than during the years of Cleveland's second administration. It explains why he could concurrently denounce cruelty to animals and revision of the Constitution.

The single most important institutional innovation discussed by the Senate in the 1890's was the proposal for popular election of federal senators. Neither the Senate nor its members could approach the topic with complete objectivity; for implicit in the demand for popular election was the belief that some senators had bought their election from state legislatures and more were guilty of favoring special interests at the expense of the general will. If senators were popularly elected, they would be true representatives of the people and the decline of congressional government would be reversed—or so reasoned the reformers. In their attacks on the membership and methods of the Senate these reformers always excepted Hoar. He refused to return the compliment. There was no senator more ardent in his opposition to a constitutional amendment providing for direct election of federal senators. On the floor of the Senate and then in the pages of the *Forum*, Hoar declared the proposed reform false to wisdom and to history.

To Hoar, those who bemoaned the alleged decline of the Senate were guilty of exaggeration and error. He believed the Senate to be at present a more dignified and industrious body than when first he had come to Washington. As chairman of the Committee on Privileges and Elections he was well aware that there had been in recent years instances of irregularity in the legislative election of

---

For Hoar's defense of the rights of the Chinese *see Congressional Record*, 47th Cong., 1st sess., 1516 (1 March 1882); 49th Cong., 1st sess., 4958–4960, 5109–5110 (26 May 1886, 1 June 1886); 57th Cong., 1st sess., 4252 (16 April 1902); Henry Abrahams, Secretary, Cigarmakers Local Union, Boston, to Hoar, 23 April 1894, Prescott F. Hall (Immigration Restriction League of Boston) to Hoar, 20 August 1894, Hoar Papers; *New York Times*, 11 April, 13 April 1902. For Hoar's interest in fair treatment and educational opportunity for the Indian *see* the *Congressional Record*, 47th Cong., 1st sess., 2454–2463 (31 March 1882); A. J. Standing, Yankton Agency, Dakota, to Hoar, 29 March 1882, Hoar Papers.

federal senators. Just because "a few millionaires clink their money bags about our State legislative halls" was no reason, however, to overthrow the careful constitutional balance arranged by the Philadelphia Convention and institute a pure democracy rather than a government of checks and balances. The charge that the Senate as presently constituted was insufficiently responsive to the popular will was erroneous. The Senate was not responsive to every mad whim or Populist passion, but to the deliberate second thought of the American people it was obedient today as yesterday.

Hoar associated his defense of the Senate with a defense of the party system, but his basic intent was to defend the wisdom of the past against the irritations of the present. Roger Sherman's grandson would not consent to the destruction of the great Connecticut Compromise. The Constitutional Fathers had intended the Senate to represent the states, and to serve as a filter for the popular will. The Senate, like the House, the presidency, and the judiciary, had its particular function. If this proposal were to be adopted, it would be followed in time by the abolition of the electoral college, the popular election of federal judges, and the overthrow of the Constitution. Government by brutal force of numbers would be the end result, and America would witness in the future examples of fraud and corruption greater by far than any she suffered at present.

He was not, he insisted, oblivious to the need of reform in the Senate, but that reform should concern its procedures, not its essential purpose and structure. He would support reforms that would restrict the power of individual senators to obstruct the majority in the exercise of its political duties. He would support reform measures designed to make certain the purity and honesty of senatorial elections. Radical alteration of the tested structure of our political institutions, however, must be prevented. He congratulated his colleagues when they buried the proposed amendment that would attempt such "radical alteration."[40]

Hoar's opposition to the popular election of senators did not reflect a lack of faith in the populace but an overabundance of faith

---

[40] *Congressional Record*, 53d Cong., 1st sess., 97, 101–110 (6 April 1893; 7 April 1893). *See*, too, G. F. Hoar, "Has The Senate Degenerated?" *Forum*, April 1897.

in the wisdom of the institutional compromises of the past. He opposed with equal fervor a movement to change the Massachusetts state constitution and provide for biennial rather than annual elections. The proposal had the support of many of the more conservative members of the business community, on the grounds that it would lend stability to state administration and reduce election holidays. Hoar, serving as vice-president of the Anti-Biennial League, denounced the proposed change. Biennial elections would diminish popular interest and influence in state politics "with many consequent evils." The present system worked well; there was no reason to tamper with it.[41]

Suspicion of institutional change was also reflected in Hoar's opposition to all schemes of proportional representation, but let the reform concern the moral or educational elevation of society and Hoar's response was always sympathetic.[42] Societies formed to oppose lotteries, drunkenness, and cruelty to animals and children found in him a ready memorialist and counselor.

Hoar had always been more prepared to support moral improvement than institutional or economic reform, and by the mid-nineties his interest in the latter was diminished by the rising strength of those he referred to as "the mad Populists." When those same Populists captured the Democratic party—or so he believed—with the nomination of William Jennings Bryan, Hoar reacted by assuming a more conservative stance. The presidential election of 1896 would see many Republican politicians confound Bryan with change and proceed to denounce both.

Hoar did not attend the Republican convention of 1896. He was in Europe at the time, and the leading figure of the Massachusetts delegation at St. Louis was the junior senator, Henry Cabot Lodge. Although Lodge, as Hoar, personally preferred Speaker Tom

---

[41] *See* broadside, "Defend the Constitution!" and Hoar to R. L. Bridgman, 20 April 1896, Hoar Papers.

[42] *See* Stoughton Cooley, Secretary, American Proportional Representation League, to Hoar, 20 January 1894, Hoar Papers. Hoar also rejected the idea of apportioning representation in the Republican national convention in accordance with the party's geographic strength. The southern Republicans often posed a danger to the sound judgment of the convention, but it would be wrong to overthrow arrangements sanctioned by long custom. Hoar to John Manley, 19 March 1894, Hoar Papers.

Reed to McKinley as the Republican nominee, he was more concerned with the platform than the candidate. Hoar's warnings that the platform must pledge the party to work for recoinage of silver by means of international agreement were judged irrelevant by Lodge; the important thing was to persuade Mark Hanna to agree that the monetary plank commit the party to gold. The Massachusetts delegation at least awarded Lodge full credit for anticipating the Democrats' conversion to free silver and emblazoning on the Republican standard the magic word, "gold."[43]

Unlike Lodge, Hoar did not at first appreciate the degree to which the Battle of the Standards would dominate the campaign of 1896. Reluctant to see the Republican party commit itself too rigidly to the gold standard, he initially hoped that the election might center about Democratic responsibility for the Panic of '93 and the dangers of free trade. Upon his return from Europe, however, Hoar was soon caught up in the exaggerations of the campaign, and was before long prepared to admit the political wisdom of specifying the Republican allegiance to the gold standard.[44] It helped to dramatize the differences between the two parties and candidates. One party desired fiscal integrity; the other a dollar that would cheat the wage earner as well as the creditor. Bryan was no better than a Populist, and the Populists had for several years waged "a crazy attempt at revolution and a passionate crusade of dishonor."[45] By election eve Hoar had convinced himself that the election of Bryan would initiate a national disaster. It would mean not only a fifty-cent dollar, but "free trade, panic, unemployment, and the appointment of John P. Altgeld to the Supreme Court."[46] McKinley's election was accordingly judged a victory for political sanity as well as the Republican party.

Hoar, like most of his countrymen, failed to appreciate the full dimensions of the Republican victory of 1896. That victory served, in fact, to confirm the results of the congressional elections of 1894; it revealed that the Republican party, having gained the increasing

[43] *See* E. W. Doherty, Secretary, Senate Judiciary Committee, to Hoar, 2 July 1896, Hoar Papers.

[44] Hoar to Lodge, 7 October 1896, Papers of Henry Cabot Lodge, Massachusetts Historical Society.

[45] *Lowell Daily Courier*, 24 October 1896; George H. Lyman, Chairman, Republican State Committee, to Hoar, 20 August 1896, Hoar Papers.

[46] *Lowell Daily Courier*, 24 October 1896.

allegiance of the urban voter, was once again a party with a clear popular majority.[47] The urban population, reacting against the industrial depression and the narrow agrarian orientation of Bryan's candidacy, had turned to the Republican party in growing numbers. If that party was identified with corporate power—and it was—it was also identified with prosperity, industrial progress, and national authority. In measure that identification was the result of Democratic default, but in equal measure it was the result of the labors and efforts in the eighties of such Half-Breed leaders as George F. Hoar.

Hoar was content in November 1896 to emphasize the victory of the moment and to congratulate the nation on its escape from Bryanism. The Republican allegiance of the millhands of New England was gratefully noted, but he appeared to take greater delight in the return to the fold of certain of the Mugwumps— including his favorite nephew. If Hoar was slow, however, to detect the beginnings of a new era of Republican ascendancy, he was quick to forecast for William McKinley a brilliant administration.

That forecast was based on his confidence that McKinley would inspire prosperity, raise the tariff, and negotiate a permanent monetary agreement among the commercial nations of the world.[48] Hoar had no suspicion that war, diplomacy, and expansion would dominate that administration, or that he would find in McKinley a foe as well as a friend. Possessed of very similar political styles and temperaments, sharing a common allegiance to high tariffs and noble sentiments, Hoar and McKinley would finally stand diametrically opposed in their interpretation of the duty and mission of America.

[47] This point is well made in two brilliant studies: Samuel P. Hays, *The Response to Industrialism, 1885–1914* (Chicago: University of Chicago Press, 1957), 47, 189; Carl N. Degler, "American Political Parties and the Rise of the City: An Interpretation," *Journal of American History,* 51 (June 1964), 41–59 (especially 42–50).

[48] Hoar was delighted when McKinley assured him and Senator William E. Chandler that he considered their bill "looking to an international conference" to be both "timely and wise." The selection of Senator Edward O. Wolcott to tour Europe as an advance man for such a conference was warmly approved. *See* McKinley to Hoar, Chandler, *et al.,* 28 December 1896, Papers of William McKinley, Library of Congress; Moreton Frewen to Hoar, 23 January 1897; Bellamy Storer to Hoar, 6 February 1897, Hoar Papers; William E. Chandler to William C. Whitney, 21 March 1897, Papers of W. E. Chandler, Library of Congress.

# 7

## *Party Unity and a War for Humanity*

From the standpoint of the Republican party the outstanding feature of William McKinley's presidency was his popularity with Republicans. Not since the days of Grant had there been a president in the White House for whom a majority of Republican senators and representatives had much use, and surely their respect for Grant had been spasmodic. Hayes had been despised by many, Garfield by some, and Arthur by more; Harrison had been far from popular, and Cleveland was a political enemy. McKinley with his wet-eyed tact and well-disguised strength of will would quietly but surely gain effective control of presidential patronage and reassert the power and leadership of the executive branch of the federal government. Certainly the recent augmentation of Republican strength and popularity—particularly with the urban voter—furthered the self-confidence of party and administration and so made easier the task of presidential leadership. A party enjoying the euphoria of victory and self-congratulation is less likely to seek the narrower pleasures of factional animosity. It would be a mistake, however, to ignore the role of McKinley in promoting the institutional efficiency of Republican organization and effecting a marked decline of party factionalism.

Republican unity was not unbroken in the McKinley years, but there was far less internecine warfare than at any time since the founding of the party at Ripon, Wisconsin, in 1854. McKinley, in many ways a weak man, was a strong party leader. Party division during his administration centered primarily around questions of policy and not around the rival claims of factional chieftains. There were no Blaines or Conklings in Congress now. In the Senate there was the "Big Three"—Aldrich of Rhode Island, Allison of Iowa, and Platt of Connecticut—but they were generally sympathetic to the policies of the administration, and McKinley in large measure controlled them even while he conciliated them. The leaders of the Senate were more than matched as political tacticians by McKinley and Hanna, and though it has been customary to think of Hanna as the master mind of the administration it is probably more accurate to view him as its executive officer. The relationship of McKinley and Hanna is, in any case, irrelevant to the two developments of the McKinley years under consideration: the revival of executive influence and power in the federal government; the increase of party unity and organizational efficiency among Republicans in Congress.[1] These developments were already apparent before the Cuban crisis reached its climax and war came with its particular stimulation to executive power and party unity. By the end of 1897, it was possible to see in McKinley's shrewd distribution of patronage and the relatively smooth passage of the Dingley Tariff that a new period in the history of the Republican party had begun.

The Massachusetts senators, like many others, anticipated that McKinley would depend on their advice in determining the state's share of presidential appointments. George Frisbie Hoar, aware

---

[1] Professor Rothman has noted the increased strength of party organization and discipline, but appears to attribute "the heightened power of party" to the general post-Civil War tendency toward "centralization" and to the political sophistication of a new breed of senatorial professionals. His analysis of "the increased importance of party government" in the 1890's ignores the degree of factionalism among Republican congressmen in the earlier half of the decade and undervalues the contribution and role of McKinley and Hanna. David J. Rothman, *Politics and Power: The United States Senate, 1869–1901* (Cambridge, Mass.: Harvard University Press, 1966), 71–72; 187–188.

of McKinley's frequent professions of respect and affection, was confident that this affection and Lodge's services at the St. Louis convention would guarantee their influence. His confidence was unwarranted. The "Massachusetts place" in McKinley's cabinet went not to T. Jefferson Coolidge, whom Lodge and Hoar had both wished to see appointed to the Treasury, but to John Davis Long, as Secretary of the Navy. McKinley's political skill was never more evident than when he convinced Lodge and Hoar that he cherished their advice and support, while appointing to his cabinet a Massachusetts man neither favored. Hoar was conciliated by a warm and lengthy handclasp; Lodge, with the appointment of his Harvard classmate, Theodore Roosevelt as Long's assistant.[2]

Hoar was soon being asked by McKinley to help select the new Librarian of Congress and to have a talk with Senator Foraker of Ohio and discover the latter's objections to the appointment of young Bellamy Storer as first assistant to the Secretary of State.[3] The way McKinley kept calling senators to the White House like so many messenger boys was admittedly disconcerting, but so humble and sincere was he when they arrived that it was impossible to view him as an enemy of senatorial prerogative. Hoar had no sympathy with those scandal mongers who accused McKinley of appointing John Sherman Secretary of State just so there would be

[2] A concerted but unsuccessful effort had been made in behalf of Coolidge. *See* Stephen M. Weld to Hoar, 18 January 1897 (telegram), Hoar Papers. *See*, too, Hoar and Lodge to McKinley, 8 March 1897, Papers of William McKinley, Series 3, Library of Congress. Although previously he had never fully trusted Long—who had opposed him in the senatorial election of 1883—Hoar, unlike Lodge, would warmly praise Long's performance as Secretary of the Navy. And Long, his senatorial ambitions currently deflected, found Hoar a charming companion. He wrote in his journal, January 11, 1898:

> Senator Hoar called upon me. He is a delightful man. His mind is stored with learning, especially on the lines of historical and biographical literature. He has the highest sense of public duty, most chivalrous and unflinching courage of his convictions, and deservedly possesses the confidence of all with whom he is associated and of the people whom he represents . . . He is inclined to be extravagant in his likings . . . which, of course, is a good fault.

Lawrence Shaw Mayo, ed., *America of Yesterday: As Reflected in the Journal of John Davis Long* (Boston: Little, Brown, 1923), 148–150.

[3] *See* Hoar to McKinley, 23 March 1897; Hoar to Bellamy Storer, 23 March 1897, Hoar Papers.

a vacancy to match the senatorial ambitions of Mark Hanna. Hoar had been a bit surprised by the selection of his aging kinsman, but Sherman assured him that his appointment had been inspired by merit alone, and Hoar was quick to denounce any press reports to the contrary. How vicious were those papers that emphasized Mr. Sherman's "little failures of memory as to names and unimportant transactions."[4] Hoar would not pretend that Hanna's appointment to the Senate served in any sense to elevate its cultural level, which he thought was declining every year—now one felt forced to translate not only Greek epigrams but Latin as well—but he was soon ready to admit that "the business of the Senate" moved more efficiently than during preceding administrations.[5] He could not escape the feeling that at times Hanna was guilty of a "town constable style of performance" in his attitude toward political appointments, and was not always respectful of the dignity of his fellow senators, but there could be no doubt that he served most effectively in supporting Nelson Aldrich and guiding the Dingley Tariff bill to victory.

The Dingley Tariff was passed in record time, largely because Aldrich, with the aid of Allison and Hanna, persuaded the Republican caucus to commit itself in advance to the decisions of a subcommittee of the Senate Finance Committee. If this pledge did not obviate antagonism between the conflicting sectional and economic interests of the Republican majority, it did abbreviate it.

Hoar and Lodge both loyally supported the agreement throughout, although displeased with the level of the duty on wool and the increased duty on hides. Hoar saw that in the case of a recorded vote on either item, it would be "a little annoying to us . . . to be compelled to stand by the engagement of the Caucus to vote with the Committee," but he believed that it would not be too difficult to make "an explanation to our people at home."[6] In anticipation of

---

[4] *See* report of Hoar's speech to meeting of the Massachusetts Club at Providence, Rhode Island, *Springfield Daily Republican* 13 August 1897. Also, John Sherman to Hoar, 16 August 1897, Hoar Papers.

[5] When Hanna was elected by the Ohio legislature to a full term in January 1898, Hoar's note of congratulation was cordial if delayed. Hoar to Hanna, 18 January 1898 (copy), Hoar Papers.

[6] Hoar to Lodge, 18 June 1897, Hoar Papers.

such an explanation, Hoar wrote a long letter to T. Jefferson Coolidge, who was undoubtedly expected to disseminate its argument:

> I think our New England manufacturers ought to understand that they will get no protection whatever as a permanent policy without a large duty on wool. The political power of this country is controlled by States that do not manufacture woolens and are not likely to for a long time to come, if ever. Right or wrong, you will not get their votes for protection unless they believe their people have some direct benefit from it. The result [of their alienation] will be not merely to overthrow the protective policy. It will be to separate them from us in matters that relate to sound money, to wise political administration, to honesty in the collection of debts, and other like matters. We can act together for a good while to come . . . while the protective policy is the issue. But if we give that up, I think we have a political chaos before us. It is for this reason that I have taken pains to emphasize . . . my willingness to let the wool-growing states determine . . . the duty upon wool.[7]

Hoar did not allow his concern for sectional compromise to prevent him from calling for greater attention to the boot and shoe industry of Massachusetts or higher protection for New England granite, but he made his pleas and protests only at informal sessions of the Republican caucus in the Senate lobby or its extension, the Arlington Hotel.

In the Senate debate over the Dingley Tariff not only was there a greater degree of regimented unity than in earlier tariff debates, but perhaps, too, a greater degree of honesty. Aldrich did not conceal his desire to pass a tariff that would afford ample protection for raw materials and still higher and compensatory protection for most every American manufacture. Hoar believed this approach would prove equally salutary to Republican unity and industrial prosperity. He scoffed at the claims of his gadfly correspondent, Edward Atkinson, that McKinley owed his victory to the Gold Democrats and that in consequence the Republicans

[7] Hoar to Coolidge, 15 May 1897, Hoar Papers.

owed the latter a revenue tariff. The Republicans owed the Gold Democrats nothing. They owed the industrialist, the workingman, and the cause of political consistency a tariff that in its sufficiency and equity would stand as the permanent capstone of the long history of Republican protectionism.[8]

Although he was absent when the final vote was taken on the Dingley Tariff, Hoar was paired in its favor and was on the whole highly pleased. He was relieved that it avoided any mention of commercial reciprocity with Canada and was convinced that he and Lodge had done wisely to follow the lead of Aldrich and his subcommittee.[9] Deciding that the best defense of the high duty on hides was a bold front, he called a reporter of the Worcester *Spy* to his home but a few days after the passage of the conference version and arranged an interview. He explained to the *Spy* and so to Massachusetts the agreement of the Republican caucus and its necessity. That agreement had required his acceptance of the regrettable duty on hides. The alternative would have been indefinite delay and delay would have been harmful to all business interests. No one valued the Massachusetts boot and shoe industry more than he, but its managers and workingmen must remember that with all America they would suffer if the business depression were allowed to continue under the auspices of the shameful Wilson tariff.[10]

Despite his confident words, Hoar worried over the possible political effects of the new tariff for the shoe towns of Massachusetts and the congressional elections of 1898. He did not foresee that those elections would be dominated not by the accustomed issues of tariffs and silver, but by the excitements and consequences of martial adventure.

George Frisbie Hoar, in company with most Americans, had given relatively little thought to international relations prior to McKinley's administration. As was true of most Half-Breed Re-

---

[8] Hoar to Atkinson, 19 April, 6 May 1897, Papers of Edward Atkinson, Massachusetts Historical Society. *See*, too, Atkinson to Hoar, 13 March, 1 May 1897, Hoar Papers.

[9] *See* Lodge to Hoar, 8 July, 10 July 1897, Hoar Papers.

[10] Worcester *Spy*, 27 July 1897, Scrap Book, VI (1897), Hoar Papers.

publicans, he had made a definite if artificial distinction between foreign commerce and foreign affairs. He favored the increasing exportation of American goods and capital, and was anxious for the reputation of America in foreign eyes, but before 1898 Hoar and his party were primarily interested in domestic developments. Excepting the question of the North Atlantic fisheries, few of his major speeches in the Senate had concerned American diplomacy. When he spoke of the progress of America it was primarily in reference to the expansion of the domestic economy; when he referred to the mission of America it was in terms of the need to maintain the strength and purity of her domestic institutions. Quick to proclaim the glory of the soldiers of Bunker Hill and the settlers of the Ohio Country, he anticipated neither war nor territorial expansion in the nation's future.

He had had no sympathy with Grant's rather quixotic expansionist designs in the 1870's and was by no means wholeheartedly admiring of the diplomacy of James G. Blaine when that gentleman strove to haul American diplomacy from the doldrums in the Harrison administration. Hoar's distaste, however, was primarily for 'Blaine's methods, and those methods he excused on the partisan ground that they were necessitated by the damage done America's reputation abroad by the "pusillanimous Cleveland administration." He assured his correspondents that in Latin America Blaine only wished "reciprocity and not war."[11] Hoar's dislike of jingoism was sincere and reasonably constant, but it was diminished at times by a reluctance to believe badly of the nation's official representatives and by a reluctance to see the Senate interfere with the prerogative of the executive in the formulation of foreign policy.[12] This was more evident when that executive was a

[11] Hoar was fully sympathetic with the desires of Blaine and American exporters to enlarge our Latin American markets, and he applauded the establishment of the Bureau of American Republics. Hoar to Edward L. Pierce, 2 January 1892; Hoar to Dean N. S. Shaler, 15 April 1892, Hoar Papers.

[12] Robert L. Beisner, in a recent and brilliant book, *Twelve Against Empire: The Anti-Imperialists, 1898–1900* (New York: McGraw-Hill, 1968), 145–146, exaggerates the distinction between Hoar's foreign policy attitudes in the early and later 1890's. Hoar's "chauvinism of the early nineties" was both infrequent and rhetorical, and his public support of Blaine's Samoan policy displayed greater evidence of loyalty than conviction.

Republican, but his limited endorsement of Cleveland's Venezuela policy offers the best example of Hoar's somewhat contradictory desires to see American diplomacy eternally just and always successful.

When Cleveland and his Secretary of State, Richard Olney determined in 1895 to thwart the presumed designs of Britain on Venezuela by projecting into the dispute our own surveyors and national honor, Hoar had deplored the "rude behavior and diplomacy of the hippopotamus in the White House," but his public criticisms were chiefly reserved for those fearful Americans who were undermining the nation's dignity as well as its diplomats. We should not have threatened Britain but everyone must agree— "with the exception of persons like Godkin, who could hardly be said to belong to the United States"—that we should "not permit a feeble American Republic to be crowded out of its rights, or territory, by any European power."[13] Hoar was equally desirous that the Monroe Doctrine be upheld and that war be avoided. His general counsel was to be firm but to go slowly and allow delay to moderate national animosities.[14]

Hoar's support of the diplomatic prerogatives of the executive was not, of course, without exception in the Cleveland years, as

[13] Hoar to T. Jefferson Coolidge, 31 December 1895, Hoar Papers; Hoar to William Claflin, 21 January 1896, Claflin Papers, Rutherford B. Hayes Library. To Claflin he wrote:

> It is certainly unwise . . . to embarrass an important diplomatic negotiation with violent and frantic criticism upon our own Executive when he is in the midst of it . . . I should have much preferred that Congress should have acted rather slowly on Cleveland's message. But I think, after a consideration of two or three weeks, they should have given him the Commission [of surveyors] he asked . . . There I would have stopped until the Commission reported . . . If I speak at all, I shall make a quiet business-like speech, the object of which will be to remove the whole matter from the domain of excitement, and get it where the opinion of the business men and the religious and peaceable and friendly people of the two countries will have its just weight, and tend to get the question settled.

*See,* too, Hoar to Edwin D. Mead, editor of the *New England Magazine,* 30 January 1896, Hoar Papers.

[14] Hoar's position was the object of criticism from Anglophiles, Mugwumps, and Theodore Roosevelt. *See* Hoar to Peter H. Walsh, 28 August 1897 (copy), Hoar Papers; Roosevelt to Lodge, 13 March 1896, Lodge Papers, Massachusetts Historical Society.

Cleveland noted with considerable bitterness during the debate over the Anglo-American Arbitration Treaty of 1897. Hoar's rather pettish conduct respecting the treaty is difficult to understand or excuse. An early advocate of international arbitration, Hoar acted to delay and confound the treaty, and though he voted in its behalf he must share the responsibility for its defeat. It would appear that he desired the establishment of arbitral procedures between England and America, but was fearful lest the freedom of the Senate be restricted and eager that the treaty be given a Republican stamp.[15] So he voted for amendments and helped assure the treaty's defeat—a defeat that sorrowed and surprised him. Later he would try to remedy matters by cooperating with the British minister to Washington in fashioning a draft for a new and weaker treaty, but the McKinley administration proved uninterested.[16] Hoar comforted himself with the thought that international good will was in any case based not upon treaties but the confidence of nations in the honorable intentions of one another.

International good will and national honor provided the chief themes of Hoar's efforts in the years 1896–1898 to persuade the more bellicose members of the Senate not to take the country to war over Cuba and then to assure that a "war for humanity" be preserved from the taint of imperialism. Before describing those efforts, however, it is necessary to evaluate Hoar's approval of the annexation of Hawaii. For here was a vote that—on the surface— appears to cast doubt upon both his posture as an anti-imperialist and the strength of his opposition to the Cuban jingoes. Can Hoar be considered a true enemy of geographic expansion or diplomatic aggression if he failed to oppose the annexation of Hawaii?

[15] Hoar associated criticism of delay with criticism of the motives of Senate Republicans, and in defense of the latter he denounced all attempts to "drive" the Senate into a quick endorsement. *See* Hoar to Charles Eliot, 20 January 1897, Hoar Papers. Also, *Congressional Record,* 54th Cong., 2d sess., 1045 (22 January 1897); Hoar to the Reverend Joseph A. Allen, 21 January 1897; Hoar to Benjamin Trueblood, Secretary, American Peace Society, 29 January 1897; Hoar to the Reverend Endicott Peabody, 4 February 1897; Hoar to Stephen Chase, 17 February 1897; Hoar to Edward Atkinson, 11 March 1897, Hoar Papers.

[16] Sir Julian Pauncefote to Hoar, 11 May, 4 June 1897, Hoar Papers.

When early in 1893 Sanford B. Dole and other American residents in Hawaii had engineered a revolt against the native monarchy of Queen Liliuokalani and applied to Washington for annexation, Hoar had expressed neither eagerness nor distaste at the prospective acquisition. He did not view Hawaiian annexation as a dangerous diplomatic departure, but when the expiring Harrison administration submitted an annexation treaty to the Senate in February 1893 Hoar recommended caution. He was aware, he declared, that there was a special connection of long standing between the United States and the Hawaiian Islands. The Senate, however, should carefully investigate the circumstances of the recent revolution in Honolulu before confirming the treaty. There had been charges that American agents had conspired to assist the insurgents, and those charges, though most probably false, should be fully disproved.

The return of Cleveland made certain that the treaty of 1893 would not suffer precipitate action. Cleveland withdrew the pact from the Senate, and prepared to investigate the provincial government in Honolulu and its origins. Hoar, with an inconsistency typical of partisan politics, denounced Cleveland's actions as discourteous to the Senate and highly improper. He was not unhappy, however, that the annexation of Hawaii had been postponed, nor was he pleased when, with the inauguration of McKinley, certain Republicans began to urge that Washington negotiate a new annexation treaty with the Hawaiian Provisional Government. Hawaiian annexation was not to be associated with an expansionist conspiracy, but Hoar was far from certain that it represented an immediate necessity. The treaty of 1897 never came to a vote in the Senate, but Hoar was informally recorded as among those "opposed." In November of that year, he informed Moorfield Storey: "I do not think it likely that either . . . [Senator Justin] Morrill or I will support the treaty for the annexation of Hawaii . . . I have never been able to see that our security in case of a war with a great naval power would be increased by a fortress three thousand miles off.[17]

[17] Hoar to Storey, 24 November 1897, Hoar Papers.

Hoar's opposition to Pacific expansion was an open secret in Washington. It inspired McKinley's excitable Assistant Secretary of the Navy to share with Captain Alfred Mahan his disgust with "men of by-gone age":

> It seems incredible that such shortsighted folly should obtain among our public men . . . I feel so deeply about it I hardly dare express myself in full. The terrible part is to see that it is the men of education who take the lead in trying to make us prove traitor to our race . . .
>
> It is bitter . . . but, as you say, it is due to the men of a by-gone age having to deal with the facts of the present, complicated in this case with the further fact that we have in America among our educated men a kind of belated survivor of the little English movement among the Englishmen of thirty years back. They are provincials, and like all provincials, keep step with the previous generation of the metropolis.[18]

Seven months later, Roosevelt would congratulate Senator Henry Cabot Lodge upon his success in converting one "provincial," and Moorfield Storey would denounce Hoar as an administration puppet who talked one way only to vote the other. For in July 1898 Hoar would cast his vote in favor of the joint congressional resolution that annexed the Hawaiian islands to the United States. It was the vote of neither a convert nor a puppet of William McKinley.

McKinley was equally determined to acquire Hawaii and to prevent its acquisition from jarring the new-found harmony of the Republican party. He shrewdly withdrew the annexation treaty of 1897 and then two months after the commencement of the Spanish-American War, with his countrymen newly absorbed in discussions of naval warfare and national defense, requested the immediate annexation of the Hawaiian islands by joint congressional resolution. If McKinley thought that the existence of a state

[18] Theodore Roosevelt to Alfred Thayer Mahan, 9 December, 11 December, 13 December 1897, Elting Morison, ed., *The Letters of Theodore Roosevelt* (Cambridge, Mass.: Harvard University Press, 1951), I, 725, 741.

of war would obviate all dissension in the Senate, he was mistaken, but his timing on this occasion as so often was excellent. On 7 July 1898 he had the satisfaction of signing the joint resolution. Two days earlier he had enjoyed the lesser satisfaction of receiving the endorsement of Senator Hoar.

McKinley had twice called Hoar to the White House to plead for that endorsement, but Hoar had refused to commit himself. Until he rose to address the Senate on the morning of 5 July no one had been certain of Hoar's vote; indeed, he had finally decided to support the resolution only three days earlier. His address reflected his indecision. It was the speech of a man attempting to reconcile his loyalties and his fears. He sought to warn the administration against the evil path of imperialism while accepting what some saw as the first step along that path.

Hoar's argument ran along three main lines: (1) Hawaii was a special case due to the suspected ambitions of Japan and the needs of national defense; (2) Hawaii was a special case because of its long-standing connection with the United States, the gradual extinction of its native population, and the known desire of the Provisional Government to be annexed to this country; (3) as the acquisition of Hawaii would be the result of special needs and circumstances it did not represent a departure from our traditional antipathy for colonialism nor offer justification for such a departure. Two passages of this long speech best illustrate the anxiety and ambiguity of its argument:

> There are two dreams of empire, two conceptions of destiny presented to the gaze of the American people to-day. One is held out to us in the Far East and in the West Indies as the result of military conquest; the other is held out to us in Hawaii by the children of the Puritans . . . The first is that which has been the ruin of the empires and republics of former times . . . [It] is forbidden to us by our Constitution, by our political principles, by every lesson of our own history and of all history . . . The second . . . is the invitation to willing and capable people to share with us our freedom, our self-government, our equality.

If this be the first step in the acquisition of dominion over bar-
barous archipelagoes in distant seas; if we are to enter into
competition with the great powers of Europe in the plundering
of China, in the division of Africa . . . if our commerce is hereafter to be forced upon unwilling peoples at the cannon's
mouth; if we are ourselves to be governed in part by peoples
to whom the Declaration of Independence is a stranger; or
worse still, if we are to govern subject and vassal states . . . then
let us resist this thing in the beginning, and let us resist it to
the death . . . But, Mr. President, I am satisfied after hearing
and weighing all arguments and much meditating on this
thing, that all this is needless alarm.[19]

Hoar's vote would provide ammunition then and later for those
who believed that his partisanship was stronger than his principles.
Some of the more bitter of his critics declared Hoar an arrant
hypocrite. Theirs was a false judgment. Whatever the subconscious
inspirations for Hoar's decision might have been, that decision was
the product of conviction. He was anxious to convince himself that
to approve the Hawaiian resolution implied no support of colonial
expansion and he succeeded.[20] In retrospect his vote was an error

[19] *Congressional Record*, 55th Cong., 2d sess., 6660–6665 (5 July 1898). Winslow
Warren, Mugwump reformer and Bostonian, wrote Hoar: "I was much interested
in your speech on the Hawaiian question & agreed with you entirely *except* as to the
conclusion. I trust that you may be right that the door has not now been opened to
so-called imperialism but if it has not the hopes of most of those who voted for
annexation will be disappointed." Warren to Hoar, 7 July 1898, Hoar Papers.

[20] That success was, if honestly obtained, not easily gained. In a later letter to
Senator Justin Morrill, a confirmed opponent of territorial expansion, Hoar would
indicate this fact as he sought his friend's understanding:

While, as you know, after great and anxious consideration and, as I am sure,
without any desire except to find what was for the public interest, I thought that
the principles upon which you and I are so thoroughly agreed did not require
me to oppose the admission of Hawaii, and while I thought that as a matter of
sound policy the great contest between imperialism and the doctrine of George
Washington ought to be fought on a wider battlefield where the enemy had no
advantage of position, yet I thoroughly agree with you in principle.

Hoar to Morrill, 26 September 1898, Papers of Justin S. Morrill, vol. 49, Library
of Congress.

—surely it would restrict his later influence with the anti-imperialist movement—but it was an error made in the certainty of his own rectitude. Hoar's subsequent opposition to McKinley's Philippines policy was not an act of penance for his Hawaiian vote.[21] He always sharply distinguished between the acquisition of Hawaii and the Philippines. American imperialism was not initiated by Hawaiian annexation, he insisted, but was the result of a tragic perversion of our just if unfortunate war with Spain. He had voted for that war, but only after repeated efforts to reprove the jingoes and promote a peaceful settlement of the Cuban insurrection.

Rebellion broke out in Cuba in February 1895. By the end of that year several members of Congress were already agitating in behalf of the insurgents and in opposition to the colonial policy of Spain. Hoar consistently opposed their clamor over the next two years. The American Congress was not a "loaded cannon which any single member can touch off at his discretion." All must sympathize with the Cubans in their struggle against "the oppression of Spanish rule," but international law and our own self-interest gave warning against precipitate recognition of the belligerency or independence of the rebels and surely against armed intervention in their behalf. America's prime duty was not to the Cubans but to her own reputation as a peace-loving nation seeking to treat fairly all friendly powers. Every American should applaud the efforts of the executive to use his good offices to secure home rule for the oppressed Cubans, but our relations with the Cuban rebels must be based on facts and not rumor; our policy must reflect our true and permanent interests and not the excitements of the moment.[22]

As late as December 1897 Hoar expressed confidence that the danger of American intervention was lessening. He asked T. Jefferson Coolidge to see his fellow financiers of Boston and tell them

[21] Hoar was prepared, however, to do penance to Queen Liliuokalani. Having called her at one point a "barbarian Queen," he subsequently publicly apologized when he learned of her Christian allegiance. He sought on several occasions to obtain a congressional annuity for the exiled queen. *See* Liliuokalani to Hoar, 9 March 1900, 18 February 1904; Hoar to Liliuokalani, 16 February 1904 (copy), Hoar Papers.

[22] *Congressional Record*, 54th Cong., 1st sess., 815, 2683–2684 (21 January 1896, 11 March 1896); 54th Cong., 2d sess., 2228–2233, 2237–2239 (25 February 1897); 55th Cong., 1st sess., 1136–1137, 1139–1140 (18 May 1897).

that the President was anxious that "benevolent persons" contribute to a fund for the relief of starving Cubans. Such a fund would serve a purpose diplomatic as well as charitable: "It will, in his opinion and in mine, have a great influence in enabling him to carry through his policy in dealing with Spain and Cuba, and in keeping this country out of war."[23] Coolidge and other Boston capitalists opposed a war with Spain, and Hoar was pleased to see that Speaker Tom Reed was standing firm against war sentiment in the House.

With the sinking of the American battleship *Maine* in Havana Harbor in February 1898, Hoar's confident predictions of a peaceful settlement ceased. He became increasingly less patient with the "foolish and obstinate" Spanish, half-heartedly negotiating with our minister, Stewart Woodford, in Madrid. Hoar continued to oppose hasty action and to warn Congress not to disturb the pacific labors of the President, but he was ready now to emphasize the evil conduct of Spain. The Spanish were responsible for sinking the *Maine*, whether the explosion was from within or without. We should demand an indemnity, perhaps seeking the good offices of some friendly power such as England to help determine the degree of Spanish complicity.[24] With the beginning of April, Hoar's hopes for the achievement of Cuban home rule through diplomatic negotiation had eroded still further. He was prepared to support military intervention if the President was convinced that there was no other way to achieve Cuban peace and liberty. War would unsettle business; it might excite the cupidity of those who wished for America a colonial empire; it might bring in its train a new wave of corruption and scandal such as had followed the Civil War, but if McKinley was convinced that justice dictated the use of American arms Hoar was prepared to follow.[25] Peace was not to be maintained at the cost of honor.

[23] Hoar to Coolidge, 28 December 1897, Hoar Papers.

[24] Hoar to Henry Marsh, 9 April 1898, Hoar Papers.

[25] As late as mid-April 1898 Hoar was the recipient of scores of letters from Boston merchants and bankers, as well as Unitarian ministers and women's rights leaders, opposing a war with Spain and urging the "wise and courageous course of negotiation." *See*, for example, George C. Houghton to Hoar, 2 April 1898; Rockwood Hoar to Hoar, 6 April 1898; H. G. Curtis to Hoar, 14 April 1898; Rufus F. Greeley to Hoar, 14 April 1898, Hoar Papers.

On 11 April 1898, McKinley sent a special message to Congress asking that body to "empower the President to take measures to secure a full and final termination of hostility" in Cuba, to establish a stable government there, and "to use the military and naval forces of the United States as may be necessary for these purposes."[26] Hoar's reaction was one of disappointment and resignation, as he explained the following day in a letter to his old friend, William Claflin:

> I have done everything I could to promote peaceful policies. I know and dread the horrors of war, of which the loss of life and health to soldiers and sailors is by no means the larger part. The corruption which always follows a war, the piling up an enormous debt, the making other wars easier . . . I had hoped and expected that the mission of this country would be to be the great Peacemaker among nations, both by example and influence. But we cannot look idly on while . . . innocent human beings, women and children and old men, die of hunger close to our doors. If there is ever to be a war it should be to prevent such things as that. The demoralization which comes to a people from preventing such things cannot be greater than that which comes to them from permitting them.[27]

Hoar was under no illusion that the congressional authorization requested by the President was not in effect a war declaration. He informed his Senate colleagues that he was prepared to vote for the resolution although aware that it "leads to war . . . no doubt about it." Regretting that the President's wise restraint and sincere efforts had failed to bring peace and justice to Cuba, he would vote for war in the certain knowledge that America's motives were

[26] Although it is probable that McKinley had made up his mind some two weeks earlier to assume the leadership of the war hawks and give the American people the war for which they appeared psychologically prepared, it is not true that McKinley asked for a declaration of war in full knowledge that Spain had already capitulated to all American diplomatic demands. Ernest R. May has proven conclusively that by 11 April Spanish capitulation was but partial and her concessions qualified. *See* Ernest R. May, *Imperial Democracy: The Emergence of America As a Great Power* (New York: Harcourt, Brace and World, 1961), 148–177.

[27] Hoar to William Claflin, 12 April 1898, Claflin Papers, Rutherford B. Hayes Library.

pure and honorable. This would be a war "in which there does not enter the slightest thought or desire of foreign conquest or of national gain or advantage . . . It is entered into for the single and sole reason that three or four thousand human beings, within 90 miles of our shores, have been subjected to the policy intended, or at any rate having the effect, deliberately to starve them to death." Intervention to stop horrors of this kind had the sanction of international law as well as the cause of humanity.[28]

Hoar was quick to support and praise the Teller Resolution, which disclaimed any intention of the United States to acquire the island of Cuba. That resolution, he believed, stood as a witness to the purity of the motives of Congress, as well as a warning to some of its more expansionist members, and on 19 April he voted with a clear conscience for the joint congressional declaration initiating the Spanish-American War.[29]

Congress formally baptized the war on the twenty-fifth of April, and Hoar—though absenting himself from the vote—declared that all division respecting its necessity should now cease. As a senator he gave an automatic affirmative to all appropriation bills and as a friend of the administration he felt at liberty to make recommendations to Secretary Russell A. Alger and the War Department. He recommended for active service Battery A, First Massachusetts Artillery—"made up of some of our best young men, from all classes in the community, including Harvard athletes"—and offered frequent suggestions respecting the care and health of "our

[28] *Congressional Record,* 55th Cong., 2d sess., 3832–3835 (14 April 1898). Hoar was undoubtedly much influenced by Senator Redfield Proctor's vivid description of the misery existent in the Cuban *reconcentrados,* which he had noted in a fleeting trip to Cuba. Hoar wrote some time later: "I suppose [Proctor's] picture of the misery and starvation . . . was in the main true, and that it was that picture which brought about the war. Certainly it was what led me to give my consent in the end to the declaration." Hoar to Edward Atkinson, 2 September 1898, Papers of Edward Atkinson, Massachusetts Historical Society.

[29] During the debate over the joint congressional declaration, Hoar strongly opposed any effort to force McKinley to grant formal recognition to the insurgent "government" in Cuba. Such recognition, he felt, would restrict the proper freedom of the executive and of the armed forces in their subsequent dealings with the Cubans and found no factual justification in the existing political turmoil in Cuba. In the Senate an amendment to grant recognition to the Republic of Cuba was attached to the "war declaration," but it was deleted by the House. On this point Hoar and Lodge stood opposed, to the worry of certain Republican papers in Massachusetts. *See* the *Fall River Evening News,* 18 April 1898.

boys in Cuba."[30] Fearful that a long war would serve to stimulate the martial fervor of his countrymen and the expansionist ambitions of his colleagues, he cheered the failure of Spanish arms and the rapidity of the war's progress.

The very fears that Hoar entertained about the possible consequences of martial victory he was prepared to denounce when expressed by others. Under the psychological necessity of acting righteously in his own sight, Hoar was often most bitter with those who, inspired by the same principles, declared themselves at a different time or in a different way. When his classmate Charles Eliot Norton criticized the Spanish-American War as unnecessary and liable to lead to disastrous consequences for the liberties and institutions of America, Hoar publicly denounced him as though determined to quiet his own fears by the fury of his assault. The senior Harvard professor was a bad influence on the youth of the nation, undermining its patriotism and loyalty. Norton could understand neither his countrymen nor their instinctive sense of honor; his was "the doctrine of arrogance, of contempt, of pessimism, of bitterness, of despair." Let the cloistered professor learn from Worcester's own Clara Barton that the guiding motive of this war was humanity, not ambition, and the inspiration of our young soldiers, the call of duty.[31]

Hoar was cruel in his treatment of Norton but not demagogic.[32] What he sought was not popularity but personal reassurance. His

[30] Adelbert Ames to Hoar, 16 June 1898; "Association of Naval Veterans, Boston" to Hoar, 30 June 1898; Hoar to Attorney General H. C. Corbin, 25 July 1898; Hoar to Surgeon General, U.S. Army, 13 September 1898, Hoar Papers; Hoar to McKinley, 8 September 1898; George B. Cortelyou to Hoar, 12 September 1898; J. A. Porter to Hoar, 19 September 1898, Papers of William McKinley, Library of Congress.

[31] *Worcester Evening Gazette,* 13 July, 18 July, 25 July 1898; C. E. Norton to Hoar, 15 July 1898; Hoar to C. E. Norton, 18 July 1898 (copy), Hoar Papers. *See,* too, Hoar to Jessie L. Gladwin, 11 August 1898, Scrap Book VI (1897–1898), Hoar Papers; Hoar to Edward Atkinson, 16 August 1898, Papers of Edward Atkinson, Massachusetts Historical Society.

[32] To *The Nation,* and particularly E. L. Godkin, Hoar was both demagogic and unprincipled. *The Nation* declared that Hoar's convictions were always subordinated to "the requirement of voting straight" and Godkin informed Norton that it was an honor to be attacked by Hoar who was an "incompetent unprincipled old rascal . . . [and] utterly unscrupulous." *The Nation,* 4 August 1898; E. L. Godkin to C. E. Norton, 4 August 1898, Norton Papers, Houghton Library, Harvard.

vote in favor of war had been right; America fought for no other desire than to do her duty by the Cuban people. There was no possibility that we would dilute the justice of our cause by seeking territorial aggrandizement. He was certain, but not wholly convinced. A month before his denunciation of Norton he had felt obliged to take the opportunity of a commencement address at Bryn Mawr College to remind his countrymen that their flag must never serve as a symbol of domination: "Let it never fly in times of peace over conquered islands or vassal states. It is the emblem of Freedom, of Self-government, of Law."[33] Surely William McKinley would never seek territorial conquest, but certain of his supporters might. Hoar had reluctantly to agree with one of his English correspondents that "America's time of temptation will come after victory."[34]

By the end of July with victory in sight and the time of temptation drawing nearer, he judged it necessary to offer more specific warning. On the occasion of a meeting of the Massachusetts Club, an organization of Republican businessmen, he urged the re-election of Henry Cabot Lodge and then denounced certain carefully hypothetical figures who would advise America to implant its flag permanently in the western Pacific.[35] The dichotomy of his speech foreshadowed the efforts and frustrations of one who over the next three years would contest the aims of an expansionist administration while proclaiming a loyal allegiance to party.

In the weeks following the armistice agreement Hoar tried to ignore all signs that President McKinley was preparing to send to Paris a peace commission composed of men sympathetic to expansion and to instruct those commissioners to obtain Pacific bases as well as Cuban independence. In his self-deception he received McKinley's full cooperation. Like Hoar, McKinley had every in-

[33] G. F. Hoar, "Influence of Educated American Women," the *American Friend*, 9 June 1898.

[34] Hoar to H. Y. J. Taylor, 28 June 1898, Hoar Papers. *See*, too, Associate Justice David J. Brewer to Hoar, 13 August 1898, Hoar Papers.

[35] The meeting was held at Marblehead Neck, 29 July 1898. Scrap Book, VI (1897–1898), Hoar Papers. To a former colleague, Hoar expressed his fears more bluntly. He wrote W. E. Chandler: "I am willing to risk much for liberty . . . but I am willing to risk nothing for mere empire." Hoar to Chandler, 28 July 1898, Papers of W. E. Chandler, Library of Congress.

tention of maintaining old political friendships while pursuing the course of righteousness. It was typical of McKinley that though he tried at one point to remove Hoar to the Court of St. James, he would subsequently grasp his hand and cry with tearful sincerity: "I shall always love you, whatever you do."[36]

McKinley formally offered Hoar the English mission on 13 September, but for two weeks or more rumors had informed Washington that the Massachusetts senator was McKinley's first choice to succeed John Hay. Lodge wrote Hoar as early as 26 August that "all the newspapers" were certain of Hoar's appointment and he remained unconvinced when Hoar dismissed these reports as baseless.[37] Hoar insisted that the President had far too many political debts to make it likely that he would offer the post to one who already possessed a place of "greater dignity and public importance," and he was genuinely surprised when he received McKinley's telegram.[38] His reply, however, was decisive and immediate:

I am honored by your confidence, for which I am grateful. But I believe I can better serve my country and better support your administration by continuing to discharge the legislative duties to which I have been accustomed for thirty years, than by undertaking new responsibilities at my age, now past seventy-two. If it were otherwise, I cannot afford to maintain the scale of living which the social customs of London make almost indispensable to an Ambassador, and I have no right to impose upon my Wife, in her present state of health, the burden which would fall upon her.[39]

It would appear that Hoar's reasons were those expressed in his telegram and that at no time did he suspect that the proferred honor was inspired by a desire to secure his removal from the

[36] G. F. Hoar, *Autobiography*, II, 315.

[37] Lodge to Hoar, 26 August, 31 August 1898, Hoar Papers; Hoar to Lodge, 29 August 1898, Lodge Papers, Massachusetts Historical Society.

[38] Hoar to Edward R. Tinker, [?] August 1898, Hoar Papers; Hoar to Senator John W. Daniel, 7 September 1898, Daniel Papers, Duke University Libraries.

[39] McKinley to Hoar, 13 September 1898, Hoar Papers; Hoar to McKinley, 14 September 1898, Papers of William McKinley, Library of Congress.

Senate prior to the struggle over the confirmation of the peace treaty.[40] Nor is it certain that McKinley's offer was exclusively inspired by a wish to eliminate a senatorial opponent of expansion. McKinley had not fully determined in mid-September how expansionist he wished the treaty to be. He knew, moreover, that few Americans would be more acceptable to London than Hoar.[41] It is difficult to believe, however, that McKinley did not guess in September that Hoar would find the future peace treaty distasteful, whatever the number of its acquisitions, and in that sense probably saw Hoar's appointment as doubly beneficial.

One man quite ready to suspect the worst of McKinley's offer to Hoar was Senator Eugene Hale of Maine. Hale had begun his congressional career as a toady to James G. Blaine but by 1898 he had gained sufficient seniority to feel entitled to independent judgment as well as an irritable disposition. Hoar must remain in the Senate; the great question that would determine the shape of America "for our sons & grandsons" would be settled in Washington, not in London. If McKinley wished to honor Hoar, why didn't "he put you on to the Peace Commission?" Who was he selecting for that commission but imperialists and weaklings? From the Senate he had chosen William P. Frye and Cushman K. Davis, admitted expansionists, and George Gray, a feeble Democrat.[42] Hoar replied that he had not been consulted by McKinley respecting the composition of the peace commission, did not think highly of its membership, and was glad to hear that at least one-half of Maine would be in "good fighting trim." Although he had respect for the integrity of Frye and Davis, he was

[40] *See* Hoar to William Claflin, 19 September 1898, Claflin Papers, Rutherford B. Hayes Library; Hoar to H. Y. J. Taylor, 6 December 1898, Hoar Papers.

[41] It was the opinion of Senator Lodge that Britain would have welcomed Hoar with "universal respect": "Mr. Hoar would have been an admirable appointment and one of the very few men who could take such a place without money. He is the representative of the type of what Emerson called 'plain living and high thinking' which I think is not to be found here outside of New England. A man of very old and distinguished family, on both sides, of the highest education and scholarship he would have commanded universal respect in England, where he is well known." Lodge to Henry White, 23 September 1898, Lodge Papers, Massachusetts Historical Society.

[42] Hale to Hoar, 2 September, 8 September 1898, Hoar Papers.

more and more satisfied of the truth of what I said in the Senate several years ago—that it is a gross impropriety and contrary to the Constitution, to employ Senators for diplomatic purposes subject to the authority and instruction of the Executive . . .

It is possible that the President . . . thinks he can get a Treaty through the Senate better by having these gentlemen on the Commission. Otherwise he is to have a pretty lively fight on his hands if my life and health shall be spared.[43]

The certainty of that fight was assured when William McKinley on 28 October 1898 instructed his commissioners in Paris to acquire the Philippine Islands, as well as Puerto Rico and an island in the Marianas. In the eyes of Hoar the treaty that incorporated these provisions stood traitor to the old faith and true mission of the nation. It aimed at nothing less than the conversion of the American Republic into an empire. The Senate must be persuaded to reject the treaty and the temptation it offered. He was prepared to lead the fight—as a loyal Republican.

[43] Hoar to Hale, 9 September 1898 (copy), Hoar Papers. In a letter to Lodge, Hoar declared that it was a violation of the doctrine of the separation of powers for senators to serve as treaty commissioners under orders of the executive and then return to Congress and as legislators deliberate upon their own handiwork. Lodge implied agreement but was in fact bitterly disappointed that he had not personally been selected for the commission. Lodge compensated for his exclusion by sending Cushman Davis and Secretary of State William R. Day a steady stream of advice. *See* Hoar to Lodge, 15 September 1898 and Lodge to John D. Long, 8 August 1898; Lodge to Cushman K. Davis, 18 November 1898; Lodge to William R. Day, 11 August 1898; Lodge to Henry White, 12 August 1898, Lodge Papers, Massachusetts Historical Society.

8

*The Start of the Last Crusade:*
*The Treaty of Paris in the Senate*

The treaty ending the Spanish-American War was signed in Paris on 10 December 1898 and submitted to the Senate for its confirmation on 4 January 1899. The senatorial debate, however, may be dated from 6 December when Senator George Vest, Democrat of Missouri, introduced a resolution denying the constitutional power of the government to acquire colonial dependencies. For the next two months the Senate argued the desired size and destiny of the American nation. The result was one of the more intelligent, reasoned, and significant debates in American history. If the members of the Senate possessed little knowledge of contemporary conditions in Asia or the Pacific, they were well aware that confirmation of the treaty would represent a turning point in the history of American foreign policy. The Treaty of Paris did not make the United States a world power—geography and economic development had done that—but it did embody a definite departure.

It was primarily the impact of territorial expansion upon the domestic institutions of America that inspired George Frisbie Hoar to oppose the Treaty of Paris. His was in a very real sense a conservative reaction—he feared for the traditions of the past and the social and political institutions of the present. He spoke in behalf of the liberties of the Puerto Rican and the Filipino, but at all times his ultimate concern was the preservation of liberty at home. Subjugation of colonial peoples was not only unjust, it was self-destructive.

The necessity of balancing the demands of justice and self-interest was from first to last the central problem raised by the Treaty of Paris, and that problem centered about the Philippines. If the Philippines were not to be returned to the alleged tyranny of Spain and so injustice, how could we avoid annexing them and thereby risk the evils of empire? The degree of Hoar's anxiety to find a solution is illustrated by his willingness to seek aid and advice from the Mugwumps. To Carl Schurz he had written on October 26, 1898:

> I don't know whether you will think that the rather sharp political differences which have existed and which, I suppose, are likely to exist hereafter between your opinions on public questions and mine might not render it improper for me to write to you now . . . It seems to me the great need . . . is to satisfy the people what ought to be done with the Philippines if we do not take them. There is a strong feeling that it would be alike humiliating and dishonorable to give them back to Spain, or to let them become the prey of European Powers . . . I should be glad for my own instruction to know what you think in this matter.[1]

---

[1] Hoar to Schurz, 26 October 1898, Papers of Carl Schurz, Volume 126, Library of Congress. At the beginning of this letter Hoar referred to Schurz's opposition to the gubernatorial campaign of Theodore Roosevelt in New York and offered a clouded prediction:

I ought to say frankly that if I were in New York I should zealously support Mr. Roosevelt now. I do not think there is the slightest possibility that he will ever be nominated for the Presidency, and if he were nominated and elected I think he would make a very good President. I think he would be a vigorous combatant of existing abuses and that all questions of imperialism would have got settled long before he would have a chance to influence them, for good or evil.

"The Modern Cassandra" from *Puck,* February 8, 1899.

Schurz eagerly accepted the invitation and suggested that "a conference of the Powers most immediately interested" in the Pacific and the Philippines might offer a way out.[2] This proposal intrigued Hoar and he endorsed it in a speech before his Worcester constituents at the close of the state election campaign.[3] Over the next weeks—while the negotiations at Paris were concluded and Congress reassembled in Washington—Hoar and Schurz sought to formulate an "honorable alternative" to annexation. Initially Hoar had hoped that the United States might simply pick up and leave the Philippines, but by mid-December he had come to the conclusion that the United States had a moral obligation to assist the Filipinos in establishing their new government, and that it would be impolitic and wrong to ignore that obligation. Not only would the American people not consent to giving the islands back to Spain; "it will be difficult to get the assent of the people to leaving them in a state of confusion and anarchy." But if America should assist the Philippines, that assistance must be coupled with a policy that sought to observe and secure the sovereign independence of the islands.[4]

The specific form that such a policy might assume was first publicly suggested by Schurz in his convocation address at the University of Chicago on January 4, 1899. The United States should give temporary assistance to the Philippines in the establishment of law, order, and stability—similar to the aid and guidance promised Cuba—and sponsor an international guarantee of Philippine sovereignty and neutrality—similar to that enjoyed in Europe by Belgium and Switzerland. Hoar expressed complete agreement. American protection of an independent Philippine republic would provide an honorable alternative to the impropriety of desertion or the disaster of annexation.[5]

---

[2] Schurz to Hoar, 30 October 1898, Hoar Papers.

[3] *Boston Journal*, 3 November 1898.

[4] Hoar to Schurz, 5 December 1898, Papers of Carl Schurz, Volume 126, Library Congress. *See*, too, Hoar to George Boutwell, 5 November, 12 November 1898, Hoar Papers.

[5] Carl Schurz, *American Imperialism: A Convocation Address delivered at the University of Chicago, January 4, 1899*, pamphlet, Hoar Papers; Schurz to Hoar, 11 January, 16 January 1899, Hoar Papers; Hoar to Schurz, 12 January, 17 January 1899, Papers of Carl Schurz, Volume 127, Library of Congress. Earlier in their correspon-

In retrospect, one of Hoar's major tactical errors in his long fight against imperialism was his failure to emphasize this alternative during the Senate debate over the Treaty of Paris. During that debate he concentrated upon the sinfulness and unconstitutionality of the acquisition of "subject states," and so forfeited the chance of discussing the merits of a limited American protectorate in the Philippines. It would not be until some weeks after the treaty had been confirmed that he would publicly advocate the alternative that he and Schurz had fashioned in their letters of December–January. Lingering doubts about the propriety of a temporary occupation of the Philippines and of negotiation with the corrupt powers of Europe partially explain this delay, but more important was his conviction that his first duty in the Senate was to denounce and defeat the treaty. Once the administration was forced to revise the treaty there would be time to demand the formal recognition of Aguinaldo and the negotiation of an international guarantee.

Before analyzing Hoar's errors, in the Senate, however, it is necessary to describe the impact of McKinley's diplomacy on the Republican party in Massachusetts and to analyze the composition of the Anti-Imperialist League. For the force of partisan loyalty and the weakness of anti-imperialist organization help to explain those errors as they helped to assure the treaty's confirmation.

When Hoar had proclaimed in Worcester on the first of November his conviction that America would never be so false to its traditions as to annex the Philippines, "treat them as booty," or "govern

---

dence they had discussed such possibilities as a special referendum on annexation, which Hoar rejected, and the loan to Aguinaldo of an international police force, which Hoar declared impractical. *See* Schurz to Hoar, 1 December 1898; William D. Sohier to Hoar, 8 December 1898, Hoar Papers; Hoar to Schurz, 5 December 1898, Papers of Carl Schurz, Volume 126, Library of Congress. Neither Hoar nor Schurz ever referred to their alternative proposal as a protectorate, for this term had incurred unpopular connotations in connection with the Samoan tangle of the previous decade. It was in fact a dual protectorate arrangement: temporary American aid and occupation terminable at the decision of the Filipinos, and permanent protection of Filipino sovereignty and neutrality by international agreement. For a more detailed examination of the inspiration of the protectorate proposal and its failure to gain contemporary recognition and support, *see* Richard E. Welch, Jr., "Senator George Frisbie Hoar and the Defeat of Anti-Imperialism, 1898–1900," *The Historian*, (26 May 1964), 362–380.

them as serfs," he had been careful to declare his certainty that his colleague, Mr. Lodge was similarily opposed to holding the Filipinos "as a conquered people."[6] He soon found that among those who wrote to praise him for his defense of the principle of national self-determination, there were few who were prepared to accept his optimistic judgment of Republican accord.[7]

Hoar's determination to veil even to himself the probable extent of his disagreement with Lodge was the result of false hope as well as partisan loyalty. Lodge, for his part, was up for re-election in January, 1899 and wished no disturbance within the Republican ranks of Massachusetts. Having skillfully and carefully achieved a position of acknowledged political predominance in Massachusetts, Lodge had no intention of endangering that predominance by waging open contest there before the battle was won in Washington. He was certain that he could count on Senator Hoar to restrain his anti-imperialist followers within the Republican ranks of Massachusetts, and events proved his confidence justified. Though Hoar made his anti-imperialist sympathies known early, he refused to encourage any moves to force either the state convention in October 1898 or the General Court in January 1899 to take a definite stand on the issue of colonial expansion and so risk division of the Republican party in Massachusetts.[8]

[6] *Boston Journal*, 3 November 1898.

[7] *See* George Ernst to Hoar, 3 November 1898; Charles Frances Adams, Jr., to Hoar, 2 November 1898; Benjamin F. Trueblood, Secretary, American Peace Society, to Hoar, 2 November 1898; Anson D. Morse to Hoar, 2 November 1898; Hoar to Edward Atkinson, 12 November, 15 November 1898 (copies), Hoar Papers.

[8] The leaders of the Republican state convention were advised that both Hoar and Lodge would be satisfied by a platform declaration that limited its attention to a denunciation of Spanish tyranny and an expression of approval for the liberation of the Spanish colonies. *See* Hoar to William S. Knox, 1 October 1898, Hoar Papers; Lodge to J. C. Hammond, 4 October 1898; Lodge to William Laffan, 12 September 1898; Lodge to Frederick Gillett, 23 September 1898, Lodge Papers, Massachusetts Historical Society.

In the Massachusetts General Court, in January 1899, rival resolutions were offered praising Hoar for his defense of human freedom and applauding the peace treaty and its provisions. Hoar and Lodge both approved a compromise solution whereby all resolutions were submitted to the legislature's Committee on Federal Relations and allowed quietly to expire. Charles G. Washburn to Hoar, 13 January 1899; D. S. Lamson to Hoar, 13 January 1899; Hoar to Willard Howland, 1 February 1899, Hoar Papers; Lodge to W. Murray Crane, 23 January 1899, Lodge Papers, Massachusetts Historical Society.

There appears to have been a clearly understood if unspoken agreement between Lodge and Hoar that they would seek to confine their contest to the national Senate.[9] When Lodge was reelected by the General Court, Hoar was quick to inform the Washington correspondent of the *Boston Journal* that he had heard the news "with great delight."[10] His comment was sincere as well as self-conscious. By mid-January Lodge and Hoar were equally determined to defeat one another in Washington and to disguise the extent of their differences in Massachusetts. Senatorial association, partisan loyalty, and personal friendship combined to persuade each that he could without sacrifice of principle isolate their battle in the Senate from the politics of the Bay State.[11]

Hoar's concern for the feelings of Lodge and the unity of Republican organization in Massachusetts did not lessen the vigor of his attack on the treaty in the Senate, but it was part and parcel of his failure to serve as a unifying agent for the anti-imperialist forces both within and without that body. Surely it could not help but lessen his influence with the Anti-Imperialist League of Boston.

The constitution of the Anti-Imperialist League was fashioned in the office of Edward Atkinson, 14 Ashburton Place, on Friday, 18 November 1898. From its beginning the league was closely associated with the Mugwump-Independent-Reform Club element of Boston society and Massachusetts politics. Its founding fathers were Gamaliel Bradford and Moorfield Storey, and its constitution welcomed the membership of all citizens, irrespective of party

[9] Hoar to Lodge, 4 November 1898, Lodge Papers, Massachusetts Historical Society; Lodge to Hoar, 5 November 1898; Hoar to William D. Sohier, 1 December 1898, Hoar Papers; clippings from *Boston Journal*, 3–10 November 1898, and *Worcester Gazette*, 30 November 1898, Scrap Book VI, Hoar Papers. *See*, too, John A. Garraty, *Henry Cabot Lodge* (New York: Alfred A. Knopf, 1953), 199–200; Richard E. Welch, Jr., "Colleagues and Opponents: George Frisbie Hoar and Henry Cabot Lodge," *New England Quarterly*, 39 (June 1966), 182–209.

[10] *Boston Journal*, 19 January 1899.

[11] Hoar had written Lodge on 5 November 1898: "You and I have the duty without any sacrifice of principle or opinion so to represent the Commonwealth of Massachusetts as first, to have her opinion expressed, and next, to keep the Republican party, in which the hope of the whole country, and especially the best hope of Massachusetts rests, from being divided." Lodge Papers, Massachusetts Historical Society.

affiliation, to join in battle against imperialism and the extension of American sovereignty over noncontiguous territory.[12]

Hoar was invited to attend the charter meeting of the league on 18 November and refused. His refusal was inspired by concern for the proprieties of his senatorial office and strong doubts as to the "wisdom and efficiency" of those in charge of the meeting. The important thing was to persuade to righteousness those Republicans who had "unguardedly and hastily" spoken in favor of expansion. Such men would not be "attracted to leaders whom they only know as men who seem to have been always wrong in the past and who are likely to be wrong-headed, obstinate and conceited in the future." Bradford, Storey, Erving Winslow, Winslow Warren, William Lloyd Garrison, Jr.—"Massachusetts Reform Club men"—were not the proper leaders for the great battle ahead.[13]

Hoar's initial suspicions were easily matched by the founders of the Anti-Imperialist League. Gamaliel Bradford's letter of 9 December 1898 was filled with praise for Hoar's objection to the treaty, but it concluded with expressions of doubt respecting his constancy and strength. Hoar must not "give up to party what was meant for mankind"; he must not allow his sense of right and duty to be outweighed again by the persuasions of the administration.[14]

---

[12] Maria C. Lanzar, "The Anti-Imperialist League," *Philippine Social Science Review*, 3 (1930), 7–18.

[13] Hoar to Edward Atkinson, 17 November 1898, E. A. Atkinson Papers, Massachusetts Historical Society.

[14] Bradford to Hoar, 6 December 1898, Hoar Papers. Bradford's reference was to Hoar's vote on Hawaiian annexation. Hoar returned a sizzling reply, declaring that his public life had been one of strife for unpopular causes and that he had never done anything that could justify Bradford's insulting exhortations. In this letter Hoar conveniently summarized his public expressions of anti-imperialism prior to the debate in the Senate:

> I have denounced this doctrine of imperialism in season and out of season, ever since it showed its head. I made a speech denouncing it at Bryn Mawr last spring; I made a speech against it at Marblehead in the early summer; I wrote an article in opposition to one of Morgan's [Senator John T. Morgan of Alabama] in the New York Independent last Spring; I made a speech against it, the only speech I made in the campaign, in the Mechanics's Hall in Worcester last month; I declared in an interview to the Boston Journal that if it were accom-

Hoar was as early and sincere an opponent of imperialism as any Mugwump member of the Anti-Imperialist League, but he was determined to seek salvation for America and justice for the Filipino primarily through the instrumentality of the Republican party. He was convinced that anti-imperialism was the true doctrine of that party and its advocacy consistent with his position as a self-proclaimed partisan. Indeed, he saw the fight as a fight for the health of party as well as nation; a battle for the salvation of the Republicans as well as the Republic.[15] Suggestions by members of the league that the opponents of imperialism should imitate the Free Soilers and form a separate party met a cold response. Hoar found little joy in political dissent and was loath to affiliate too closely in the anti-imperialist cause with those who were habitual dissenters. Anti-imperialism must not be identified with the Mugwumps.[16]

Hoar's correspondence with three Bostonians in the months between the formation of the league and the confirmation of the Treaty of Paris illustrates the limited cooperation possible between Hoar and the Independents, as it reflects the self-defeating divisions that existed within the anti-imperialist ranks. These Bostonians were Charles Francis Adams, Jr., Edward Atkinson, and Erving Winslow, and the degree of confidence accorded to them

---

plished the downfall of the American Republic would date from the administration of William McKinley.

And now you write me this letter in which you ask me to do as I think William Bradford and George Washington and Samuel Hoar would have done, as if I needed to be reminded whose son I am by you.

Hoar to Bradford, 9 December 1898, Hoar Papers.

[15] To Nathan Mathews, Sr., he wrote: "You say that you think I shall not agree with you that our party will suffer defeat in the elections of the year 1900 if we should take possession of the Philippine Islands. I fully agree with you. I further think that not only the party, but the country, the cause of Republicanism, what the party stands for and what the Republic stands for will suffer defeat if we take possession," 23 November 1898, Hoar Papers.

[16] When one supporter wrote, "Think of the company you are in, Charley Eliot, a free trade & free silver mugwump, Edward Atkinson the free trade oil stove crank, George Ernst the liar, Garrison the growler, 'Bug' Norton the sneerer, all of them inveterate haters of the Republican party and its great leaders," Hoar vigorously defended his position but made no defense of his "allies." Charles Gilbert to Hoar, 6 December 1898; Hoar to Gilbert, 11 December 1898, Hoar Papers.

by Hoar was in inverse relationship to the extent and duration of their mugwumpery.

Hoar entertained considerable respect for Adams as a fellow student of colonial Massachusetts and as the descendant of a "noble line." Hoar was sure that at heart he supported the basic principles and beliefs of the Republican party. It was consequently agreeable to receive Adams's opinion that Hoar stood in the position of "my grandfather . . . during the early anti-slavery days." Like John Quincy Adams, he was "the old warrior" who would spark the crusade. Hoar thought the analogy just but inexact. The current danger was the greater; for imperialism once consummated would be "irrevocable." It was for that reason that he was prepared to demand that Adams exert discipline among his Independent and Democratic friends in Boston. If the Democrats and Mugwumps would redeem their past errors, they must stop chattering about free trade and confine themselves to the battle against colonialism. Adams should "speak to Brother Atkinson" in this connection.[17]

Edward Atkinson was a source of perpetual frustration for Hoar. He considered Atkinson to be too sound a businessman to be a real Mugwump, but why when asked for a few summary figures in support of the potential cost of imperialism must Atkinson insist on producing reams of complicated statistics and pacifist diatribes against "the hell of war"? Certainly there was no one more industrious in the cause, but what was wanted was the persuasion of the average Republican voter in time to secure the defeat of the treaty, and many of Atkinson's friends did not seem to care to succeed "so much as to show their own wisdom." When Atkinson suggested that Hoar "hold a consultation" with Erving Winslow, the better to "give the true direction" to the league, Hoar replied with irritation that the fight would be determined in the halls of the Senate and not the committee room of Mr. Winslow.[18]

[17] *See*, especially, Adams to Hoar, 26 October, 20 December 1898, 3 January 1899; Hoar to Adams, 29 November, 9 December, 31 December 1898, Hoar Papers.
[18] Atkinson to Hoar, 28 November, 12 December, 19 December, 27 December 1898, 5 January 1899, Hoar Papers; Hoar to Atkinson, 16 December 1898, Atkinson Papers, Massachusetts Historical Society.

If Adams and Atkinson were viewed as allies of dubious strength, Winslow, secretary of the New England Anti-Imperialist League in Boston, was a source of positive disdain. He was a typical Reform Club enthusiast, and his suspicion of Hoar's partisanship was positively insulting. Did he think the senior senator from Massachusetts was but "a piece of dull or dead metal," of no use but to serve as a congressional errand boy for the league? What did he mean by asking if Hoar was "still with us"? Hoar would assist the league in the presentation of its petitions and the distribution of his speeches, but while Winslow was its manager he could never fully cooperate with it nor expect that it would serve as a useful weapon in defeating the treaty or effecting a solution for American disengagement in the Philippines.[19] Neither the labors of the league nor those of Hoar were confined to their restricted efforts at cooperation. The contribution of each lay outside that relationship, but the limit of their respective achievement was foreshadowed in the mutual suspicions of Erving Winslow and George Frisbie Hoar.

The anti-imperialist movement was characterized throughout its history by heterogeneity. The diversity of its membership, however fascinating to later historians, was a serious hindrance to its contemporary effectiveness. It is probably true that the inspirations of the leaders of the movement were as personally unselfish as those of any group in the history of American political debate. Purity of motive was not matched, however, by clarity of purpose. Such spokesmen of the Anti-Imperialist League as Moorfield Storey wished to bury McKinley while saving America. George Hoar sought to preserve both the Declaration of Independence and the virtue of his party. If the goals of neither were self-contradictory, they were far from identical. Those of Hoar made it almost certain that his famous fight in the Senate against the Treaty of Paris would be a personal battle, courageous but also nostalgic. It was the battle of a man who sought the collaboration of men dead and past, and who fought not only a treaty but a sense of personal alienation.

[19] Winslow to Hoar, 8 December, 9 December, 10 December, 21 December 1898; Hoar to Winslow, 31 December 1898 (copy); George S. Boutwell to Hoar, 8 December 1898, Hoar Papers.

When Hoar began to speak at 12:15 on Monday, 9 January he not only formally opened his campaign against the Treaty of Paris in the Senate, but he inaugurated the last and most famous phase of his career. There is always a certain inherent drama in the sight of a man torn between the loyalties of party and principle, and both the Senate floor and gallery were filled as Hoar rose to address his colleagues and the nation. For those who liked their heroes handsome and youthful, there must have been a certain sense of disappointment. Hoar had fortunately given up the scraggly sidewhiskers that some years earlier had given him a resemblance to Horace Greeley, but at 72 he was, with his round face, white hair, and appreciable stomach, an unlikely figure for a crusader as he stood facing Vice-President Hobart, unconsciously jiggling a large key ring in his left hand. Hoar's usual custom was to carefully prepare his speeches but to bring to the Senate only a handful of notes containing key topic sentences and quotations. On this day he read from a typewritten manuscript. He made a conscious effort to read slowly and to curb his high-pitched voice, but to his attentive audience on the floor and in the gallery the anxiety and passion of the speaker were unmistakable.[20]

The central theme of Hoar's argument was that annexation of the Philippines was unconstitutional as well as unjust and unwise; for the Constitution could only be interpreted in accordance with the immutable principle that "governments derive their just powers from the consent of the governed." He prefaced that argument, however, with a purposeful digression. He would have no one believe that he was deserting the Federalist-Whig-Republican tradition of constitutional construction. He believed in the doctrine of implied powers and always would, but the powers of Congress were "limited to the one supreme and controlling purpose" expressed in the preamble of the Constitution:

The question with which we now have to deal is whether Congress may conquer and may govern, without their consent and against their will, a foreign nation, a separate, distinct, and

[20] *New York Tribune*, 10 January 1899.

numerous people, a territory not hereafter to be populated by Americans, to be formed into American States and to take its part in fulfilling and executing the purposes for which the Constitution was framed, and whether it may conquer, control, and govern this people, not for the general welfare, common defense, more pacific union, more blessed liberty of the people of the United States, but for some real or fancied benefit to be conferred against their desire upon the people so governed.

He did not deny the contention that this country had the power to acquire territory and to govern its inhabitants, but this power could only be exercised to effect a recognized constitutional purpose. To hold a purchased people in colonial vassalage was not a constitutional purpose. The Constitution was always to be construed in the light of the Declaration of Independence. So interpreted it forbade the purchase of Philippine sovereignty, the acquisition of a subject people.[21]

In the final analysis, Hoar declared that Philippine annexation would be unconstitutional because immoral. He spoke of cost, of tropical disease, and of alien races, but only briefly. The overriding objection to annexation of the Philippines was that it was "wicked." Hoar's argument against imperialism would eventually develop strategic and economic as well as constitutional and humanitarian objections, but fundamentally it was based on abstract political principle. Above all else he spoke in behalf of the political ideals of America as he understood those ideals to have been articulated by Sam Adams and Jefferson, and by Abraham Lincoln on the battlefield of Gettysburg.

Advance copy of Hoar's speech had been requested by most of the major papers in the East and it received wide publicity. Its content was announced by the New York *World* in a series of banner heads: "Hoar Attacks Imperialism And Treaty"; "Our Constitution Gives No Power to Hold Vassal States and Govern Them"; "No Nation Was Ever Created Good Enough to Own Another"; "Flag Raised in The Far East Means It Must Be Lowered

[21] *Congressional Record*, 55th Cong., 3d sess., 493–503.

from Independence Hall"; "No American Workman, No American Home Will Be Better For The Philippines."[22] Other papers, if less exuberant with their capitals, accorded Hoar almost equal attention. Many of his personal correspondents called him false to McKinley and others false to Christ and the Anglo-Saxon missionary, but a majority forwarded praise and congratulation.[23] Andrew Carnegie sent a thousand dollars "to aid in distributing your speech."[24]

Hoar failed to offer in that speech any positive suggestions for American policy in the Philippines; particularly, he failed to discuss the solution of a limited protectorate. For the moment he considered it sufficient to denounce the treaty and demand its rejection and revision. It would be time to spell out our responsibility for the Philippines after we had renounced any designs upon them and declared them "of right free and independent."[25]

The latter phrase lay at the heart of the resolution Hoar offered in the Senate on 14 January. That resolution demanded that the United States government proclaim the right of the people of the Philippines to independence and "to institute a new govern-

---

[22] *The World* (New York), 9 January 1899. *See,* too, Scrap Book, Personal, VI (1898–1900).

[23] Those correspondents who criticized Hoar and supported expansion fell into one of four categories: Protestant clergymen, professional patriots, exporters, and textile and shoe manufacturers. *See,* for example, the Reverend S. L. Blake to Hoar, 13 January 1899; G. B. Addison to Hoar, 26 January 1899; Levi B. Santer to Hoar, 27 January 1899; Carl Adams to Hoar, 28 January 1899, Hoar Papers. Among those who praised Hoar and opposed expansion were certain Boston bankers, farm society spokesmen, labor officials (fearing the competition of cheap Filipino labor), Mugwump intellectuals, and self-styled "Old Abolitionist Republicans." Letters from the last group Hoar found particularly gratifying. *See,* for example, Memorial of the Union League of New Bedford to Hoar, 16 January 1899; Hoar to William Claflin, 19 January 1899 (copy), Hoar Papers.

[24] Andrew Carnegie to Hoar, 18 January 1899, Hoar Papers. Hoar returned Carnegie's check and asked him to arrange the matter of distribution through the agency of a third party, as less susceptible to erroneous interpretation. Carnegie replied that he was acting under "the advice of your friends, and was only too glad to spend money in such missionary work." Hoar to Carnegie, 19 January 1899 (copy); Carnegie to Hoar, 20 January 1899, Hoar Papers.

[25] Hoar wrote Schurz that *after* the treaty was voted down, he would try "to amend it by making it exactly what we want." Hoar to Schurz, 17 January 1899, Carl Schurz Papers, Volume 127, Library of Congress.

ment for themselves, laying its foundation on such principles . . . as to them shall seem most likely to effect their happiness."[26] Hoar was by mid-January in correspondence with the Philippines committee in London and was increasingly convinced that the Filipinos had the capacity as well as the right of self-government.[27] If Hoar's chief fears concerned the effect of imperialism on the institutions and ideals of America, he demonstrated from the first an honest if not equal anxiety for the liberties and self-respect of the Filipino.[28]

That the expansionists were equally prepared to associate the needs of the nation at home with its duty abroad was made clear by the speech of Senator Lodge on 24 January. Lodge's effort was to all intents and purposes a direct answer to the speech and resolution of his colleague. It was also the most concise and forceful address made during the treaty debate in support of the administration and its treaty. Lodge was not yet ready to expound in full his long-range design for the diplomatic power and position of America. Rather he gave a brief summary of the constitutional

[26] *Congressional Record*, 55th Cong., 3d sess., 677. Hoar's resolution of 14 January 1899 was never brought to a vote.

[27] "The Philippine Islands Committee in Europe" and a British businessman in Hong Kong served as the chief instruments in convincing Hoar that the Filipinos were politically capable. Felipe Agoncillo, Sixto Lopez, and other Filipino diplomats in London selected Hoar as the most sympathetic and influential of the anti-imperialists in the Senate and sent him a steady stream of suggestions. *See,* for example, F. Madrigal to Hoar, 2 December, 13 December 1898; Felipe Agoncillo to Hoar, 10 December 1898, Hoar Papers. Concurrently, Hoar was in receipt of letters from Howard W. Bray of Hong Kong informing him that he had lived in the Philippines for sixteen years and knew the Filipinos to be an intelligent people, "with all the Pride and Chivalry of the Malay race," who unitedly desired independence and would be content with nothing less. *See* Bray to Hoar, 13 January 1899, Hoar Papers.

Hoar was almost alone among the anti-imperialists in the Senate in advocating as well the right of the Puerto Ricans to self-determination. *Congressional Record,* 55th Cong., 3d sess., 1384.

[28] These two distinct but connected concerns—his fear of what imperialism would do to the ideals and institutions of his countrymen; his belief that it was impractical and unjust to dictate the political goals and institutions of any people abroad—were explicitly described in a long letter to Beverly K. Moore, Secretary of the Boston Merchants' Association, 27 December 1898, Hoar Papers. *See,* too, Hoar to the Reverend Francis E. Clark, President, United Society of Christian Endeavor, 11 January 1899, Hoar Papers.

justification for territorial expansion and then confined his attention to the "practical" considerations that should dictate the decision of the Senate: the humiliation that our President and diplomats would suffer if the treaty were not confirmed; the impossibility of returning the islands to Spain; the incapacity of the untutored Filipinos to govern themselves; the danger of renewed warfare were the treaty rejected. That treaty did not restrict the United States to any particular path respecting the Philippines; it simply gave the United States the right to determine the fate of the Philippines in due course and proper time. The opponents of the treaty were men of little faith; they were distrustful of the future and the nation's ability subsequently to do justice to itself and to its wards. Their dire predictions were false. The social ideals and economic institutions of Americans at home would be strengthened and vitalized as the nation did its civilizing duty abroad.[29]

The speeches of Hoar and Lodge during the month of January 1899 reflected, as both men were now aware, more than an incidental difference of views. Lodge saw his country poised for a new century and saw himself as the statesman-intellectual who anticipated the new role that century demanded of America. Hoar saw his country tempted by false doctrines and saw himself as the appointed prophet who would remind his party and country of the old truths and commandments. In a broader sense, it was but another chapter in the long warfare between the conflicting ideals of Manifest Destiny and Mission. Both men believed America to be unique and the American experiment to be of continuing and international significance. For Lodge, however, the American dream was subject to the laws of evolution and now demanded that America pursue its destiny on a worldwide scale. Power politics would assure America the naval strength, the island bases, the coaling stations and markets necessary to insure the health and spread of American institutions. For Hoar, the superiority of American institutions was undeniable, but they could not be forcibly exported; they would spread only by example. The mission of America demanded that it be true to its old faith and high ideals.

---

[29] *Congressional Record*, 55th Cong., 3d sess., 958–960.

Only so would it be of inspiration and therefore service to the world.[30]

As the debate in the Senate continued, Hoar's initial certainty that the treaty would be defeated sharply declined. The administration was "moving Heaven and earth . . . to detach individual Senators from the opposition"; Senators Spooner and Burrows had deserted, and he suspected that Stewart of Nevada had been persuaded to change his mind by the most blatant promises of administration patronage. Senator Gorman was doing his best to rally the Democrats in opposition to the treaty, but Bryan's mischievous visit had quite demoralized the western Democrats and Populists. Hoar was certain that Bryan, whatever his protestations of anti-imperialism, had advised his followers to confirm the treaty from the worst and most partisan of motives.[31]

At one point, Hoar became convinced that the administration was determined to delay a vote on the treaty until late March and a special session of the new Congress with its increased Republican majority. Acting on this assumption he applauded the efforts of Gorman to force the treaty from committee and to pressure its floor managers to schedule a vote for the sixth of February. The present Congress offered the best opportunity to "record the

[30] It is currently fashionable to deny the width and significance of the division between the expansionists of 1898 and their opponents. Such historians as Thomas J. McCormick have argued that both groups favored American expansion into world markets and the only difference between them was that while the one favored formal colonization, the other considered it unnecessary to the expansion of trade. Certainly both the anti-imperialists and expansionists favored trade, but whether the nation's flag should follow the nation's trade was and remains a significant question of national policy. Thomas J. McCormick, "A Commentary on the Anti-Imperialists and Twentieth-Century Foreign Policy," *Studies on the Left*, 3 (1962), 28–33. *See*, too, William A. Williams, *The Contours of American History* (Cleveland: World Publishing Company, 1961), 367–368; J. Rogers Hollingsworth, *The Whirligig of Politics: The Democracy of Cleveland and Bryan* (Chicago: University of Chicago Press, 1963), 144n, 249.

[31] Hoar to Schurz, 12 January 1898, Carl Schurz Papers, Volume 127, Library of Congress. Andrew Carnegie was equally convinced of the "mischief" occasioned by Bryan. He wrote to him: "Your advocacy of ratification has disorganized matters . . . I wish you were here to be satisfied that you have the power to defeat the treaty thus giving the Country time to reflect." Carnegie to Bryan, 10 January 1899, William Jennings Bryan Papers, Library of Congress.

strength" of anti-expansionism.[32] He was equally convinced that the Senate offered the only effective means of recording that strength and that the anti-imperialists in the Senate should concentrate on preventing confirmation of the treaty. Hoar opposed all suggestions that the treaty be ratified and independence of the Philippines subsequently arranged by congressional statute. If the Treaty of Paris were to be approved in its present form, it would become the supreme law of the land, and the task of "unannexing" the Philippines and so alienating a part of the territory of the United States made more difficult.

Of all the many arguments offered in behalf of the treaty perhaps none was more effective in persuading the waverers than the argument that confirmation of the treaty involved no permanent commitment. It might be described as the argument of practical expediency and paraphrased as follows: "Let us officially end the war and subsequently we can deal with this island empire by our own independent action, safely relying upon the intelligence of the American people and their representatives. It is not a question of taking the Philippines; we have them. In the absence of any more sure or advantageous solution, let us stand fast." The force of inertia found support in considerations of self-interest and duty. In support of the argument of practical expediency there were the arguments of national dignity, strategic necessity, commercial advantage, and moral obligation.

The argument of national dignity was the most general and surely the most simplistic. Support the President; stand by the flag! Don't force the President to apologize for the victory of American arms or beg Spain to take back the Philippines. Palsied the hand that would lower the flag where once it had been raised. Such sentiments often cloaked considerations of national power and strategic necessity. There was relatively little indication of *Realpolitik* in the Senate debate itself, but such senators as Lodge were

[32] Hoar to Carl Schurz, 17 January, 28 January 1899, Carl Schurz Papers, Volume 127, Library of Congress. To George Boutwell, president of the Anti-Imperialist League, Hoar wrote: "If we have a vote now, I think the treaty is pretty sure to be beaten and then that there are enough of those who will vote for the treaty from a desire to support the President, who really sympathize with us, to pass an amendment which shall absolutely pledge the country against retaining the Philippine Islands." Hoar to Boutwell, 17 January 1899, Hour Papers.

surely as interested in the diplomatic authority of the nation as the *amour propre* of the President. The nation that held the Philippines would not only have the harbor of Manila for its navy but the right to be consulted in all diplomatic arrangements respecting the Far East.

Senatorial expansionists thought it best, however, to emphasize the commercial rather than the diplomatic advantages of Manila Bay. Big Navy advocates were already in camp; it was the manufacturers of excess production that must be persuaded. Commercial necessity demanded the acquisition of new and assured markets. The Philippines would provide such a market and more importantly a vestibule to increased trade with the Orient. Various segments of that real if elusive object, "the business community," were persuaded that possession of the islands would be commercially advantageous. Businessmen were as divided on expansion as they had been earlier on war, but a majority of business journals in the winter of 1899 supported acquisition of the Philippines.[33] Certain of the manufacturers and investors who supported expansion had to be reassured that it would not necessarily be followed by free trade between the United States and its new colonies, and others were probably as interested in the domestic distraction that imperialism would provide as in any economic advantage, but however segmented the character of "the business community," its supposed interests received considerable attention from the treaty supporters in the United States Senate.[34]

It is of course impossible to determine with any accuracy which of the many arguments used by those supporters had the greatest influence, and quite possibly those of practical expediency, national dignity, strategic necessity, and commercial advantage would have been sufficient in themselves. They did not, however, provide the supporters of the treaty with a suitable counter to the

[33] Julius Pratt, *Expansionists of 1898* (Baltimore: Johns Hopkins Press, 1936), 266–278.

[34] A. Whitney Griswold is probably correct in his judgment that for the framers of the "Large Policy" the desire to acquire territory in the Pacific fathered the thought of commercial advantage, but this probability need not deny the fact that the economic potential of the Philippines was frequently urged in the winter of 1899. Griswold, *The Far Eastern Policy of the United States* (New York: Harcourt, Brace, 1938), 24–26.

anti-imperialists' appeal to tradition. Against that appeal, the expansionists offered the argument of moral duty. Possessed of superior institutions and strength we could not shirk our obligation to the Filipino. In the words later attributed to William McKinley, we must "uplift and Christianize them, and by God's grace do the very best we could by them." This argument was composed of a rather uneasy mixture of Social Darwinism and international altruism. Its two-sided nature was perhaps never more vividly expressed than by Theodore Roosevelt, when he excoriated the anti-imperialists for their wicked suggestion that the Philippines be turned over to the Filipinos:

> If the men who have counseled national degradation, national dishonor, by urging us to leave the Philippines . . . could have their way, we should merely turn them over to a rapine and bloodshed until some stronger, manlier power stepped in to do the task we had shown ourselves fearful of performing. But, as it is, this country will keep the islands and will establish therein a stable and orderly government, so that one more fair spot of the world's surface shall have been snatched from the forces of darkness.[35]

The arguments of the treaty supporters were not without an element of self-contradiction. They spoke simultaneously of historical determinism and the need to shape the future. They assumed the identity of morality and self-interest and confused the honor of the nation with the reputation of its chief executive. And surely they talked too little of specific foreign policy objectives. Given the needs of time and politics, however, they offered an intelligent and skillful defense of colonial expansion.

For each of the arguments of the expansionists their opponents had an equivalent. As indicated by Hoar's speech of 9 January, they countered the argument of national dignity with that of national faithfulness; strategic advantage with the danger of diplo-

---

[35] Theodore Roosevelt, "Expansion and Peace," *The Works of Theodore Roosevelt* (New York, 1900), XII, 23–36. *See,* too, the analysis of Albert K. Weinberg on the force of "moral imperatives" in *Manifest Destiny: A Study of Nationalist Expansionism in American History* (Baltimore: Johns Hopkins Press, 1935), 273–282.

matic embroilment; commercial gain with economic waste; and destiny and duty with mission and liberty. The anti-imperialists did not ignore the possibility that the Philippines might prove both an economic and a military liability, but they placed chief stress on the cost of imperialism to the political traditions of America.[36] Imperialism was in direct contradiction to our heritage of government by compact and consent; it must subvert our mission to serve as an example of republican virtue, which all the world might emulate in time.

For some opponents of expansion a conviction of the superior virtue of America was undoubtedly re-enforced by a conviction of white superiority.[37] The anti-imperialists were not immune to the racist conceptions and currents of the 1890's. Unlike their opponents, however, they were inclined to emphasize the alien nature of the Tagalog rather than the civilizing duty of the white man. There were, moreover, very real differences among the anti-imperialists on this score. In the Senate, Arthur Pue Gorman was a white supremacist; George Frisbie Hoar was not. Hoar was in point of fact one of the first senators to be educated to a respect for the abilities of Aguinaldo and other Filipino leaders. There was a certain element of noblesse oblige in his attitude toward the Filipino, but the chosen adviser of the Filipino exile committee in London did not categorize peoples by the classifications of Social Darwinism. By February 1899 he was convinced that the Filipinos were civilized, capable, and Christian. Under the leadership of Aguinaldo they had established a civil administration that enjoyed and deserved wide popular support.

[36] Several students of the Philippines debate have made this charge. *See* Louis J. Halle, *Dream and Reality: Aspects of American Foreign Policy* (New York: Harper and Brothers, 1959), 210–212; Griswold, *Far Eastern Policy of the United States*, 33; Tyler Dennett, *Americans in Eastern Asia: A Critical Study of the Policy of the United States* (New York: Macmillan, 1922), 627–631.

[37] The charge that the anti-imperialists shared a strong sense of racial superiority and a Social Darwinian frame of reference with their opponents was first made by Christopher Lasch; it has been endorsed by Professors James P. Shenton and J. Rogers Hollingsworth. *See* Christopher Lasch, "The Anti-Imperialists, the Philippines, and the Inequality of Man," *Journal of Southern History*, 14 (August 1958), 319–331; James P. Shenton, "Imperialism and Racism," *Essays in American Historiography*, Donald Sheehan, Harold C. Syrett, eds. (New York: Columbia University Press, 1960), 233–237; Hollingsworth, *The Whirligig of Politics*, 149.

George Frisbie Hoar opposed the annexation of the Philippines as an ideological conservative not as a racist. His errors were not personal but political; his failure was a failure in political leadership. In the Senate debate Hoar demonstrated his courage, but he failed to construct a bipartisan alliance.

With the last days of January, there were but three Republicans in the Senate who were still to be counted against the Treaty of Paris, Walter Mason of Illinois, Eugene Hale of Maine, and Hoar. With the first days of February, there were but two; Mason had deserted. If more than one third of the Senate was to be counted against the treaty, opposition senators—Democrats and Populists—must furnish almost the entire complement. The anti-imperialists in the Senate needed a figure who could cross the aisle: who would seek to persuade Republican senators to resist the blandishments of McKinley while coordinating the tactics and bolstering the resolution of the Populist and Democratic opponents of the treaty. Hoar failed to fulfill the role, or indeed to attempt it. As he saw his Republican colleagues succumb to the convictions and coercion of the administration, he made only limited efforts to cooperate with his political opponents. His inherited suspicion of the motives of southern Democrats and his long-standing reputation as a partisan Yankee circumscribed his spasmodic efforts of collaboration with such men as Gorman of Maryland and James K. Jones of Arkansas. Bipartisanship was limited to informal cloakroom discussion and the tabulation of probable vote lists. Requests by outsiders and political Independents that they be allowed to play the role of "intermediaries" in procuring "united action," Hoar dismissed as improper and irrelevant.[38]

Principle demanded that he vote against the administration; the force of partisan loyalty restricted his ability to persuade others to follow. Hoar firmly repudiated all suggestions that he recant, but the very features of personality that assured his constancy denied

---

[38] Winslow to Hoar, 12 January 1899; Hoar to Winslow, 13 January 1899; Bradford to Hoar, 27 January 1899; Hoar to Bradford, 30 January 1899; Edward Atkinson to Hoar, 23 January 1899, Hoar Papers.

his ability to lead a bipartisan effort.[39] And when the day came for the vote in the Senate, and he realized for perhaps the first time the probability of defeat, he saw himself as a man deserted by his political friends and regarded still as a political enemy by his anti-imperialist allies. It was not in the Concord tradition, however, to be maudlin. His anxiety was not for himself, but for his countrymen:

> Today is the fateful day when the Senate of the United States is to vote upon the policy of entering upon the acquisition of an empire in the East which . . . is to abandon all the ideals and policies which have made our Republic so great . . . [This vote will determine] whether we shall continue to dwell in our borders bounded by the two great seas, and have our relations to the rest of the world peaceful and our influence that of a great example of justice and freedom. I am very anxious about the result.[40]

At four o'clock on 6 February 1899 the Senate voted to confirm the Treaty of Paris, by a vote of 57 to 27, one vote in excess of the required two thirds. The majority was composed of 42 Republicans, 10 Democrats, 3 Populists, and 2 Silver "Independents." A shift of two votes would have defeated the treaty—at least for that session of Congress—and students of the Philippines debate have long argued the question of responsibility for the victory of the expansionists in the United States Senate.

For a long time it was upon the confusing figure of William Jennings Bryan that attention centered, and the judgment rendered that Bryan, by persuading his followers to vote for the treaty, gave McKinley his victory. Recently, however, there has been an effort to minimize the role of Bryan. The opinion of Hoar and other anti-imperialists that Bryan swung the votes of 17 sena-

[39] *See,* especially, Hoar to Representative William C. Lovering, 3 February 1899, Hoar Papers.
[40] Hoar to H. Y. J. Taylor, 6 February 1899, Hoar Papers.

tors, and was inspired by selfish and partisan motives, is now usually rejected.[41]

In all likelihood Bryan was inspired more by conviction than by calculation; indeed, if judged by the criteria of partisan advantage his course was stupid and incomprehensible.[42] It would appear, however, that though Hoar, Carnegie, and others exaggerated his influence with individual senators, Bryan must share responsibility for the confirmation of the treaty; not for what he did but for what he failed to do. If Bryan had come out strongly against the treaty and had worked with Gorman, probably at least three fourths of the 37 Democratic and Populist senators would have followed their lead, and the treaty would have been defeated. As it was, his advice was most likely the determining factor in the decision of two senators, William V. Allen of Nebraska and John P. Jones of Nevada, to vote for confirmation.

The degree of Bryan's responsibility must remain conjectural. More certain is the fact that the man most responsible for the passage of McKinley's treaty was McKinley himself. Aldrich and Lodge might have thought they engineered the victory, but the instruments they used so skillfully were furnished by the President.[43] The contribution of McKinley, however, lies not so much in the patronage he distributed as in the persuasion he exerted. Undoubtedly there was some purchasing of votes—Senator George

[41] Hoar, *Autobiography*, II, 322–323; "Memorandum: Supporters of Bryan who Voted on Treaty," Hoar Papers; Paola E. Coletta, "Bryan, McKinley, and the Treaty of Paris," *Pacific Historical Review*, 26 (May 1957), 131–146.

[42] Professors Merle Curti and Fred Harrington, as well as Professor Coletta, have argued persuasively in behalf of Bryan's sincerity. Merle Curti, *Bryan and World Peace* (Northampton, Mass.: Smith College Studies, 1931), 121–132; Fred H. Harrington, "The Anti-Imperialist Movement in the United States, 1898–1900," *Mississippi Valley Historical Review*, 22 (1935), 221–222.

[43] Lodge informed his friend and collaborator, Theodore Roosevelt, that he felt "exactly as if I had been struggling up the side of a mountain and as if there was not an ounce more of exertion left in any muscle of my body . . . It was the closest, hardest fight I have ever known, and probably we shall not see another in our time where there was so much at stake." Lodge to Roosevelt, 9 February 1899, H. C. Lodge, ed., *Selections from the Correspondence of Theodore Roosevelt and Henry Cabot Lodge, 1884–1918* (New York: Charles Scribner's Sons, 1925), I, 391–392. The irony of Lodge's last judgment in the light of his own opposition to another president and another treaty twenty years later is instructive as well as obvious.

Gray was rewarded for his compliance by a seat on a United States Circuit Court and two of the last three converts, Democratic Senators Samuel McEnery and John Lowndes McLaurin, were subsequently given wide patronage powers by a Republican president in the states of Louisiana and South Carolina—but more senators were out-maneuvered than were corrupted.[44] By appointing three senators to the Peace Commission, McKinley had assured a favorable vote from the Foreign Relations Committee and made more difficult the task of those who would reject the treaty. By seizing the initiative and proclaiming the sovereignty of the United States over the entire Philippine archipelago, in executive orders of 21 December and 5 January, he had made sure that the only option offered the Senate was to accept the treaty or lower the flag. In his two tours about the country, moreover, McKinley had not been content just to keep his ear to the ground. He had helped inspire popular sentiment in behalf of expansion and so in behalf of a favorable vote in the Senate.

It is also true that McKinley's policy of phased duplicity towards the Filipino was responsible, in good measure, for the irruption of the Filipino Insurrection forty-eight hours before the Senate roll call. There is no evidence, however, that the clash of pickets outside the lines at Manila exerted any decisive influence on the vote in the Senate. It certainly further inflamed the last hours of the debate— as each side proclaimed the responsibility of the other. It brought upon Hoar and other anti-imperialists further abuse and obloquy, and one might expect the death of American soldiers at the hands of the Filipino to have generated a wave of senatorial support for

[44] Richard Olney wrote his former chief, Grover Cleveland, that he had heard Hoar declare Gray's conduct to be "perfectly awful." Olney to Cleveland, 22 March 1899, Papers of Richard Olney, Library of Congress. Hoar never blamed McKinley for the administration's pressure tactics, but attributed all "questionable means" to Nelson Aldrich and Mark Hanna. *See* Hoar to Francis Wayland, dean of the Yale Law School, 16 February 1899, Hoar Papers.

Mark Hanna wrote McKinley, 7 February 1899: "In securing the votes of McEnery and McLaurin yesterday I made myself your representative to the extent of a personal plea." William McKinley Papers, Library of Congress. It would seem clear that for "plea" one might read "promise."

The floor managers for the administration were Senators Aldrich and C. K. Davis, but more active in the lobby were Senators Lodge, Elkins, and Hanna.

the administration.[45] In all probability, however, the four men who were converted in the last two days of the debate—Henry Heitfeld, the Idaho Populist; McLaurin; McEnery; and John P. Jones—were inspired by other considerations.

The point to be made, however, is that whatever one's judgment respecting the legality or impact of McKinley's orders to the American army at Manila, his was the most influential and persuasive voice in the United States Senate.

The political skill of the McKinley administration and its influence in determining the decision of the Senate in the Philippines debate was exhibited not only by the treaty vote of 6 February but also in the disposition of various resolutions that sought to limit that victory. Although it is likely that a secret poll of the Senate would have shown that a clear majority of the senators opposed permanent ownership of the Philippines by the United States, the McKinley administration, operating through its senatorial supporters, was able to defer, delay, and defeat all efforts to obtain from Congress a promise to foreswear such ownership. The Vest and Hoar resolutions were never allowed to come to a vote; the Gorman resolution was routed; the Bacon resolution delayed and then defeated; and the McEnery resolution allowed to pass the Senate as a meaningless sop and then buried in the House.[46]

---

[45] The editor of the *New York Sun* during the first week of February, 1899 listed daily "the roll of dishonor." It was a short list that began with the names of Charles Lee and Benedict Arnold and ended with those of Gorman, Hale, and Hoar. *See, too,* the editorial of *New York Mail and Express,* 5 February 1899, Scrap Book, Personal, VII (1899), Hoar Papers.

One of Hoar's admirers was so upset by the charges of the *New York Sun* that he composed a poem, of dubious accuracy:

> A traitor? Yea, if it be Treason's fame
>    To throttle schemes that Avarice and Greed
>    Beneath a hallow'd flag conceive and breed
> Then sanctify with Patriotism's name!
>    Ay coward, traitor, ay, your curse is o'er,
>    Since ye were coupled, to the name of Hoar!

William H. Tomkins to Hoar, 14 February 1899, Hoar Papers.

[46] The resolution introduced by Senator Gorman was in the shape of an amendment to the treaty and bore the character of a rather makeshift effort. It called

Although Hoar labored in behalf of an expression of congressional opinion that might diminish the victory of the expansionists, he was well aware that the first chapter of the Philippines debate had come to an end with the vote of 6 February. He had fought not to supplement the treaty with promises of future generosity but to defeat the treaty and secure American recognition of Aguinaldo's republic. Confirmation of the treaty, he wrote Schurz, committed America to a course that would be "very hard indeed to retrace." How inferior was the conduct of the American Senate to that of the Philippine patriots:

> Aguinaldo's provisional constitution . . . is a masterpiece of a temporary form of government for persons engaged in a revolution for the achievement of their liberties. I do not believe there are ten men now living who could have improved upon it . . . These people were in possession of their own country . . .

---

upon Spain to relinquish authority over the Philippines and went on to indicate, somewhat vaguely, that the United States should withdraw from the Philippines once the Filipinos had a free government. Hoar considered it insufficient and ambiguous, but voted in its favor. It was defeated by a sizeable margin, 30–53, on the sixth of February, shortly before the vote on the treaty. *Journal of the Executive Proceedings of the Senate,* 55th Cong., 3d sess., 1283.

The most publicized effort was that of Augustus Bacon of Georgia. On 24 January Bacon offered a resolution disclaiming any disposition on the part of the United States to exercise permanent control over the islands, and promising independence to the Philippines *after* stable government was established there. Hoar was prepared from the first to vote for the resolution but did not consider it a proper substitute for renegotiation of the treaty; the Filipinos were independent by right and not favor. The Bacon resolution was not allowed by the Republican majority to come to a vote until eight days after the treaty was confirmed. It was then offered in the form of an amendment to the McEnery Resolution and was defeated by the tie-breaking vote of Vice-President Garret Hobart. *Congressional Record,* 55th Cong., 3d sess., 561, 1845–1846.

The McEnery resolution took the form of a vague explication of the treaty. It declared that in consenting to the Treaty of Paris Congress did not intend to annex the Philippine Islands indefinitely, but "in due time" would dispose of the Philippines in a manner that would "best promote the interests of the citizens of the United States and the inhabitants of the said islands." On 6 February Hoar tried, unsuccessfully, to strengthen the resolution by inserting a specific promise that any government established in the Philippines must be "with the consent of the people thereof" and none could be imposed "upon them against their will." The McEnery resolution passed the Senate on 14 February by a vote of 26–22, with forty-two abstentions, but then died quietly in the House. *Congressional Record,* 55th Cong., 3d sess., 1487–1488, 1835–1840, 1848.

A single word of sympathy or encouragement, or of disclaimer of a purpose to subjugate them and govern them without any regard to their wishes, would have prevented this bloodshed.[47]

Hoar appreciated that with the outbreak of the Filipino Insurrection, praise of Aguinaldo would appear to an increasing number of his countrymen as purest treason. Within forty-eight hours of his vote of 6 February he was in receipt of at least five letters proclaiming him "an infamous traitor, conspirator and murderer."[48] Hoar did not flinch before these accusations. If in the course of duty he must suffer slander, he would continue to obey the dictates of conscience. But while doing his duty he wished, if possible, to retain the good opinion of his party chieftain. On the day after the treaty vote there occurred in the White House a meeting symbolic of the character of McKinley Republicanism and George F. Hoar.

Hoar wrote his son on the evening of 7 February: "I had a full talk with the President this morning. He expressed himself with great kindness and even affection toward me personally. I feel strongly inclined to believe that he wishes to accomplish in the matter just what I do."[49] Hoar's colleague Lodge had blundered into this meeting and had expressed his surprise to Henry Adams, who recounted it with a typical lack of charity:

> Only a few hours before, in the full belief that his single vote was going to defeat and ruin the administration, Hoar had voted against the treaty . . . [And now] . . . sitting by the President's side . . . unctuous, affectionate, beaming, the virtuous Hoar! . . . There he was, slobbering the President with assurances of his admiration, pressing on him a visit to Massachusetts, and distilling over him the oil of his sanctimony.[50]

[47] Hoar to Schurz, 9 February 1899, Papers of Carl Schurz, Volume 127, Library of Congress.

[48] *See,* for example, "An American" to Hoar, 7 February 1899; Arthur S. Sadler to Hoar, 8 February 1899, Hoar Papers.

[49] Hoar to Rockwood Hoar, 7 February 1899, Hoar Papers.

[50] Adams to Elizabeth Cameron, February 12, 1899, W. C. Ford, ed., *Letters of Henry Adams* (Boston: Houghton Mifflin, 1938), II, 217.

Adams possessed far too convoluted a personality to appreciate the more simple motivations of Hoar and McKinley. Hoar did not go to McKinley to beg forgiveness but rather to reassure himself that he was a member in good standing of the party of Sam Hoar and Abraham Lincoln, the party which in his eyes had accomplished more for liberty than any political instrument in the history of mankind. And McKinley had recognized this and had beamed away. For McKinley party harmony and good will were not only expedient, but the very principles of his administration. There was in both men a strong quality of what might be called political pietism. McKinley felt more at home with Hoar, the enemy of his foreign policy, than ever he would with Lodge and Roosevelt, its champions.[51]

Hoar would not desert the Filipinos in order to be assured of McKinley's regard—that would be dishonorable—but he was quite prepared to rebuff the Mugwump anti-imperialists. That was only sound politics. He thanked Gamaliel Bradford for his offer of a public dinner in Boston, and dismissed the project as undesirable.[52] Only to a fellow Republican could he express fully his fear that McKinley's treaty was not only unjust but disastrous. Shortly after the Senate vote he sent Eugene Hale a large steel engraving depicting the signing of the Declaration of Independence. He inscribed it as follows:

> To the Honorable Eugene Hale, who alone of my colleagues voted with me against the repeal of the Declaration of Independence,
>
> with the affectionate regard of
> Geo. F. Hoar[53]

---

[51] Lodge carefully refrained from direct criticism of his colleague, but the ebullient Roosevelt was positively creative in his denunciation of Hoar: "It is difficult for me to speak with moderation of such men as Hoar. They are a little better than traitors . . . He can be pardoned only on the ground that he is senile. His position is precisely that of the cotton whigs whom he so reprobated forty years ago." Roosevelt to Lodge, 26 January 1899, 7 February 1899, Elting E. Morison, ed., *The Letters of Theodore Roosevelt* (Cambridge, Mass.: Harvard University Press, 1951), II, 923, 935.

[52] Hoar to Gamaliel Bradford, 8 February 1899, Hoar Papers.

[53] Hoar to Eugene Hale, 1 March 1899 (copy), Hoar Papers.

Hoar exaggerated the revolutionary quality of the Treaty of Paris, but he was correct in his belief that its confirmation heralded the assumption of new responsibilities by the American nation and marked the conclusion of the first phase of the Philippines debate. That debate continued, however, as Americans continued to divide in their definition of those responsibilities. Its second phase would reach a noisy and confused climax with the election of 1900.

# 9

## The Election of 1900 and
## the Inevitable Decision

Hoar's well-publicized fight against the treaty had made him one of
the best known of American senators, and he found prominence a
burden as well as a consolation. Renown he enjoyed, but he was
suspicious of power, and had no desire to capitalize upon his new
fame to forge a bipartisan coalition or transform the anti-imperialist movement into a third party. Gratified by the recognition
given his efforts by his fellow anti-imperialists, he was impatient at
their insistence that he direct those efforts along unfamiliar lines.
A traditionalist where moral principles were concerned, Hoar
would continue to oppose colonialism; a dogmatist where party
loyalties were concerned, he must continue to hope that the
McKinley administration would reverse its policy in the Philippines.[1] Determined from the first to wage his battle within the
accustomed ranks of party, he could not but disappoint those who
sought to make him a political martyr.

[1] To the Secretary of the Massachusetts Club, Hoar wrote: "Oh, how Sumner and
Wilson would both have hated this massacre of these poor, ignorant peoples strug-
gling for their liberties at Iloilo." Hoar to S. S. Blanchard, 23 February 1899,
Hoar Papers.

"The Bugaboo of the Anti-Expansionist" from *Puck*, January 18, 1899. Hoar is shown kneeling on the left, shedding tears of sorrow or anger.

By the spring of 1899 the cause of anti-imperialism offered serious political risk. As Filipino resistance developed into organized insurrection and reports of American casualties mounted, it was increasingly easy for the declamatory patriot to associate anti-imperialism with cowardice if not treason. There was considerable interest within the anti-imperialist ranks to see whether or not Hoar would dilute his initial defense of Aguinaldo.

Hoar's first public statement after the beginning of the insurrection came in the form of a letter addressed to George S. Boutwell, president of the Anti-Imperialist League, and some one hundred other Boston anti-imperialists. In this letter, released to the press on the fourth of April, Hoar declared his conviction that the blame for the insurrection rested not on Aguinaldo nor the opponents of the Treaty of Paris, but upon the diplomacy of the McKinley administration and the duplicity of our military officers in the Philippines. The Filipinos knew that we had solicited their military assistance against the Spanish and that we had subsequently demanded "their absolute surrender." Treated in such fashion, would not any brave people feel tricked and entitled to resort to arms in defense of their liberties. "The blood of the slaughtered Filipinos, the blood and wasted health and life of our own soldiers" was upon the head of those who would violate "the principles upon which the American republic itself rests." America should protect the Filipino Republic, not seek its destruction. "Let us do what we pledged ourselves to do for Cuba—compel other nations to keep their hands off, and keep our own hands off as well."[2]

Though determined to defend the rights of the Filipino, Hoar was not prepared actively to collaborate with their spokesmen.[3] However just their cause they were men in armed contest with the soldiers of his own country. While vacationing on the Isle of

[2] "Letter from Hon. George F. Hoar, 29 March 1899, declining invitation to a public reception" (Boston, 1899), pamphlet, Hoar Papers. Hoar's letter was given wide publicity by the Boston Anti-Imperialist League, which arranged for its publication in pamphlet form. The league's secretary forwarded to Hoar a specially prepared cardboard map of the Philippine islands with the preamble of the Declaration of Independence superimposed across its face.

[3] Charges by an unfriendly Worcester editor that Hoar continued to be "in conference with Aguinaldo's agents in Washington" brought forth private but heated denials. Hoar to Daniel B. Howland, 18 April, 22 April 1899, Hoar Papers.

Wight in June 1899, Hoar received a request from Sixto Lopez to come to London, consult with the Filipino exiles there, and receive their "homage." Hoar declared that he was "deeply touched" by the invitation but believed such a meeting inadvisable "while the relations of the American people and the Philippino people are in their present unhappy condition."[4]

If negotiation between the Filipinos and a private American citizen was indictable under the Logan Act, no such restriction was imposed on official diplomacy. Hoar wished the McKinley administration to arrange an immediate armistice and invite Filipino representatives to Washington for discussions looking toward a permanent settlement. As the months passed, however, he was made aware that many of his countrymen believed that negotiations had to await the unconditional surrender of the Filipino and that sympathizers of the latter were faithless to the American soldier.

Such insinuations became more frequent as the insurrection continued. John Barrett, a minor politico and former minister to Siam, sought notoriety in the summer of 1899 by appearing before the Boston Chamber of Commerce and proclaiming Hoar an accomplice in the death of every American soldier on Luzon. Pleased by the stir that this occasioned, Barrett later declared in Chicago that it had been Hoar's Senate speech of 9 January, cabled to Aguinaldo by way of Hong Kong, that had precipitated the Filipino insurrection. Who had paid the four-thousand-dollar cost of the infamous cable, which had lent aid and comfort to "the rebellious Tagals?" The question was readily answered by the expansionist *Philadelphia Press.* It claimed to have discovered from "a prominent member of Congress" that Andrew Carnegie was the guilty party. The charge was groundless and the cable imaginary, but it remained good copy for several weeks, receiving a great play in several midwestern papers.[5]

After each attack by a fellow Republican, Hoar received a fresh vote of approval from the Mugwump members of the Anti-Imperialist League. Their strained alliance through the year 1899 and the

---

[4] Hoar to Lopez, 7 June 1899 (copy); Lopez to Hoar, 5 June, 9 June 1899, Hoar Papers.

[5] *See* Edward Atkinson to Hoar, 26 June 1899; clippings from *Philadelphia Press,* January 1900, Scrap Book, VII, Hoar Papers.

early months of 1900 was supported by a shared sense of outrage at those who would deny their patriotism as well as their counsel. Every time the correspondence of Hoar and Edward Atkinson appeared about to end in irritated disagreement over anti-imperialist tactics, it would burst into fresh volubility under the inspiration of some new assault by an expansionist spokesman. In his famous battle with the Postmaster General, Atkinson received indeed more sympathy from Hoar than from his fellow officers of the Anti-Imperialist League.

The seizure of Atkinson's tracts from the United States mails constituted one of the more sensational if minor episodes in the unhappy history of the anti-imperialist movement. In the spring of 1899 Atkinson sent the Secretary of War copies of his three most bitter anti-imperialist pamphlets, informing him of his intention subsequently to send them to American soldiers fighting in the Philippines. When he received no reply, Atkinson addressed copies of these pamphlets to seven persons in the Philippines—four of them United States army officers. The Postmaster General, Charles Emory Smith, then ordered his subordinates in San Francisco to remove them from the Manila mail. Never happier than when persecuted, Atkinson was in his glory. The order of the Postmaster General represented a direct threat to the constitutional liberty of free speech. Atkinson informed Hoar that the postal inspectors of San Francisco were rifling the mails for copies of the printed speeches of Hoar, George Boutwell, and former Senator George Edmunds, as well as his own pamphlets, and that this was only the beginning of the militaristic oppression that was to come.[6] Hoar was convinced that Atkinson exaggerated the danger, but unlike Erving Winslow, the nervous secretary of the Anti-Imperialist League, Hoar refused to repudiate or criticize either Atkinson or his pamphlets. Atkinson was grateful for his support and would remember it when a year later other members of the Anti-Imperialist League would denounce Hoar as a cowardly apostate.

During the year 1899 the history of the Anti-Imperialist League was marked by a growth in membership and continued confusion

---

[6] Atkinson to Hoar, 9 May 1899, Hoar Papers; Harrington, *Anti-Imperialist Movement*, 224–225.

of strategy. By May it claimed thirty thousand members and had moved its headquarters to Chicago and rechristened itself the American Anti-Imperialist League.[7] Hoar's grievance against the league had from the beginning been its Mugwump coloration, and its effort to assume a more national status did not alter his prejudice. He continued convinced that the league would be of influence in changing the policy of the McKinley administration only if it were identified with "responsible Republicans."

He was probably right, but he did little to correct the error of which he complained. As he was informed by both Moorfield Storey and George Boutwell, it was far easier to call for "an organization of Republican resistance to the President's policy," than to achieve it: "The difficulty is that the organization of the Republican party is so strong and the rewards which it can offer are so great, and the Democratic alternative is so unattractive that it is very difficult to make Republicans take the stand which they wish to. They dislike to weaken their own administration and to incur the penalties of independent action." Could not Hoar give them the names of Republicans whom they might approach; could he not persuade former Speaker Thomas B. Reed to "come out as he should."[8]

Suspicious of political amateurism and unduly conscious of his own legislative dignity, Hoar refused to proselytize for the league or associate too closely with it. He was determined to oppose McKinley's Philippines policy not only as a Republican but as a senator: "If I can be useful at all, my work must be done in the Senate, and I do not wish to have another person responsible for what I say or do, or to be myself responsible for what other people say or do."[9] It was an honest position, but one that denied him the opportunity to influence the strategy of the only significant organization within the anti-imperialist movement.

For the Anti-Imperialist League, however diverse and divided its membership, was composed of some of the best minds and pens

[7] Its charter branch in Boston now assumed the name of the New England Anti-Imperialist League. Lanzar, "The Anti-Imperialist League," *Philippine Social Science Review*, 3 (August 1930), 24–29.

[8] Boutwell to Hoar, 15 February 1899; Storey to Hoar, 9 March 1899, Hoar Papers. *See,* too, Storey to Hoar, 28 February 1900 (copy), Moorfield Storey Papers, Library of Congress.

[9] Hoar to Erving Winslow, 1 January 1900, Hoar Papers.

in the country, and time and again Hoar would be compelled to forget his suspicions respecting its political reliability and seek the assistance of certain of its members. Moorfield Storey was instructed to find a lawyer who would compile opinions on the status of Spanish authority in the Philippines at the time of their transfer; Samuel Bowles, Jr., publisher of the *Springfield Republican*, was requested to forward materials collected by a member of his staff "on the present conditions" in the islands; and Herbert Welsh, the industrious Philadelphia propagandist, was asked to match his memorial from the bishops of the Episcopal church with one from Methodist clergymen—McKinley being a Methodist.[10] These requests were always eagerly accepted; for these men were all educators at heart. They shared with Hoar a common conviction that if only enough information could be collected and disseminated, the people must turn against imperialism and repledge their allegiance to the old faith and creed.

But how best to convince the administration and Congress? Here division succeeded agreement, and Hoar and the league managers worked at cross purposes. Underlying their differences was a basic disagreement over the role of the league itself. Hoar was determined to make anti-imperialism a Republican crusade, the crusade of a party redeemed from temporary error. The function of the league should be that of an information service, subordinate if perhaps necessary. Edward Atkinson, on the other hand, believed that the anti-imperial crusade must supersede all party loyalties and that the league should dominate the crusade. It was essential that Congress and the President feel the whip of the league's wrath and be driven publicly to confess their sins.[11] Seemingly convinced that denunciation alone would stop "the accursed war," Atkinson showered upon McKinley and "his masters" an amazingly varied selection of epithets, and with each he lost that much more of the confidence of the leading anti-imperialist in the United States Senate.

The pattern of Hoar's relations with Atkinson was repeated time and again with other officers of the league, and in New York and

[10] Hoar to Moorfield Storey, 20 February 1900; Samuel Bowles to Hoar, 31 October 1899; Hoar to Herbert Welsh, 22 December 1899, Hoar Papers.

[11] Hoar to Atkinson, 21 November 1899, Atkinson Papers, Massachusetts Historical Society; Atkinson to Hoar, 26 February 1900, Hoar Papers.

Philadelphia as well as Boston. In Philadelphia it was Herbert Welsh and George C. Mercer who sought to make him their spokesmen and who were frustrated in the attempt. The Philadelphia league planned a giant banquet for 14 December 1899, the centennial anniversary of the death of Washington, and made an intensive effort to gain Hoar as their stellar attraction. Initially he refused—disinclined to attend a meeting where "I might very probably hear severe criticism of the conduct of my associates in the Senate"—but he subsequently relented to the point of sending the honorary president of the league a long letter which was read to great acclaim at the dinner.[12] The honorary president was George F. Edmunds, the Half-Breed Republican for whom Hoar had voted at the Republican conventions of 1880 and 1884. In Hoar's eyes his name on the letterhead gave promise that the meeting would be politically respectable and salutary. It was in fact a meeting that featured some of the most vituperative criticism of the entire anti-imperialist campaign, and Hoar soon regretted that he had released his letter through such a controversial media. At no time did he apologize for its argument:

> If we had dealt with the people of the Philippine Islands as we undertook to deal with the people of Cuba who we declared . . . of right ought to be free and independent; if instead of undertaking to buy them, and then undertaking to subjugate them by force, we had assured them of our purpose to respect their rights, to protect them against foreign interference, to aid them to restore order and to leave them whenever they should desire to the blessing of Freedom and of self-government, we should have had no war [and] . . . we should not have trampled on the doctrines upon which our own institutions are founded . . . We should have had the glory—with which the glory of no other country in history could be compared—of being the great liberator in both hemispheres.[13]

[12] George G. Mercer to Hoar, 27 November 1899; Hoar to Mercer, 8 December 1899, Hoar Papers.

[13] Hoar to George F. Edmunds, 13 December 1899, pamphlet of the American Anti-Imperialist League, Hoar Papers.

Less than a month later Hoar would express an identical opinion in reply to Senator Albert J. Beveridge. Their confrontation on the floor of the United States Senate, 9 January 1900, was possibly the most dramatic personal encounter of the long and tangled Philippine debate. Symbolic of the shifting leadership of the Republican party, that encounter also reflected the changing rationale of the imperialist argument. For if under the impact of defeat and slander many anti-imperialists turned savagely against the person of McKinley, so under the stimulus of success and popularity the expansionists were persuaded to reveal more boldly their aims and ambitions.

The Senate and press had anticipated Beveridge's Philippines speech with considerable interest. Recently returned from a visit to the islands and newly elected to the Senate, Beveridge was the self-conscious personification of Young America. It was anticipated that he would defend colonial expansion without apology or disguise, and he did not disappoint. Never was the economic argument for imperialism offered more unashamedly. Appeals to duty and service were overshadowed in his exposition by descriptions of untapped raw materials and limitless markets. The incapable Filipino resided in a land that could furnish the technology of America with magnificent opportunity for economic profit and expansion. By our occupation of the Philippines we should fulfill our mission of regeneration, but let none believe that once the Filipino was improved he would be released. On the contrary, we would "establish the supremacy of the American Republic over the Pacific and throughout the East till the end of time." That supremacy would secure our role as carriers of Anglo-Saxon civilization, and it would be to our advantage and profit.[14]

Read today Beveridge's oration does not appear remarkable for either its organization or its language. It was heard, however, with rapt attention and when the orator finished he met a storm of applause from the galleries and the immediate congratulation of dozens of his colleagues. The handsome, boyish Indianan was a student of elocution and the dramatic gesture, and the Senate of 1900 and its audience still appreciated both. Many minutes passed

[14] *Congressional Record*, 56th Cong., 1st sess., 704–712.

before Senator Frye in the chair saw the excited hand of Senator Hoar and still more before the Senate was restored to sufficient order to hear his warning:

> I have listened, delighted, as have, I suppose all the members of the Senate, to the eloquence of my honorable friend from Indiana . . . Yet Mr. President, as I heard his eloquent description of wealth and glory and commerce and trade, I listened in vain for those words which the American people have been wont to take upon their lips in every solemn crisis of their history. I heard much calculated to excite the imagination of the youth seeking wealth, of the youth charmed by the dream of empire. But the words Right, Justice, Duty, Freedom were absent, my friend must permit me to say, from that eloquent speech. I could think as this brave young Republic of ours listened to what he had to say of but one occurrence:
> "Then the devil taketh Him up into an exceeding high mountain and sheweth Him all the kingdoms of the world and the glory of them.
> And the devil said unto Him, 'All these things will I give Thee if Thou wilt fall down and worship me.'
> Then said Jesus unto him, 'Get thee behind me Satan.'"[15]

Despite interruptions from Senators Teller and Cockrell, Hoar was allowed to expand his reprimand and recite again his objections to the course of empire, but the glory of the day belonged to Senator Beveridge in the eyes of the Washington press. Indeed the *Washington Post* was so admirous of the forthright declaration of Beveridge that it was emboldened to declare: "We annexed these possessions in cold blood" and we "intend to utilize them to our own profit."[16]

Beveridge's speech was symbolic of the evolving arguments of the expansionists, but by no means were all as forthright in detailing the advantages of colonial expansion for a nation possessed of an increasing economic surplus. William McKinley, always seeking the broadest consensus possible, was far too shrewd to discard the

---

[15] *Ibid.*, 712.
[16] *Washington Post*, 14 January 1900, cited in Weinberg, *Manifest Destiny*, 310.

arguments of moral duty and humanitarian service while increasing his references to foreign markets and Oriental commerce. And Henry Cabot Lodge, although no longer concealing the extent of his expansionist convictions from his Massachusetts constituents and prepared by the spring of 1900 to offer a full-dress review of the "Large Policy," would continue to place chief emphasis upon the arguments of national strength and diplomatic duty.

On 7 March 1900, Lodge addressed the Senate and offered the most detailed brief imperialism was ever to receive in America. Colonial expansion found justification in morality, the Constitution, and international law. It offered economic advantages to the farmers, workingmen, and manufacturers of America; it was demanded by the needs of military defense and the manifest destiny of the nation. Especially on the last score did Lodge offer a significant contribution to the evolution of imperialist rationale. Others had spoken of mission and duty, but Lodge went beyond these concepts to defend imperialism as an essential long-term national policy:

> We are told that the possession of these islands brings a great responsibility upon us. This . . . I freely admit. A great nation must have great responsibilities. It is one of the penalties of greatness. But the benefit of responsibilities goes hand in hand with the burdens they bring. The nation which seeks to escape from the burden also loses the benefit, and if it cowers in the presence of a new task and shirks a new responsibility the period of its decline is approaching . . . It was neither chance nor accident which brought us to the Pacific and which has now carried us across the great ocean even to the shores of Asia, to the very edge of the cradle of the Aryans, whence our far distant ancestors started on the march which has since girdled the world . . . What we have done was inevitable because it was in accordance with the laws of our being as a nation, in the defiance and disregard of which lie ruin and retreat.[17]

McKinley spoke seldom of the "laws of our being," but he shared in full the determination not to "retreat." In some measure

[17] *Congressional Record*, 56th Cong., 1st sess., 2616–2630.

McKinley stumbled into the Philippines, but it was with purposeful intent that he stayed there. If McKinley never realized the full implications of the new diplomatic departure, he was increasingly convinced of the association between territorial expansion and an exportable surplus, and quite prepared to initiate that departure. Certain of his contemporaries were well aware of the determination beneath the platitudes. In the opinion of George Boutwell, McKinley was able as well as wrong: "I give him credit for great ability guided by purpose;" the purpose, "to found a colonial, republican empire."[18]

McKinley's continuing effort to ignore Republican dissension over his foreign policy was not a reflection of timidity but the response of a man determined to be a consensus president. McKinley's great contribution to his party, as he saw it, lay in his ability to promote unity and harmony: between the executive and Congress, between the West and East, between its agrarian supporters and industrial contributors. Foreign expansion could serve to heal domestic divisions, at least if one was careful not to make martyrs of dissidents such as Senator Hoar. And McKinley was a careful man.[19]

Hoar for his part proclaimed an unshaken conviction in the purity of McKinley's motives and a continuing opposition to his Philippines policy. Hoar's stand was misunderstood by many, but never by McKinley.[20] Yet if both men were determined to be conciliatory, each drew a careful if subconscious line between conciliation and appeasement. Hoar would instinctively issue a new denunciation of imperialism every time he made a propitiatory gesture toward the person and office of the president. Indeed in the months just prior to his public endorsement of McKinley's re-

[18] Boutwell to Hoar, 9 October 1899, Hoar Papers.

[19] After the confirmation of the treaty by the Senate, McKinley had made a trip to Massachusetts where he had combined a short visit to Hoar's veranda in Worcester and a speech in defense of his foreign policy before the Home Market Club of Boston. *New York Tribune,* 17 February 1899; Albert Clarke, Secretary, Home Market Club, to Hoar, 4 March 1899, Hoar Papers.

[20] It was the opinion of William Croffut, Secretary of the Washington Anti-Imperialist League, that Hoar stood alone in "denouncing the crime and praising the criminal." Croffut to George Boutwell, 27 May 1900, Boutwell Papers, Massachusetts Historical Society.

election, Hoar made his greatest effort to wrench his party back to virtue. The culmination of that effort was his Senate speech of 17 April 1900, but earlier there had been the Senate resolutions of December 1899 and the "Letter to Mr. Quigg."

Hoar's resolutions of 20 December 1899, were not introduced with any thought that they would be adopted. They were intended as a warning and a plea to the McKinley administration. Hoar offered them in his role of a contemporary Jeremiah elected to remind the chosen party of its true purpose and covenant. That covenant embraced the following injunctions for the Republic:

> To grow and expand . . . just so fast and no faster, as we can bring into equality and self-government, under our Constitution, people and races who will share [our] ideals and help to make them realities.

> To set a peaceful example of freedom which mankind will be glad to follow, but never to force even freedom upon unwilling nations . . .

> To abstain from interfering with the freedom and just rights of other nations or peoples, and to remember that the liberty to do right necessarily involves the liberty to do wrong; and that the American people has no right to take from any other people the birthright of freedom because of a fear that they will do wrong with it.

Hoar's resolutions expressed his continuing conviction that however sincerely McKinley might wish to help the Filipino, the actions of his administration were dangerous as well as misguided.[21]

McKinley passed the word that the supporters of the administration should ignore Hoar's resolutions, but certain of those supporters felt obliged to denounce the resolutions and their author. Of the attacks received, perhaps none more irritated Hoar than those implying that he had no plan for the Philippines and sought

---

[21] *Congressional Record*, 56th Cong., 1st sess., 601–602 (20 December 1899); *Boston Journal*, 21 December 1899.

simply to counsel his countrymen to ignore their duty. He was particularly incensed when these attacks were waged within the precincts of Massachusetts and by foreigners, such as the former New York Congressman, Lemuel E. Quigg.

On the last day of December 1899, Mr. Quigg made a speech to the Essex County Republican Club, in the course of which he charged that "Senator Hoar wants us to skulk from our duty."[22] In a public letter published by all the Boston papers, Hoar sought to repudiate the charge once and for all. He insisted that he had maintained from the beginning that America should stand by the Philippines, "a defender and protector," until their government was "established in freedom and in honor." Only let us recognize their rightful claim to independence and a cease fire could be easily negotiated. Then General Miles could go to the Philippines, "gather about him a cabinet of the best men among the Filipinos," and begin the process of turning over to the Filipinos the direction of their own government: "I would by degrees withdraw the authority of the United States, making a treaty with them that we would protect them against the cupidity of any other nation and would lend our aid for a reasonable time to maintain law and order. I would not hesitate, if it were needful . . . to vote to make them a loan of a moderate sum to replenish their wasted treasury.[23]

The publication of this letter brought a fresh burst of applause from such political independents as Samuel Bowles, Jr., but elicited a mixed reception among Republican regulars in Massachusetts.[24] All could unite in questioning Congressman Quigg's manners, but such partisan organs as the *Boston Journal* now openly recognized the division of Massachusetts Republicans and awarded Hoar the blame. By April 1900 the *Journal* would publicly question whether "love for Senator Hoar" could be long sustained if he did not change his ways. "If Massachusetts remain loyal to the man, the state will be charged with open disloyalty to the president, for it

[22] *Boston Herald*, 2 January 1900.
[23] *Boston Globe*, 10 January 1900; *Boston Journal*, 11 January 1900. A more detailed statement of Hoar's position on "Our Duty To the Philippines" will be found in *The Independent* of 9 November 1899.
[24] *Springfield Republican*, 3 January 1900.

will be hard indeed to convince the country that we support the president while we are supporting the one man who has done most to injure him."[25] Praise and criticism would reach new heights with the publication of Hoar's Senate speech of 17 April—his supreme effort in the anti-imperialist cause.

Hoar offered neither new arguments nor new solutions. What he offered was a synthesis of the beliefs and difficulties of a Republican anti-imperialist. From the beginning Hoar made clear that he addressed himself primarily to his own party; for the party and person of Bryan offered neither promise nor sincerity.

With imagery and illustration refined by the practice of many months, Hoar reviewed the anti-imperialist contentions over American annexation and conquest of the Philippines. Such conquest was contrary to the Constitution, economically inexpedient, strategically unwise, and morally unjustifiable. It was false to our historic traditions and indeed to the very nature of republican liberty:

As the Christian religion was rested by its author on two sublime commandments on which hang all the laws and the prophets, so [our Founding Fathers] rested republican liberty on two sublime verities . . . in which it must live or bear no life. One was the equality of the individual man with every other in political right. The other is that you are now seeking to overthrow—the right of every people to institute their own government and organize its powers in such form as to them shall seem most likely to effect their safety and happiness, and so to assume . . . the separate and equal station to which the laws of nature and of nature's God entitle them.

These two secular commandments were necessarily associated. A nation that was prepared to deny the rights of Filipinos abroad would soon deny the rights of certain of its citizens at home. Already it was evident that Republican leaders who insisted upon

[25] Scrap Book, VI (1897–1900), Hoar Papers.

the incapacity of the Filipino no longer dared to question the disfranchisement of the southern Negro.[26]

Our true mission was to set for the world an example of republican virtue, freedom, and equality. To call for a policy faithful to the past was not to deny the power and influence of America but to preserve it. The opponents of imperialism sought not to deny the nation's duty but to perform that duty in a manner respectful of the natural rights of others and our own fundamental principles. The Republican party was the very embodiment of those principles. It could deny them for the moment, but surely not for long. All must soon come right.

> The stars in their courses fight for freedom. The ruler of the heavens is on that side. If the battle to-day go against it, I appeal to another day, not distant and sure to come . . . I appeal from the Present, bloated with material prosperity, drunk with the lust of empire, to another and a better age. I appeal from the Present to the Future and to the Past.[27]

To the accompaniment of the prolonged applause of the Senate, Hoar slowly gathered the ninety pages of his manuscript and retired to his rented room at the Hotel Richmond. He had done what he had to do, and having denounced the administration and warned his party, he could now support both in good conscience in

---

[26] Hoar was well aware of the historical connection between the declining concern for the rights of the American Negro and the conviction of many Americans respecting the incapacity of the Tagalogs. A month before he had written to his friend Susan B. Anthony:

> At present the sense of justice and righteousness and the love of liberty which abolished slavery and put down the Rebellion and gave citizenship and suffrage to the colored people seems dead. Senator Morgan made his bid for re-election by a speech in the Senate in which he declared the unfitness of the negro for citizenship and demanded that the 14th and 15th amendments to the Constitution be rescinded. And now it is said that the Republicans in his State are to support him for Senator . . . as he is too valuable a supporter of expansion policies to be spared from public life.

Hoar to Susan B. Anthony, 14 March 1900, Hoar Papers.

[27] *Congressional Record,* 56th Cong., 1st sess., 4278–4306.

the forthcoming election. He was not to blame if certain of his fellow anti-imperialists saw fit to overlook his castigation of Bryan's conduct and party and assume that he would take another course.

Most members of the Anti-Imperialist League gave Hoar's speech the tribute of unreserved praise, but before three months had passed many would damn him as an apostate.[28] When Hoar formally announced his support of McKinley, they would proclaim him a political captive, prepared to sacrifice principle to party. It was not an unnatural judgment; neither was it accurate. If political honesty can be defined as the consistent application of professed beliefs, Hoar's decision was quite as honest as the contrary choice of his critics. It was, even more certainly, inevitable.

Time and again Hoar had made clear his determination to enunciate the cause of anti-imperialism as a Republican and to continue to demand the rights and influence of party affiliation.[29] Whatever its present errors, the Republican party was to his mind the party of economic progress and honest government. It was the party of Jefferson as well as Lincoln, the party of rural virtues as well as Negro emancipation. Republican affiliation was not a political convenience but a moral necessity, and desertion would be not only wicked but harmful to the anti-imperialist cause. The deserter lost

---

[28] See, for example, Boutwell to Hoar, 19 April 1900; Erving Winslow to Hoar, 18 April, 2 May 1900; Gamaliel Bradford to Hoar, 18 April, 21 April 1900; Winslow Warren to Hoar, 18 April 1900; Moorfield Storey to Hoar, 20 April 1900, Hoar Papers.

Professor William James, writing from Mauheim, Germany, was careful to balance his praise of Hoar with a blunt accusation of McKinley's personal responsibility for crushing "the sacredest thing on earth: the successful attempt of an aspiring people to embody its own ideals in its own institutions." James offered the opinion that Hoar's speech made him "one of the few vital figures of American history," and agreed that our Philippine policy had diminished our power among the nations of the world. We had lost "our unique past position among the nations, of the only great one that could be a trusted mediator and arbiter, because the only one that was not a professional pirate." "Having puked up our ancient national soul after 5 minutes," we were now prisoners in "the chain of international hatreds, and every atom of our moral prestige lost forever." James to Hoar, 11 May 1900, Hoar Papers.

[29] See, for example, Hoar to George Boutwell, 23 December, 29 December 1899; Hoar to Henry B. Blackwell, 26 December 1899; Hoar to Gamaliel Bradford, 20 April 1900, Hoar Papers.

all opportunity to accomplish good or lessen evil.[30] All Republican anti-imperialists must stay in the party. If they did, then no man could with justice confuse the expected re-election of McKinley with an endorsement of the administration's course in the Philippines. All men would judge his re-election for what it would truly be, a second repudiation of Bryan and Bryanism.

Hoar publicly urged the re-election of William McKinley in a speech at Marshfield, Massachusetts on 6 July 1900. With this speech he inaugurated the presidential campaign in Massachusetts and enunciated the rationale for all Republican anti-imperialists who chose to stand by their party. The election of Bryan would endanger social order, financial honesty, and domestic prosperity without compensating advantage for the nation's foreign policy. The Democratic party, whatever the professions of certain of its politicians, was riddled with the infection of expansion. Bryan offered no hope for the Filipino and only depression and danger for his own countrymen.

The Marshfield address was greeted with relief by the Republican organization in Massachusetts and with a sharp sense of grievance by the Anti-Imperialist League. Henry Cabot Lodge wrote that he was delighted by the "force, power and eloquence of the whole speech." Lodge knew his elder colleague sufficiently well to expect his endorsement of McKinley and to appreciate that neither ambition nor cowardice had determined it.[31] The anti-imperialist *Springfield Republican*, on the contrary, had not expected it and excoriated its logic. For Hoar to cast the chief blame for the Treaty of Paris on Bryan was outrageous; it was to declare more guilty a man

---

[30] To Moorfield Storey he had written: "I think the men who left the Republican party in 1872 to vote for Greeley, and the men who left the Republican party in 1884 to vote for Cleveland made it much harder to accomplish the good they conscientiously desired to accomplish than it would have been if they had stayed. If these men had been with us, were with us now, we should have stopped the imperialistic business long ago. If the persons who wish to put a stop to it now quit the Republican party . . . the only reasonable hope that we may stop it will be extinguished." Hoar to Storey, 6 March 1900, Hoar Papers. *See*, too, Hoar to Gustav Mayer, editor of *Prosperity*, 9 May 1900; Hoar to William Endicott, 9 May 1900, Hoar Papers.

[31] *See* George H. Lyman to Lodge, 10 July 1900; Lodge to Lyman, 16 July 1900, Lodge Papers, Massachusetts Historical Society.

who failed to defeat evil than the man who conceived it. Fortunately, Hoar's endorsement of McKinley would have little practical effect—its impact on popular opinion would be balanced by his earlier anti-imperialist addresses—but it must damage "his standing as a statesman and patriot."[32]

Some of Hoar's critics were content to register sorrow and bewilderment; others preferred anger. Thomas B. Reed, now safe in the profitable retreat of private law, implied that Hoar had deserted his principles from a wish "to die in the Senate," and an Ohio Republican insisted that Hoar's decision was in flagrant contradiction to his words and labors of the past year.[33] The more significant criticisms, however, were those of such political Independents as Erving Winslow and Edward Atkinson and such Democrats as Allen Thurman and William Jennings Bryan. To summarize their accusations is to indicate the varying shades of criticism occasioned by Hoar's decision and to offer yet another illustration of the fatal disunity of the anti-imperialist movement.

Three days after Hoar's Marshfield Address, Erving Winslow sent Hoar a letter by courtesy of the Associated Press. It was a lengthy letter but its general tenor was embodied in the following paragraph:

> You have thought proper to make a bitter attack upon the character of the Democratic candidate. He is not the candidate of the anti-imperialist organization; we as yet have none. We are simply pledged so far to defeat the author and representative of imperial policy . . . President McKinley . . . We are even content to leave the motive unimpugned of one whose championship of the right has been carried just exactly far enough to aid in the highest degree the cause of wrong . . . It is a melancholy fact that your venerable hand has been the first to be sullied with the mud-slinging of the campaign of 1900, but it has done

[32] *Springfield Republican*, 9 July 1900.

[33] "Reminiscences of George H. Lyman," Massachusetts Historical Society *Proceedings*, LXV (1932–1936), 230–231; Samuel P. Butler to Hoar, 26 August 1900, Hoar Papers. *See*, too, Nathaniel T. Allen to Samuel Bowles, 3 November 1900, Scrap Book #2, Moorfield Storey Papers, Library of Congress.

much, thank Heaven, to weaken the effect of your apostasy to the cause of liberty.[34]

Winslow's castigation was answered not only by Hoar, but by Edward Atkinson.[35] Atkinson, like Winslow, was a Republican-turned-Mugwump, but Atkinson was a man who could appreciate Hoar even while contesting the logic of his decision. Atkinson, moreover, was an amateur economist and gold bug and had little use for Bryan and free silver. Consequently, Atkinson was in the unfortunate but not illogical position of a man who desired the defeat of both McKinley and Bryan; alternately criticizing Hoar for supporting McKinley and admonishing various members of the Anti-Imperialist League for their praise of Bryan. Throughout he attempted to make clear the difference between his comradely chastisement of Hoar and that of such "small fry" as Erving Winslow:

I have been rebuking certain persons for their foolish attacks upon you, they not being capable of believing that a man can be sincere in his opposition to Imperialism and yet support the Republican party under its present control . . .

I have dealt with facts, not persons. I think the facts are undisputed. What McKinley's motive may have been does not concern me; but the man who could take the course that he has taken in consideration of these facts is in my judgment incapable, unfit, dangerous . . . He may be as sincere as you think him, but he is the type of man of whom it has been said in old time, that "Hell is paved with their good intentions," and he has paved a very large area in that way.[36]

[34] Worcester *Spy*, 10 July 1900. *See*, too, Captain Patrick O'Farrell to Hoar, 30 July 1900, Hoar Papers; *Springfield Republican*, 18 July 1900.

[35] *The Spy* (Worcester), 10 July 1900; *Boston Advertiser*, 11 July 1900.

[36] Atkinson to Hoar, 15 August 1900, Hoar Papers. Harold F. Williamson, Atkinson's biographer, declares that of the two candidates, Atkinson "preferred McKinley." Atkinson's correspondence with Hoar shows that he disliked both candidates intensely, but disliked McKinley the more. Harold F. Williamson, *Edward Atkinson: The Biography of an American Liberal, 1827–1905* (Boston: Old Corner Book Store, 1934), 230.

If for Atkinson, Hoar's course was illogical and for Winslow, traitorous; for Allen W. Thurman, it was at least disappointing. Having used certain of Hoar's speeches as campaign documents in 1899, Thurman and other Democratic politicians hoped to use their author in the campaign of 1900.[37] It was a strained hope and in the case of Thurman one shattered two months before the Marshfield address.

Thurman, an Ohio Democrat and the son of Cleveland's running mate in 1888, had been quick to note in Hoar's Senate speech of 17 April the theme of continuing allegiance to the Republican party. He had written Hoar that he found the speech both eloquent and contradictory. Surely Hoar did not believe that the victory of the Democrats would represent a greater danger than the present evil of colonialism. If Thurman's letter was designed as a "feeler," Hoar's response left no doubt of his unwillingness to enlist under Bryan's banner. The question, Hoar wrote, was not which was worse for the country, imperialism or Bryanism, but whether the election of the Democratic candidate, harmful in all other respects, would offer advantage to the cause of anti-imperialism. It would not: "I know there are many good, honest and patriotic Democrats who have been misled in the past and are now misled into the support of the Democratic party, just as McKinley has been misled into the support of a wrong and disastrous policy. But there is nothing to be hoped from that party as an organization, and there is little to be hoped from any man whom that organization will make its candidate for the Presidency."[38]

Apprised by Thurman of Hoar's charge that Bryan had counseled ratification of the treaty for reasons of partisan advantage, Bryan wrote to Hoar to protest the charge and to persuade him of the similarity of their views respecting American policy in the

[37] *See* Thurman to Hoar, 12 January 1900; C. G. Heifner to Hoar, 19 April 1900, Hoar Papers.

[38] Thurman to Hoar, 30 April 1900; Hoar to Thurman, 2 May 1900 (copy), Hoar Papers. *See*, too, Thurman to Hoar, 5 May 1900 (photocopy), Bryan Papers, Library of Congress.

Philippines.[39] By implication he requested Hoar's sympathy and cooperation. He received neither. Hoar began his reply on a note of conciliation, but it ended with a full-scale repetition of his initial charge. Dismissing Bryan's advocacy of a temporary American protectorate in the Philippines as but colonialism in disguise—and quite foreign to his own proposals for gradual American withdrawal—Hoar concentrated on the past sins of Bryan and his divided party:

> The fact remains that, so far as you had power to influence the result—and your influence seems to me to have decided the result—you induced the Senate . . . to affirm the right to purchase sovereignty over an unwilling people, to pay for it in gold, and to affirm that the Congress of the United States would thereafter dispose of that people according to its pleasure. . . . Under these circumstances you can hardly expect that any kindly personal feeling will induce me to support a party or a candidate from whom I differ so widely as to all other important questions, including the recognition of the humanity, equality and citizenship of ten millions of our own countrymen; or to hope that a gentleman who thought the Spanish treaty right, will now be able to undo the terrible wrong which that treaty caused, especially when so large and influential a number of his own supporters disagree with him.[40]

Bryan again sought to deny that he ever thought the Spanish treaty "right" or ever feared to fight the forthcoming campaign on domestic issues, but the effort was brief. Convinced that there was no hope of Hoar's support, Bryan dismissed him as a hopeless partisan: "I do not write to argue the case with you. The National plat-

---

[39] Thurman to Bryan, 5 May 1900 (photocopy), Bryan Papers, Library of Congress; Bryan to Hoar, 10 May 1900, Special Collection, Hoar Papers.

[40] Hoar to Bryan, 15 May 1900 (copy), Hoar Papers. There were in fact differences between the policy proposed by Hoar and Schurz in the winter of 1899 and the protectorate scheme advocated by Bryan and later incorporated in the Democratic platform of 1900. Bryan's exposition of a temporary protectorate seemed to imply that the United States would *grant*, not acknowledge, Filipino independence and this *after* aid had been given and orderly government established. *See* Hoar to Edward Atkinson, 30 July 1900, Hoar Papers.

forms will soon be adopted and then each citizen must decide for himself."[41]

Each citizen who bothered to vote in the election presumably "decided for himself," but the character of the platforms and campaigns of 1900 makes it doubtful that he decided primarily upon the issue of imperialism.

The Republican platform of 1900 supported the gold standard and the protective tariff, favored an isthmian canal and the subsidization of shipping, and spoke rather airily of eliminating monopoly. The Democrats, at Bryan's insistence, declared again for free silver, and advocated tariff reform, the direct election of fedderal senators, an enlargement of the regulatory powers of the Interstate Commerce Commission, and an end to "government by injunction." The Republicans issued a strong endorsement of McKinley's Philippine policy; the Democrats proclaimed imperialism "the paramount issue" of the campaign and promised the Filipinos peace now and independence later. Specifically, the Democratic platform read: "We favor an immediate declaration of the nation's purpose to give to the Filipinos, first, a stable form of government; second, independence; and third, protection from outside interference such as has been given for nearly a century to the republics of Central and South America." The Republican platform declared that with the destruction of Spanish authority in the Philippines it became the duty of America "to provide for the maintenance of law and order, and for the establishment of good government and for the performance of international obligations. Our authority could not be less than our responsibility; and wherever sovereign rights were extended it became the high duty of the Government to maintain its authority, to put down armed insurrection, and to confer the blessings of liberty and civilization upon all the rescued peoples."[42]

In the heat of the campaign Hoar would declare on several occasions that he found "little practical difference" between the protectorate notions of Bryan and the imperial benevolence of the

[41] Bryan to Hoar, 1 June 1900, Hoar Papers.

[42] Kirk H. Porter; Donald B. Johnson, *National Party Platforms, 1840–1960* (Urbana: University of Illinois Press, 1961), 113, 124; *Congressional Record*, 71st Cong., 2nd sess., 1023.

Republican platform, and several authors have subsequently expressed a similar judgment. According to one historian Bryan's program for the Philippines represented a "kind of imperial anticolonialism;" another has declared that there was "after all, little difference between Tweedledum and Tweedledee."[43] As with most exaggerations, there is a degree of truth here. Bryan, the author of the Democratic plank, did disappoint Winslow and other self-appointed advisers from the Anti-Imperialist League by not demanding immediate independence for the Philippines. The essential theme of the Democratic plank, however, was a denunciation of imperial expansion, and the essential theme of its Republican counterpart was a defense of a foreign policy of expansion. By the shifting emphases of his campaign Bryan would subsequently becloud the issue of imperialism, but the respective foreign policy planks of the two major parties were not indistinguishable. If they had been, it is possible that the third-party efforts of such uncompromising anti-imperialists as Moorfield Storey would have been more successful because more necessary.

As early as December 1899 there had been talk of a third-party movement within the ranks of the anti-imperialists, particularly among those who were strong gold men and consequently loath to support Bryan. Edwin Burritt Smith, chairman of the executive committee of the American Anti-Imperialist League, had from his Chicago headquarters issued a call for a meeting of anti-expansionist Republicans and others at the Plaza Hotel in New York on 6 January 1900 to explore the possibilities of fashioning the anti-imperialist movement into a separate political organization. Hoar was asked repeatedly to attend and refused, but the list of acceptances was impressive if small.[44] Former senators George Edmunds

---

[43] William A. Williams, *The Tragedy of American Diplomacy* (Cleveland: World Publishing Company, 1949), 36; Leon Wolff, *Little Brown Brother* (Garden City, N.Y.: Doubleday, 1961), 327.

[44] Edwin Burritt Smith to Hoar, 18 December, 30 December 1899, Hoar Papers. Hoar was the recipient of several letters in the winter and early spring of 1900 urging that he head a third ticket and run on a platform comprised solely of the Declaration of Independence. Among those who envisioned Hoar as a presidential candidate was Moreton Frewen, amateur British diplomat and tireless friend of the great. Frewen's suggestion afforded Henry Adams the opportunity for another epistolary gossip:

and Donelson Caffery, Andrew Carnegie, Carl Schurz, Senator Richard Pettigrew, George S. Boutwell, Franklin Henry Giddings, Edwin Burritt Smith, and Herbert Welsh were all in attendance, along with some dozen others. The meeting accomplished little, and whatever expectations it generated among its participants were soon dashed when Andrew Carnegie withdrew his support and his money.[45] By June, when the Democratic platform emphasized anti-imperialism, the ranks of the third-party faction were further reduced. But a few anti-imperialists continued to pursue the idea, and as late as August they made an effort to persuade the "Liberty Congress" to adopt their views.

The Liberty Congress that met in Indianapolis on 15–16 August was primarily the work of Erving Winslow and Carl Schurz. Its purpose was to coordinate the efforts of the members of the anti-imperialist leagues in the campaign then underway, and, in the view of its chief sponsors, to unite that membership behind the Democratic party and Bryan. John Jay Chapman, the erratic poet and essayist from Cambridge, and his friends had other ideas, however. They proposed to meet in Indianapolis on 14 August and generate such excitement in behalf of a third-party movement that the Liberty Congress would be forced to agree. Chapman's meeting was an unmixed failure. A mere handful attended and when a small delegation visited Moorfield Storey and offered him their presidential nomination, he sorrowfully informed them they had best forget the whole thing.[46] In the Liberty Congress itself there

---

Poor dear Moreton Frewen has turned up . . . His stupidity is divine—portentous—volcanic . . . As we were innocently talking of his democratic friends and their best candidate, he said, seriously, solemnly, with sublime good faith, that they ought to unite the best elements of both parties, and nominate—guess! I'll give you twenty guesses! fifty! a hundred! He would be, according to Frewen, sure of election. He would command the confidence and support of Wall Street, State Street, South Dakota, and Jones of Arkansas–Nevada . . . For Frewen's candidate was the senior senator, Cabot's colleague, your own adored cousin, George Frisbie Hoar . . . The Major's luck is great, but, after all, not so colossal as that.

Adams to Elizabeth Cameron, 5 February 1900, Worthington C. Ford, ed., *Letters of Henry Adams*, II, 262–263.

[45] Harrington, *Anti-Imperialist Movement*, 225–226; Richard F. Pettigrew, *Imperial Washington* (Chicago: C. H. Kerr, 1922), 272–273.

[46] *New York Evening Post*, 14 August 1900; Mark DeWolfe Howe, *Storey*, 199–201.

was little third-party sentiment. After a certain amount of lobbying by Winslow, it endorsed a resolution which declared: "While we welcome any other method of opposing the re-election of Mr. McKinley, we advise direct support of Mr. Bryan as the most effective means of crushing imperialism."[47]

The resolution of the Liberty Congress effectively quashed the idea of a separate anti-imperialist party for the election of 1900. The anti-imperialists would divide between McKinley and Bryan. Some, like Andrew Carnegie, Charles Eliot, George Edmunds, and Hoar would, with varying degrees of difficulty, endorse McKinley. A clear majority, however, would follow the recommendations of the managers of the Liberty Congress and, again with varying degrees of satisfaction, vote for Bryan.

In the campaign of 1900 Hoar, as a Republican anti-imperialist, actively supported the author of the Republican policy of imperialism. In the performance of that role was he honest; was he justified? His sincerity was, of course, frequently questioned by other anti-imperialists. Throughout the campaign they doubted his professions of respect for the natural rights of the Filipino and anticipated his recantation of the anti-imperialist faith. Hoar did not recant. Never did he publicly accept McKinley's contention that the Filipinos must be led by a benevolent Mother Country toward an indeterminate degree of self-government. And in private he faltered only once. Early in September, worried that Bryan might win and anxious lest McKinley commit himself irrevocably to a policy of permanent American dominion in the Philippines, Hoar approached McKinley and advocated a compromise that, at least by implication, would have delayed if not diluted the natural rights of the Philippine people. The letter was marked "Highly Confidential" and was sent to McKinley's campaign manager, Senator Mark Hanna:

My Dear Mr. Hanna:
    I direct this letter to you, instead of sending it direct to the President because I believe he would trust your judgment

---

[47] Lanzar, *Anti-Imperialist League,* III, 37; *New York Times,* 17 August 1900.

rather than mine in the matter to which it relates, and if it could be re-inforced by your endorsement, and the President should be willing to act upon it, it will in my opinion render his re-election absolutely certain. I do not think you or he can know how profoundly a very great number of his Republican supporters feel in regard to the Philippine question . . .

I believe if he will say in his letter of acceptance that while he "conceived it his duty under the Constitution and laws to enforce order and obedience to the authority of the United States, and while he had not heretofore deemed himself authorized to make pledges which should bind Congress, and did not think the period of hostility the time for such pledges, still there could not in his judgment be any doubt that when hereafter the people of the Philippine Islands, having an orderly and free Government established, which should prove itself able to maintain peace and order and civilization, and the Philippine Islands through such Government should desire to take an independent place among the nations of the earth, that of course the people of the United States would not put forth their power to prevent it,"—such a declaration, in my opinion, would remove the last chance for the election of Mr. Bryan, or for a Democratic House.[48]

Hanna promised to forward this letter at once to McKinley and did so. According to the diary of George B. Cortelyou, the President's secretary, McKinley not only studied it carefully but at one point sketched out a one-page revision of his letter of acceptance "largely on the lines of Senator Hoar's suggestion." However that might be, the letter of acceptance did not incorporate a promise of future independence for the Filipinos, but only a vague wish that America "prepare them for self-government."[49] Hoar was bitterly

[48] Hoar to Hanna, 3 September 1900, McKinley Papers, Series 1, Vol. 61, Library of Congress. *See*, too, Hoar to Senator John Coit Spooner, 14 August 1900 (copy); Hoar to William E. Chandler, 6 September 1900 (copy), Hoar Papers.

[49] Hanna to Hoar, 5 September 1900, Hoar Papers; C. S. Olcott, *Life of William McKinley* (Boston: Houghton Mifflin, 1916), II, 287–288; Leach, *In the Days of McKinley*, 552.

disappointed, but he sought to give the term "self-government" the broadest construction possible.[50]

It would appear that in the early weeks of September, Hoar, at least in private, was half-prepared to compromise his conviction of the natural *right* of the Filipino people to national self-determination. His faltering was of brief duration, however. In his last campaign speeches, as in those of July and August, he identified diplomatic justice with America's explicit recognition of the Filipino Republic.

The campaign speech is a poor vehicle for the discovery of clues to a man's consistency or sincerity. Read on the stump the telephone directory would appear suspiciously exaggerated. A more satisfactory field of evidence is a man's personal correspondence. One cannot read through the hundreds of letters Hoar wrote in the summer and fall of 1900—especially those to his son and such old friends as Edward Everett Hale—without a growing conviction that whether Hoar was right or wrong in supporting McKinley he was honestly persuaded that his decision was in complete sympathy with his professions as an anti-imperialist. He found the campaign an ordeal, but an ordeal without shame.

To declare that Hoar's decision was the product neither of dishonesty nor cowardice is not, of course, to prove that it was correct or without elements of self-deception. Its justification must in large measure depend upon one's judgment of Hoar's belief that neither Bryan nor the Democratic party offered any valid hope for Aguinaldo's republic or American foreign policy. It was Hoar's contention that as president Bryan would be "worthless as an Anti-Imperialist . . . and thoroughly mischievous in every other respect."[51] It was a contention entertained by many who were neither

---

[50] Hoar to Charles Dick, chairman of the Ohio Republic State Executive Committee, 11 September 1900, Hoar Papers. *See,* too, Hoar to T. L. Long, 15 August 1900; Hoar to Samuel P. Butler, 26 August 1900, Hoar Papers.

[51] Hoar to Edward Atkinson, 14 August 1900, E. A. Atkinson Papers, Massachusetts Historical Society. Hoar's case against Bryan was most fully articulated in an article he prepared for the *International Monthly.* G. F. Hoar, "Party Government in the United States," *International Monthly,* October 1900. *See,* too, interviews in *Boston Herald,* 16 February 1900 and *Boston Journal,* 10 August 1900; typed rough draft, "Campaign Speech, Summer of 1900," Hoar to Albert E. Smith, 11 October 1900, Hoar Papers.

partisans nor office holders. Not only did such Republican "regulars" as George Edmunds, Walter Mason, and Samuel McCall
agree with Hoar in denouncing Bryan but so did such indepen-
dent-minded, lay Republicans as Charles Eliot of Harvard and
Charles Francis Adams, Jr. Although Adams considered McKinley's
policy not only misguided but opportunistic, he could not bring
himself to endorse the candidate of free silver and Tammany
Hall.[52] And many of the anti-imperialists who did, such as Carl
Schurz and David Starr Jordan, found reason to deplore Bryan's
campaign strategy and complain of his failure sufficiently to emphasize the issue of imperialism.[53]

Bryan's opposition to imperialism was genuine, but his conduct
during the campaign, as earlier during the fight over the treaty,
offered justification to those who considered him a false champion
of the anti-imperialist cause. Bryan began by emphasizing the issue
of colonialism, but almost at once veered about to the trust problem and then in the latter stages of his campaign appeared determined to resurrect the battle of the standards. There was no
necessary contradiction in the various causes he professed, but his
haphazard juggling of issues, like his praise at one point of Richard
Croker, the Tammany chieftain, was confusing and unwise. Hoar
found in Bryan's conduct agreeable confirmation of the wisdom of
his own decision.

It is the judgment of one student of the election of 1900 that
many voters doubted the sincerity of Bryan's anti-imperial pro-
nouncements and "cast their ballots for McKinley because they felt
that under his leadership the United States would be able to get out
of the Philippines sooner than under that of Bryan."[54] This was
Hoar's position and the stand of "the more intelligent Republican
Anti-Imperialists in New England," or so he insisted in a long and

[52] Adams, with Thomas B. Reed, Grover Cleveland, Edward Atkinson, and
Donelson Caffery, refused to support either Bryan or McKinley. *See* C. F. Adams,
Jr. to Hoar, 3 March 1900, 12 December 1900, Hoar Papers; Adams to Carl Schurz,
14 July 1900, Papers of Carl Schurz, Library of Congress.
[53] *See* Schurz to Edward M. Shepard, 7 October 1900; Schurz to Charles Francis
Adams, Jr., 5 November 1900, Schurz Papers, Library of Congress.
[54] Thomas A. Bailey, "Was the Presidential Election of 1900 a Mandate for Imperialism?" *Mississippi Valley Historical Review*, 24 (June 1937), 51.

acidulous correspondence with George S. Boutwell.[55] It was not an unreasonable position. The historical record did not oblige the electorate in 1900 to believe that Bryan or the Democratic party would bring to American foreign policy superior resources of imagination or experience.

If McKinley's re-election did not represent a clear expression of opinion on the part of the American people in behalf of colonial expansion, what then was the historical significance of the election of 1900? The most obvious answer is that the election offered further proof that the Republican party was the majority party of the nation. The elections of 1894 and 1896 had shown this to be true; the election of 1900 offered additional evidence. Both Bryan and Hoar were incorrect in their evaluation of the election. The voters identified the Republican party neither with "criminal aggression in the Philippines" nor with "the truest hope for the liberty of the Filipinos," but rather with economic improvement and full dinner pails. For the student who would emphasize the motive force of ideology, the election of 1900 is an exercise in frustration. The cautionary doctrines of anti-imperialism were confronted by the optimistic arguments of expansionism, and each largely canceled the electoral influence of the other. McKinley won the election of 1900 not because he had embraced the "Large Policy" of Mahan and Lodge, nor because he had wrapped that policy in the gauze of political piety, but because he and Hanna had improved the majority position of the Republican party by perfecting its organization and strengthening its popular association with the twin goals of individual economic security and national industrial expansion.

[55] The controversy with Boutwell centered about Hoar's declaration that Boutwell, who endorsed Bryan, knew and approved Hoar's decision to stand by the Republican party and McKinley. Boutwell insisted that he had been misquoted and Hoar insisted he had not. The dispute, which was revived after the publication of Hoar's autobiography, was both pettish and unnecessary, but it allowed both men a final opportunity to detail the righteousness of their respective stands in the campaign of 1900. The more interesting letters are: Hoar to Boutwell, 23 April, 23 July, 26 October 1900; 21 March, 8 June, 20 July 1904 (copies); Boutwell to Hoar, 25 April, 25 October, 29 October 1900; 16 March, 23 May, 9 July 1904, Hoar Papers.

The issue of imperialism provided the rhetoric and intellectual interest of the campaign of 1900; party management and economic identification determined its result.

After the election, the cause of anti-imperialism declined in political importance. It continued as a moral not a political issue. Hoar was slow to recognize this fact and many of his correspondents refused altogether. When his friends congratulated him in January 1901 on his election to a fifth term in the United States Senate, they expressed an unwarranted assurance that the event marked a new day for the great crusade. In point of fact, Hoar's re-election was itself a sign that by January 1901 anti-imperialism, like Negro suffrage, was no longer a significant source of political division.

Hoar's re-election was predicted on all sides. For many citizens of Massachusetts, Hoar was viewed as a foster grandfather. Though neither poetic nor bearded, he was held in almost the same regard as those figures who, clustered in a circle and encased in a gilded frame, graced the walls of the Victorian parlors of Massachusetts bearing the title, "Our Poets: Whittier, Bryant, Lowell, and Longfellow." The *Cambridge Chronicle* declared in July 1900 that though a large majority of the Republicans running for the state legislature were not in agreement with Hoar on questions of foreign policy, there was no doubt that most would support his re-election: "Senator Hoar holds a peculiar position . . . He has no 'machine' behind him, and needs none . . . His popularity is based upon the record of a long life full of splendid services for his party and his country; upon the consciousness that he is a man who does what he believes to be right, and upon the universal belief in his abilities."[56]

There was only one man who could perhaps have blocked Hoar's re-election, and he decided against it. Not only did Henry Cabot Lodge not seek Hoar's defeat, he actively urged his re-election. At the October state convention of the Republican party, he advised his followers to send Hoar back to Washington "with the most splendid majority that any senator has ever received at the hands of

[56] *Cambridge Chronicle*, 28 July 1900.

a Massachusetts Legislature."[57] Lodge's endorsement was inspired in part by a distaste for John Davis Long—Hoar's most likely replacement—but Lodge entertained a real if often strained affection for Hoar.[58] Unlike in so many ways, they were both sons of the Puritans, victims of Mugwump attack, and alumni of Harvard—similarities of sufficient power to cover if not erase a multitude of differences.

Hoar had feared that he would not be returned to Washington, and he was highly gratified when on 14 January 1901, he was easily re-elected, receiving the unanimous support of the Republican majority in both houses of the Massachusetts General Court. He took great pains, however, to make clear to all that he had not begged for the honor nor received it at the sacrifice of principle. A week before his election he cast his vote against an army appropriation bill, as an expression of his continued opposition to the presence and conduct of American troops in the Philippines. If Hoar would ever vacillate it would be in behalf of the victory of party, not of self. Hoar would continue over the next three years to champion the cause of anti-imperialism. His efforts, however, offered only a postscript to a battle already recorded.

In the winter of 1901 Hoar scored two rather meaningless victories as he sought to revive the issue of army censorship in the Philippines and to restrict the power of the Taft Commission to grant franchises and other commercial privileges in the islands, but his chief concern then and for the next eighteen months was to accumulate evidence of the "inevitable marks of despotism" that

57 *Boston Herald*, 5 October 1900. Hoar wrote his colleague, "I will not undertake to tell you how much your kind words at the Convention have gladdened me. If I can retain your respect and good-will I should care little for the rage of Democratic or Mugwump mobs," Hoar to Lodge, 6 October 1900, Lodge Papers, Massachusetts Historical Society.

58 Wendell Garrett, "John Davis Long, Secretary of the Navy, 1897-1902," *New England Quarterly*, 31 (1958), 304. After his re-election Hoar sent a grateful note to Long, praising his "disinterestedness." The ambitious Long had felt obliged to forswear an open campaign but his code of political gentility now deserted him—for a moment. He tore Hoar's letter into several pieces, and then—with an admirable regard for the needs of history—filed the pieces. Hoar's letter of 21 January 1901, now repaired, will be found in the John D. Long Papers, Box #56, Massachusetts Historical Society; Long's admirably calm reply of 22 January 1901, in the Hoar Papers.

accompanied the colonial activities of the American soldier and
civilian in the Philippines.[59] Among his papers are two thick files
containing evidence and rumor of such atrocities as the famous
"water cure."[60] Certain of these materials make grisly reading,
particularly those which viewed the conduct of American troopers
in the bushwacking war as an expression of boyish high spirits.
Writing to his mother, a young Texan reported:

> The first battle was here at San Fabian. After the gunboats had
> shelled the wood and town we landed and formed a skirmish
> line and charged the breastworks. When we turned our Krags
> on them and then put up that Indian war-whoop you can't
> imagine how those negroes did run. They almost flew through
> those bamboo and cocanut trees. We had a picnic out of them,
> for they can't stand our yell. If it wasn't for the officers the boys
> would kill every negro on the islands. We don't care for a negro
> at all, and it's the boys' delight to spy a negro head in the rice.
> He won't stay there but a few seconds until you'll find an empty
> cartridge somewhere . . . We live in the natives' houses and I
> like this life. Every one is jolly, and our officers are the kindest
> men there are over here.[61]

[59] *Congressional Record*, 56th Cong., 2d sess., 3127–3128, 3144–3146 (27 February
1901). *See*, too, Hoar to E. B. Stoddard, 27 February 1901, Gamaliel Bradford to
Hoar, 5 March 1901, Hoar Papers; Hoar to Benjamin Harrison, 15 March 1901,
Benjamin Harrison Papers, Library of Congress; *Boston Herald*, 5 March 1901.

[60] Files marked "Philippine Material Preserved by Sen. George F. Hoar," Hoar
Papers.

[61] R. O. Fatheree to Mrs. A. J. Fatheree, 12 November 1899, printed in the *Dallas
News*, 8 January 1900, P.I. File #2, Hoar Papers. Letters like this lend justification
to the innumerable parodies by anti-imperialist poets of Kipling's "The White Man's
Burden." Hoar's files (Scrap Book IX, Hoar Papers) contain at least a half-dozen
of these parodies; the most effective, that of Henry Labouchère printed in the
London journal, *Truth*. Its first two verses indicate its mixed tone of disgust and
despair:

Pile on the brown man's burden
    To gratify your greed;
Go, clear away the "niggers"
    Who progress would impede;
Be very stern, for truly
'Tis useless to be mild

In January 1902 Hoar introduced in the Senate a resolution demanding an investigation of the conduct of the war, and over the next few months he labored to bring anti-imperialist witnesses to Washington to appear before Lodge's Philippine Committee.[62] As he informed Herbert Welsh, who was performing a similar task for the Anti-Imperialist League, it was frustrating work; for though there were many soldiers and relatives of soldiers who would write "in strict confidence" of water tortures and reconcentrado camps, there were relatively few who were willing to declare themselves in public.[63] Hoar was persuaded of the truth of these allegations, how-

> With new-caught, sullen peoples,
> Half devil and half child.
>
> Pile on the brown man's burden,
>   And if ye rouse his hate,
> Meet his old-fashioned reason
>   With maxims up to date;
> With shells and dum-dum bullets,
>   A hundred times make plain
> The brown man's loss must ever
>   Imply the white man's gain.

[62] *Congressional Record,* 57th Cong., 1st sess., 597 (13 January 1902); Hoar to Isaac Bridgman, 18 January 1902; Lodge to Hoar, 30 January 1902; Edward Atkinson to Hoar, 14 April 1902; Hoar to John Bellows, [?] April 1902, Hoar Papers; Hoar to Lodge, 22 January, 28 January 1902, Lodge Papers, Massachusetts Historical Society; Hoar to Carl Schurz, 13 February 1902, Carl Schurz Papers, Vol. 141, Library of Congress; M. K. Sniffen to Moorfield Storey, 12 April 1902, Moorfield Storey Papers, Box 1, Library of Congress.

[63] *See* Hoar to Herbert Welsh, [?] March 1902, 16 April 1902 (copies); Hoar to Phoebe W. Cousins, 18 January 1902, Hoar Papers. One anonymous correspondent sent Hoar a picture of two American soldiers administering the "water cure" to a Filipino, clipped from the *Manila Times* of 4 May 1902 [?]. The accompanying and undated letter read:

> This hombre is getting what is known as the "water cure" which consists of laying him on his back and pouring canteen full after canteen full of water down his throat. A hollow bamboo pole is sometimes used. When his stomach is full to bursting the canteen is taken out of his mouth and a good hevy [*sic*] man jumps on his stomach sending a gush of water from his mouth into the air as high as six feet. Then he is asked to speak, and if he refuses the operation is continued until he is either dead or until he speaks. This is the way the U.S. Army finds out where so many rifles are hidden and so many Insurrectos are camped.
>
> J.V.C.

P.I. File #2, Hoar Papers.

ever, and reluctantly convinced that the investigation of the Lodge committee was slanted by design in favor of the Army and its officers. Hoar's response to the whitewash of the Lodge committee was typical. He would address the Senate and, by educating his colleagues, perform his duty.

The theme of his address was that military misconduct was the logical product of colonialism. When printed, that address bore the awkward title, "The Attempt to Subjugate a People Striving for Freedom, Not the American Soldier, Responsible for Cruelties in the Philippine Islands," and its argument was summed up in one short paragraph:

> Now all this cost, all these young men gone to their graves, all these wrecked lives, all this national dishonor . . . the devastation of provinces, the shooting of captives, the tortures of prisoners and of unarmed and peaceful citizens, the hanging men up by the thumbs, the carloads of maniac soldiers that you bring home—are all because you would not tell and will not tell now whether you mean in the future to stand on the principles which you and your fathers always declared in the past . . . If you try to keep order by military despotism you suffer from it by revolution and by barbarity in war.[64]

The words were angry and underlying their anger was a sense of bewilderment and defeat, an unacknowledged suspicion that he spoke in behalf of a dead cause.

The reaction of the press lent support to the suspicion. A few organs of expansionism took time to denounce the speech, but for the most part they were content to praise Hoar's integrity while dismissing his assumptions.[65] Certain Mugwump anti-imperialists, swinging round once more, praised "our noble Nestor" and proclaimed the beginning of a new day for an old crusade, but their voices were worn thin with false hope. The Washington correspondent of the *Boston Evening Transcript* was more sensitive to political realities when he wrote: "Mr. Hoar's loneliness on the Republican

[64] *Congressional Record*, 57th Cong., 1st sess., 5788–5798 (22 May 1902).
[65] *See Philadelphia Inquirer*, 23 May 1902; *New York Daily Tribune*, 23 May 1902; Scrap Book, Personal, IX, Hoar Papers.

side of the Senate will long remain an interesting historical picture."[66]

The dimensions of that "historical picture" have been the object of frequent analysis. Was the great debate over imperialism only an ideological facade behind which the needs of economic growth worked their inevitable result? Was the anti-imperialist movement but an effort in futility and Hoar's role only a study in failure? Most observers, however personally sympathetic to the idealistic temper of the anti-imperialist movement, have emphasized the ineffectuality of the movement and its leaders. In 1899 Finley Peter Dunne, speaking through the deceptively carefree brogue of Mr. Dooley, symbolized the posture of McKinley in the Philippines as that of "th' indulgent parent kneelin' on th' stomach iv his adopted child," and the anti-imperialists as but "a dillygation fr'm Boston, basten him with an umbrella."[67] A similar if more somber judgment was offered by Professor Fred Harrington a generation later: "The tangible results achieved by the anti-imperialists were few indeed. They may have had some slight influence on the American administration in the islands, by drawing attention to conditions in the Philippines, and, in the course of their long-continuing battle for Philippine independence, they may have helped secure the enactment of the Jones Act of 1916. The movement also acted as the agency for restoring many Gold Democrats to party ranks, and

[66] Winslow Warren to Hoar, 23 May 1902, Moorfield Storey to Hoar, 23 May 1902, Hoar Papers; *Boston Evening Transcript*, 24 May 1902. The reaction and praise most gratifying to Hoar was that offered by an English-language paper in Tokyo. A correspondent of the *Japan Times* wrote in its issue of 17 June 1902:

> The speech of Mr. Hoar, though an address to his own countrymen, is a message of hope to the whole world which sank with despondency at the sight of Republican America behaving like a cruel, tyrranical and rapacious Empire in the Philippines and particularly to the broken-hearted people of Asia who are beginning to lose all confidence in the humanity of the white races . . . Hence all papers in Asia should reprint his speech, translate it, and distribute it broadcast. Let it be brought home to the Asiatic people so that they may work and [may] worship their champion and his forefathers.

Scrap Book, Personal, IX, Hoar Papers.
[67] Finley Peter Dunne, *Mr. Dooley in the Hearts of His Countrymen* (Boston, 1899), 6.

for depriving certain Republicans of their influence in the party. But that is all."[68]

But is that all? The anti-imperialist movement had more influence in the shaping of subsequent foreign policy than is usually admitted, and it had a significance for the history of the Republican party greater than is often recognized. In the first connection, there is some truth in Hoar's professed belief that the effort of the anti-imperialists, although a failure in the Philippines, had a certain restraining influence on the foreign policy designs of the McKinley and Roosevelt administrations. Hoar was, of course, desperately anxious to detect such influence and surely he exaggerated when he attributed to the labors of anti-imperialist Republicans the restrained response of America to the Chinese Boxers, and, later, the withdrawal of American troops from Cuba.[69] It is probable, however, that one among many considerations persuading Theodore Roosevelt to pursue as president a foreign policy less aggressive than that once championed, was an awareness of the reluctance of certain Americans to share his conception of our international destiny.[70] That reluctance had been both propagated and publi-

---

[68] Harrington, *Anti-Imperialist Movement*, 229.

[69] In a letter to George Boutwell (8 June 1904 [copy], Hoar Papers) Hoar wrote:

When the [imperial] question first came up . . . the air about Washington, in and out of the Senate Chamber, was full of talk in favor of an Oriental Empire. That talk has all ended and disappeared. It was, in my judgment, the result of the strenuous resistance made in the matter of the Philippine Islands. It would not have ended unless that resistance had come from Republicans. Instead of buccaneering in China, we had one of the most creditable chapters in our history. The United States sent her forces, with those of other nations, to the relief of their beleaguered Ambassadors and triumphantly liberated them. We restrained ourselves and restrained other countries within bounds by an unexampled moderation and justice. If anything could have effaced the injury done by what we did in the Philippines, it was that chapter of our military and diplomatic history.

[70] For Secretary John Hay's concern with anti-imperialist dissent in connection with the proposed purchase of the Danish West Indies, *see* Lodge to Hay, 28 October 1901, Lodge Papers, Massachusetts Historical Society. Hoar declared himself opposed to the Danish Treaty unless it specifically provided for a plebiscite among the West Indians. *See* Hoar to Lodge, 16 February 1902, Lodge Papers, Massachusetts Historical Society. This treaty was never confirmed.

cized by the anti-imperialist movement. Politically, that movement was an unquestioned failure, but as a moral and educational force its failure must be qualified. It helped, if indirectly, to persuade at least some Americans that jingoism and belligerence need not accompany an acceptance of international power and duty: an admission that would culminate in the figure of Woodrow Wilson and his effort to combine the doctrines of self-determination and international responsibility.

For the history of the Republican party, the anti-imperialist crusade serves as another and important chapter in its periodic struggles with party dissidents—dissidents always seemingly ignored but never too completely nor for too long. The strength of the party was illustrated once again in its ability to absorb the division inspired by anti-imperialism, as earlier those generated by the Grangers, the Greenbackers, the Civil Service reformers, and the Silverites.

That "absorption" can, of course, be viewed as an illustration not only of institutional elasticity but of individual failure. Surely no Republican anti-imperialist offered a serious threat to the political leadership of McKinley. Schurz, Adams, and Winslow lacked the necessary political base; Hale, Reed, and Hoar had such a base, potentially, but possessed neither the temperament nor the desire to organize a protest movement that might endanger their party or disturb the two-party system. Hoar's was perhaps the greatest opportunity and so the greatest failure. Certainly he must share the blame for the dissensions and disunity that existed within the anti-imperialist ranks and did so much to assure the limitations of anti-imperialism as a political movement. Unable to cooperate with the Mugwump officers of the Anti-Imperialist League, unwilling to cooperate with the distrusted Bryan, Hoar failed to provide the political strategy or leadership that might have forced revision of American policy in the Philippines.[71]

[71] It was the exaggerated opinion of "An American" in the British journal, *Westminster Review* that Hoar was as much to blame for colonial expansion as McKinley:

> Senator George F. Hoar was opposed to it, and could have prevented it through his immense influence in the Republican party, had he not made it certain that in no case would his opposition go far enough to disrupt the party. There is a very

In the final analysis, Hoar decided to settle for moral leadership. He can be criticized for believing that the validity of past traditions was proven by their antiquity; he can be criticized for demanding that a nation's foreign policy be shaped by the precedents of the past rather than the challenges of the present, but such criticisms however just are in some measure irrelevant. Hoar determined, in part unconsciously, that his contribution in the great debate over imperialism would be the historical contribution of the moralist and educator. He could not seriously threaten the new-found strength of his party, but by his eloquent defense of the natural rights of the Filipino he would remind his future countrymen of their unique mission among nations.

---

real sense in which McKinley, Bryan, and Hoar may be named together as the triumvirate of American expansion.

*Westminster Review*, March 1902, Scrap Book, Personal (1901), Hoar Papers.

# 10

## The Uncertain Patriarch
## and the Cautious Innovator

I receive the most exuberant assurances of kind feeling from the President and those about him, yet I am very much in the condition of the old country minister who said his congregation always praised his sermons, but never put anything in his contribution box.[1]

The last three years of Hoar's life and public career were overshadowed by the boisterous figure of Theodore Roosevelt and the first manifestations of the Progressive movement. They were for Hoar years of honor and confusion. The respected dean of his party in the Senate, he was often praised and frequently bypassed. His efforts in behalf of the Filipino, no longer a threat to party unity, were viewed as a personal crotchet, and his suspicions of America's canal diplomacy were judged irrelevant. His continued opposition to tariff reciprocity and executive legislation was no longer typical of his party or its leadership, and his opinions re-

[1] Hoar to Richard Olney, 11 January 1904 (copy), Hoar Papers.

specting trusts and labor unions were usually dismissed as insufficient or self-contradictory.

While certain of the younger Republican leaders began to edge toward the Progressive movement, others in reaction became more obdurate in their resistance to change, and the sing-song voice of Hoar calling now as earlier for limited and cautious reform would be ignored by both. Hoar's views became on balance more conservative in his last years, but the leit motif of those years was not reaction but uncertainty. He did not actively oppose the Muckrakers and other early participants of the Progressive movement, but he was bewildered by their clamor and doubtful of their intentions. Seeking as he always had to promote both economic incentives and social harmony, identifying as he always would economic prosperity and social well-being, Hoar was not so much opposed to the new currents of political agitation as mystified by their direction and fearful of their ultimate result. His response was neither to advance nor to recant, but rather to fumble. His relations with Theodore Roosevelt reflect in a very real sense not only the changing patterns of leadership within the Republican Party but also the bewilderment of the old liberalism when confronted with one version—personalized and limited though it was—of the new. The Half-Breed tradition that Hoar continued to represent provided in fact ideological background for the national orientation and regulatory ambitions of Theodore Roosevelt, but this fact was never understood by Hoar nor ever acknowledged by Roosevelt.

The assassination of McKinley was for Hoar a source of sincere grief, but his sorrow was personal not political in nature. He had admired the character of McKinley and even in opposition had felt at home with him.[2] He did not, on the other hand, anticipate

[2] Hoar was designated as chairman of the Senate committee appointed to attend the obsequies for McKinley in Washington and five days after McKinley's death presided at a memorial service in the Mechanics' Hall of Worcester. In the heat of the moment, Hoar used the latter occasion to denounce not only anarchism but "those bitter and uncharitable critics" who had incited Czolgosz and "shotted his weapon." *Boston Daily Advertiser*, 19 September 1901. This excited effort on Hoar's part to associate Mugwumpery and anarchism was soon dropped, however. More intelligent was his effort in Congress to provide greater personal protection for the President.

that the accession of Roosevelt would mark a new chapter for the Republican party. He took at face value Roosevelt's initial pledge to continue the policies of the McKinley administration. From the first, however, Hoar entertained strong doubts whether he would ever feel at ease with McKinley's exuberant successor.

Prior to the Spanish-American War relations between Roosevelt and Hoar had been cordial if infrequent. Hoar had admired Roosevelt's performance as civil service commissioner and had been highly gratified by Roosevelt's offer of assistance during his fight against the A.P.A. in Massachusetts. Roosevelt in turn had respected Hoar as one of the more cultured and principled elder statesmen of the party, although quite prepared to see the latter superseded by a more dynamic style of leadership. In the late 1890's, their relations had, of course, sharply deteriorated. For Roosevelt, Hoar was now an obstructionist and a traitor to progress; for Hoar, Roosevelt's bellicosity and expansionist rhetoric were repugnant. Hoar's decision to support the ticket of McKinley and Roosevelt in the campaign of 1900 served, however, to remind Roosevelt that Hoar was indeed "one of the grand old men of the party," and Hoar had made every effort during the campaign to speak well of Roosevelt's "manliness and courage," and to criticize only by indirection his expansionist doctrines.[3]

Following the campaign both men made overtures in behalf of political courtesy. Hoar took pains to inform Roosevelt that he meant no personal disrespect by his declaration before a Harvard student audience that there was more manliness in legal combat than in fighting grizzly bears, and Roosevelt in turn made special point to praise a magazine article by Hoar that had proclaimed

---

[3] To an admirer of Roosevelt, Hoar wrote in July 1900:

> I like Roosevelt very much. But what I like him for is not what he did in the late war . . . The Roosevelt that I like is Roosevelt the Civil Service Reformer; Roosevelt the New York Police Commissioner; Roosevelt the organizer of the movement which defeated the Grant men and the Blaine men both in the State Convention; and the Roosevelt who when beaten in the national Convention in 1884 had sense and wisdom not to go over and leave the Republican party for a worse one . . . It is these qualities, and not the running up a hill and hallooing at Santiago, or wherever else, that command my admiration and support.

Hoar to Edward A. Kelly, 27 July 1900, Hoar Papers.

Washington a strong party man and Mugwumps of little value.[4] Harvard and its Mugwumps provided the means for a limited rapprochement. Each man proudly served on the university's Board of Overseers and together they denounced the cowardice that denied Henry Cabot Lodge an honorary degree. Both men agreed that fellow alumnus Moorfield Storey was "utterly lost to the feeling of national self-respect," although Hoar was not prepared to go quite so far as Roosevelt who declared Storey "utterly unTeutonic" and possessed of "a Southern Latin frame of mind."[5]

Upon his elevation to the presidency, Roosevelt saw fit not only to review his initial message to Congress with the powerful senatorial quartet of Aldrich, Spooner, Allison, and Platt, but tactfully to ask Hoar's advice as well. Hoar was particularly requested to forward his opinions respecting tariff revision and reciprocity. Pleased by this consideration, Hoar declared his confidence that "your administration is to be one of . . . great blessing and prosperity to the country." He suggested that Roosevelt promise to promote the expansion of America's export trade while avoiding any rash endorsement of reciprocity agreements.[6] Both men, of course, were well aware that Roosevelt had been careful not to ask for advice respecting questions of foreign policy, but there was little hypocrisy in their careful exchange of compliments. Roosevelt, if not prepared in fact to "continue absolutely unbroken" the domestic policies of McKinley, was quite ready to concentrate for a time on party harmony. Hoar was correspondingly convinced that it was the duty of all Republicans to wish the new administration well and not to excite the fears of business or the electorate in the party's new leader.

Massachusetts's portion of the new administration's patronage was at the disposal of Lodge, but Roosevelt, not insensitive to the

[4] G. F. Hoar, "Conditions of Success in Public Life: An Address delivered in Sanders Theatre before the Students of Harvard University, November 21, 1900" (pamphlet), Hoar Papers. Hoar subsequently included Roosevelt's essay, "The Strenuous Life" in a juvenile anthology, *Book of Patriotism*, which he edited in 1902. It followed Hoar's own introductory tribute to "Love of Country."

[5] Hoar to Roosevelt, 11 December 1900, 16 April 1901 (copies); Roosevelt to Hoar, 18 March, 13 April, 17 April, 8 June 1901, Hoar Papers.

[6] Roosevelt to Hoar, 9 November, 14 November 1901; Hoar to Roosevelt, 18 November 1901 (copy); George B. Cortelyou to Hoar, 22 November 1901, Hoar Papers.

significance of small gestures, made great point of complying with Hoar's wishes on minor matters. Worcester would be included in the President's New England itinerary and he would be delighted to lunch at Oak Avenue; the postmaster at Millbury, an old friend of Mr. Hoar's, would be retained despite a low merit rating. Hoar was the recipient of immediate presidential compliments when the Senate, upon Hoar's recommendation, appointed Edward Everett Hale as its chaplain. Hale, of course, was not only Hoar's friend and former pastor, but the author of *The Man Without a Country*, a book which both Roosevelt and Hoar admired as a splendid lesson in civic morality for the nation's youth. And it was perhaps here alone—on questions of morality and concern for the young and the helpless—that Roosevelt and Hoar established any real rapport. When Hoar asked Roosevelt to intervene in behalf of the immigrant children of a Worcester citizen and free them from the red-tape of the customs officials at Ellis Island, there was no pretense or calculation in Roosevelt's booming promise of "instant action" nor any stiffness or restraint in Hoar's gratitude. Each could agree that the other was a "warm-hearted man," one who would not place the regulations of government above the requirements of personal morality.[7] Whatever their differences over the proper method of regulating trusts and railroads or the proper conduct of a President toward the Senate and the elders of his party, each man entertained a sincere appreciation for the moral worth of the other. And here were two men who placed a high value on moral worth. Neither could be quite satisfied with his position unless convinced that it was not only wise but righteous.

The need they shared was clearly illustrated in Hoar's long and unsuccessful effort to gain a commitment from Roosevelt respecting America's ultimate intention in the Philippines. In the last months of his life Hoar directed his secretary to prepare a memorandum recording his conversations and correspondence with Roosevelt about the Philippines.[8] This memorandum has slight

[7] Hoar to Rockwood Hoar, 5 March 1902; Hoar to Roosevelt, 9 August, 14 October, 15 October, 1 December 1902 (copies); Theodore Roosevelt to Hoar, 10 March, 5 June 1902; George B. Cortelyou to Hoar, 2 August, 13 August, 27 September, 1 November 1902; Hoar to John Hay, 4 December 1902 (copy), Hoar Papers.

[8] "Record-Keeping by Senator Hoar concerning his correspondence with President Roosevelt," stapled typescript, Hoar Papers.

significance for the history of the islands and their administration, but it offers considerable insight respecting the political skill of Roosevelt and the need of both men to articulate their position in terms of moral principles.

On 1 March 1902 Hoar requested an opportunity to have a private meeting with the President, and one week later, at 8:30 in the evening, he was ushered into the President's private study on the second floor of the White House. Hoar proceeded to read a seven-page statement, the heart of which was a request that Roosevelt reidentify American foreign policy with the Declaration of Independence and pledge the determination of the United States to accord full independence to the Filipinos once there had been established in the islands "a stable, orderly, and peaceable Government." Hoar had sought the same declaration from McKinley during the campaign of 1900 and would once again seek to spin success from the straw of personal sympathy.

According to Hoar's later recollection, Roosevelt had been most impressed by his statement. "Mr. Hoar, every word of that paper is engraved on my memory. You may be sure I shall not forget it." Hoar should believe that the President earnestly hoped the time would come when he could make such a declaration. There were difficulties, however. Although the administration had no patience with the flamboyant imperialism of Senator Beveridge—"Beveridge is perfectly disgusting"—it would be most unwise to make such a declaration without consulting Governor Taft and Secretary Root. They might believe that a declaration of our ultimate purpose in the Philippines would be misunderstood by the Filipinos, and by exciting political competition among the natives increase their own responsibilities. Governor Taft was soon to arrive in Washington for consultation with Secretary Root. Roosevelt would arrange a meeting where "we will talk over the whole matter and see what we can do."

Taft came to Washington and stayed several weeks. Hoar was not invited to meet him. It was not until 18 May—after the Philippines Government Act was assured safe passage and the Lodge Committee had the investigation of the conduct of American troops in

---

[9] Memorandum, Hoar-Roosevelt Correspondence, Hoar Papers.

the Philippines under firm control—that Roosevelt again renewed the discussion. Catching sight of Hoar out for a Sunday morning stroll, Roosevelt insisted on walking back with him to the Hotel Richmond. As they paced in unison the block between Sixteenth and Seventeenth Streets, Roosevelt disclosed that Governor Taft believed that any declaration now of "our purpose to give the Filipinos ultimate independence" would be "misunderstood." Parties would spring up of men scheming to get political power once independence came. If independence was not awarded as soon as they hoped, they would accuse the United States of bad faith, and it was, of course, unusually difficult to predict the pace of progress where Orientals were concerned. "He repeated with great warmth his expressions of confidence and affection for me. He said that I occupied a very high ground which he entirely approved."[10]

A high ground and a lonely one. Hoar attempted to make much of a brief reference to the possibility of Filipino independence in a Memorial Day speech by Roosevelt at Arlington, but he gradually became convinced that "the act of great statesmanship" that he had urged upon the President was to be indefinitely postponed.[11] Roosevelt had decided that moral as well as strategic considerations demanded that the nation deal with the Filipinos in "good faith," and by his definition this excluded for the foreseeable future the selfish course of setting them free.[12] With the spring of 1903 Hoar informed Roosevelt, "it is not likely that I shall trouble you again

[10] *Ibid.* A more contemporary confirmation of this conversation will be found in a letter from Hoar to Carl Schurz, 3 June 1902. Carl Schurz Papers, vol. 143, Library of Congress. *See,* too, Hoar to Lodge, 15 July 1903, Lodge Papers, Massachusetts Historical Society.

[11] Memorandum, Hoar-Roosevelt Correspondence, Hoar Papers; Andrew Carnegie to Hoar, 4 June 1902, Hoar Papers; Hoar to Carl Schurz, 19 June 1902, Carl Schurz Papers, vol. 143, Library of Congress.

[12] In a short but revealing letter, Roosevelt assured Hoar:

> I am encouraging in every way the growth of the conditions which now make for self-government in the Philippines and which if the Filipine people can take advantage of them, will assuredly put them where some day we shall say that if they desire independence they shall have it. But I cannot be certain when that day will be, and of course there is always the possibility that they may themselves behave in such a fashion as to put it off indefinitely. Now I do not want to make a promise which may not be kept. Above all things, I want for myself and for the nation that there shall be good faith. Senator Hoar, I honor you and revere you . . . I hate to seem in your eyes to be falling short of my duty

on this subject"; a year later, he wrote his friend Josephine Shaw Lowell that it appeared impossible to persuade the leaders of the Republican party to do "what you and I think right in the matter of the Philippine Islands."[13]

At no time, however, did Hoar judge the President's declarations of personal regard as insincere, or believe he had been deceived. Nor is it certain that he was. Roosevelt surely exaggerated his admiration for Hoar's political purity, and there was guile as well as tact in his expressions of gratitude for Hoar's advice, but Roosevelt as president was not the belligerent imperialist of San Juan Hill. Not only did he want party harmony and an uncontested nomination in 1904, but he was at times uncertain of the permanent advantage of a Pacific empire. This uncertainty was not sufficient to induce him to renounce the idea of permanent annexation, as Hoar desired, but it lends probability to the judgment that Hoar's last disappointment respecting his party's intentions in the Philippines was more the result of self-deception than presidential duplicity. Certainly it was the product of historical chronology. Roosevelt probably appreciated, surely Hoar failed to see, that the time was both too late and too early for a reversal of American foreign policy in the Philippines.

Roosevelt's Panama diplomacy represented an issue of far greater political sensitivity for his administration, and Hoar's objections to that diplomacy—though restricted in substance and duration—met neither courtesy or sympathy. Those objections added little to Hoar's reputation in any camp. They represented the uncertain efforts of a man worried that his country had violated the code of international decency and fearful lest he be proved correct.

Hoar was enough of a nationalist to desire to see his country the sole builder and possessor of a transisthmian canal. As early as

---

on a great question. I ask you to believe that after much painful thought, after much groping and some uncertainty as to where my duty lay, I am now doing it as light has been given me to do it.

Roosevelt to Hoar, 16 June 1902, Morison, *Letters of Theodore Roosevelt*, III, 277.

[13] Hoar to Theodore Roosevelt, 4 March 1903 (copy); Hoar to Mrs. Charles Russell Lowell, 4 May 1904, Hoar Papers.

1895. Hoar had advocated diplomatic efforts to abrogate the restraining Clayton-Bulwer Treaty, and he subsequently endorsed the Second Hay-Pauncefote Treaty, which had released the United States from the requirement of joint action.[14] Hoar's anti-imperialism glorified tradition not inaction, and when in 1903 Roosevelt began negotiations with the Republic of Colombia for the purchase of a canal zone through the Colombian province of Panama, Hoar initially saw no danger to that tradition. A trans-isthmian canal had for a long time been an American interest; its accomplishment would not subvert the liberties of another people nor threaten the institutions and genius of our own.

When, however, the Colombian senate determined to hold out for a larger price and there followed in embarrassingly quick order a revolution in Panama, orders from Washington to three conveniently stationed war vessels not to allow Colombian troops to violate the "neutrality" of the isthmus, presidential recognition of Panamanian independence, and the negotiation of a canal treaty with the new republic, Hoar was understandably less certain of the immunity of American tradition.

On 9 December 1903, Hoar offered a Resolution of Inquiry. The President should be requested to submit all papers concerning his dealing with Colombia and the new Republic of Panama, so far as they related to the canal treaty now before the Senate for its confirmation. Hoar informed his friends at home that though he was reluctant to believe Roosevelt could have been guilty of any misconduct respecting the origins of the Panamanian revolt, "the unwillingness on the part of persons in the President's confidence to have the facts known" inspired "grave apprehension."[15] Debate on this resolution was delayed until 17 December, and it was then the object of sharp attack by Republican Senator Joseph B. Foraker and warm commendation by Senator Arthur Pue Gorman, leader of the Democratic opposition.

Foraker, engaged at this time in undermining Mark Hanna in

[14] *See* Hoar to Henry I. Sheldon, 22 November 1898, Hoar to editor of *Springfield Republican*, 10 February 1900, Hoar Papers; Hoar to Lodge, 31 May 1901, Lodge to Hoar, 7 June 1901 (copy), Lodge Papers, Massachusetts Historical Society.
[15] Hoar to the Reverend Daniel Merriam, 11 December 1903, Hoar Papers. *See*, too, *Springfield Republican*, 11 December 1903.

Ohio with the aid of administration patronage, accused Hoar of disloyalty to his president and his party. Gorman declared that the Democrats were ready to stand shoulder-to-shoulder with the noble Nestor of Massachusetts and prevent the impulsive Roosevelt from staining the nation's honor. Hoar found the remarks of his two colleagues equally embarrassing. He demanded the right to be understood and in a rambling speech, made much longer by frequent interruption, attempted to explain his belief that he was performing a loyal service to his party's leader by demanding a full investigation. He wanted it understood that he spoke as a Republican and not as the ally of Senator Gorman. As a Republican he wished the President to present proof that there was no American complicity in the Panamanian revolution, no unseemly haste in our recognition of the independent status of the new republic, and no reason to believe that any American official involved in the treaty negotiation had a financial interest in the construction of the proposed canal. Though confident that the President was incapable of intrigue, he was deeply troubled by the seeming injustice of our treatment of Colombia, and particularly by our action in preventing Colombian troops from landing on the isthmus. Whatever our responsibilities for preserving peace and justice in the Caribbean, they must never be perverted into the actions of "a policeman who would manacle the intended victim of a robbery and then claim his pocketbook."[16]

Hoar's speech was assailed by spokesmen for the administration, praised by the Independent press, and misunderstood by all sides. Admittedly reluctant "to again separate myself from my party," Hoar cautioned certain of his more laudatory correspondents not to jump to hasty conclusions.[17] They ignored his advice and were in consequence quick to proclaim his subsequent vote in behalf of the Panama treaty an act of desertion.

[16] *Congressional Record*, 58th Cong., 2d sess., 316–318 (17 December 1903). H. H. Kohlsaat's Chicago paper, *The Inter-Ocean*, 19 December 1903, declared that as Hoar's speeches in the winter of 1899 had incited the Filipinos to rebellion so this unpatriotic address must now bear the blame if Colombian troops attacked the United States marines in Panama.

[17] *See*, for example, Hoar to George S. Boutwell, 8 January 1904 (copy), Hoar Papers.

Hoar announced his decision to vote for the treaty on 22 February 1904, and the following day was counted with the majority. There are various possible explanations for Hoar's change of face. Perhaps he was persuaded of the administration's innocence by Roosevelt, who called Hoar to the White House in an effort to disabuse him of any impression that the hands of the executive were less than spotless.[18] Perhaps Hoar spoke no more than the truth when he insisted in his Senate speech of the twenty-second that he considered his earlier objections to have been met by the papers subsequently forwarded to the Senate by the State Department.[19] Perhaps Hoar, grown weary with battle, wished so hard for his persuasion that he convinced himself of its accomplishment.

If Hoar anticipated that his vote would win the warm approval of Senator Foraker and other administration spokesmen, he was quickly corrected. Foraker felt obliged to interrupt Hoar's professions of support for treaty and party to quote from the record portions of Hoar's December speech and the accompanying compliments of Senator Gorman—an act of malice that infuriated its object.[20] Foraker's jibes were of little importance for the history of American diplomacy, but they offered additional illustration of

---

[18] The recollection of Senator Cullom would seem to indicate, however, that the influence of this conference was at best delayed:

> The President wanted the Senator to read a message which he had already prepared, in reference to Colombia's action . . . which message showed very clearly that the President had never contemplated the secession of Panama, and was considering different methods in order to obtain the right of way across the Isthmus from Colombia . . . The President was sitting on the table, first at one side of Senator Hoar, and then on the other, talking in his usual vigorous fashion, trying to get Senator's attention to the message. Senator Hoar seemed adverse to reading it, but finally sat down, and without seeming to pay any particular attention to what he was perusing, he remained for a minute or two, then arose and said: "I hope I may never live to see the day when the interests of my country are placed above its honor." He at once retired from the room without uttering another word.

Shelby Cullom, *Fifty Years of Public Service*, 212–213.

[19] *Congressional Record*, 58th Cong., 2d sess., 2191–2200 (22 February 1904).

[20] *Ibid.; New York Tribune*, 23 February 1904. The Democratic *New York Globe* observed: "It was very heartless of Senator Foraker . . . when Senator Hoar was executing with the facile grace of life-long practice his right-about-face on the Panama question to embarrass the movement by citations from the Massachusetts Senator's speech of a few months ago. Mr. Hoar has been through this performance many times, but never before has he been nagged and annoyed by a member of his own party while doing it." Reprinted in the *Washington Post*, 29 February 1904.

Hoar's unwilling estrangement from the changing leadership of his party.

The change of Republican leadership was in some ways not so much a change of philosophy as of temper. In economic philosophy Hoar was neither more nor less "conservative" than Henry Cabot Lodge, but in Roosevelt's view Lodge was one of the strong men who represented the party's new promise, while Hoar was a relic—however honorable—of another era. Not only did Hoar fail sufficiently to follow Roosevelt's lead on such domestic policies as those concerning the trusts and the railroads, but he displayed a sorry inability to see the importance of introducing to Washington men possessed of new ideas and a certain intellectual boldness, such as Lodge's friend, Oliver Wendell Holmes.

Hoar was unquestionably disgruntled by Roosevelt's appointment of Holmes to the Supreme Court in August 1902. Probably he had hoped that his nephew, Samuel Hoar, would be appointed to the vacancy; surely, he considered that his own dignity was injured by the abrupt manner in which Roosevelt informed him of his intentions. He was careful to make clear to Roosevelt that in former days the chairman of the Senate Judiciary Committee had been treated with greater respect.[21] Though Hoar stiffly refused to discuss Holmes's qualifications with Roosevelt, he felt no such inhibition when writing to Lodge:

> Judge Holmes personally is a very agreeable and pleasant man ... But his accomplishments are literary and social, and as an investigator of the history of jurisprudence, and not judicial. He lacks strength. I do not think that any considerable number of persons in the profession attach any weight to his opinions whatever ... In his opinions he runs to subtleties and refinements ... His appointment will be in my opinion ... a lowering of the strength of the Court and a diminution of its authority and of the public security in times of great danger when the judgments of the Court should be a bulwark.[22]

[21] *See* Hoar to Samuel Hoar, 20 May 1902; Lodge to Hoar, 26 July 1902; Roosevelt to Hoar, 26 July 1902; Hoar to Roosevelt, 28 July 1902 (copy); Roosevelt to Hoar, 30 July 1902, Hoar Papers.

[22] Hoar to Lodge, 29 July 1902, Hoar Papers. Unknown to Hoar, Lodge had been instrumental in securing Holmes's appointment.

Roosevelt most probably considered Hoar's disgruntlement with Holmes's nomination to be the reaction of a conservative mossback, who was disturbed by certain of Holmes's opinions on the Massachusetts bench respecting the rights of labor. Here Roosevelt misjudged Hoar. It was not Holmes's presumed pro-labor sympathies of which Hoar was suspicious, but rather his notions respecting historical jurisprudence and the relativity of judicial truth and precedent. Judges had not talked in such subtle and devious fashion when he was practicing before the courts of Worcester and Hoar was far from certain they need do so now.

Hoar made no effort in the Senate to block Holmes's appointment and voted in its behalf, but as late as July 1903 he was still complaining to Lodge of "the greatest personal affront I have ever known put upon a member of the Senate."[23]

Hoar's declining influence in the United States Senate was not the result of any conquest of that body by the Progressive movement or the forces of reform. The inner council of the Senate in Roosevelt's first administration—Nelson W. Aldrich, John C. Spooner, Mark Hanna, Orville H. Platt, William B. Allison, Matthew Quay—was not composed of men perceptibly worried by the abuses of big business or convinced of the propriety of the legislative alteration of society. The streamlining of the procedures of the House of Representatives under the guidance of Thomas B. Reed had indirectly increased the power of the Senate and so of its conservative leaders, and the cooperation of the latter after 1903 with the new czar of the House, Joseph G. Cannon, assured their continued influence over the legislative process in both houses of Congress. It is by no means illogical that as the Progressive Era began the United States Congress was dominated by men unsym-

[23] Hoar to Lodge, 15 July 1903, Lodge Papers, Massachusetts Historical Society. Hoar never relented in his opinion that Holmes's appointment was a serious error. He considered Holmes's first opinions on the Supreme Court to be most unsatisfactory. Holmes's opinion in the Giles case, that the discriminatory election laws of the state of Alabama represented "a political question," was "worse than the Dred Scott decision." If disregard of the Fifteenth Amendment was a sign of the new jurisprudence, Hoar was content to be "old fashioned." Convocation Address, Clark University Summer School, 13 July 1903, reported in *Boston Herald,* 27 July 1903; Hoar to Albert Pillsbury, 18 July 1903, Hoar Papers.

pathetic to the aspirations and fears that inspired the Progressive movement.

Washington was not, of course, without its advocates of change. Progressivism during the first Roosevelt administration was still primarily a local or statewide movement, but the Muckrakers had begun to move to the national level in their exposures of wrong-doing, and in Congress such figures as Albert Beveridge and Jonathan Dolliver were beginning to identify themselves with the idea of federal responsibility for social improvement. In certain of his executive recommendations and actions, Roosevelt was similarly prepared to play the role of the cautious innovator. None of these men saw in Hoar a potential ally, however; nor did Hoar express approval or awareness of the reform movement gradually taking shape. He would have disclaimed the title of Progressive, if he had recognized its validity, and the early Progressives made no effort to claim Senator Hoar. Yet in several ways Hoar's silhouette was not very dissimilar to what has been called the Progressive profile.

The typical Progressive was a well-educated member of the middle class who contested the sanctity of laissez-faire economics but had no quarrel with free-enterprise capitalism. Equally fearful of plutocracy and proletarian class-consciousness, he sought to improve the political and economic health of the nation through institutional innovation and legislative reform. The legislative process should be more efficient and more responsive to the public will, and the improved political machinery then used to correct the abuses of capitalistic monopoly. The role of government as social arbiter should be enlarged—though always in behalf of individual liberty and never under the inspiration of minority pressures or class consciousness.[24]

Granting the accuracy of such a "profile," it is clear that Hoar shared the fears of the Progressives, if not their hopes. He was worried by the growing political and economic power of the Morgans and Rockefellers and equally suspicious of the potential power of the larger unions. He deplored all talk of class division

[24] One of the best of many efforts to draw the "Progressive profile" will be found in George E. Mowry, *The Era of Theodore Roosevelt* (New York: Harper & Brothers, 1958), 85–105. *See*, too, Richard M. Abrams, *Conservatism In A Progressive Era: Massachusetts Politics, 1900–1912* (Cambridge: Harvard University Press, 1964), ii.

and all examples of class consciousness, and like many of the Progressives he shared a certain nostalgia for the agrarian past and a distaste for the new materialism. Few were more ready to declare the old standards threatened and none more convinced that the dictates of morality were as important for the legislative chamber as for the fireside.

And yet there were differences. Hoar wished America to rediscover the values of Jefferson, but he doubted that Congress could legislate their reapplication. He continued to believe that social improvement was primarily the product of education and the contagion of sound principles, and he entertained strong doubts about the desirability of tinkering with proven political instruments in an effort to make them more efficient or scientific.[25] A self-assessed nationalist, Hoar was also a "constitutionalist." He recognized the abuses in the political and economic life of America, but as he grew older he was increasingly convinced that it was safer for the federal government to do too little than too much. More particularly, Hoar found the style and temper of the new Progressives uncongenial. They, in turn, viewed him as an honest but old-fashioned conservative. Hoar's fluctuating posture on the issue of the trusts did not alter their judgment.

As one who claimed authorship of the Antitrust Act of 1890, Hoar considered himself obligated to take cognizance of the increasing agitation against the trusts. Personal conviction and political apprehensions combined to persuade him that this agitation could not be ignored. The Sherman Act did need supplementation. The type and degree of supplementation needed, however, was difficult to determine. In the years 1902–1903, Hoar earnestly sought to reconcile his fear of plutocracy with his faith in industrial expansion. The effort was painful and ultimately unsuccessful.

Hoar's correspondence during these years reflected his bifocal view of industrial combination, as did his speeches in the congressional campaign of 1902.[26] In that campaign he spoke in contra-

[25] For Hoar's suspicion of legislation by "experts," *see* Hoar to Nathaniel Mathews, 24 December 1902; Hoar to Wharton Barker, 26 December 1902, Hoar Papers.
[26] *See*, especially, Hoar to Charles Washburn, 26 May 1902; Hoar to G. Stanley Hall, 29 December 1902; Hoar to Rockwood Hoar, 4 May, 11 November, 14 November 1903; Hoar to Henry A. Marsh, 3 April 1903, 14 April 1904, Hoar Papers.

puntal style of the evils of the trusts and the danger of disturbing prosperity:

> What now must we do with great combinations of capital, powerful as States, if they undertake to put forth their combined power, on the one side, to prevent lawful competition, which is to healthy manufacture and healthy trade as the breath of their nostrils; and on the other side, try to compel labor to submit to their oppressive and unjust terms?
>
> I like to hear of Pierpont Morgan buying up foreign steamship companies. I do not object very much to hear . . . that the knees of the old lady of Threadneedle Street tremble and strike together when she hears that he is coming to England . . . We are dependent on great combinations of capital to do all things for which individual strength is totally inadequate. We are dependent on them to perform public service and to take great risk.[27]

After cautioning each audience against undue alarm, Hoar proceeded to enumerate the specific evils of which the trusts were often guilty: the destruction of competition, absentee management, indifference to public sentiment, political manipulation, fraudulent capitalization, and secrecy. It was his opinion that if only the last two could be cured, the other evils would automatically be corrected. The requirements of inspection and publicity offered the most likely and proper solution.

By the end of 1902 Hoar was sufficiently confident of the safety of that solution to seek a national audience. On 17 December he introduced in the Senate a bill to amend the antitrust statute, and three weeks later offered a lengthy explanation of its provisions and merits.[28]

[27] Memoranda for Political Speech, 1902; Draft of Speech to Chickawbut Club, Boston, 27 October 1902, Hoar Papers.

[28] *Congressional Record*, 57th Cong., 2d sess., 6659. Although Hoar noted that he spoke for neither the Senate Judiciary Committee nor the administration, he had made quiet efforts to obtain information and advice from Attorney General Philander C. Knox respecting the constitutionality of placing federal restrictions upon the interstate commerce of corporations established under state charter. Copies of the following "confidential" letters will be found in the Hoar Papers: Hoar to Knox, 16 December, 18 December 1902, 3 January 1903; Knox to Hoar, 20 December 1902, 5 January 1903.

Hoar began his speech of 6 January with a description of the various evils of which the trusts were capable, "when in bad hands." To his earlier list of evils he now added another: the danger of the spread of monopolistic practices to labor. A potential consequence of the industrial trust was that workingmen would in emulation "catch the spirit of monopoly and unlawful combination." The result of such contagion was fearful to contemplate: "The whole manufacture of the country in any branch [of industry] on one side and the whole labor of the country in that manufacture on the other are to be controlled by two great corporations, by which, as between the upper and nether millstone, the liberty of the individual, which has made alike the glory and the strength of the Republic is gone."

Such a picture, he hastened to add, was drawn only as a warning, not as a representation of the contemporary scene. He would indeed be badly misunderstood if it was thought to be his intention to indict those men "who hold the great fortunes in this country to-day." It was neither wealth nor corporate power that need worry his fellow Americans, but rather the abuse of corporate power by a. few. Such abuse was best corrected by cautious but sufficient additions to the antitrust law of 1890. The proposals he now offered could be enacted without fear of unconstitutionality or judicial challenge.

In summary, those proposals required all corporations engaged in interstate commerce to file with the Interstate Commerce Commission a full statement of their financial condition; prescribed penalties for unfair business practices judged by the courts to represent a conscious conspiracy to drive competitors from the market; and established a special fund for the Attorney General for the better enforcement of all laws regulating interstate commerce. Hoar evidently had in mind, too, an informal federal licensing system; for one section of his bill required a signed pledge by the "officers, general managers and Directors" of an interstate corporation to accept all the obligations and liabilities imposed by the act.[29]

---

[29] *Congressional Record*, 57th Cong., 2d sess., 518–524 (6 January 1903); *New York Times*, 7 January 1903. *See*, too, Thorelli, *The Federal Antitrust Policy*, 532.

Hoar's bill and the speech with which he defended it represented the most advanced position he ever took on the issue of big business regulation. If that bill included certain escape clauses respecting the determination of unfair corporation practices, and kept the task of enforcement in the hands of a conservative federal judiciary, it nonetheless called for more direct and embracive federal intervention than Hoar had previously been willing to consider.[30] Indeed, Hoar was before long rather apprehensive that he had gone too far, too fast. He did not express any sharp sense of grievance when his bill was later buried in the Judiciary Committee.

The public reception of his bill probably dampened the pride of authorship. Most of his business correspondents expressed various shades of disagreement or alarm; the Muckrakers and other proto-Progressives offered neither interest nor approval; and Roosevelt—though he was later to adopt it—labeled the notion of a federal licensing system, "idiotic."[31] Hoar had anticipated, of course, that his speech would arouse some apprehension within the business community, but he was probably surprised at its extent.[32] If the criticisms of certain New England manufacturers did not frighten him, they strengthened already existing doubts as to the necessity of any major assault by the federal government on the trusts.[33]

Hoar's failure to push his bill and the solution it proposed more vigorously was the result primarily of continuing intellectual confusion over the problem of big business and its regulation. He was as much disturbed as gratified when, in the early days of February 1903, Senator Nelson Aldrich stopped by his desk in the Senate and informed him that a delegation of sightseers from Providence

---

[30] Several papers proclaimed Hoar's bill "the most drastic yet offered in Congress." See *New York Herald*, 3 January 1903; *The Spy* (Worcester), 7 January 1903; and clippings from *Minneapolis Times* in Scrap Book, Personal, IX, Hoar Papers.

[31] Roosevelt to Joseph B. Bishop, 17 February 1903, Morison, *Letters of Theodore Roosevelt*, III, 429.

[32] Shortly before his speech he had warned the president of Clark University that he was about to "say something in the Senate on the subject of Trusts" that might well be "displeasing" to such prospective donors to Clark as Mr. Carnegie and Mr. Rockefeller. Hoar to G. Stanley Hall, 29 December 1902, Hoar Papers.

[33] *See*, for example, William F. Draper to Hoar, 9 January 1903; F. W. Pitcher to Hoar, 19 January 1903; Kidder, Peabody & Company to Hoar, 21 February 1903, Hoar Papers.

had asked Aldrich to point out to them, "Hoar, the trust buster."[34] That the conservative Aldrich was not particularly perturbed by the request is illustrative of the ultimate ineffectiveness of Hoar's long and earnest effort to grapple with the problem of industrial combination.

Closely associated with Hoar's views on the trust problem were those he entertained on such other issues of the early Roosevelt years as the coal strike and the relations of the federal government and labor.

When, during his antitrust speech of 6 January 1903, Hoar made reference to a future where the interests of the public were crushed between great monolithic combinations of capital and labor, many members of his audience were probably reminded of the recently concluded Anthracite Coal Strike. Fifty thousand anthracite coal miners in northeastern Pennsylvania had gone on strike early in May 1902. They demanded union recognition and improved hours and wages, and their demands were rejected by the six railroads that controlled the anthracite fields. By autumn the nation had been given an opportunity to witness the effectiveness of both union discipline and managerial solidarity. The refusal of George F. Baer and his fellow railroad operators to accept the offer of John Mitchell, president of the United Mine Workers, to arbitrate the issues in dispute swung many citizens behind the miners, although others continued to label the strike an insurrection and to view Mitchell as a power-hungry labor boss. Early in October Roosevelt entered the picture. He called the leaders of both sides to the White House for a day-long conference and by means of public threat and private negotiation subsequently persuaded the operators to accept arbitration. With the establishment of a seven-member arbitral board, the strike was over and Roosevelt basked in the praise of a relieved public.

The most interesting feature of this first labor crisis of the Roosevelt years was his threat to send ten thousand federal troops into the mines to dig the coal and dispossess the operators if the latter remained obdurate. This threat had both broken the resistance of

[34] *Atlanta Constitution*, 8 February 1903, Scrap Book, IX, Hoar Papers.

the operators and worried George F. Hoar. Hoar was not unsympathetic to the striking miners and would endorse the decision of the arbitral board to award the miners a modest wage increase and a reduction of the workday. When he had heard, however, that Roosevelt contemplated government seizure of the mines, he had expressed strong disapproval. The Constitution gave the government no right to seize private property except under conditions of military emergency; government operation of the anthracite mines would be nothing less than state socialism.[35] Relieved that Roosevelt never had reason to make good his threat, Hoar remained convinced that the threat alone established a dangerous precedent.

In their general views respecting the needs and responsibilities of labor, however, Roosevelt and Hoar were quite similar. Each expressed a cautious sympathy for union labor and a strong opposition to labor violence, boycotts, and the closed shop. Both men saw the inevitability of labor combination in an age of industrial expansion and both opposed certain of its aims and tactics.[36]

Hoar was convinced that a workingman had the right voluntarily to combine with his fellow laborers in an effort to bargain more effectively with management, and no right whatever to interfere with the freedom of other workingmen who did not choose to join the effort. Such interference would be "pure despotism" and was "destructive alike to republican liberty and republican government." Labor had, in short, the right to strike in orderly fashion to improve its "wages, comfort and safety," but no right to infringe the liberties of strike breakers.[37] The state legislatures, in Hoar's view, had primary responsibility for protecting the rights and curbing the abuses of union labor, but it was proper for Congress to lend its assistance. He was unsure, however, of how this should be done, and his one effort in Roosevelt's first administration to author

[35] *See* Memoranda for Political Speech, 1902, Hoar Papers.

[36] *See* Theodore Roosevelt to Hoar, 17 October 1902 (copy), Hoar Papers. Hoar willed the original of this letter to his friend Carroll D. Wright, as it contained Roosevelt's exuberant praise of Wright's role in helping to settle the Anthracite Coal Strike.

[37] *See* report of Hoar's speech to the Chickawbut Club of Boston, 27 October 1902 in the *Herald Tribune* (New York), 28 October 1902; Hoar to Thomas Perkins, 7 July 1903, Hoar Papers.

a labor bill did not increase his confidence that it could be done easily.

On 3 February 1902, Hoar as chairman of the Senate Judiciary Committee reported out a bill proposing "to limit the meaning of the word 'conspiracy'" as applied to the activities of labor unions and to offer the federal judiciary certain guidelines for the issuance of restraining orders to unions and their officials. It was the intent of the bill to restrict the use of injunctions against labor combinations and, at the same time, to protect the rights of the nonunion laborer against "criminal intimidation." In the eyes of certain union leaders the bill was a dangerous measure, likely to serve as a legislative weapon against the union shop. The magazine, *American Industries*, on the contrary, damned it as "Hoar's Anti-Injunction bill." Hoar spent considerable time and ink in an effort to erase the misunderstanding of correspondents on both sides.[38] It was a fruitless effort. The bill never came to a vote and its chief significance was to reflect the indecision Hoar shared with many Americans—Theodore Roosevelt among them—about the rights and needs of organized labor.

Roosevelt, like Hoar, saw reform as a conservative necessity, and he favored a carefully restricted amount of it. Roosevelt, however, dressed his demands for cautious innovation in battle rhetoric and sounded more radical than he was. Hoar expounded his doubts more clearly than his hopes and appeared more conservative than he was. Indeed, it was Hoar's reaction to various proposals for constitutional revision and political reform, rather than his stand on such issues as the trusts, labor unions, or the powers of the I.C.C., that most clearly differentiated his views from those who would become known as the Insurgents or Progressives.

On the floor of the Senate and in several magazine articles Hoar proclaimed and reiterated his objections to the popular election of federal senators. Those objections were inspired by a conviction that the popular election of his colleagues would result in increased

---

[38] *See,* for example, Hoar to Holyoke Machine Company, 7 March 1902; Hoar to C. H. Bell, secretary, Brotherhood of Carpenters and Joiners, Great Barrington, 30 December 1902, Hoar Papers. Also, *American Industries,* 1 January 1903.

electoral corruption, the selection of men of inferior talent and virtue, and the subversion of the masterful system of checks and balances authored in 1787. To alter the Constitution in so radical a manner would create a dangerous precedent. Certainly it would decrease the influence and change the very nature of the Senate— the body entrusted to effect the sober, second, and best thought of the American people.[39]

Hoar's opposition to what would eventually become the Seventeenth Amendment was an opposition of long standing and did not reflect the influence of advancing years. That influence was more perceptible in his attitude toward certain other institutional reforms. At one time a champion of parliamentary reform in the Senate and an opponent of the filibuster, he was by 1901 "inclined to leave matters as they are." It was proper to have one branch of Congress where both debate and the opportunity for legislative amendment was without restriction of any kind.[40] The devices of the initiative and referendum Hoar judged unnecessary and potentially disturbing to the independence of the constitutionally elected law makers. For much the same reasons, he questioned the propriety of quasi-judicial commissions when they were allowed to exercise legislative functions, and he resented the efforts of Roosevelt to exert pressure upon Congress by means of public appeals and press conferences.

Fully aware that in the eyes of certain younger members of his party he was judged an old fogey, Hoar considered the charge natural but without foundation. It was, of course, true that "as men grow older they often become more timid," and "difficulties and objections seem more formidable," but opposition to unwise political innovations was not a sign of age but rather of wisdom.[41]

Hoar's last three years in the Senate were passed in the political shadow of a man whom he tried hard to admire, but never under-

[39] Hoar was additionally convinced that the popular election of senators would "be a violation in spirit of the agreement on which the small States assented to the Constitution." *Congressional Record*, 57th Cong., 1st sess., 2616–2618 (11 March 1902); *Chicago Record-Herald*, 12 March 1902; Hoar to Elmer Beach, 15 April 1902, Hoar Papers.

[40] Hoar to Charles E. Adams, 11 April 1901, Hoar Papers.

[41] Hoar to W. W. Williams, 3 February 1904, Hoar Papers.

stood. They were not, on the whole, particularly happy years. Hoar could not help but appreciate that though frequently referred to by the press as "the dean of the Senate," his advice was disregarded more often than not by his country's president and his party's leadership. There were times when Hoar sought to attribute his fading influence to the general decline of New England's role in the national councils, but there were moments of discouraging clarity when he appreciated that a new cycle in the political history of his party and country was beginning and that he had been judged irrelevant to its progress. New men, younger and more politically adaptable, had the places of power and the ear of the "brave but sometimes rash" Mr. Roosevelt.[42]

It had been Republicans like Hoar who, by keeping alive some spark of ideology and program, had prepared the Republican party for the ideas and policies of the Roosevelt era, but the inheritance was unacknowledged. Political successions by their very nature insist on their differences and ignore their debts.

[42] Hoar to Rockwood Hoar, 31 October 1902, Hoar Papers.

# 11

## *The Man and the Partisan*

George Frisbie Hoar spent his entire adult life in an effort to be true to his God, his party, and his ancestors. He died convinced that he had done his best by each, and probably he had.

A rationalist as well as a sentimentalist, Hoar quite consciously shaped his religious convictions to coincide with his historical understanding. It would not be just to say that Hoar viewed God as a heavenly George Washington, but it would be fair to say that he believed the God of his Puritan Fathers to have been instructed and improved by William Ellery Channing. An equitable and benevolent God sought the improvement of society and the greater happiness of man, believing, as did His worshipper George F. Hoar, that progress, if not inevitable, was surely very likely. Hoar's God was not an angry Jehovah nor a watcher of sparrows; rather he was the embodiment of morality, truth, honor, and goodness. God was something of an isolationist, forever concerned but seldom interfering. Similarly, the Bible was not a literal transcription of revealed truth, but an inspiration to spiritual improvement and the finest literary expression of moral teachings the world had ever known.[1]

[1] *See* Hoar to Walter Williams, 15 July 1901, Hoar Papers.

By inheritance and choice, Hoar was a Unitarian. By today's definitions, however, Hoar must be considered a right-wing Unitarian. He saw the Unitarian emphasis on reason and free will as furnishing not a substitute but a support "for faith in the divine mysteries which surround all life."[2] It was reason, however, that allowed one to determine which were and were not satisfactory explanations of these mysteries. Hoar believed neither in the Trinity nor the Virgin Birth, but he endowed Christ's ministry with the quality of divinity and took violent exception to all suggestions that the Unitarian lay outside the Christian pale.[3] Though Jesus was but man, His labor of redemption was a miracle. With Jesus there came into the world "a spiritual power" that "revolutionized empires and lifted mankind from degradation."[4]

During the last twenty years of his life, Hoar was the most prominent Unitarian layman in the country, serving as president of the National Unitarian Conference from 1895 through 1901. His strong identification with the Unitarian church, however, only served to accentuate his natural tolerance of other sects and faiths. Hoar was not a religious equalitarian—if all faiths spoke to God, the most musical to His ears was that enunciated by Edward Everett Hale—but he had no use for intolerance. Religious prejudice he considered narrow-minded and unintelligent, and, in a pluralistic society such as the United States, highly impolitic and dangerous. Careful at all times to draw a sharp line between his senatorial position and denominational preference, Hoar believed that public men had a duty to promote morality and an obligation to keep inviolate the separation between Church and State.[5] The First Amendment protected the nation against official religious discrimination; private prejudices would gradually diminish through the agencies of education and good example. By his fight against the

---

[2] Hoar to Dr. I. K. Funk, 29 December 1902, draft of "Address to Worcester Fire Society on its One Hundredth Anniversary," Hoar Papers; Calvin Stebbins, "George Frisbie Hoar, A Discourse: Address Delivered at the First Parish Church of Framingham, 9 October 1904," pamphlet, Hoar Papers.

[3] *See* Hoar to P. W. Wood, secretary, Y.M.C.A. of Worcester, 15 February 1901, Hoar Papers.

[4] Hoar to The Reverend Charles L. Page, 25 February 1904; draft of address (undated), "The Unitarian View of Christ," Hoar Papers.

[5] *See* Hoar to the Reverend Arthur A. Woodell, 9 March 1904, Hoar Papers.

A.P.A. and by his friendship with certain Catholic and Jewish leaders Hoar consciously tried to set such an example.[6]

Hoar's second wife was an Episcopalian, but if ever he had recanted his Unitarian affiliation he would undoubtedly have become a Congregational Calvinist. It was hard to understand how any of the Puritans could have believed literally in "the terrible faith of Jonathan Edwards," but Calvinism was the creed of those both in the New World and the Old who had accomplished most in the long battle for constitutional liberty. The inspiration for their political intelligence and courage was not to be found in the frightening notions of predestination and infant damnation. It was the Puritan's moral orientation and discipline that had inspired his keen sense of liberty, justice, and constitutional order:

> This is the secret of their greatness . . . that they governed themselves, and they believed that a free people should govern itself, by a law higher than their own desire. Duty and not self-indulgence, and future good in this world and the other, and not a present and immediate good, were the motives upon which they acted. It was of this temper, in spite of their intellectual error, that their greatness was born.[7]

Not religious doctrine but secular illustration made glorious the example of the Puritans. The Colony of Massachusetts Bay was a political community governing itself by general rules derived from a free-born understanding of the Moral Law.

The example of the Puritans formed an important part of what might be called Hoar's secular creed. If he was not at times as certain as his Puritan forbears of how best to apply the Moral Law, no more than they did he doubt its existence or its ultimate applicability to the social and political relations of men.

---

[6] *See*, for example, Hoar to Julius Meyer, chairman, Zionist Council of Boston, 11 June 1903; Hoar to Morris L. Katz, chairman, Committee of Hebrew Citizens of Worcester, 29 May 1903; Hoar to Professor H. S. Carruth, Boston College, 12 December 1903, Hoar Papers; Speech of G. F. Hoar before the Father Mathew United Benevolent & Total Abstinence Society of Worcester, as reported in *The Spy* (Worcester), 29 August 1903.

[7] Hoar to James W. Johnson, 2 March 1903; draft of address before the Connecticut Valley Congregational Club, Greenfield, Massachusetts, 29 November 1887, Hoar Papers.

The "natural laws" of the Social Darwinists had little appeal for Hoar but Natural Law capitalized by its association with the purposes of Providence was indeed the proper criteria for assessing the rightfulness of political policies and institutions. The spirit of democracy, with its components of freedom, justice, and constitutionalism, found validity as well as genesis in the Moral Law. Hoar seldom made any speech that did not reflect this belief, but perhaps its most concise expression was embodied in a single paragraph of his address to the Massachusetts General Court, 12 February 1901:

> I have no belief in fatalism, in destiny, in blind force . . . I believe that the God who created this world has ordained that His children may work out their own salvation, and that his nations may work out their own salvation, by obedience to his laws. I believe that Liberty, good government, free institutions cannot be given by one people to any other, but must be wrought out each for itself . . . in the progress of years . . . I believe that the Moral Law and the Golden Rule are for nations as well as Individuals.[8]

A nation's great men were those who by their character as well as their work undertook to reflect the guiding power of inherited ideals and spiritual laws. When Hoar on one occasion was asked by a Massachusetts antiquarian to indicate his preference among "Americans most deserving representation" in a future hall of fame, he submitted a list of twelve: Washington, Jefferson, Lincoln, Jonathan Edwards, John Adams, Sam Adams, Hamilton, Webster, Marshall, Sumner, Emerson, and John Greenleaf Whittier. Such men as Longfellow and Hawthorne he would exclude, for to be a great man one must possess "more than the quality of a great artist," and Benjamin Franklin was "without idealism, without lofty principle, and, on one side of his character, gross and immoral."[9]

---

[8] "Address of G. F. Hoar before The General Court of Massachusetts, February 12, 1901," pamphlet, Hoar Papers.

[9] Edward A. Kelley to Hoar, 25 July 1900; Hoar to Kelley, 27 July 1900, Hoar Papers. *See*, too, Hoar to Lodge, 20 April 1901, Lodge Papers, Massachusetts Historical Society. It was with the greatest difficulty that Hoar excluded from the list his grandfather Roger Sherman and General Rufus Putnam, a native of Worcester County. Hoar believed Putnam almost solely responsible for saving the Old Northwest from Slavery, and he organized a successful campaign to restore and enshrine Putnam's homestead in Sutton, Massachusetts.

Of the twelve elected, Washington was the noblest; Jefferson, the most influential. Washington was integrity and patriotism incarnate —indeed his monument in Washington marked "the prime meridian of pure, exalted, human character"—but the author of the Great Declaration had equal claim to reverence. He had expressed for the ages the duty of a state to conduct itself by spiritual laws and "abide neither injustice nor evil as part of its foundation."[10]

Hoar was sufficiently provincial to believe that no section had given more greatness to America than New England, and that no other nation could boast as many statesmen concerned with the application of justice and moral truth. He would admit Lafayette and Bolivar, and possibly Mazzini, to the highest court of honor, and surely Kossuth and Miss Nightingale, but the public men of Europe were too little concerned with the reality of political ideals. His favorite European nation, England, had but one statesman who could compare with his friend Sumner: "Mr. Gladstone was one of the few Englishmen since Milton died whose life was inspired by the loftiest ideals of public duty and public service . . . So he is our best witness in modern public life that conscience and the moral law are the best guides for public men, as well as private men, in the greatest difficulties and perplexities."[11] Gladstone, not the bombastic Palmerston or the clever Disraeli, was the true statesman, the public man who would not separate policy from morality. Gladstone knew, as did Jefferson, Lincoln, and George F. Hoar, that in Hoar's words "Freedom, self-government, justice, the welfare of humanity are still the tests by which we mark the progress of the nation and the race."[12]

When Hoar wished to thank Andrew Carnegie for a generous gift to Clark University, he sent him a copy of John Trumbull's engraving, "The Signing of the Declaration of Independence." In

[10] Draft of "Speech of G. F. Hoar at the Celebration of the Centennial Anniversary of the Establishment of the Permanent Seat of the Government in the District of Columbia, December 12, 1900," Hoar Papers; G. F. Hoar, "Thomas Jefferson: An Address Delivered, April 13, 1903, in Washington, at a Banquet of the Thomas Jefferson Memorial Association," pamphlet, Hoar Papers; Hoar to Thomas Nelson Page, 3 August 1904, Thomas Nelson Page Papers, Duke University Libraries, Durham, North Carolina.

[11] Hoar to The Right Honorable John Morley, 23 June 1904 (copy), Hoar Papers.

[12] "Address of G. F. Hoar before the General Court of Massachusetts, February 12, 1901," pamphlet, Hoar Papers.

the enclosing letter he took care to point out that Carnegie would find in the central group, between Jefferson and Adams, Roger Sherman, "my own grandfather from whom I inherited the love of Liberty and my opinions as to the rights of men and of nations."[13] The comment contained truth as well as pride. In the final analysis, Hoar's political faith was more the product of inheritance than of experience or study. His ideas respecting particular policies, men, and events evolved under the impact of changing conditions and partisan pressures, but the set of political certitudes that were his by inheritance remained his at death. The ideal statesman was always cast in the mould of that wise patriot, Roger Sherman; the ultimate task of statesmanship was to show an equal passion for liberty and an equal respect for constitutional order.

The pragmatic quality of Hoar's religious beliefs and the idealistic temper of his political creed reflected a life-long conviction in the value of education. Education bred religious tolerance and moral probity. All true statesmen of American history had seen the importance of education for the moral and political health of their countrymen, and had seen its promotion as one of their first duties. By education he referred to instruction that inspired improvement of character as well as intellect:

> The final purpose of all scholarship, as of all life, is character . . . Let the university teach ignorance—not knowledge; let her teach error—not truth, unless the result of all its doctrine be to improve the moral quality of the soul of men and women who make the State . . . The friends of sound learning have claimed for her that she not only clarifies and strengthens the intellect, but that she sweetens and tempers the heart, by teaching that Divine charity, which is not only the chief of the Christian graces but is the chief grace of the scholar, also.[14]

Although such sentiments were liable to criticism on the ground that they confused education with indoctrination, such was not

[13] Hoar to Carnegie, 20 April 1903 (copy); Carnegie to Hoar, 17 June 1903, Hoar Papers.
[14] "Lesson of the University to the Republic: An Address by G. F. Hoar before the Students of Harvard College," March 1902, typed draft, Hoar Papers.

Hoar's intention. A founder and trustee of Worcester Polytechnic Institute and Clark University and an overseer of Harvard University, he was as concerned with the freedom of intellectual inquiry as with the development of moral character. If not a scholar, Hoar was a man of scholarly interests and one who found relaxation in preparing his own translation of Thucydides' history of the Peloponnesian Wars. A study of the classics was fundamental to the instruction of an educated man.[15] There was no affectation or pretense in Hoar's frequent quotations from Aristotle and Horace; nor were the Greek and Latin mottoes over the door and fireplace in his paneled library intended for display. The study of ancient languages improved one's style and was a pleasant relaxation from the study of coinage bills and tariff schedules. It was a pleasurable duty, and Hoar was never more content than when he discovered that what he liked to do was what he ought to do.

Hoar was not intellectually adventurous, but natural curiosity and continuous application made him one of the more learned men of his time. A strong sense of duty made him study subjects for which he had little inherent interest or sympathy—money and banking, socialism, Darwinism—and neither his conscience nor his education would allow him to disregard the weight of evidence when, as with biological evolution, it ran counter to inherited beliefs. He was intellectually honest and if his mind was not bold, it was well disciplined. His enthusiasms were reserved for causes rather than abstract ideas, but he was a moralist who had trained as a lawyer. Ideals were never more welcome than when supported by logic and sound reason.

Hoar was by instinct a virtuous man. Under the pressures of politics, virtue had occasionally to be shaded, but as a private citizen it could be allowed greater freedom. The clubs and organizations he most enjoyed were those where he had a chance to do good while enjoying the companionship of contemporaries who possessed an equal sense of "right conduct." His membership in such seemingly diverse organizations as the Massachusetts Society for

---

[15] Hoar to Charles Eliot, 5 April 1899; Hoar to John Bellows, 30 May 1902, Hoar Papers.

the Prevention of Cruelty to Animals, the Anti-Tenement League, the American Antiquarian Society, and the Smithsonian Institution all had this inspiration in common. It was wrong for hunters to slaughter "gentle and harmless wild creatures;" it was wrong to corrupt the hearth with sweatshop labor. It was equally right to encourage an understanding of our history and the preservation of its records.[16] And it was the obligation of public-spirited men formally to band together to oppose injustice and encourage virtue.

The man of good will should, however, also be a man of good sense. Fanaticism was no true part of virtue; there must be balance in everything, including good works. One must stand forth boldly against sportsmen who "hunt defenseless animals with dogs and torture them with deadly fear," but there was no call to become an antivivisectionist and infringe the rights of scientific research.[17] Central to Hoar's character was a reverence for order and balance. With the possible exception of the Free Soil years, he always found radicals distasteful, whether their reforms were moral or economic. The public men most to be admired were those who possessed ideals and horsesense.

In the capacities of disciple and friend, however, Hoar was an enthusiast. Here balance usually deserted him. Jefferson and Sumner were not only to be admired but revered. Those among his contemporaries who were fellow members of the Fire Society and the Worcester Club were not merely fine fellows but men without fault or blemish. Hoar held the quality of loyalty in great esteem, and for old and faithful friends he would go to great lengths to select a gift or perform a kindness. Susceptible to flattery himself, Hoar was prepared to laud his intimates and by the force of supe-

---

[16] Hoar was a member of both the Massachusetts Historical Society and the American Historical Association. He was elected a resident member of the former in 1886 and published several papers in its *Proceedings*; he became a member of the American Historical Association in October, 1884—one month after it was organized at Saratoga, New York. Hoar was the public man most responsible for securing a congressional charter for the AHA in 1889, and chiefly in recognition of that fact was elected president of the association in 1895. His inaugural address was a plea to the historical profession to avoid iconoclasm and to write history in the vein of his late friend, George Bancroft. History should be elevating as well as accurate. *Annual Report of the American Historical Association for 1895*, 21–43.

[17] Hoar to G. O. Shields, League of American Sportsmen, 11 April 1902; Hoar to S. N. Cleghorn, 29 June 1904, Hoar Papers.

rior intellect to dominate them. Several times a summer he would send forth a call to some ten or twelve and organize a short antiquarian junket. Hoar would insist on serving as tour guide, host, and chief raconteur.[18]

Hoar's temperament was at the same time serious and boyish. There was little frivolity in his makeup but he never lost a taste for what he would have called, "wholesome fun." The new electric trolley cars and the recurring mysteries of nature were equally a source of pleasure. Like a small boy he wanted to own a part of the horizon, and he purchased the crest of Asnebumskit Ridge, three miles west of Worcester. To the top of his very own mountain he would take his young granddaughters to identify bird calls, or would go to read in solitude his favorite poets, George Herbert and Robert Burns.

With adults he did not know well or favorably, Hoar was stiff and reserved, but with children he was always at ease. Although as psychologically assured as any man with political ambitions, he both needed and craved affection. He took immense pride in the warm but respectful greetings of children as he strolled the streets of Worcester, and in the weeks before Christmas would always have his pockets full of shiny new quarters, which he would distribute to his youthful admirers.

Hoar possessed a sense of fun but very little sense of wit. His efforts at humor ranged from the pawky to the corney. He enjoyed puns, vocabulary jests, and jokes about the insufficient humor of others. But wit was far too near frivolity to be comfortable. Jokes that found their humor in either the bodily functions or sexual appetites of his fellow man were anathema. Idealizing woman and the state of holy matrimony, Hoar had nothing but repugnance for those who would make light of either. At one point he was prepared to investigate the possibility of congressional legislation "to break up the habit of divorces for light reasons," and when he

[18] F. F. Dresser, "George Frisbie Hoar," reprint from *Reminiscences and Biographical Notices of Past Members of the Worcester Fire Society* (Worcester, 1917), pamphlet file, Hoar Papers.

The essential kindliness of Hoar's nature is illuminated by the letters he exchanged with Helen Keller when she was a student at Radcliffe College. Hoar to Helen Keller, 21 November, 3 December 1901 (copies); Helen Keller to Hoar, 25 November, 7 December 1901, Hoar Papers.

heard a rumor to the effect that a Massachusetts man whom he had recommended to McKinley had been seen dining and wining a young actress, Hoar did not rest content until he had proven to his own satisfaction that the lady was of "the highest character" and had not imbibed a drop.[19]

Hoar's instinctive sense of balance, however, restrained his natural prudishness. If he was disgusted by drunkenness, he enjoyed a glass of wine, and at his annual stag dinner at Wormley's Restaurant he always served champagne. He believed in the old virtues of hard work and thrift, but was tolerant of the expenditures of his son when the latter was a Harvard undergraduate and was ready to make every excuse for two impecunious relatives who by their financial carelessness cost him over a thousand dollars. When the instinct to censure confronted the demands of loyalty, it usually lost.

Hoar had little difficulty practicing the morality he preached. Training and circumstances supported high principle. The ideals to which he had been bred in his youth were viewed as sources of happiness as well as goodness, and as his life was generally happy there was little temptation to deny them. Worshipped by his family, admired by his constituents, fulfilled by the satisfaction of public service, Hoar had perhaps little reason to doubt that virtue was its own reward.

It would not appear that Hoar was ever seriously tempted by the seven deadly sins, and surely not by lust or sloth. Both of his wives —the first, young and pretty; the second, plain and intelligent— considered him the kindest and wisest of men, and their reverence was gratifying and sufficient. The habit of intellectual application was acquired at the Harvard Law School, and conscience and ambition served to sustain it. The duties of office had paramount claim. Only the illness of his wife would draw him away from Washington before the congressional session formally adjourned.

In Washington he allowed himself few distractions from the congressional routine. Sports, art museums, and concerts held no interest for him, and the health of his wife and the limits of his purse sharply restricted his participation in Washington society.

[19] Hoar to Charles Eliot Norton, 7 January 1904; Hoar to Archbishop John Ireland, 2 May 1904, Hoar Papers; Hoar to George B. Courtelyou, 7 November 1900, McKinley Papers, Series 1, vol. 70, Library of Congress.

That restriction was not a deprivation. As he became older and more famous Hoar became less stiff, but he was never comfortable at a large formal dinner and enjoyed dancing not at all. His tastes were generally simple and though on occasion he loved an elaborate meal, those occasions seldom involved a large or a mixed company. He would have felt deeply offended if the reigning president ever failed to ask Mrs. Hoar and himself to the annual Judiciary Committee–Supreme Court dinner, but he derived greater pleasure from the baked kidney beans and New England–style codfish cakes that his friend Mrs. Patterson served at her Washington boarding house on Sunday mornings.

Surely in comparison with many of his contemporaries Hoar was little given to conspicuous consumption. Neither an ascetic nor a miser, he was financially cautious. Generous with his friends and with dozens of local charities, he had a dread of debt and financial dependence that grew appreciably in his last years. This was in part the result of his decision in 1902 to purchase a house in Washington and in the process give the Worcester National Bank his personal note for twenty thousand dollars. He had deliberated this step for years and when elected to a fifth term in the Senate decided to take the plunge, influenced by the wishes of his wife. He never regretted the purchase, but the last years of his life saw him exhibit an untypical and apologetic concern for income and compensation. For the first time he would accept an honorarium when delivering an historical address, and he asked Scribner's for immediate remission of $2,500 when sending them the completed manuscript of his autobiography.

The financial concerns of his last years reflected above all else Hoar's determination that his daughter Mary—an emotionally immature spinster—should never suffer want.[20] It was part of the

[20] Hoar would leave an estate valued at approximately $100,000 but most of that sum represented real estate holdings: his house and land at Oak Avenue, Worcester, an apartment house and part interest in an office building in Worcester, and his house on Connecticut Avenue in Washington. Roughly two thirds of Hoar's estate went, as a life interest, to his daughter Mary; the balance, to his son Rockwood. His estate was the product of inheritance and slow accumulation, not of speculation or inside information. Most of his small holding of stocks and bonds had been purchased from rental income; his senatorial salary of $5,000 per annum being largely consumed by living expenses in Washington. *See* Hoar to Rockwood Hoar, 24 December 1902; 15 January, 24 April 1904, Hoar Papers. Also, Hoar to Daniel De Leon, Marxist editor of the *Daily People*, 9 March 1904 (copy), Hoar Papers.

moral code he inherited and practiced that though "high thinking and simple living" were more to be admired than wealth and display, still it was a sorry man who died in debt and left nothing to his children.

Hoar's moral and intellectual dispositions were displayed against two seemingly diverse backgrounds: his home, where he was increasingly the patriarch, and Congress, where he was most often the partisan. Family and party were the prime objects of loyalty as they furnished the chief sources of personal identification and fulfillment.

On a spring morning in the last year of his life, Hoar called to his bedside his daughter, daughter-in-law, and two young grand-daughters and, propped erect by the aid of three horsehair bolsters, delivered the following oration:

> Ladies, this is the 19th of April. One hundred and twenty-nine years ago, to-day, your Grandfathers, to wit, my Grandfather Samuel Hoar, my Great-grandfather John Hoar, my Great-grandfather Abijah Peirce, with our Great-uncle Leonard Hoar, and our Great-uncle Samuel Farrar, and a few others, went to the Bridge at Concord and drove the British Army back to Boston.
> Three cheers!

The orator spoke without notes, for the speech had been delivered many times before, and, as he wrote his absent son, he hoped it would be long continued by his descendants. Perhaps, he added, "as time goes by, it may be unnecessary to state that anybody helped our Great-grandfathers and Uncles in this important achievement."[21] The postscript was intended to lighten but not erase the injunction.

Hoar inherited a deep pride and pleasure in his ancestry and was determined to increase and transmit that inheritance. He obtained the services of the genealogist Henry Stedman Nourse to trace the "Hoar Family in America and Its English Ancestry," a

---

[21] Hoar to Rockwood Hoar, 20 April 1904, Hoar Papers.

task made relatively easy by his own notes and research; he restored the gravestone of his first American ancestress, Joanna Hoar; he uncovered the shield and motto of a collatoral ancestor, Henry Hoare; and he subsequently drove two American consuls mildly insane by his efforts to purchase and import to Worcester various relics associated with Sheriff Charles Hoare of Gloucestershire.[22] There was, as with most antiquarian piety, a note of the ridiculous in all of this—most particularly perhaps in Hoar's unsuccessful efforts to prove collatoral descent from Geoffrey Chaucer—but little of snobbishness.[23]

Hoar was not a social equalitarian, but he was a social democrat. Some men were more morally upright and deserving than others and among these he would choose his friends, but far less than most of his contemporaries was he impressed by wealth and social position. He did not engage in genealogical research in an effort to prove his blood was blue, but rather to reassure himself and his descendants that they came from a long line of honorable men and women. Hoar took far less pleasure in a distant connection with Lady Alice Lisle—and this chiefly because she and her husband were martyrs to royal tyranny—than in his connection with the Minute Men. If he enjoyed securing a few relics from Gloucestershire, he took greater pride in purchasing Redemption Rock and deeding it to his nephew John. Redemption Rock had been the scene of Mrs. Mary Rowlandson's return from Indian captivity, a return accomplished through the reputation for fair dealing of John Hoar, farmer-settler of Concord, Massachusetts.[24]

It was honest yeoman stock in which Hoar took pride; such stock had provided the greatest heroes of both Old England and New. To revere such men as John Hoar and grandfather Roger Sherman was an act of patriotism, not of snobbishness. Roger Sherman had authored the Connecticut Compromise, and it was consequently a positive duty to try and restore the old Sherman tomb in England. He could not understand the "lack of romance and

---

[22] *New-England Historical and Genealogical Register,* January, April, July 1899; separately printed in pamphlet form (Boston, 1899). And *see* Hoar to Mrs. John Bellows, 2 December 1902; Hoar to Loren A. Lothrop, 22 July 1903, Hoar Papers.

[23] Hoar to Mrs. E. W. Whitney, 14 July, 31 December 1902, Hoar Papers.

[24] Hoar to Mrs. Elizabeth Bowles, 4 June 1901, Hoar Papers.

feeling" that dissuaded his friend John Sherman from participating in such a noble undertaking.[25]

Ancestral piety was not for Hoar a substitute for family affection but rather its nourishment. With the death of his brother Ebenezer Rockwood Hoar, whom he admired above all his contemporaries, Hoar became in 1894 the senior male representative of his family. He informed his nephews and great-nephews that he stood ready as their guide and protector; their claim to his care and affection was only exceeded by that of their cousins Mary and Rockwood and their Aunt Ruth.

Hoar was a devoted and solicitous husband to his second wife, Ruth Miller Hoar, for forty-one years. A quiet sensible woman, devoted to her husband and stepchildren, she was a careful manager of her household and her husband's comfort. Although not without a sense of independent judgment in family matters, she dutifully echoed her husband's political prejudices and literary tastes. A periodic sufferer of angina pectoris throughout the last fifteen years of her life, she died on Christmas Eve, 1903. Her death left Hoar "feeling like a man strangely lost and empty," and he found only limited solace in the flood of condolences that came from political friend and foe alike.[26] He found chief consolation in the companionship of his son.

With his wife's death, Hoar was increasingly conscious of his own mortality, and before he died he wished to see the son emulate the father and take a seat in the national House of Representatives. As much to gratify his father as his own ambition, Rockwood consented to run. Hoar was delighted and troubled. Had he persuaded his son to a course that would bring defeat and mortification? In the late spring and early summer of 1904, the ailing father made applications for aid for his son, which if undertaken on his own behalf he would have judged improper. Lodge was success-

[25] G. F. Hoar, "The Connecticut Compromise: Roger Sherman the Author of the Plan of Equal Representation of the States in the Senate and Representation of the People in Proportion to Numbers in the House," *American Antiquarian Society Proceedings*, 15 (1903), 233–258; Hoar to Edward D. Mead, 25 May 1904, Hoar Papers.

[26] Carl Schurz and Grover Cleveland were among the first to express sympathy. An eloquent expression of Hoar's grief will be found in his letter to Mrs. Daniel Kent, 4 June 1904, Hoar Papers.

fully solicited to bestow his blessing and his influence; the leading editor of Worcester County was carefully sounded out; and Rockwood's campaign placed in the hands of Hoar's friend, Frank Roe Batchelder.[27] Hoar would die before the congressional elections of 1904 were held, but not before his son's election was predicted on all sides. There was no political news he found more gratifying —as a father and as a partisan. Family tradition would be served and the district reclaimed from the Democrats.

Hoar would have loved his son whatever his politics, but he would not have lent him aid and encouragement had he not been a member of the Grand Old Party, the most admirable political organization of modern history. Loyalty to family implied loyalty to party, for had not Samuel Hoar and other Free Soilers been the true founders of the Republican party and its principles. The leaders of that party might occasionally go astray, but its principles—human equality; federal citizenship; liberty under constitutional restraint; the national encouragement of individual economic initiative—were as eternal as the fame of Roger Sherman. Hoar's ideals and prejudices as a partisan were not in conflict with those of the private man but their natural extension.

To his dying day he thanked his good fortune to have been born in time to be a Republican and to have participated in "the great achievement of my generation": the frustration of the slave power and the liberation of the slave.[28] As the members of that generation died and Hoar proudly succeeded Justin Morrill as the senior Republican member of the Senate, he took increased pains to repudiate all slurs against its accomplishments. Elihu Root was quickly corrected when, in a public address, he implied that Reconstruction and its "experiment in universal negro suf-

[27] During the same months, Hoar was laboring to obtain for Lodge an honorary degree from Harvard. Although this undoubtedly gratified Lodge, there was no "corrupt bargain." Hoar had long urged the Harvard Corporation and Overseers to give Lodge a degree, and Lodge's own sense of family pride made him instinctively sympathetic to Hoar's ambitions for his son. Hoar to Rockwood Hoar, 22 March, 10 April 1904; Lodge to Hoar, 29 April, 12 May 1904; Hoar to Lodge, 9 May, 7 July 1904 (copies), Hoar Papers. And *see* Hoar to Rockwood Hoar, 9 March, 19 March, 26 March, 14 April 1904, Hoar Papers.

[28] Hoar to William F. York, 18 March 1904, Hoar Papers.

frage" had been a failure. Hoar was prepared on occasion to extend the olive branch to old congressional opponents from the South and to agree that probably not even time would reconcile the southern white to "social equality and companionship with the Negro," but he never denied the justice or practicality of the goals of Sumner and Radical Reconstruction. When old veterans of the Confederacy thanked him for his "new charity," they were informed that courteous references to certain of their former leaders implied no recantation.[29] To admit the existence of irremediable racial antipathy was not to share it. The Fourteenth and Fifteenth Amendments were landmarks in the advance of liberty and the consolidation of the nation, and central to the faith of all true Republicans.

The obverse of loyalty is suspicion, or so it was for Hoar. Loyalty to the crusades of the past demanded continued antipathy toward Bourbon Democrats and Mugwumps. It also implied displeasure with the increasing orientation of his own party to the politics and diplomacy of power. The mistakes of his party, however, were the subject of sorrow not scorn.

Partisan prejudice and self-deception were evident in Hoar's refusal to judge the errors and men of the Republican party as harshly as those of the political enemy, but there was more. There was his conviction that constructive legislation and reform were only secured through the operations of the party system and that the operations of party government required allegiance to majority decision. There was, too, his sincere if exaggerated belief that the rank-and-file membership of the Republican party was superior in wisdom and virtue to its Democratic counterpart and offered security against the long continuance of error by its leaders.

Hoar's repeated declaration that "the Democratic Party was ever the creator of grievances and never their redresser" was campaign cant, but the divided Democratic party under Tilden and Cleveland seldom offered a convincing alternative to Republican policies and under Bryan it offered an alternative philosophically unclear

---

[29] "Speech of G. F. Hoar before the Union League Club of Chicago, February 22, 1903," pamphlet; Adjutant of Camp George Moorman, Forney, Texas, to Hoar, 23 March 1903; Hoar to C. E. Merrill, 26 March 1903; Donelson Caffery to Hoar, 13 June 1903, Hoar Papers.

and, to Hoar's mind, economically dangerous. The Republican party had suffered the misdemeanors of Conkling and Belknap and the embarrassment of Blaine; it had insufficiently persevered in behalf of the southern Negro; and it had participated in the shame of the Philippines, but though conscience required protest, patriotism as well as prudence forbade desertion to the enemy. The children of the Democratic party were slavery, rebellion, fiat money, free trade, electoral fraud, and social discontent. Not only must the voters be told this, but inheritance, repetition, and sectional prejudice convinced Hoar that it was true.

Hoar was less violent in his distrust of Democrats, however, than many of his Republican colleagues. It was when he addressed himself to the Mugwumps of the Northeast that Hoar appeared most partisan and narrow-minded. The Mugwumps were "the worst of our Pharisees," men querelous, unpatriotic, and intolerant of the opinions of others. And what is more, they were men who belonged in the Republican party! As Republican regulars they might have made a constructive contribution. By their carping criticism of everything and everyone they hurt the reputation and influence of independent partisans, such as G. F. Hoar. They gave independence a false definition and a poor name. Indeed, it was partly from a desire to disassociate his own course from that of the Mugwumps that Hoar denounced them so often and so harshly. More significantly, however, he believed that the Mugwumps undermined Republican strength and threatened the two-party system.[30] It was possibly the major inconsistency of Hoar's political creed that while he praised the party system as essential to the progress of liberty under law, he believed that America had best be governed by but one party, his own.

This inconsistency, however, was shared by many Americans, Republicans and Democrats alike. It did not prevent his contemporaries from recognizing what was yet more typical of Hoar, his determination to remain loyal to his party's past as well as its present. If the labor of reconciliation was difficult, Hoar never doubted that it must be accomplished, though by the fall of 1904 he was prepared to bequeath the task to others.

[30] Hoar to James C. Carter, 5 February, 10 March 1903; Hoar to Charles A. Moody, 15 April 1904, Hoar Papers.

When Hoar was stricken with a severe attack of lumbago in February 1904, his initial reaction was one of irritation. Except for periodic inflammation of the eyes, he had enjoyed excellent health all his life, and like most persons of strong constitutions he viewed ill health as a minor insult. A series of atropine injections and "electrical treatments" brought little relief, and by June he was at home in Worcester complaining of "an unaccustomed fatigue." With the first of July he was put to bed and was writing to George Lyman that his nights were torture and his days scarcely more comfortable.[31] He never left his bed again.

On the fifteenth of August he suffered a stroke and fell into a sudden coma. The papers predicted his death hourly. To the surprise of his doctors he recovered consciousness but the onset of pneumonia in his left lung steadily wore away his strength. For a month and a half he lingered, increasingly resigned but resisting by instinct the defeat of death.[32] In the last weeks of September the memory in which he had taken such pride began to fail; in the early hours of the morning of the thirtieth of September the church bells of Worcester in prearranged unison announced his death.

The funeral of George Frisbie Hoar was without the accompaniment of military fanfare; yet better than half the population of Worcester lined the streets in silent tribute as the coffin went from the City Hall, where it had lain in state, to the services at the Church of the Unity and then to the special train that would take it to Con-

---

[31] Hoar to Lyman, 26 July 1904; Hoar to Mrs. Emily C. Lyon, 6 August 1904, Hoar Papers.

[32] His son Rockwood reported: "My father . . . is fully possessed of the belief that he had done his work in life . . . He said that his part of the great work was over and that the campaign this year would be on the question of power and not on the great questions of freedom and equality and constitutional restraint with which he had dealt so intimately." Rockwood Hoar to William E. Rice, 22 August 1904, Hoar Papers.

Rockwood Hoar dutifully kept a diary of his father's last injunctions and benedictions. The entry of 24 August is typical: "Father asked me what messages had come. I told him that messages had come from Senators and friends, and from the President. 'I supposed that the President would,' he said. 'He is a strong, brave man; a man of steel. He is all right.'" Memorandum of Rockwood Hoar (copy), courtesy of the late Mrs. Reginald Foster. *See,* too, Theodore Roosevelt to Rockwood Hoar, 18 August 1904; Rockwood Hoar to Roosevelt, 18 August 1904 (copy); Lodge to Rockwood Hoar, 30 August 1904; John Hay to Rockwood Hoar, 9 September 1904, Hoar Papers.

cord and the family plot. Though not a vain man, Hoar would have been deeply pleased by the tributes that poured in upon his death.[33] Lacking personal magnetism or the flamboyance of personality that can move crowds to demonstrative displays of allegiance, he had always praised the kindness of his constituents without ever being quite certain of their affection. Now he would have been delighted to see among the floral tributes not only a great spray from the White House but a blanket of roses from the Ancient Society of Hibernians, and near them a large silk pillow that described in its elaborate embroidery the loss of the Armenian Citizens of Worcester. Representatives of local, state, and national governments stood in tribute; the hymns were his declared favorites, "Our God, Our Help in Ages Past" and "Awake Our Souls!", and the pastor was his friend of fifty years, Edward Everett Hale. Hale spoke of the spirit of the Puritans, the progress of man, and the quality of loyalty. Hoar had a strong feeling for what was "fitting," and both ceremony and address were appropriate to the man they honored.[34]

Among the many distinguished Massachusetts figures who bowed their heads at the closing benediction were three honorary pallbearers who wished to succeed the deceased in the United States Senate, W. Murray Crane, William D. Moody, and William F. Draper. A fourth claimant, John Davis Long was absent, though possibly the most eager of all. Hoar's own preference would most likely have been Moody, Roosevelt's Attorney General, but it was generally predicted that Governor John L. Bates would select the wealthy paper manufacturer, Murray Crane, which he did. Crane had established a reputation during three terms as governor as one

[33] Within twenty-four hours of his father's death Rockwood Hoar received telegrams of condolence and eulogy from over two hundred public men and organizations. Roosevelt wired: "The loss is not yours only nor that of Massachusetts only but that of all who believe in a lofty standard of purity, integrity and fearlessness in public life." Roosevelt to Rockwood Hoar, 30 September 1904, Hoar Papers. All public men are assured of some praise upon their death, but few were the Republican regulars who received the simultaneous praise of the editors of the *New York Tribune* and the *Springfield Republican*, Senator Augustus Bacon and Booker T. Washington. Rockwood Hoar Collection, Hoar Papers.

[34] Rockwood Hoar to George A. Goulding, 29 September 1904; Charles Allen to Rockwood Hoar, 5 October 1904; Edward Everett Hale to Rockwood Hoar, 12 October 1904, Hoar Papers.

of the most quietly effective political managers in the history of Massachusetts. An honest conservative, he was at home with corporate power and its political associations.

With the death of Hoar and the succession of Murray Crane, the last personal connection of the Massachusetts Republican Party with its Free Soil past was formally severed.

A large and benevolent statue of Hoar by Daniel Chester French is prominently stationed in front of the Worcester City Hall. Hoar is seated in a great bronze chair, a sheaf of manuscript upon his knee, the whole supported by a granite pedestal with inscriptions on each of its four sides. Those inscriptions proclaim Hoar a Statesman, Scholar, Lawyer, Orator, Puritan, Patriot, Lover of Liberty, Champion of the Oppressed, and Citizen of Worcester. They do not mention that he was a Republican.

This omission was corrected but slightly in the parade of speeches that accompanied the formal dedication of the statue on 26 June 1908. Their chief purpose was to eulogize Hoar as an example of political purity and moral courage. Each speaker discovered for himself that the statue now unveiled bore the image of the Last Puritan.[35] Their eulogies were inaccurate not in their praise but in their insistent implication that Hoar's position in post-Civil War politics was that of an honorable relic. There was, of course, an element of truth in their portrait of Hoar as the displaced Puritan, but Hoar's character was less simple than they implied and his political career more interesting.

It is perhaps to be expected that speeches accompanying the unveiling of a monument would ignore the politician in favor of the patriot. It is more surprising that the memorial addresses delivered several years earlier in Senate and House had displayed a similar limitation. The integrity, purity, independence, and learning of a former colleague were dutifully acknowledged, but it appeared that the man they honored had been a visitor from the past who had spent eight years in the House and almost twenty-seven years in the Senate in a state of spiritual alienation. If one were to sum-

[35] Trustees of the George F. Hoar Memorial Fund, eds., *Dedication of the Statue of the Hon. George Frisbie Hoar, Worcester, June Twenty-Sixth 1908* (Worcester, 1909).

marize in a single paragraph some thirty-three pages of prepared eloquence in the *Congressional Record*, the result might be as follows:

> George Frisbie Hoar, America's Grand Old Man, lived a life governed by spiritual laws, deaf to the calls of compromise and commercial profit. The last of the Human-Rights statesmen, he was forever a Man of '48. Only questions of human freedom and the rights of man could excite his interest; the issues and concerns of the present generation were foreign to his sympathy. Every act of his public career was influenced by his love for the wisdom and institutions of the Past. Thus inspired he could not but offer heartfelt protest against political experiment, commercial greed, and the more materialistic standards of a later day. His like will not be seen again. All honor to Senator Hoar; for in honoring him, America does homage to its Past.[36]

Certainly some of his eulogists must have known that his was a more complicated character and career than the above paraphrase would indicate. If Hoar was solicitous of the heritage of the past, he was equally ambitious for his country's economic future. His career was not an exercise in nostalgia; rather it describes the story of a man who like his party was torn between old ideals and new realities. He spent much of his public life attempting to reconcile Concord and Worcester, the American dream of Emerson and the market requirements of Washburn and Moen. In the process he sought the simultaneous comforts of partisan regularity and political independence. Neither the Stalwarts nor the Mugwumps understood or fully trusted him, but far more than Roscoe Conkling or Carl Schurz did he represent the tensions of change and continuity that accompanied the post-Civil War evolution of the Republican party.

[36] *See* the *Congressional Record,* 58th Cong., 3d sess., 1503–1523; 2434–2445 (28 January 1905, 12 February 1905)—especially the memorial addresses of Senators Lodge, Daniel, Platt, Cullom, Bacon, McComas, and Depew and Representatives Keliher, Driscoll, and Tirrell. *See,* too, Charles Francis Adams, Jr., "Remarks by the President," Massachusetts Historical Society, *Proceedings,* 2nd series, vol. 18 (1903–1904), 377–378.

During that evolution, Hoar appeared now the reformer, now the conservative. He was labeled a radical by some for his early interest in the hours of labor and the votes of women; by others he was judged reactionary for his antipathy to executive power and constitutional revision. In measure these varying characterizations were the result of chronology—the moral exhortations that had appeared relatively bold in the years of Grant appeared less satisfactory in the age of Roosevelt. They were also the result, however, of a continuing uncertainty respecting the propriety of government intervention in the social and economic concerns of its citizens—an uncertainty shared with many genteel reformers of the post-Civil War generation.

Throughout his life Hoar accepted the prevailing social and economic order, while anticipating its improvement. In an open society, change must always occur, but in America social harmony must always prevail. As a reformer he was primarily concerned with perpetuating the expected harmony of American society. The reforms he primarily understood were those to be accomplished through increased educational opportunities, moral improvement, or the restricted application of government power in behalf of individual rights. This concern for social harmony, however, inspired periodic dissatisfaction with the industrial abuses that threatened to upset it. If Hoar sought less to reform than to reconcile, he was an advocate of cautious change, convinced that while the demands of social continuity forbade radical experimentation they occasionally required legislative revision.

In the last analysis the historical significance of George Frisbie Hoar depends neither upon the degree of his Puritanism nor his liberalism. It was as a legislator and as a Republican that he spent his public life, and it is here that one must make final assessment of Hoar's relevance and importance.

Hoar's contribution to the work of House and Senate between 1869 and 1904 was not of the type easily dramatized. While most of his congressional eulogists spoke of his "great services," few sought to retard the pace of their eloquence by reciting them. Many newspaper editors, failing to recall any great public measures to which Hoar had given his name, were content to label Hoar a "speculative statesman," with the implication that he had bothered little with

legislative carpentry.[37] Hoar was, in fact, a conscientious professional who took considerable pride in his abilities as a legislative
craftsman. If no single act that he authored significantly affected
the course of congressional history, they form in sum a creditable
product. His major contribution, however, was not as a draftsman
or manager of congressional bills but as a master and expediter of
congressional routine. It was in the committees of the Senate rather
than its corridors that he performed most effectively. He served at
various times on the Rules Committee, the Committee on Privileges and Elections, the Committee on Woman Suffrage, and committees on claims and patents. His major service, however, was as a
member of the Judiciary Committee and for fourteen years its
chairman. Virtually every investigation made by that committee in
these years was conducted by Hoar, and every bill it forwarded to
the Senate floor was revised by his pen.

Possibly the chief paradox of his legislative career is that he
gained national recognition not for the thousand tasks he quietly
performed for his party in behalf of its legislative effectiveness but
for his relatively infrequent outbursts against the misdeeds of its
leaders. His speeches against the conduct of Secretary Belknap, the
restriction of Chinese immigration, and the purchase of the Philippines fashioned Hoar's reputation in the public at large, with the
result that not only was his constructive contribution as a legislator
underrated, but his relationship to his party oversimplified and
misunderstood. During his thirty-five years in the national legislature, Hoar served more frequently as a reflection of his party's
contemporary tensions than as a reminder of its idealized past.

Hoar wished to punish the Bourbons and promote sectional
good-will, to encourage industrialism and check plutocracy, to expand American markets and denounce American jingoism, and
these conflicting aims were not untypical of the rank and file of the

---

[37] *See*, for example, E. Harlow Russell, "George Frisbie Hoar (1826–1904)," pamphlet; sketch by "Savoyard" in *Washington Post*, Scrap Book IX, Hoar Papers.
  *See also Boston Herald*, 26 September 1903; *New York Evening Post*, 21 November
1903; William Everett to James Schouler, 21 February 1905, James Schouler Collection, Massachusetts Historical Society; Thomas Wentworth Higginson, "George F.
Hoar," American Academy of Arts and Sciences, *Proceedings*, 15, 761–769 (May
1905); Talcott Williams, "George Frisbie Hoar: A Character Sketch," *American
Monthly Review of Reviews*, 30 (November 1904), 551–557.

Republican party during the greater part of his public career. His ambitions for his party exceeded those of its leadership when first he entered Congress as they were exceeded in turn by those of Theodore Roosevelt a generation later, but contrasts were seldom as sharp in reality as in appearance. For the transformation of the Republican party in the generation after Appomattox was a more subtle process than is usually recognized. It was not the transformation of a party descending from unblemished idealism to corporate reaction, only to be redeemed at a stroke by the magnetic example of Theodore Roosevelt. Despite significant changes in the leadership and policies of the Republican party in this period, there was a strong note of continuity. And that note was provided by the mixed ambitions and motives of Half-Breed Republicanism.

When first fashioned, the Republican party was a composite of materialism and idealism. Its founders were men who combined antislavery sentiment and Whig economics; they sought the economic consolidation of the nation as well as the restriction of slavery. As the economic demands of the eastern manufacturing community were from the first an object of interest to the Republican politicians, so its influence after the war though appreciably larger was seldom the sole determinant of Republican policy. The Republican party from conviction and financial self-interest adopted policies generally favorable to the entrepreneurial class, but the realities of national politics and public opinion prohibited the party from sustaining any concerted posture of subservience. The party's dependence on its political base in the Mississippi Valley required sporadic efforts to conciliate the heresies and grievances of the western farmer. The political demands of eastern capitalists were, moreover, often confused and frequently self-contradictory. Particularly in the 1870's and 1880's bankers and manufacturers, exporters and importers, speculators and creditors, large industrialists and small-town businessmen offered conflicting prescriptions for government policies respecting the South, the Negro, the tariff, banking regulation, and monetary policy.

It is true that by the Harrison years industrial consolidation and fears of agrarian radicalism had succeeded in strengthening the unity and political prestige of eastern industry, and for about a dozen years after the inauguration of Harrison the influence of big business was the strongest single influence in determining the power structure and legislative policies of the Republican party. But it was never the sole influence. The Republican party continued to try and balance its traditions and opportunities, the promises of the past and the needs of the New Industrialism. The point of balance had perceptibly shifted—the McKinley Tariff passed; the elections bill did not—but the effort to maintain the balance continued. And that effort indicates the essential nature of Half-Breed Republicanism.

Half-Breed Republicanism existed both before and after the rise and eclipse of the particular faction that fought and bested Roscoe Conkling and his Stalwart cohorts. It most clearly represented the leadership and policies of the Republican party in the 1880's, but in the form of such figures as George Frisbie Hoar it was not without influence in the decade preceding and following. The limited progressivism of the Roosevelt administration was its natural extension. Like most examples of political compromise, Half-Breed Republicanism is most clearly defined in terms of its opponents, the Stalwarts, the Independents, the western Radicals, the monopolists, but its spokesmen articulated a creed by the very ambivalence of their desires.

The Republican Half-Breeds scorned the role of industrial lobbyists and insisted that the growth of industry offered the best security for economic progress and social harmony. They favored economic bigness but judged monopoly un-American. They wished to see America gain an ever larger share of the world markets but were suspicious of military adventure. They refused to judge Reconstruction a failure yet sought the economic advantages of sectional reconciliation. They opposed the excesses of patronage politics and abhorred political independents. They distrusted professional reformers and supported the ICC and the Sherman Antitrust Act.

The Republican Half-Breeds can be faulted on several counts: they had but a limited understanding of the forces of industrialism and urbanization that were re-shaping America; they were reluctant to accept the logic of their own beliefs about the economic intervention of the federal government; they entertained an exaggerated concern for social harmony and too often allowed their fears to circumscribe their labors. Despite their limitations, however, these political pragmatists were a constructive force in the legislative history of the post-Civil War generation. If they failed fully to understand either the danger or the utility of party government in Congress, they contributed to its creation. By their limited efforts at federal intervention, moreover, they paved the way for the more ambitious if no less self-contradictory efforts of the Progressive period. The Half-Breeds were politicians who sought equilibrium rather than new frontiers. They were men like George F. Hoar.

Hoar was more ready to acknowledge the rights of unions than Garfield, more constant in his support of civil service reform and the rights of the Freedman than John Sherman, and more idealistic and independent than H. L. Dawes or George F. Edmunds, but all of these men were representative of Half-Breed Republicanism and its effort to adjust the mixed goals of the founders of their party to the social and economic complexities of late-nineteenth-century America. Their understanding of those complexities was limited and their adjustment incomplete and quickly outmoded, but their careers, spanning in the aggregate the first half century in the life of the Republican party, illustrate the veiled consistency of an important element of its congressional leadership.

It is only by understanding the nature and duration of Half-Breed Republicanism, that one can understand the relationship of Hoar to his party. A study of his career is a study of the limitations, compromises, and convictions of the Republican Half-Breeds, and the Republican Half-Breeds provide a necessary transition in the postwar evolution of the Republican party. By the administration of Theodore Roosevelt, Hoar had fulfilled his function and suffered political exclusion. His significance is not that of the spiritual exile, however; it is that of a politician who typified an important and misunderstood transition in the history of the Republican party.

In the generation after Appomattox the party of Lincoln and Sumner became in turn the party of Grant and Conkling, of Harrison and Quay, of McKinley and Hanna, of Roosevelt and Aldrich.

The evolution was not illusory but neither was it abrupt. Like all political generations, that between Lincoln and Roosevelt witnessed the uneasy and incomplete reconciliation of the forces of continuity and change. In the task of reconciliation the Half-Breed Republicans found their role. In his efforts to understand and occasionally to challenge the evolution of his party the political career of George Frisbie Hoar gains meaning and historical significance.

*Bibliography and Index*

# Bibliography

MANUSCRIPT COLLECTIONS

*Massachusetts Historical Society:*

Papers of Edward A. Atkinson (1895–1904).
Papers of George S. Boutwell (1872–1877, 1898–1904).
Papers of Richard H. Dana (1894, 1901).
Papers of George Frisbie Hoar.
Papers of Henry Cabot Lodge (1893–1904).
Papers of John Davis Long (1882–1883, 1897–1901).
Papers of Robert C. Winthrop (1885, 1891).

*Library of Congress:*

Papers of Nelson Aldrich (1890–1891, 1902–1903).
Papers of Thomas F. Bayard (1885–1886).
Papers of James G. Blaine (1877–1888).
Papers of Benjamin F. Butler (1873–1876, 1882–1883).
Papers of William E. Chandler (1876–1877, 1890–1891, 1897).
Papers of Zachariah Chandler (1875–1881).
Papers of Grover Cleveland (1886–1887, 1894–1897).
Papers of Henry L. Dawes (1876–1885, 1891–1892).
Papers of William M. Evarts (1877, 1885).

*Bibliography*

Papers of Moreton Frewen (1896–1897, 1900–1901).
Papers of James Garfield (diary and correspondence, 1876–1878, 1880–1881).
Papers of Edward Everett Hale (1903–1904).
Papers of Benjamin Harrison (1889–1891).
Papers of William McKinley (1897–1899).
Papers of Justin Morrill (1880, 1884, 1888).
Papers of Carl Schurz (1877–1878, 1898–1900).
Papers of John Sherman (1877–1878, 1889–1890).
Papers of John Coit Spooner (1890–1891).
Papers of Moorfield Storey (1898–1900).
Papers of Henry Wilson (1851–1878).

*Harvard Archives, Harvard University:*

Faculty Records; Class of 1846, Secretary's File; Corporation Papers, with scattered materials concerning Hoar's student days at Harvard, 1843–1846 and his service as an Overseer, 1873–1879, 1896–1904.

*Houghton Library, Harvard University:*

Papers of William W. Clapp (1883–1884).
Papers of Charles Eliot Norton (1898–1900).

*Rutherford B. Hayes Library:*

Papers of William Claflin (1869–1883, 1898–1901).
Papers of Rutherford B. Hayes (1877–1879).

*Indiana University Library:*

Papers of Charles W. Fairbanks (1901–1903).

*Cincinnati Historical Society:*

Papers of Joseph B. Foraker (1903).

*New York Historical Society:*

Papers of Chester A. Arthur (1881–1883).

*Duke University Libraries:*

Papers of John W. Daniel (1898–1900).

*New York Public Library:*

Scattered materials in Anthony Collection; Edward Atkinson Papers; Century Collection; Miscellaneous Papers.

## NEWSPAPERS

*Boston Advertiser; Boston Daily Globe; Boston Evening Transcript; Boston Evening Traveller; Boston Herald; Boston Journal; Civil Service Record* (Boston); *The Inter-Ocean* (Chicago); *Lowell Daily Courier; New York Times; New York Tribune; The World* (New York); *Philadelphia Evening Telegraph; Daily Republican* (Springfield); *The Spy* (Worcester); *Worcester Evening Gazette.*


## PERIODICALS

*Century Illustrated Magazine*
*International Monthly*
*Puck*
*Scribner's Magazine*
*The American Monthly Review of Reviews*
*The Forum*
*The Independent*
*The Nation*
*The North American Review*


## PUBLIC DOCUMENTS

*Congressional Globe*, March 1869–February 1873.
*Congressional Record*, March 1873–May 1904.
*Journal of the Executive Proceedings of the Senate of the United States of America.* Washington, 1901.
*Journal of the House of Representatives of the Commonwealth of Massachusetts* (1852–1853).
*Official Proceedings of the National Republican Conventions of 1868, 1872, 1876 and 1880.* Minneapolis, 1903.
"Report of the Select Committee of the House of Representatives Appointed under the Resolution of January 6, 1873, to Make an Inquiry in Relation to the Affairs of the Union Pacific Railroad Company, the Credit Mobilier of America and Other Matters," *House Report*, 42d Cong., 3d sess., no. 78.
"The Proceedings of the Electoral Commission," *Congressional Record*, 44th Cong., 2d sess. (1877).
"The Trial of William W. Belknap," *Congressional Record*, 44th Cong., 1st sess. (1876).
United States Bureau of the Census, *Historical Statistics of the United States, Colonial Times to 1957.* Washington, 1960.

## WRITINGS OF G. F. HOAR

Hoar, G. F. *Autobiography of Seventy Years.* 2 vols. New York, 1903.

An essential source and a difficult one, Hoar's *Autobiography* is in some ways most interesting for its omissions. There are few conscious misstatements of fact, but it offers selected reminiscence not self-analysis. Except for Ben Butler, Hoar treats all political friends and foes with an almost suffocating generosity. Whatever the frustrations it offers to a student of post-Civil War politics, it is charmingly written. Its organization, however, is chaotic, reflecting the fact that much of it first appeared as separate articles in *Scribner's Magazine.*

Hoar, G. F., ed. *Book of Patriotism.* Boston, 1902. Introductory essay by Hoar on "Love of Country."

A lengthy but selective list of Hoar's public speeches was published by the American Antiquarian Society in its *Proceedings*, 17 (October 1905), 159–166. A few additional addresses, not cited in that listing, will be found among the eighteen bound volumes of pamphlets among the Hoar Papers at the Massachusetts Historical Society. Because of the listing in American Antiquarian Society *Proceedings,* cited above, there would appear no value in listing each of these pamphlet titles. The more important are cited in the text and footnotes, together with certain magazine articles, campaign speeches, and newspaper interviews not published in pamphlet form.

"The Hoar Family in America and Its English Ancestry," *New England Historical and Genealogical Register,* January, April, July 1899. Though submitted by Henry Stedman Nourse and published under his name, this genealogy was in large part the work of Hoar.

## BOOKS AND ARTICLES

Aaron, Daniel. *Men of Good Hope: A Story of American Progressives.* New York: Oxford University Press, 1951.

Abrams, Richard M. *Conservatism in a Progressive Era: Massachusetts Politics, 1900–1912.* Cambridge: Harvard University Press, 1964.

Adams, Charles Francis, Jr. "Remarks by the President," Massachusetts Historical Society, *Proceedings,* 2d Series, 18 (1904), 377–378.

Bailey, Thomas A. "America's Emergence as a World Power: The Myth and the Verity," *Pacific Historical Review,* 30 (February 1961), 1–16.

———— "Was the Presidential Election of 1900 a Mandate on Imperialism?", *Mississippi Valley Historical Review,* 24 (1937), 43–52.

Bancroft, Frederic, ed. *Speeches, Correspondence and Political Papers of Carl Schurz.* 6 vols. New York: G. P. Putnam's Sons, 1913.

Barnard, Harry. *Rutherford B. Hayes and His America*. Indianapolis: Bobbs-Merrill, 1954.

Barnes, James A. "Myths of the Bryan Campaign," *Mississippi Valley Historical Review*, 34 (1947–1948), 367–404.

Beale, Howard K. *Theodore Roosevelt and The Rise of America to World Power*. Baltimore: Johns Hopkins Press, 1956.

Beer, Thomas. *Hanna*. New York: Alfred A. Knopf, 1929.

Beisner, Robert L. *Twelve Against Empire: The Anti-Imperialists, 1898–1900*. New York: McGraw-Hill, 1968.

Blake, Nelson M. *William Mahone of Virginia*. Richmond: Garrett & Massie, 1935.

Blodgett, Geoffrey. *The Gentle Reformers: Massachusetts Democrats in the Cleveland Era*. Cambridge: Harvard University Press, 1966.

_____ "The Mind of the Boston Mugwump," *Mississippi Valley Historical Review*, 48 (March 1962), 614–634.

Blum, John M. *The Republican Roosevelt*. Cambridge: Harvard University Press, 1954.

Boutwell, George S. *Reminiscences of Sixty Years in Public Affairs*. 2 vols. New York: McClure, Phillips, 1902.

Bowers, Claude. *Beveridge and the Progressive Era*. Boston: Houghton Mifflin, 1932.

Buck, Paul H. *The Road to Reunion, 1865–1900*. Boston: Little, Brown, 1937.

Bumphrey, Marvin H. *Authorship of the Sherman Antitrust Law, report of an investigation of the official records*. Cincinnati, 1912.

Burnham, W. Dean. *Presidential Ballots, 1824–1892*. Baltimore: Johns Hopkins Press, 1955.

Butler, Benjamin F. *Autobiography and Personal Reminiscences of Major General Benj. F. Butler: Butler's Book*. Boston: A. M. Thayer, 1892.

Campbell, Charles S., Jr. *Anglo-American Understanding, 1898–1903*. Baltimore: Johns Hopkins Press, 1957.

_____ *Special Business Interests and the Open Door Policy*. New Haven: Yale University Press, 1961.

Chase, Philip P. "A Critical Juncture in the Political Careers of Lodge and Long," Massachusetts Historical Society, *Proceedings*, 70 (1950–1953), 107–127.

Clancy, Herbert J. *The Presidential Election of 1880*. Chicago: Loyola University Press, 1958.

Clark, John D. *The Federal Trust Policy*. Baltimore: Johns Hopkins Press, 1931.

Coletta, Paola E. "Bryan, McKinley, and the Treaty of Paris," *Pacific Historical Review*, 26 (May 1957), 131–146.

Coolidge, Louis A. *An Old-Fashioned Senator: Orville H. Platt of Connecticut*. New York: G. P. Putnam's Sons, 1910.

Coolidge, Mary R. *Chinese Immigration*. New York: Henry Holt, 1909.

Cox, J. D. "How Judge Hoar Ceased to be Attorney-General," *Atlantic Monthly*, 76 (August 1895), 162–173.

Cullom, Shelby. *Fifty Years of Public Service*. Chicago: A. C. McClurg, 1911.

Curti, Merle. *Bryan and World Peace*. Northampton, Mass. Department of History of Smith College, 1931.

Dawes, Henry L. "Garfield and Conkling," *Century Illustrated Monthly*, 47 (January 1894), 341–344.

Dearing, Mary R. *Veterans in Politics*. Baton Rouge: Louisiana State University Press, 1952.

Degler, Carl N. "American Political Parties and the Rise of the City: An Interpretation," *Journal of American History*, 51 (June 1964), 41–59.

Dennett, Tyler. *Americans in Eastern Asia: A Critical Study of the Policy of the United States* . . . New York: Macmillan, 1922.

DeSantis, Vincent P. *Republicans Face the Southern Question: The New Departure Years, 1877–1897*. Baltimore: Johns Hopkins Press, 1959.

Dresser, F. F. *G. F. Hoar: Reprint from Reminiscences and Biographical Notices of Past Members of the Worcester Fire Society*. Worcester, 1917.

Duberman, Martin B. "Some Notes On the Beginning of the Republican Party in Massachusetts," *New England Quarterly*, 34 (September 1961), 363–365.

Dulles, Foster Rhea. *America's Rise to World Power, 1898–1954*. New York: Harper & Brothers, 1955.

———— *The Imperial Years*. New York: Thomas Y. Crowell, 1956.

Dunne, Finley Peter. *Mr. Dooley in the Hearts of His Countrymen*. Boston: Small, Maynard, 1899.

Ellis, Elmer. *Henry Moore Teller, Defender of the West*. Caldwell, Iowa: Caxton Printers, 1941.

Faulkner, H. U. *The Decline of Laissez Faire, 1897–1917*. New York: Rinehart, 1951.

Fine, Sidney. *Laissez Faire and the General Welfare State: A Study of Conflict in American Thought, 1865–1901*. Ann Arbor: University of Michigan Press, 1956.

Fite, Gilbert C. "Republican Strategy and the Farm Vote in the Presidential Campaign of 1896," *American Historical Review*, 65 (1959–1960), 787–806.

Fogel, Robert William. *The Union Pacific Railroad: A Case in Premature Enterprise*. Baltimore: Johns Hopkins Press, 1960.

Foraker, Joseph B. *Notes of a Busy Life*. 2 vols. Cincinnati: Stewart & Kidd, 1916.

Ford, Worthington C., ed. *Letters of Henry Adams*. 2 vols. Boston: Houghton Mifflin, 1930–1938.

Garraty, John A. *Henry Cabot Lodge, a Biography*. New York: Alfred A. Knopf, 1953.

Garrett, Wendell D. "John Davis Long, Secretary of the Navy, 1897–1902: A Study in Changing Political Alignments," *New England Quarterly*, 31 (September 1958), 291–311.

Gillett, Frederick. *George Frisbie Hoar*. Boston: Houghton Mifflin, 1934.

Ginger, Ray. *The Age of Excess: The United States from 1877 to 1914*. New York: Macmillan, 1965.

Glad, Paul W. *The Trumpet Soundeth: William Jennings Bryan and his Democracy, 1896–1912*. Lincoln: University of Nebraska Press, 1960.

Graebner, Norman A. "The Year of Transition—1898," in *An Uncertain Tradition: American Secretaries of State in the Twentieth Century*, Norman A. Graebner, ed. New York: McGraw-Hill, 1961.

Grenville, John A., and Young, George B. *Politics, Strategy, and American Diplomacy*. New Haven: Yale University Press, 1966.

Griswold, A. Whitney. *The Far Eastern Policy of the United States*. New York: Harcourt, Brace, 1938.

Grunder, Garel A., and Livezey, William E. *The Philippines and the United States*. Norman: University of Oklahoma Press, 1951.

Hale, Edward Everett. "George F. Hoar," American Antiquarian Society, *Proceedings*, 17 (October 1905), 150–158.

Hale, Edward E., Jr. *The Life and Letters of Edward Everett Hale*. 2 vols. Boston: Little, Brown, 1917.

Halle, Louis J. *Dream and Reality: Aspects of American Foreign Policy*. New York: Harper & Brothers, 1959.

Harrington, Fred H. "The Anti-Imperialist Movement in the United States, 1898–1900," *Mississippi Valley Historical Review*, 22 (1935) 211–230.

———— "Literary Aspects of American Anti-Imperialism, 1898–1902," *New England Quarterly*, 10 (1937), 650–667.

Hays, Samuel P. *The Response to Industrialism, 1885–1914*. Chicago: University of Chicago Press, 1957.

Healy, David F. *The United States in Cuba, 1898–1902*. Madison: University of Wisconsin Press, 1963.

Hess, James W. "John D. Long and Reform Issues in Massachusetts Politics, 1870–1889," *New England Quarterly*, 33 (March 1960), 57–73.

Hicks, John. *The Populist Revolt*. Minneapolis: University of Minnesota Press, 1931.

Higginson, Thomas Wentworth. "George Frisbie Hoar," *Proceedings* of the American Academy of Arts & Sciences, 15 (May 1905), 761–769.

Higham, John. *Strangers in the Land: Patterns of American Nativism, 1860–1925*. New Brunswick: Rutgers University Press, 1955.

Hirshson, Stanley P. *Farewell to the Bloody Shirt: Northern Republicans and the Southern Negro, 1877–1893*. Bloomington: Indiana University Press, 1962.

Hofstadter, Richard. *The Age of Reform, From Bryan to FDR*. New York: Alfred A. Knopf, 1955.

———— "Manifest Destiny and the Philippines," in *America in Crisis*, Daniel Aaron, ed. New York: Alfred A. Knopf, 1952.

———— *Social Darwinism in American Thought, 1860–1915*. Philadelphia: University of Pennsylvania Press, 1944.

Hollingsworth, J. Rogers, ed. *American Expansion in the Late Nineteenth Century: Colonialist or Anticolonialist?* New York: Holt, Rinehart, and Winston, 1968.

───── *The Whirligig of Politics: The Democracy of Cleveland and Bryan.* Chicago: University of Chicago Press, 1963.

Holloway, Jean. *Edward Everett Hale.* Austin: University of Texas Press, 1956.

Holt, W. Stull. *Treaties Defeated by the Senate.* Baltimore: Johns Hopkins Press, 1933.

Hoogenboom, Ari. *Outlawing the Spoils: A History of the Civil Service Reform Movement, 1865–1883.* Urbana: University of Illinois Press, 1961.

Howe, George F. *Chester A. Arthur: A Quarter-Century of Machine Politics.* New York: Dodd, Mead, 1934.

Howe, M. A. DeWolfe. *Later Years of the Saturday Club, 1870–1920.* Boston: Houghton Mifflin, 1927.

───── *Portrait of an Independent: Moorfield Storey, 1845–1929.* Boston: Houghton Mifflin, 1932.

Hughes, Sarah Forbes, ed. *Reminiscences of John Murray Forbes.* 3 vols. Boston: Houghton Mifflin, 1902.

Josephson, Mathew. *The Politicos, 1865–1896.* New York: Harcourt, Brace, 1938.

Kennan, George F. *American Diplomacy, 1900–1950.* Chicago: University of Chicago Press, 1951.

Kerr, Winfield S. *John Sherman: His Life and Public Services.* 2 vols. Boston: Sherman, French, 1908.

Kinzer, Donald L. *An Episode in Anti-Catholicism: The American Protective Association.* Seattle: University of Washington Press, 1964.

Kirkland, Edward C. *Charles Francis Adams, Jr., 1835–1915: The Patrician at Bay.* Cambridge: Harvard University Press, 1966.

───── *Industry Comes of Age: Business, Labor, and Public Policy, 1860–1897.* New York: Holt, Rinehart and Winston, 1961.

Knoles, George. *The Presidential Campaign and Election of 1892.* Palo Alto: Stanford University Press, 1942.

Kohlsaat, Herman H. *From McKinley to Harding.* New York: Charles Scribner's Sons, 1923.

Kolko, Gabriel. *The Triumph of Conservatism: A Reinterpretation of American History, 1900–1916.* New York: Free Press of Glencoe, 1963.

LaFeber, Walter. *The New Empire: An Interpretation of American Expansion, 1860–1898.* Ithaca: Cornell University Press, 1963.

Lambert, John. *Arthur Pue Gorman.* Baton Rouge: Louisiana State University Press, 1953.

Lanzar, Maria C. "The Anti-Imperialist League," *Philippine Social Science Review,* 3 (August 1930), 7–41.

Lanzar-Carpio, Maria C. "Anti-Imperialist Activities between 1900 and Election of 1904," *Philippine Social Science Review,* 4 (July 1932; October 1932), 182–198; 239–254.

Lasch, Christopher. "The Anti-Imperialists, the Philippines, and the Inequality of Man," *Journal of Southern History,* 14 (August 1958), 319–331.

Leech, Margaret. *In the Days of McKinley.* New York: Harper & Brothers, 1959.

Leopold, Richard W. "The Emergence of America as a World Power: Some Second Thoughts," in *Change and Continuity in Twentieth-Century America,* John Braeman, Robert H. Bremner, Everett Walters, eds. Columbus: Ohio State University Press, 1964.

Leuchtenberg, William E. "Progressivism and Imperialism: The Progressive Movement and American Foreign Policy, 1898–1916," *Mississippi Valley Historical Review,* 39 (1952), 483–504.

Lodge, H. C.; Powderly, T. V. "The Federal Election Bill," *North American Review,* 151 (September 1890), 257–273.

Lodge, Henry Cabot. "George Frisbie Hoar," Massachusetts Historical Society, *Proceedings,* 2d Series, 18 (1904), 385–390.

————, ed. *Selections from the Correspondence of Theodore Roosevelt and Henry Cabot Lodge, 1884–1918.* 2 vols. New York: Charles Scribner's Sons, 1925.

Long, Margaret, ed. *The Journal of John D. Long.* Rindge, N.H.: R. R. Smith, 1956.

Lyman, George H. "Reminiscences," Massachusetts Historical Society, *Proceedings,* 3d Series, 65 (1932–1936), 217–232.

McCall, Samuel W. *Thomas B. Reed.* Boston: Houghton Mifflin, 1917.

McCormick, Thomas J. "A Commentary on the Anti-Imperialists and Twentieth-Century Foreign Policy," *Studies on the Left,* 3 (1962) 28–33.

McPherson, James. *The Struggle for Equality: Abolitionists and The Negro In The Civil War and Reconstruction.* Princeton: Princeton University Press, 1964.

Mallam, William D. "Butlerism in Massachusetts," *New England Quarterly,* 33 (June 1960), 186–206.

Mann, Arthur. *Yankee Reformers in the Urban Age.* Cambridge: Harvard University Press, 1954.

Marvin, Abijah P. *History of Worcester in the War of Rebellion.* Worcester, 1870.

May, Ernest R. *Imperial Democracy: The Emergence of America as a Great Power.* New York: Harcourt, Brace & World, 1961.

Mayer, George. *The Republican Party, 1854–1964.* New York: Oxford University Press, 1964.

Merk, Frederick. *Manifest Destiny and Mission in American History: A Reinterpretation.* New York: Alfred A. Knopf, 1963.

Merriam, George S. *The Life and Times of Samuel Bowles.* 2 vols. New York: The Century, 1885.

Merrill, Horace S. *Bourbon Leader: Grover Cleveland and the Democratic Party.* Boston: Little, Brown, 1957.

Millis, Walter. *The Martial Spirit: A Study of Our War with Spain.* Boston: Houghton Mifflin, 1931.

Morgan, H. Wayne. *From Hayes to McKinley: National Party Politics, 1877–1896.* Syracuse: Syracuse University Press, 1969.

———, ed. *The Gilded Age: A Reappraisal,* rev. ed. Syracuse: Syracuse University Press, 1970.

——— *William McKinley and His America.* Syracuse: Syracuse University Press, 1963.

Morison, Elting, ed. *The Letters of Theodore Roosevelt.* 8 vols. Cambridge: Harvard University Press, 1951–1954.

Mowry, George E. *The Era of Theodore Roosevelt, 1900–1912.* New York: Harper & Brothers, 1958.

Muzzey, David S. *James G. Blaine: A Political Idol of Other Days.* New York: Dodd, Mead, 1934.

Nelson, James W. *Shelby M. Cullom, Prairie State Republican.* Urbana: University of Illinois Press, 1962.

Nevins, Allan. *Grover Cleveland: A Study in Courage.* New York: Dodd, Mead, 1932.

Nichols, Roy. *The Stakes of Power.* New York: Hill and Wang, 1961.

Norton, Sarah, and Howe, M. A. DeWolfe, eds. *The Letters of Charles Eliot Norton.* Boston: Houghton Mifflin, 1913.

Ogden, Rollo. *Life and Letters of Edwin Lawrence Godkin.* 2 vols. New York: Macmillan, 1917.

Olcott, Charles S. *The Life of William McKinley.* 2 vols. Boston: Houghton Mifflin, 1916.

Paine, Nathaniel P.; Hall, G. Stanley. "George Frisbie Hoar," Massachusetts Historical Society, *Proceedings,* 2d Series, 19 (1905), 258–267.

Parker, William Belmont. *The Life and Public Services of Justin Smith Morrill.* Boston: Houghton Mifflin, 1924.

Pearson, C. C. *Readjustor Movement in Virginia.* New Haven: Yale University Press, 1917.

Pearson, Henry G. *An American Railroad Builder, John Murray Forbes.* Boston: Houghton Mifflin, 1911.

Perkins, Dexter. *The Monroe Doctrine, 1867–1907.* Baltimore: John Hopkins Press, 1937.

Pettigrew, Richard F. *Imperial Washington.* Chicago: C. H. Kerr, 1922.

Pierce, Edward L. *Memoir and Letters of Charles Sumner.* 4 vols. Boston: Roberts Brothers, 1877–1893.

Pletcher, David M. *The Awkward Years: American Foreign Relations Under Garfield and Arthur.* Columbia: University of Missouri Press, 1962.

Pollack, Norman. *The Populist Response to Industrial America: Midwestern Populist Thought.* Cambridge: Harvard University Press, 1962.

Porter, Kirk H., and Johnson, Donald B., eds. *National Party Platforms, 1840–1960.* Urbana: University of Illinois Press, 1961.

Pratt, Julius W. *Expansionists of 1898: The Acquisition of Hawaii and the Spanish Islands.* Baltimore: Johns Hopkins Press, 1936.

Richardson, Leon B. *William E. Chandler: Republican.* New York: Dodd, Mead, 1940.

Robinson, Edgar E. *The Presidential Vote, 1896–1932.* Palo Alto: Stanford University Press, 1934.

Robinson, William A. *Thomas B. Reed: Parliamentarian.* New York: Dodd, Mead, 1930.

Robinson, William S. *"Warrington" Pen Portraits . . . from 1848 to 1876.* Boston: p.p., 1877.

Rothman, David Jay. *Power and Party: The United States Senate, 1869–1901.* Cambridge: Harvard University Press, 1966.

Sage, Leland L. *William Boyd Allison: A Study in Practical Politics.* Iowa City: Historical Society of Iowa, 1956.

Shaffer, A. W., "A Southern Republican on the Lodge Bill," *North American Review,* 151 (November 1890), 601–609.

Sharkey, Robert P. *Money, Class, and Party: An Economic Study of the Civil War and Reconstruction.* Baltimore: Johns Hopkins Press, 1959.

Shenton, James P. "Imperialism and Racism," in *Essays in American Historiography: Papers Presented in Honor of Allan Nevins,* Donald Sheehan and Harold C. Syrett, eds. New York: Columbia University Press, 1960.

Sherman, John. *Recollections of Forty Years in the House, Senate and Cabinet.* 2 vols. Chicago: Werner, 1895.

Sievers, Harry J. *Benjamin Harrison, Hoosier Statesman: From the Civil War to the White House, 1865–1888.* New York: University Publishers, 1959.

———— *Benjamin Harrison, Hoosier President: The White House and After.* Indianapolis: Bobbs-Merrill, 1968.

Smalls, Robert. "Election Methods in the South," *North American Review,* 151 (November 1890), 593–600.

Smith, Theodore C. *Life and Letters of James Abram Garfield.* 2 vols. New Haven: Yale University Press, 1925.

Sproat, John G. *"The Best Men": Liberal Reformers in the Gilded Age.* New York: Oxford University Press, 1968.

Stebbins, Calvin. "George Frisbie Hoar: A Discourse Spoken at the First Parish Church, Framingham, October 9, 1904." (pamphlet) Hudson, Mass.: E. F. Worcester Press, 1904.

Stephenson, N. W. *Nelson W. Aldrich: A Leader in American Politics.* New York: Charles Scribner's Sons, 1930.

Stern, Clarence. *Republican Heyday: Republicanism Through the McKinley Years.* Ann Arbor: Edwards Brothers, 1969.

Storey, Moorfield, and Emerson, Edward W. *Ebenezer Rockwood Hoar: A Memoir.* Boston: Houghton Mifflin, 1911.

Sumner, William Graham. *The Conquest of the United States by Spain.* Boston: D. Estes, 1899.

Thorelli, Hans B. *The Federal Antitrust Policy: Origination of an American Tradition.* Baltimore: Johns Hopkins Press, 1955.

Tompkins, E. Berkeley. "The Old Guard: A Study of the Anti-Imperialist Leadership," *The Historian*, 30 (May 1968), 366–388.

———— "Scylla and Charybdis: The Anti-Imperialist Dilemma in The Election of 1900," *Pacific Historical Review*, 36 (May 1967), 143–161.

Trustees of the George F. Hoar Memorial Fund, eds. *Dedication of the Statue of the Hon. George Frisbie Hoar, Worcester, June Twenty-Sixth 1908.* Worcester, 1909.

Unger, Irwin. *The Greenback Era: A Social and Political History of American Finance, 1865–1879.* Princeton: Princeton University Press, 1965.

Vanderbilt, Kermit. *Charles Eliot Norton: Apostle of Culture in a Democracy.* Cambridge: Harvard University Press, 1959.

Vevier, Charles. "Brooks Adams and the Ambivalence of American Foreign Policy," *World Affairs Quarterly*, 30 (April 1959), 3–18.

Walters, Everett. *Joseph Benson Foraker: An Uncompromising Republican.* Columbus: Ohio History Press, 1948.

Ware, Edith Ellen. *The Political Opinion in Massachusetts, During the Civil War and Reconstruction.* New York: Columbia University Press, 1916.

Weinberg, Albert. *Manifest Destiny: A Study of Nationalist Expansion in American History.* Baltimore: Johns Hopkins Press, 1935.

Weinstein, Allen. "Was There a 'Crime of 1873'?: The Case of the Demonetized Dollar," *Journal of American History*, 54 (September 1967), 307–326.

Welch, Richard E., Jr. "The Federal Elections Bill of 1890: Postscript & Prelude," *Journal of American History*, 52 (December 1965), 511–526.

———— "George Edmunds of Vermont: Republican Half-Breed," *Vermont History*, 36 (May 1968), 64–73.

———— "Opponents and Colleagues: George Frisbie Hoar and Henry Cabot Lodge, 1898–1904," *New England Quarterly*, 39 (June 1966), 182–209.

———— "Senator George Frisbie Hoar and the Defeat of Anti-Imperialism, 1898–1900," *The Historian*, 26 (May 1964), 362–380.

Wellborn, Fred A. "The Influence of the Silver-Republican Senators, 1889–1891," *Mississippi Valley Historical Review*, 14 (1927–1928), 462–480.

West, Richard S., Jr. *Lincoln's Scapegoat General: A Life of Benjamin F. Butler, 1818–1893.* Boston: Houghton Mifflin, 1965.

White, Leonard D. *The Republican Era, 1869–1901: A Study in Administrative History.* New York: Macmillan, 1958.

Wiebe, Robert H. *Businessmen and Reform: A Study of the Progressive Movement.* Cambridge: Harvard University Press, 1962.

———— *The Search for Order, 1877–1920.* New York: Hill and Wang, 1967.

Williams, Charles R., ed. *Diary and Letters of Rutherford Birchard Hayes.* 5 vols. Columbus: Ohio State Archaeological and Historical Society, 1922–1926.·

Williams, Talcott. "George Frisbie Hoar: A Character Sketch," *American Monthly Review of Reviews*, 30 (November 1904), 551–557.

Williams, William A. *The Contours of American History.* Cleveland: World Publishing Company, 1961.

──────── *The Tragedy of American Diplomacy.* Cleveland: World Publishing Company, 1959.

Williamson, Harold F. *Edward Atkinson: The Biography of an American Liberal, 1827–1905.* Boston: Old Corner Book Store, 1934.

Wolff, Leon. *Little Brown Brother: How the United States Purchased and Pacified the Philippine Islands at the Century's Turn.* Garden City, N.Y.: Doubleday, 1961.

Wood, Gordon S. "The Massachusetts Mugwumps," *New England Quarterly,* 33 (December 1960), 435–451.

Woodward, C. Vann. *Reunion and Reaction: The Compromise of 1877 and the End of Reconstruction.* Boston: Little, Brown, 1951.

──────── *The Strange Career of Jim Crow,* rev. ed. New York: Oxford University Press, 1957.

# Index

Abolitionists, 9, 191, 234n23
Adams, Charles Francis, Jr., 41, 42, 45, 50n, 229–231, 279, 288
Adams, Henry, 248–249, 274n44
Adams, John Quincy, 230
Agoncillo, Felipe, 235n27
Aguinaldo, Emilio, 225, 241, 247, 248, 253, 254, 278
Aldrich, Nelson W., 145, 158–159, 162, 200, 307–308; and Roosevelt, 293, 302; and tariffs, 154, 202–204; and Treaty of Paris, 293, 302
Aldrich, P. Amory, 10
Alger, Russell A., 215
Allen, Charles, 9–10
Allen, William V., 185, 244
Allison, William B., 37, 88, 139, 140, 200, 202, 293, 302
Altgeld, John P., 197
American Antiquarian Society, 300
American Bell Telephone Company, 120
American Historical Association, 320n16
*American Historical Review*, 125
American Indians, 193n
*American Industries*, 310

American Iron and Steel Association, 143
American party, *see* Know-Nothing movement
American Protective Association (APA), 188–193
Ames, Oakes, 49
Andrew, John A., 14, 15–16
Anglophiles, 206n14
Anthony, Susan B., 266n26
Anthracite Coal Strike, 308, 309n36
Anti-Imperialist League (American Anti-Imperialist League), 225, 227–231, 238n, 253, 254–258, 267–268, 274, 283, 288
Anti-imperialist movement, 212, 225, 226, 227–231, 240–241, 253–258, 269–271, 274–276, 286–288
Anti-Monopolists, 41
Anti-Tenement League, 320
Arthur, Chester A., 97, 104–109, 111–116, 124, 132, 136, 199
Atkinson, Edward, 191–192, 203, 229–231, 269, 270, 279n52; and anti-imperialism, 227, 255, 257

Bacon, Augustus, 246, 331n33

Baer, George F., 308
Bailey, W. H., 84
Balfour, Arthur James, 176n
Bancroft, George, 320n16
Banks, Nathaniel P., 12
Barker, Wharton, 168
Barrett, John, 254
Barrett, W. E., 105
Batchelder, Frank Roe, 327
Bates, John L., 331
Bates, Theodore C., 94, 107
Battle of the Standards, 197
Bayard, Thomas F., 135
Beard, Alanson W., 70, 74n28, 76, 105
Beecher, Henry Ward, 131
Belknap, William W., 51–54, 71, 329
Beveridge, Albert J., 162, 259–260, 295, 303
Bird, Frank W., 10, 12
Bishop, Robert R., 105
Blackwell, Henry B., 30
Blaine, James G., 103, 121, 139, 145, 219; and Hoar, 81, 107, 205; and Stalwarts, 90, 91; role of, in Republican conventions, 55–58, 95, 96–98; as Secretary of State, 100, 104; on labor, 118n; nominated for presidency, 124–133
Blair, Henry, 91
Bland, Richard, 87, 88
Blodgett, Geoffrey, 126
*Book of Patriotism,* 293n4
*Boston Advertiser,* 72, 73, 138
Boston and Albany Railroad, 121
Boston Chamber of Commerce, 254
*Boston Evening Transcript,* 285
*Boston Globe,* 73
*Boston Herald,* 72, 73
*Boston Journal,* 106n20, 107, 112, 227, 228n14, 264–265
*Boston Post,* 73
Boston Stock Exchange, 174
Boutwell, George S., 38, 56, 74n28, 105; and anti-imperialism, 238n, 253, 255, 262, 275; and Hoar, 70–72, 256, 280
Bowles, Samuel, Jr., 41, 73, 257, 264
Bradford, Gamaliel, 227, 228, 249
Bradley, Charles, 68n
Bray, Howard W., 235n27
Bristow, Benjamin, 55–58, 71
Britain, 206, 207
Brown, B. Gratz, 42
Bryan, William Jennings, 196, 268, 269, 270, 274, 328; and Hoar, 267, 271–273, 278, 288; and the imperialism

issue, 279; and the Treaty of Paris, 243–244
Bryn Mawr College, 217
*Buffalo Evening Telegraph,* 131
Burchard, Samuel, 132
Burden, F. L., 105
Bureau of American Republics, 205n11
Bureau of Labor Statistics, 34
Burlingame, Anson, 12
Burns, Robert, 321
Butler, Benjamin, 39, 56, 75, 85, 86, 105; and Hoar, 35, 40, 45–48, 70, 76, 106–107, 170n
Butler, Matthew C., 155

Caffery, Donalson, 275, 279n52
*Cambridge Chronicle,* 281
Cameron, Don, 57, 92, 94–95
Cameron, Simon, 36
Cannon, Joseph G., 302
Carlisle, John Griffin, 181
Carnegie, Andrew, 234, 237n31, 244, 254, 275, 276, 307n32, 317–318
Central Labor Union of Boston and Vicinity, 174–175
Chamberlain, Daniel H., 61n3
Chandler, Archie, 191
Chandler, William E., 105, 106, 145, 160, 172, 176n, 198n48, 217n35
Chandler, Zachariah, 36, 60–62, 66, 92
Channing, William Ellery, 313
Chapman, John Jay, 275
Chicago, University of, 224
Chinese Boxers, 287
Chinese immigration to U.S., 193n
Civil Service Commission, 108–110
Civil service reform, 134, 288
Civil war, 14–15
Claflin, William, 46, 70, 103, 214
Clapp, W. W., 106n20, 107
Clark University, 182, 190, 307n32, 317, 319
Clarke, Albert, 161n
Clarkson, James S., 140
Clay, Henry, 177
Cleveland, Grover, 129, 134–138, 205, 206–207, 279n52; and Hawaii annexation, 208; and Hoar, 171n3, 326n26; second administration of, 169–198; and silver question, 172–173; and tariffs, 116
Clothing Manufacturers Association, 174
Coletta, Paola E., 244n42
Colombia, 298–299

Committee for the Promotion of International Bimetallism, 176
Commonwealth Club, 133
Compromise: of 1850, 8, 152; of 1877, 65, 80n; Connecticut, 195, 325
Conkling, Roscoe, 57, 89–105 *passim,* 111, 333, 337; and Grant, 39
Conway, Thomas M., 82
Cooke, Alvin, 84
Coolidge, Thomas Jefferson, 85n, 201, 203, 212–213
Cortelyou, George B., 277
Coxey, Jacob, 35, 181, 183–186
Crane, W. Murray, 331–332
Crapo, William W., 105
Crédit Mobilier, 41, 48–51
Crocker, Richard, 279
Croffut, William, 262n20
Cuba, 212–217, 224, 253, 258, 287
Cullom, Shelby M., 121–123, 300n18
Curti, Merle, 244n42
Curtis, H. G , 174

Danish West Indies, 287n70
Davenport, John P., 147
Davis, Cushman K., 219, 220n, 245n
Davis, David, 64–65
Davis, Jefferson, 82
Dawes, Henry L., 46, 47n, 51, 74, 91, 100n3; and Arthur, 105; and Bland-Allison Act, 88; on civil service reform, 109–110; and Hoar's election to Senate, 71–72, 106–107
Day, William R., 220n
Debs, Eugene, 186
Democratic party, 51, 92n62, 93, 111, 130–134, 237, 273–274; and the federal elections bill, 155–162; Hoar's opinion of, 9, 10, 14, 43, 85, 116, 268, 271, 278, 328–329; and Treaty of Paris, 242, 243, 244
Democrats: Anti-Nebraska, 12, Bourbon, 129, 136, 148, 328; Gold, 203–204, 286; Massachusetts, 30, 105, 230
Depew, Chauncey, 140
Devens, Charles, Jr., 14–15, 16, 56, 74
Disputed Election, 62
Dole, Sanford B., 208
Dolliver, Jonathan, 303
Donnelly, Ignatius, 179
Douglas, Stephen, 13
Douglass, Frederick, 60
Draper, William F., 331
Dunne, Finley Peter, 286

Eaton, Dorman B., 170n
Edmunds, George F., 91, 279; anti-imperialism of, 255, 258, 274, 276; and Electoral Commission, 65; and Republican conventions, 93, 97n69, 123, 124; and Sherman Antitrust Act, 164–167
Electoral Commission, 62–69, 80n
Eliot, Charles, 129, 229n16, 276, 279
Emancipation League, 16
Emancipation Proclamation, 16
Endicott, William, Jr., 85n, 115, 116
Ernst, George, 229
Evans, T. C., 190–191
Evarts, William M. (Hoar's cousin), 48n29, 74, 76, 91, 124, 133, 164
Expansionism, 217, 219, 221, 235–236, 238–240, 259–262, 274; supporters and opponents of, 234n23, 237n30. *See also* Philippines

Farrar, Samuel (Hoar's great-uncle), 324
Fifteenth Regiment, Massachusetts Volunteers, 14, 15
Fifteenth Amendment, 17, 141, 162, 302n, 328
Filipino Insurrection, 245, 248, 253–255. *See also* Philippines
Fire Society, 320
First Amendment, 314
Fish, Hamilton, 94
Foraker, Joseph B., 144, 163, 201, 298–300
Forbes, John Murray, 57, 66, 97, 115, 116; and Hoar, 46, 75, 85n, 123
*Forum,* 194
Foster, Dwight, 10
Fourteenth Amendment, 17, 18–19, 21, 328
Free Kansas Convention, 11
Free Soil party, 5–12, 16, 70, 128, 152, 229, 327
Frelinghuysen, Frederick, 65, 94, 104
French, Daniel Chester, 332
Frewen, Moreton, 176n, 274n44
Frye, William P., 172, 219, 260
Fugitive Slave Law, 8
Fullam, L., 84–85

Garfield, James, 65, 66, 94–115 *passim,* 199, 338
Garrison, William Lloyd, Jr., 45, 228, 229n16
Geneva Award, 84n48

Giddings, Franklin Henry, 275
Gilman, Daniel Coit, 129
Gladden, Washington, 191
Godkin, E. L., 170, 206, 216n32
Gold Democrats, 203–204, 286
Gorman, Arthur Pue, 152n, 298–300;
  and federal elections bill, 147–148,
  155, 158–159; on the Treaty of Paris,
  237, 241, 242, 244, 246
Gould, Jay, 41, 64, 113
Grand Army of the Republic (GAR),
  107, 136
Grant, Ulysses S., 21, 26–27, 95, 102,
  108, 205; and Hoar, 23, 38–40; and
  Republican Convention of 1880, 94–
  97; scandal in administration of, 45–
  54; and the Stalwart leaders, 37–39
Grant and Wilson Club of Worcester, 43
Gray, George, 155, 219, 244–245
Gray, Horace, 100
Gray, William, 85n
Greeley, Horace, 42, 43, 45, 80, 268n30
Greenbacker party, 41, 85, 115, 288
Greenbacks, 17, 21, 83–88
Greene, J. Evarts, 94, 171n3
Greenhalge, Frederic T., 190
Gresham, Walter Q., 139
Griswold, A. Whitney, 239n34

Hale, Edward Everett, 22, 278, 288,
  294, 314, 331
Hale, Eugene, 92, 97, 219, 242, 246n45,
  249
Half-Breed Republicans, 56, 73, 204–
  205, 291, 336–338; on big business,
  166; brief history of, 2–4; compared
  to other factions, 90–91; on labor,
  118n; skirmishes with Stalwarts, 102–
  108
Halpin, Maria, 131
Hancock, Winfield, 98
Hanna, Mark, 202, 245n, 299, 302; and
  McKinley, 200, 276–277, 280; and
  the silver question, 150, 197
Harvard University, 127, 129, 142–143,
  171n2, 293, 319, 327n27; Law School,
  6, 322
*Harper's Weekly*, 125
Harrington, Fred H., 244n42, 286
Harrison, Benjamin, 138–168, 199, 205,
  208
Hawaii, 207–212, 228n14
Hawthorne, Julian, 162
Hay, John, 191, 218, 287n70

Hayes, John L., 115n36
Hayes, Rutherford B., 57–58, 74, 107,
  111, 199; campaign and election, 60–
  69; New Departure, 77–83, 101;
  Stalwart hate for, 91–92
Heitfeld, Henry, 246
Herbert, George, 321
Hewitt, Abraham, 68n
Higginson, Thomas Wentworth, 56,
  128, 191
Hill, Ben, 101
Hoar, Ebenezer Rockwood (Hoar's
  brother), 7, 12, 16, 38–39, 40, 87n52,
  121, 326
Hoar, George Frisbie: and the American Protective Association (APA),
  188–193, 292, 314–315; and the Anti-
  Imperialist League, 228–231, 254–
  258; and the Arthur administration,
  104–116; and William W. Belknap,
  51–54; and big business, 118–121,
  181–182, 304–308; birth and education, 5–6; and Bryan, 267, 271–273,
  278, 288; and Benjamin F. Butler,
  45–48; and civil service reform, 35–
  36, 88–89, 108–111; and Cleveland,
  134–138, 172–173, 206; and Jacob
  Coxey, 183–186; and the Crédit
  Mobilier/Union Pacific scandal, 48–
  50; death and funeral of, 330–332;
  and defeat of Conkling, 54–58; on
  the Democrats, 9, 10, 14, 43, 85, 116,
  268, 271, 278, 328–329; as editor of
  *Book of Patriotism*, 293n4; and the
  Electoral Commission, 62–69; and
  the federal elections bill, 146–148,
  152, 153–162; and federal regulation
  of railroads, 121–123; on the Fourteenth Amendment, 18–19, 21; and
  the Free Soil party, 7–10, 320; and
  Grant, 23, 38–40; as Half-Breed, 90–
  91; Hawaii annexation, 207–212,
  228n14; and Hayes policies, 77–88;
  in the House of Representatives, 20–
  24, 49–50, 52–54; on income tax,
  180–181; interest in family and ancestry, 324–327; on labor, 31–35,
  117–119, 186–187, 309–310; and
  Liberal Republicans, 42–45; and
  Lodge, 190, 217, 218, 219n41, 226–
  227, 268, 281–282, 301–302, 327n27;
  and McKinley, 210, 217–219, 245n,
  248–249, 262–263, 267–271, 276–
  278, 291, 295; and mass demonstra-
  tions, 183–186; on Mugwumps, 127–

133, 169–172, 329; and Negro rights, 17–27, 77–83, 136, 146–148, 161–162; opposition to imperialism, 229, 232–233, 236–237, 265–267; on Panama policy, 297–300; and the Philippines issue, 222–248 *passim*, 253–254, 259–266, 282–285, 295–297; on popular election of federal senators, 194–195, 310–311; and presidential election campaigns, 93–98, 42–45, 123–133, 138–142, 276–279; as a Radical Republican, 16–25; reelection to Senate of, 105–108, 281–282; religious convictions of, 313–315; and the River and Harbor Act of 1882, 112–114; and Roosevelt, 292–297; secular creed of, 315–318; the Senate candidacy and election of, 70–74; and the Sherman Antitrust Act, 163–168; and the silver question, 149–150, 173–176; on slavery, 8–9; on the Spanish-American War, 212–217; and the Stalwarts, 40, 45–58; on tariffs, 114–116, 135–136, 151–155, 177–179, 202–204; and the Treaty of Paris, 221–250; and universal education, 22–25; and the woman's rights movement, 29–31

Hoar, Joanna (Hoar's first American ancestress), 325

Hoar, John (Hoar's great-grandfather), 324

Hoar, John (Hoar's nephew), 325

Hoar, Leonard (Hoar's great-uncle), 324

Hoar, Mary (Hoar's daughter), 323

Hoar, Rockwood (Hoar's son), 278, 323n, 326–327, 330n32, 331n33

Hoar, Ruth Miller (Hoar's second wife), 326

Hoar, Samuel (Hoar's father), 5, 7, 9, 228n, 229n14, 327

Hoar, Samuel (Hoar's grandfather), 324

Hoar, Samuel (Hoar's nephew), 128, 301

Hoar, Sarah (Hoar's mother), 5

Hoar, Sherman (Hoar's nephew), 128

Hoare, Charles, 325

Hoare, Henry, 325

Hobart, Garret, 232, 247n

Hollingsworth, J. Rogers, 241n37

Holmes, Oliver Wendell, 301–302

Home Market Club of Boston, 262n19

Immigration Restriction League, 193n

Independents, 2, 73, 242, 299, 337; and anti-imperialism, 227, 229, 230

Ingalls, John J., 160

*International Monthly*, 278n51

Internationale (International Association of Workingmen), 32

Interstate Commerce Commission, 273, 306

Irish Home Rule Movement, 189

Jackson, Sherman, 146

James, William, 267n28

*Japan Times*, 286n66

John Brown's Raid, 11n12

Johnson, Andrew, 18, 19, 111

Jones, James K., 242

Jones, John P., 244, 246

Jordan, David Starr, 279

Josephson, Matthew, 166–167

Julian, George W., 42

Kansas Emigrant Aid Society, 11

Keller, Helen, 321n

Kellogg, William P., 61n3, 82n43

Key, David M., 79

Kidder, H. P., 85n

Know-Nothing (American party) movement, 10, 11–12, 13, 188, 190

Knox, Philander C., 305n28

Labouchère, Henry, 283n

Lasch, Christopher, 241n37

Labor marches of 1894, 181, 183–186

Liberty Congress, 275–276

Liliuokalani, 208, 212n21

Lincoln, Abraham, 13, 14, 15

Lisle, Lady Alice, 325

Little Rock and Fort Smith Railway, 56, 121, 125

Lloyd, Henry Demerest, 166, 183

Loco Focos, 83

Lodge, Henry Cabot, 74n28, 201, 261, 280; at 1896 convention, 196–197; on Cuba, 215n29; denied Harvard honorary degree, 293, 327n27; and federal elections bill, 147; and Hoar, 190, 217, 218, 219n41, 226–227, 268, 281–282, 301–302, 327n27; in Massachusetts Republican politics, 105, 124; and the peace commission, 220n; Philippine Committee, 284–285, 295; and Roosevelt, 209; and Senate Philipines debate, 235–236, 244n43, 245n; on tariffs, 180, 202, 204

Logan, John, 36, 91, 95

Long, John Davis, 70, 100n4, 106–107, 124, 282, 301, 331
Lopez, Sixto, 235n27, 254
Lowell, Josephine Shaw, 297
Lyman, George, 330

McCall, Samuel, 279
McClure, S. S., 117
McCormick, Thomas J., 237n30
McCrary, George W., 63, 65, 91
McEnery, Samuel, 245–246
McKinley, William, 140, 197–220 *passim*, 244–249 *passim*, 257, 259, 260–263, 291; and Hoar, 262–263, 267–271, 295; and patronage, 200–202; and peace commission, 217–220; Philippine policy of, 253–254, 273; reelection, 280; Tariff Act, 146, 151–155, 179
McLaurin, John Lowndes, 245–246
McMillan, James, 154
Mahan, Alfred, 209, 280
Mahone, William, 101–102
*Maine*, 213
*Man Without a Country*, 294
Manning, Daniel, 137
Mason, Walter, 242, 279
Massachusetts Club, 217, 251n
Massachusetts General Court, 9, 13, 38n, 64, 226, 282; and Fourteenth Amendment, 18–19; and Hoar election to Senate, 71–72; and Hoar reelection in 1883, 105–107; Hoar speech to, 316
Massachusetts Historical Society, 320n16
Massachusetts Labor party, 84
Massachusetts Reconstruction Association, 19–20
Massachusetts Reform Club, 179, 227, 228, 231
Massachusetts Society for the Prevention of Cruelty to Animals, 319–320
Massachusetts Telegraph Company, 120
Matthews, Stanley, 69n16, 91
May, Ernest R., 214n26
Mercer, George C., 258
Mexican Cession, 8
Mexican War, 7n, 82
Missouri Compromise, 10
Miles, N., 264
Mitchell, John, 308
Moen, Philip L., 84, 85n
Monroe Doctrine, 206

Moody, William D., 331
Morgan, John T., 159, 162, 228n14, 266n26
Morrill, Justin, 47, 88n54, 124, 168, 327; and Hawaii annexation, 208, 211n20
Morton, Levi P., 66, 158–159
Morton, Oliver, 36, 57, 65
Muckrakers, 166, 183, 291, 303, 307
Mugwumps, 41, 45, 126–133, 134, 206n14, 222, 234n23, 282, 333; in anti-imperialist movement, 227, 249, 254, 285, 288; in Harvard faculty, 142, Hoar's opinion of, 169–171, 230, 291n, 293, 328, 329

*Nation*, 125, 128, 191, 216n32
National Association of Wool Manufacturers, 115n36
National Unitarian Conference, 314
Negro rights, 17–27, 77–83, 132–136 *passim*, 141–162 *passim*, 266, 329
New Departure, 77–83, 101
New England Anti-Imperialist League, 256n7
New England Woman's Suffrage Association, 29, 30
*New York Post*, 170
*New York Sun*, 246
*New York Times*, 61, 191
*New York Tribune*, 331n33
*New York World*, 233
Northwest Alliance, 160
Norton, Charles Eliot, 73, 112, 216, 229n16
Nourse, Henry Stedman, 324

Olney, Richard, 171n3, 206, 245n
Oregon and Hayes election, 66–67
O'Reilly, John Boyle, 189

Panama, 297–300
Panic of 1873, 59
Panic of 1893, 172, 173, 181
Paris Commune, 32
Pendleton, George, 108
People's Party Club, 174
Pettigrew, Richard F., 154n13, 275
*Philadelphia Press*, 254
Philippines, 212, 220–226 *passim*, 232–246 *passim*, 259–266, 273–289 *passim*, 295
Philippine Islands Committee in Europe, 235n27
Phillips, Wendell, 33

Pierce, Abijah (Hoar's great-grand-father), 324
Platt, Orville H., 200, 302
Platt, Thomas C., 103, 170n, 293
Plumb, Preston, 149, 160
Poland, Luke, 49–50
Populists, 41, 179, 237; Hoar's opinion of, 181, 185, 196, 197; and the Treaty of Paris, 242, 243, 244
Porter, Fitz John, 107
Proctor, Redfield, 215n28
Progressive movement, 290, 291, 302–304, 307, 310
Prohibitionists, 132
Puerto Rico, 220, 235n27
Pugh, James L., 147
Pullman strikers, 186–187
Puritans, 6, 315
Putnam, Rufus, 316n9

Quay, Matt, 140–142, 151–154, 302
Quigg, Lemuel E., 264

Radical Reconstruction, 78, 80
Randall, Samuel J., 68
Readjusters, 101
Reed, Thomas B., 149, 196–197, 213, 256, 269, 279n52, 288, 302
Republican party, 101, 199–200, 273, 288, 329, 333, 336–338; Massachusetts, 10–11, 15–16, 30, 76–77, 78, 82, 93–94, 97n69, 104–107; National Committee, 92, 130; national conventions, 30n, 38, 54–58, 94, 196–197; post-war transformation of, 145–162
Republicans: Liberal, 40–45, 56, 77, 91; Old Abolitionist, 243n23; Radical, 13, 16–25, 145. See also Free Soil party, Half-Breed Republicans, Stalwarts
Rice, William W., 48n27
Ripley, Mrs. Sarah, 30
Robertson, W. H., 102–103
Robinson, George D., 124
Rockefellers, 303, 307n32
Roosevelt Progressives, 91
Roosevelt, Theodore, 166, 201, 209, 221n, 287, 307; and Hoar, 171, 192, 206n14, 292–297, 301–302, 311; and labor, 308–310; Panama policy of, 297–300; on the Philippines issue, 240, 244n43, 295–297
Root, Elihu, 295, 327–328
Rothman, David J., 200n

Rowlandson, Mary, 325
Russia, 133n

Saint Anthony's Society, 189
Schurz, Carl, 41, 42, 130–131, 247, 275, 279, 288, 326n26; and the Philippines, 222, 224–225, 272n40
Secession Crisis of 1860, 13
Secret Six, 11n12
Senate: Philippine debate in, 232–248, 259–260; reform, 194–195; vote on Treaty of Paris, 243
Seventeenth Amendment, 311
Shellabarger, Samuel, 49
Shenton, James P., 241n37
Sheridan, Phil, 139
Sherman, John, 83–97 passim, 111, 137–140, 149, 160, 201, 326
Sherman, Roger (Hoar's grandfather), 5, 195, 316n9, 318, 325, 327
Silver, 149–151
Silver "Independents," 243
Silverites, 288
Slavery, 8–9
Slavocracy Power, 8, 14
Smith, Charles Emory, 255
Smith, Edwin Burritt, 274, 275
Smithsonian Institution, 320
Socialist Labor party, 186
Sons of Ireland, 131
Southern Redeemers, 69
Spain, 212–213, 222, 224, 226n8, 236, 247n
Spanish-American War, 209, 212–217, 221
Spooner, John C., 162, 190, 237, 293, 302; and federal elections bill, 146, 154n13, 158
Springfield Republican, 73, 112, 257, 268–269, 331n33
Stalwarts, 2, 36–58, 70–71, 73, 75, 92, 133, 333, 337; attitudes of, toward Hayes, 88, 90, 91–92; election of 1876, 59–69; and Half-Breeds, 91–98
Standard Oil Trust, 163
Stearns, George L., 11n12
Stearns, M. L., 61n3
Steward, Ira, 32n
Stewart, William M., 151, 157, 158, 185, 237
Storer, Bellamy, 201
Storey, Moorfield, 56, 70, 127, 275, 293; anti-imperialism of, 227, 228, 231, 257, 274; and Hoar, 45, 256

Sumner, Charles, 13, 14, 25, 45, 161, 190; and Grant, 43–44
Swift, Morrison I , 184

Taft, William Howard, 166, 295–296; Commission, 282
Tammany Hall, 279
Tariffs, 114–116, 135–136, 141–142, 151–155, 176–181, 202–204
Taylor, Zachary, 7
Teller, Henry Moore, 151, 157, 158, 215, 260
Thayer, Adin, 64, 70, 72, 74n28, 107
Thayer, Eli, 11
Thurman, Allen, 267, 271
Tilden, Samuel, 59, 61, 62, 63, 328
Tinker, Edward R., 72, 74n28, 107
Townsend, Washington, 88n53
Transcendentalism, 6
*Traveller,* 105
Treaty: Anglo-American Arbitration (1897), 207; Clayton-Bulwer (1850), 298; of Paris, 112, 221–250, 253, 268; Second Hay-Pauncefote (1901), 298; Sino-American (1886), 193n
Trumbull, John, 317
Trumbull, Lyman, 41, 42
*Truth,* 283n
Tweed Ring, 49

Union Army, 107, 136
Union Pacific, 49–50
Union Republican Congressional Committee, 19
Unitarian church, 6, 314
United Mine Workers, 308
United States Supreme Court decisions, 122, 181, 302n

Venezuela, 206
Vest, George, 221, 246

Walker, Francis A., 176
Wallace, Lew, 66
Warren, Winslow, 211n19, 228
Washburn, John D., 70, 72, 107
Washburn, Moen and Company, 114, 167
Washburn, William B., 46, 47
Washington, Booker T., 331n33
*Washington Post,* 260
Webster, Daniel, 8, 112
Welles, Gideon, 42
Welsh, Herbert, 257, 258, 275, 283
Western Radicals, 337
West Point, 82
Wheeler, William A., 55, 57, 58, 91
Whig party, 7, 8, 10, 69, 152
White, Horace, 41
Wilmot Proviso, 8
Wilson, Henry, 12, 45, 71, 74n28
Wilson, Jeremiah, 50
Winslow, Erving, 228, 229–231, 255, 269–270, 274, 275–276, 288
Wolcott, Edward O., 159, 198n48
*Woman's Journal,* 30
Woodford, Stewart, 213
Woodward, C. Vann, 69
Worcester, 8, 13, 15, 330–331, 332
Worcester and Nashua Railroad, 87n52, 121
Worcester Club, 320
Worcester *Daily Spy,* 112, 204
Worcester Free Institute for Industrial Science, 47
Worcester Polytechnic Institute, 319
Wormley conference, 68–69
Worthington, Roland, 105, 106
Wright, Carroll D., 309n36

Young Men's Independent Republican Club, 80